*The Evolution of Mind*

# The Evolution of Mind

*Edited by*
DENISE DELLAROSA CUMMINS
AND COLIN ALLEN

New York   Oxford     Oxford University Press   1998

Oxford University Press

Oxford   New York
Athens   Auckland   Bangkok   Bogota   Bombay
Buenos Aires   Calcutta   Cape Town   Dar es Salaam
Delhi   Florence   Hong Kong   Istanbul   Karachi
Kuala Lumpur   Madras   Madrid   Melbourne
Mexico City   Nairobi   Paris   Singapore
Taipei   Tokyo   Toronto   Warsaw

and associated companies in
Berlin   Ibadan

Copyright © 1998 by Oxford University Press, Inc.

Published by Oxford University Press, Inc.
198 Madison Avenue, New York, New York 10016

Oxford is a registered trademark of Oxford University Press

Library of Congress Cataloging-in-Publication Data
The evolution of mind / edited by Denise Dellarosa Cummins,
Colin Allen.
p. cm.
Includes bibliographical references and index.
ISBN 0-19-511053-6
1. Cognition.   2. Behavior evolution.   3. Cognition and culture.
4. Psychology, Comparative.   5. Genetic psychology.   I. Cummins,
Denise D.   II. Allen, Colin.
BF311.E876 1998
155.7—dc21      97-28321

9 8 7 6 5 4 3 2 1

Printed in the United States of America
on acid-free paper

# Contents

*Contributors*, vii

*Introduction*, 3,
DENISE DELLAROSA CUMMINS & COLIN ALLEN

1   *Ecological Intelligence:* An Adaptation for Frequencies, 9
GERD GIGERENZER

2   *Social Norms and Other Minds:* The Evolutionary Roots
      of Higher Cognition, 30
DENISE DELLAROSA CUMMINS

3   *Building a Cognitive Creature from a Set of Primitives:*
      Evolutionary and Developmental Insights, 51
MARC HAUSER & SUSAN CAREY

4   *An Evolved Capacity for Number*, 107
KAREN WYNN

5   *Cognitive Ethology:* The Minds of Children and Animals, 107
CAROLYN A. RISTAU

6   *Playing with Play:* What Can We Learn about Cognition,
      Negotiation, and Evolution?, 162
MARC BEKOFF

7   *The Evolution of Reference*, 183
COLIN ALLEN & ERIC SAIDEL

8   *Some Issues in the Evolution of Language and Thought*, 204
PAUL BLOOM

9   *Morgan's Canon*, 224
ELLIOTT SOBER

10   *Do's and Don'ts for Darwinizing Psychology*, 243
LAWRENCE A. SHAPIRO

Index, 260

# Contributors

COLIN ALLEN
Department of Philosophy
Texas A&M University

MARC BEKOFF
Department of Environmental,
Population, and Organismic Biology
University of Colorado, Boulder

PAUL BLOOM
Department of Psychology
University of Arizona

SUE CAREY
Department of Psychology
New York University

DENISE CUMMINS
Department of Psychology
California State University,
Sacramento

GERD GIGERENZER
Center for Adaptive Behavior
and Cognition
Max Planck Institute for
Psychological Research, Berlin

MARC HAUSER
Departments of Anthropology and
Psychology, Harvard University

CAROLYN A. RISTAU
Department of Psychology
Columbia University

ERIC SAIDEL
Department of Philosophy
Southwestern Louisiana University

LAWRENCE A. SHAPIRO
Department of Philosophy
University of Wisconsin, Madison

ELLIOT SOBER
Department of Philosophy
University of Wisconsin, Madison

KAREN WYNN
Department of Psychology
University of Arizona

*The Evolution of Mind*

# Introduction

DENISE DELLAROSA CUMMINS & COLIN ALLEN

This book is an interdisciplinary endeavor, a collection of essays by ethologists, psychologists, anthropologists, and philosophers united in the common goal of explaining cognition. The challenge facing the reader of interdisciplinary works is to develop greater sophistication in fields beyond one's academic speciality. There are sometimes terminological barriers to comprehension of other disciplines, but we hope that this volume has minimized those. In other cases the barriers are ideological. For instance, those with backgrounds in philosophy and psychology are often prone to regard the human mind as a pinnacle of evolutionary development. Biologists, however, frequently point out that all forms of intelligence on this planet are specially engineered solutions to specific ecological problems, all of which have been developing for exactly the same amount of time.

Taking an evolutionary approach to the explanation of cognitive function follows naturally from the growing body of neuroscientific evidence showing that the mind is divisible. The picture that is emerging from both noninvasive studies of normal brain function and from clinically defined syndromes resulting from brain damage from strokes, injury, and neuro-developmental disorders is one of different neurological substrates serving different cognitive functions. This picture has provided philosophers a glimpse into the possibility that Descartes was mistaken about the unity of consciousness. The neurological divisibility of mind also provides the key to understanding its evolution. The Cartesian view of a seamless whole makes it hard to see how such a whole could have come into being, except perhaps by an act of divine creation. By recognizing the modularity of mind, however, it is possible to see how human mentality might be explained by the gradual accretion of numerous special function pieces of mind.

An evolutionary perspective forces two changes in the traditional approach to human cognitive psychology. First, the functional modules of human mentality are evaluated in a biological context. Human reasoning, human language, and human intentionality are all aspects of neurological substrates with an evolutionary history—substrates that have evolved with one or more specific jobs to do. A better understanding of these jobs leads to a deeper understanding of the strengths and weakness of the human cognitive apparatus. The second shift is toward a greater emphasis on comparative studies of cognition in other species. Neither brains nor cognitive mechanisms fossilize, hence it is not possible to look to the fossil record for information about the phylogenetic trajectory of the human mind. Instead, one must look to other species to see how their cognitive capacities suit their ecological requirements. From such investigation, one may draw inferences about the likely ecological context in which human cognitive modules evolved. These inferences are, of necessity, highly tenuous. Yet scientific progress requires bold conjecture, and bold conjectures are exciting.

By having leading figures describe their current research, we hope to convey this excitement and to help set the agenda for the future development of evolutionary psychology. Some of our contributors are psychologists who have employed ideas about the biological functions of human cognition both to illuminate otherwise puzzling discoveries about human cognition, and to suggest new avenues for research. Other contributors are ethologists concerned with understanding the nature and function of non-human animal cognition, thereby drawing parallels to human cognitive abilities. The remainder of our contributors are philosophers concerned with the theoretical underpinnings of evolutionary psychology and the light that comparative methods can shed on some traditional philosophical claims about human uniqueness.

A number of topics are threaded through the various chapters of this book. Several of the authors show that an evolutionary perspective helps us understand why humans sometimes seem to have cognitive blindspots. For example, our abilities to reason through certain kinds of problems can seem quite poor when the problem information is presented in a way that differs significantly from the way it would have been presented during our evolutionary past. Reasoning abilities also seem specially geared toward handling social relationships, a context that ethologists have suggested is especially important for the evolution of higher cognitive functions.

Other essays in this volume examine the extent to which the cognitive capacities of other species are homologous to those of humans, and the extent to which the capacities are merely analogous or "homoplastic" to human traits (homologies have common evolutionary origins and functions, while homoplasies have common functions but different evolutionary origins). This issue is closely related to the question of how far one must go back to find the ecological conditions that best account for any particular feature of the mind. In some cases, it appears sufficient to consider adaptation to the conditions of our hominid, hunter-gatherer ancestors. In other cases, the roots of cognitive function may be very much older indeed.

Gerd Gigerenzer (chapter 1) begins the challenge by asking the following question: For which information formats have mental algorithms been designed? He points out that most studies that purport to show human statistical reasoning to be error-ridden, biased, heuristically driven, and even irrational, typically present reasoning problems in terms of probabilities and percentages. Yet, evolutionarily speaking, these are quite recent forms of representation of uncertainty, emerging as a human invention in the mid-seventeenth century. He then presents an impressive body of data showing that when these same problems are presented in terms of frequencies, human reasoning appears statistically sound. He argues that this paradox is readily explained by taking an evolutionary perspective: Mental algorithms evolved in an environment with fairly stable characteristics, and hence are adaptations for manipulating representations of event frequencies acquired by natural sampling. When numerical information is represented as frequencies, Bayesian computations reduce to a minimum, rendering them computable in real time by an organism of finite reasoning capacity.

Denise Cummins (chapter 2) continues the challenge by focusing on another paradox in human reasoning performance: Just as statistical reasoning improves dramatically when problems are presented in frequency rather than probability format, logical reasoning improves dramatically when problems are presented as social norms rather than truth- or validity-testing problems. She presents a large body of evidence showing that this social-nonsocial distinction emerges early in human development, colors reasoning performance throughout the lifespan, and is neurologically separable from other types of intelligent reasoning. She explains this distinction in human reasoning as an adaptation in cognitive architecture that emerged in response to pressure to reason about social dominance hierarchies, the social organization that characterizes most social mammals. She argues that the problems one must repeatedly solve when living in a dominance hierarchy fall into two categories. The first is recognizing what one may, must, or must not do given one's rank. These are implicit social norms. The second category consists of strategies for circumventing the constraints of the hierarchy by dint of guile, particularly through successful manipulation of others' beliefs and behaviors. This is called theory of mind reasoning. She concludes that these domain-specific adaptations constitute the origins of higher cognition.

In chapter 3, Marc Hauser and Sue Carey describe their collaboration on an extensive comparative study of human infants and various nonhuman primates. They emphasize the importance of distinguishing homology and homoplasy in selecting species and capacities for comparison. In light of this distinction, they consider two major areas of cognitive capacity: the development of concepts of object and number, and the capacity for a theory of mind that includes the attribution of mental states to other individuals. Hauser and Carey have made extremely innovative use of a technique they call the "preferential looking time paradigm" which measures the amount of time a young child or other organism spends looking at a novel display. Because changes in presentation affect the time spent looking, researchers can find out which features and relationships organisms can discriminate. Using this technique, Hauser and Carey have argued that several capacities often thought to be unique to humans are shared by our simian relatives.

In her chapter on an evolved capacity for number (chapter 4), Karen Wynn argues that humans possess a domain-specific mechanism for representing and reasoning about the abstract concept of number. This mechanism was designed through natural selection, and is independent of language or cultural transmission. To support her claim, she presents evidence on the numerical reasoning capacities of human infants and nonhuman animals. She also discusses in detail a possible mechanism called an "accumulator model" through which this numerical competence might be realized in the cognitive architecture. Wynn cites predation-defense as a likely candidate in the evolution of this cognitive capacity.

Carolyn Ristau (chapter 5) also compares the cognitive capacities of human infants and nonhuman animals, though the range of animals that she considers is broader than the nonhuman primates. She considers the importance of object classification schemes to a wide variety of organisms, suggesting that the roots of human language and cognition may lie in some very basic, shared cognitive capacities both to detect motion and to discriminate animate motion from other forms of motion. These capacites are likely to have been evolutionarily important in anti-predator behavior. She then suggests how these more basic capacities might form a foundation for the joint attention that is essential for shared intentionality in social cooperation tasks, and ultimately for the development of theories of mind.

In chapter 6, Marc Bekoff looks at how communicative abilities function to allow cooperation in social play. Animals such as dogs play with each other by engaging in behaviors that, in other contexts, would demand rather different responses. Somehow, playing wolves, coyotes, and domestic dogs manage to communicate to each other that a bite or mount is playful not serious. In focusing on canids, Bekoff feels a heavy burden to argue that his cognitive approach to these animals is not excessively anthropomorphic. He argues that a cognitive approach to these interactions yields testable hypotheses about the placement of "play signals" relative to other actions and suggests that only by forthrightly embracing the possibility of animal cognition can the approach be thoroughly tested.

Colin Allen and Eric Saidel in chapter 7 also consider communication, casting their net wide enough to include the vocalizations of chickens and monkeys for comparison to human linguistic abilities. They argue that looking far into the evolutionary past can yield insights into both the phylogeny and ontogeny of human language. Concerned with the issue of homology versus homoplasy, they too suggest that whether homologous or homoplastic, the vocalizations of chickens can show the way to understand the roots of linguistic reference. Like Ristau and Wynn, Allen and Saidel suggest that anti-predatory capacities have importantly shaped the evolution of communication and reference.

Paul Bloom (chapter 8) considers the co-evolution of human language and thinking capacity. He argues that although the capacity for language and the particular characteristics of human language are related to culture, social cognition, and abstract thought, language is nevertheless a distinct biological adaptation for the function of communication. Citing linguistic, psychological, and anthropological evidence, Bloom considers and rejects other theoretical positions that explain language as a cultural invention or as a by-product of hominid brain expansion. Taking this one step further, he argues for the independence of language and the quality of mental life. While not rejecting the possibility that language and other aspects of human mental capacity co-evolved through a bootstrapping feedback loop, he nonetheless argues strongly that they evolved as independent functions. He summarizes evidence that many of the unique aspects of human mental life cannot be explained as by-products of the evolution of language, and that too many of the unique morphological and syntactic aspects of human language play no role in the richness of mental life.

In chapter 9 Elliott Sober takes on the comparative method, in particular the topic of Lloyd Morgan's canon: "In no case may we interpret an action as the outcome of the exercise of a higher psychical faculty, if it can be interpreted as the outcome of the exercise of one which stands lower in the psychological scale" (Morgan 1894, p. 53). Sober argues that the best way to interpret this principle is neither as a statement of parsimony, nor as a specifically evolutionary principle. This is an important move, for divorcing the principle from the theory of evolution opens the way to make testable, noncircular hypotheses about the evolution of higher psychological abilities from lower ones, as well as claims about homology and homoplasy.

In chapter 10, Lawrence Shapiro explains the particular role of Darwin's theory of evolution in discussions of psychological function. For Shapiro, all functional attributions in psychology are underwritten by Darwin's theory of adaptation by natural selection. Psychology is ultimately much richer for it because Darwinian theory suggests substantive hypotheses about our mental capacities. This Shapiro illustrates in his discussion of color vision. He is skeptical, however, of views that suggest a cognitive module for every function, for some functions can be carried out by mechanisms requiring little cognitive ability at all. Caution in inferring modules from functions is required.

As we mentioned earlier, the work in these chapters is clearly interdisciplinary. Once the ideological and terminological differences have been bridged, the chief challenge is to make evolutionary psychology into an experimental science. Several of the chapters in this volume describe experimental techniques and results consistent with this aim; our hope and intention is that they lead by example in the development of evolutionary psychology from the realm of speculation to that of established research program.

# 1

# Ecological Intelligence
## An Adaptation for Frequencies

GERD GIGERENZER

When I left a restaurant in a charming town in Tuscany one night, I looked for my yellow-green rented Renault 4 in the parking lot. There was none. Instead, there was a blue Renault 4 sitting in the lot, the same model, but the wrong color. I still feel my fingers hesitating to put my key into the lock of this car, but the lock opened. I drove the car home. When I looked out the window the next morning, there was a yellow-green Renault 4 standing in bright sunlight outside. What had happened? My color-constancy system did not work with the artificial light at the parking lot. Color constancy, an impressive adaptation of the human perceptual system, normally allows us to see the same color under changing illuminations, under the bluish light of day as well as the reddish light of the setting sun. Color constancy, however, fails under certain artificial lights, such as sodium or mercury vapor lamps, which were not present in the environment when mammals evolved (Shepard, 1992).

Human color vision is adapted to the spectral properties of natural sunlight. More generally, our perceptual system has been shaped by the environment in which our ancestors evolved, the environment often referred to as the "environment of evolutionary adaptiveness," or EEA (Tooby & Cosmides, 1992). Similarly, human morphology, physiology, and the nervous and immune systems show exquisite adaptations. The tubular form of the bones maximizes strength and flexibility while minimizing weight; bones are, pound for pound, stronger than solid steel bars, and the best man-made heart valves cannot yet match the way natural valves open and close (Nesse

*9*

& Williams, 1995). Like color constancy, however, these systems can be fooled and may break down when stable, long-term properties of the environment to which they were adapted change.

In this chapter, I propose that human reasoning algorithms are, like those of color constancy, designed for information that comes in a format that was present in the EEA. I will focus on a class of inductive reasoning processes technically known as *Bayesian inference*, specifically a simple version thereof in which an organism infers from one or a few indicators which of two events is true.

## Bayesian Inference

David Eddy (1982) asked physicians to estimate the probability that a woman has breast cancer given that she has a positive mammogram on the basis of the following information:

> The probability that a patient has breast cancer is 1% (the physician's prior probability).
>
> If the patient has breast cancer, the probability that the radiologist will correctly diagnose it is 79% (sensitivity or hit rate).
>
> If the patient has a benign lesion (no breast cancer), the probability that the radiologist will incorrectly diagnose it as cancer is 9.6% (false positive rate).
>
> QUESTION: What is the probability that a patient with a positive mammogram actually has breast cancer?

Eddy reported that 95 out of 100 physicians estimated the probability of breast cancer after a positive mammogram to be about 75 percent. The inference from an observation (positive test) to a disease, or more generally, from data D to a hypothesis H, is often referred to as "Bayesian inference," because it can be modeled by Bayes's rule:

$$p(H|D) = \frac{p(H)p(D|H)}{p(H)p(D|H) + p(\bar{H})p(D|\bar{H})} = \frac{(.01)(.79)}{(.01)(.79) + (.99)(.096)} = .077 \quad (1)$$

Equation 1 shows how the probability $p(H|D)$ that the woman has breast cancer (H) after a positive mammogram (D) is computed from the prior probability $p(H)$ that the patient has breast cancer, the sensitivity $p(D|H)$, and the false positive rate $p(D|\bar{H})$ of the mammography test. The probability $p(H|D)$ is called the "posterior probability." The symbol $\bar{H}$ stands for "the patient does not have breast cancer." Equation 1 is Bayes's rule for binary hypotheses and data. The rule is named after Thomas Bayes (1702[?]–1761), an English dissenting minister, to whom this solution of the problem of how to make an inference from data to hypothesis (the so-called inverse problem; see Daston, 1988) is attributed.[1] The important point is that Equation 1 results in a probability of 7.7%, not 75% as estimated by the majority of physicians. In other words, the probability that the woman has breast cancer is one order of magnitude smaller than estimated.

This result, together with an avalanche of studies reporting that lay people's reasoning does not follow Bayes's rule either, has (mis-)led many to believe that Homo Sapiens would be inept to reason the Bayesian way. Listen to some influential voices: "In his evaluation of evidence, man is apparently not a conservative Bayesian: he is not a Bayesian at all" (Kahneman & Tversky, 1972, p. 450). "Tversky and Kahneman argue, correctly, I think, that our minds are not built (for whatever reason) to work by the rules of probability" (Gould, 1992, p. 469).[2] The literature of the last twenty-five years has reiterated again and again the message that people are bad reasoners, neglect base rates most of the time, neglect false positive rates, and are unable to integrate base rate, hit rate, and false positive rate the Bayesian way (for a recent review see Koehler, 1996). Probability problems such as the mammography problem have become the stock-in-trade of textbooks, lectures, and party entertainment. It is guaranteed fun to point out how dumb others are. And aren't they? There seem to be many customers eager to buy the message of "inevitable illusions" wired into our brain (Piattelli-Palmarini, 1994).

### Ecological Bayesian Inference: An Adaptation for Frequencies

Back to color constancy. If a human visual system enters an environment illuminated by sodium vapor lamps, its color constancy algorithms will fail. This does not mean, however, that human minds are not built to work by color-constancy algorithms. Similarly, if a human reasoning system enters an environment in which statistical information is formatted differently from that encountered in the environment in which humans evolved, the reasoning algorithms may fail. But this does not imply that human minds are not built to reason the Bayesian way. The issue is not whether nature has equipped our minds with good or with bad statistical software, as the "optimists" versus "pessimists" discussion about human rationality suggests (Jungermann, 1983). The issue I address here is the adaptation of mental algorithms to their environment. By "mental algorithms," I mean induction mechanisms that perform classification, estimation, or other forms of uncertain inferences, such as deciding what color an object is, or inferring whether a person has a disease.

For which information formats have mental algorithms been designed? What matters for an algorithm that makes inductive inferences is the format of numerical information. Eddy presented information (about the prevalence of breast cancer, the sensitivity, and the false positive rate of the test) in terms of probabilities and percentages, just as most experimenters did who found humans making irrational judgments. What was the format of the numerical information humans encountered during their evolution? We know too little about these environments, for instance, about the historically normal conditions of childbirth, or how strong a factor religious doctrines were, and most likely, these varied considerably between societies. But concerning the format of numerical information, I believe we can be as certain as we ever can be—probabilities and percentages were not the way organisms encountered information. Probabilities and percentages are quite recent forms of representations of uncertainty. Mathematical probability emerged in the mid-seventeenth century (Hacking, 1975), and the concept of probability itself did not gain prominence over the primitive notion of "expectation" before the mid-eighteenth century (Daston, 1988). Percentages became common notations only during the nineteenth century, after the metric system was introduced during the French Revolution (mainly, though, for interest and taxes rather than for representing uncertainty). Only in the second half of the twentieth century did probabilities and percentages become entrenched in the everyday language of Western countries as representations of uncertainty (Gigerenzer et al., 1989). To summarize, probabilities and percentages took millennia of literacy and numeracy to evolve as a format to represent degrees of uncertainty. In what format did humans acquire numerical information before that time?

I propose that the original format was *natural frequencies*, acquired by *natural sampling*. Let me explain what this means by a parallel to the mammography problem, using the same numbers. Think about a physician in an illiterate society. Her people have been afflicted by a new, severe disease. She has no books nor statistical surveys; she must rely solely on her experience. Fortunately, she discovered a symptom that signals the disease, although not with certainty. In her lifetime, she has seen 1,000 people, 10 of whom had the disease. Of those 10, eight showed the symptom; of the 990 not afflicted, 95 did. Thus, there were 8 + 95 = 103 people who showed the symptom, and only 8 of these had the disease. Now a new patient appears. He has the symptom. What is the probability that he actually has the disease?

The physician in the illiterate society does not need a pocket calculator to estimate the Bayesian posterior probability. All she needs to do is to keep track of the number of symptom and disease cases (8) and the number of symptom and no disease cases (95). The probability that the new patient actually has the disease can be "seen" easily from these frequencies:

$$p(H|D) = \frac{a}{a + b} = \frac{8}{8 + 95} \qquad (2)$$

Equation 2 is Bayes's rule for natural frequencies, in where $a$ is the number of cases with symptom and disease, and $b$ is the number of cases having the symptom but lacking the disease. The chance that the new patient has the disease is less than 8 out of 100, or 8%. Our physician who learns from experience cannot be fooled as easily into believing that the chances are about 75%, as many of her contemporary colleagues did.

The comparison between Equations 1 and 2 reveals an important theoretical result: Bayesian reasoning is computationally simpler (in terms of the number of operations performed, such as additions and multiplications) when the information is in *natural frequencies* (Equation 2) rather than in *probabilities* (Equation 1) (see Kleiter, 1994). Incidentally, as Equation 2 shows, the base rates of event frequencies (such as 10 in 1,000) need not be kept in memory; they are implicit in the two frequencies, *a* and *b*.

Let me be clear how the terms "natural sampling" and "natural frequencies" relate (Gigerenzer & Hoffrage, 1995). Natural sampling is the sequential process of updating event frequencies from experience. A foraging organism who, day after day, samples potential resources for food and learns the frequencies with which a cue (e.g., the presence of other species) predicts food, performs natural sampling by updating the frequencies *a* and *b* from observation to observation. Natural sampling is different from systematic experimentation, in which the sample sizes (the base rates) of each treatment group are fixed in advance. For instance, in a clinical experiment, one might select 100 patients with cancer and 100 without cancer, and then perform tests on these groups. By fixing the base rates, the frequencies obtained in such experimental designs no longer carry information about the base rates. This is not to say that controlled sampling in systematic experiments is useless; it just serves a different purpose. Brunswik's (1955) method of "representative sampling" in a natural environment is an example of applying the idea of natural sampling to experimental design.

Natural frequencies report the final tally of a natural sampling process. There is more than one way to present the final tally. In the case of the physician in the illiterate society, I specified the total number of observations (1,000), the frequency of the disease, and the frequencies *a* and *b* of hits and false positives, respectively: "In her lifetime, she has seen 1,000 people, 10 of whom had the disease. Of those 10, eight showed the symptom; of the 990 not afflicted, 95 did." This is a straightforward translation of the base rates, hit rates, and false positive rates into natural frequencies. Alternatively, one can communicate the frequencies *a* and *b* alone: "In her lifetime, she has seen 8 people with symptom and disease, and 95 people with symptom and no disease." The former natural frequencies use a *standard menu* ("standard" because slicing up the information in terms of base rate, hit rate, and false positive rate is deeply entrenched today), the latter use a *short menu* (Gigerenzer & Hoffrage, 1995). Both lead to the same result.

Natural frequencies must not to be confused with a representation in terms of relative frequencies (e.g., a base rate of .01, a hit rate of .79, and a false positive rate of .096). Relative frequencies are, like probabilities and percentages, normalized numbers that no longer carry information about the natural base rates (Gigerenzer & Hoffrage, 1995). Relative frequencies, probabilities, and percentages are to human reasoning algorithms (that do Bayesian-type inference) like sodium vapor lamps to human color-constancy algorithms. This analogy has, like every analogy, its limits. For instance, humans can be taught, although with some mental agony, to reason by probabilities, but not, I believe, to maintain color constancy under sodium vapor illumination.

Note that the total number of observations—communicated only when natural frequencies are expressed in the standard menu—need not be the actual total number of observations. It can be any convenient number such as 100 or 1,000. The computational simplicity of natural frequencies holds independently of whether the actual or a convenient number is used. For example, if the actual sample size was 5,167 patients, one can nevertheless represent the information in the same way as above. "For *every* 1,000 patients we expect 10 who have breast cancer, and 8 out of these 10 will test positive."[3]

The hypothesis that mental algorithms were designed for natural frequencies is consistent with (a) a body of studies that report that humans can monitor frequencies fairly accurately (Barsalou & Ross, 1986; Hintzman & Block, 1972; Jonides & Jones, 1992), (b) the thesis that humans process frequencies (almost) automatically, that is, without or with little effort, awareness, and interference with other processes (Hasher & Zacks, 1984), (c) the thesis that probability learning and transfer derive from frequency learning (Estes, 1976), and (d) developmental studies on counting in children and animals (e.g., Gallistel & Gelman, 1992). This is not to say that humans and animals count all possible events equally well, nor could they. A conceptual mechanism must first decide what the units of observation are so that a frequency encoding mechanism can count them. This preceding conceptual process is not dealt with by the hypothesis that mental algorithms are designed for natural frequencies (but see the connection proposed by Brase, Cosmides, & Tooby, in press).

Thus, my argument has two parts: evolutionary (and developmental) primacy of natural frequencies, and ease of computation. First, mental algorithms, from color constancy to inductive reasoning, have evolved in an environment with fairly stable characteristics. If there are mental algorithms that perform Bayesian-type inferences from data to hypotheses, these are designed for natural frequencies acquired by natural sampling, and not for probabilities or percentages. Second, when numerical information is represented in natural frequencies, Bayesian computations reduce themselves to a minimum. Both parts of the argument are necessary. For instance, the computational part could be countered by hypothesizing that there might be a single neuron in the human mind that almost instantaneously computes Equation 1 on the basis of probability information. The evolutionary part of the argument makes it unlikely that such a neuron has evolved that computes using an information format that was not present in the environment in which our ancestors evolved.

### Predictions

This argument has testable consequences. First, laypeople—that is, persons with no professional expertise in diagnostic inference—are more likely to reason the Bayesian way when the information is presented in natural frequencies than in a probability format. This effect should occur without any instruction in Bayesian inference. Second, experts such as physicians who make diagnostic inferences on a daily basis should, despite their experience, show the same effect. Third, the "inevitable illusions" (Piattelli-Palmarini, 1994), such as base rate neglect should become evitable by using natural frequencies. Finally, natural frequencies should provide a superior vehicle for teaching Bayesian inference. In what follows, I report tests of these predictions and several examples drawn from a broad variety of everyday situations.

This is not to say that probabilities are useless or perverse. In mathematics, they play their role independent of whether or not they suit human reasoning, just as Riemannian and other non-Euclidean geometries play their roles independent of the fact that human spatial reasoning is Euclidean.

*Breast Cancer*

Eddy (1982) provides only a scant, one-paragraph description of his study of physicians' intuitions, and refers to a study by Casscells, Schoenberger, and Grayboys (1978) with similar results. Both studies used a probability format. Would natural frequencies make any difference to experts such as physicians? Ulrich Hoffrage and I tested 48 physicians in Munich, Germany on the mammography problem. These physicians had an average professional experience of 14 years. Twenty-four physicians read the information in a probability format as in Eddy's study, the other 24 read the same information in natural frequencies. Physicians were always asked for a single-event probability (as in Eddy's study) when the information was in probabilities; they were always asked for a frequency judgment when the information was in natural frequencies. The two formats of the mammography problem are shown in Table 1. Each physician got four diagnostic problems (including the mammography problem), two in a probability format and two in natural frequencies (the details are in Gigerenzer, 1996b; Gigerenzer & Hoffrage, forthcoming; Hoffrage & Gigerenzer, 1996).

In the probability format, only 2 out of 24 physicians (8%) came up with the Bayesian answer. The median estimate of the probability of breast cancer after a positive mammogram was 70%, consistent with Eddy's findings. With natural frequencies, however, 11 out of 24 physicians (46%) responded with the Bayesian answer. Across all four diagnostic problems, similar results were obtained—10% Bayesian responses in the probability format, and 46% with natural frequencies.

Natural frequencies also changed the physicians' non-Bayesian inferences. When information was in the form of probabilities, the two dominant non-Bayesian strategies consisted of subtracting the false positive rate from the sensitivity, or simply taking the sensitivity. Both strategies ignore base rates. With natural frequencies, however, these two strategies largely disappeared, and physicians' dominant non-Bayesian strategies focused exclusively on base rates—the base rate of the disease, or the base rate of a positive test. Natural frequencies not only changed physicians' reasoning but made them also feel less nervous, more relaxed, and in need of less time to complete the task.

*Table 1.1   The Mammography Problem: Probability Format and
Natural Frequencies*

To facilitate early detection of breast cancer, women are encouraged from a
particular age on to participate at regular intervals in routine screening, even if
they have no obvious symptoms. Imagine you use mammography to conduct
such a breast cancer screening in a certain region. For symptom-free women
age 40 to 50 who participate in screening using mammography, the following
information is available for this region:

*Probability format*

The probability that one of these women has breast cancer is 1%.

If a woman has breast cancer, the probability is 80% that she will have a positive
mammogram.

If a woman does *not* have breast cancer, the probability is 10% that she will still
have a positive mammogram.

Imagine a woman (age 40 to 50, no symptoms) who has a positive mammogram in your breast cancer screening. What is the probability that she
actually has breast cancer?    _____%

*Natural frequencies*

Ten out of every 1,000 women have breast cancer.

Of these 10 women with breast cancer, 8 will have a positive mammogram.

Of the remaining 990 women *without* breast cancer, 99 will still have a positive
mammogram.

Imagine a sample of women (age 40 to 50, no symptoms) who have positive
mammograms in your breast cancer screening. How many of these women do
actually have breast cancer? _____ out of _____.

---

We obtained essentially identical results when we tested lay people
(Gigerenzer & Hoffrage, 1995). Lay people and experienced physicians
were equally helpless with probabilities, and did not by themselves spontaneously translate probability information into natural frequencies. Some
even retranslated frequencies into percentages, because they believed that
doing so was the only right way to represent uncertainty. A remarkable result
was that when students worked on 30 problems in which natural frequencies and probability formats alternated randomly from problem to problem, students continued to fail on the probability formats and to solve the
frequency formats at about the same rate, with little spontaneous transfer
(Gigerenzer & Hoffrage, 1995).

Even those who are experienced with statistics can have problems "seeing" through probabilities as easily as through frequencies. Colleagues who
work with Bayes's rule on a daily basis often falter when confronted with a
specific problem to be solved on the spot. I grant that few people are skilled
at mental arithmetic under any circumstances, but it is nevertheless note-

worthy that experts as well as laymen seem to do better when calculations involve natural frequencies rather than probabilities.

The lesson of these results is not to blame physicians' or students' minds when they stumble over probabilities. Rather, the lesson is to represent information in textbooks, in curricula, and in physician-patient interactions in natural frequencies that correspond to the way information was encountered in the environment in which human minds evolved.

### Colon Cancer

The fecal occult blood test is a widely used and well-known test for colon cancer. Windeler and Köbberling (1986) report that while physicians overestimated the (posterior) probability that a patient has colon cancer if the fecal occult blood test is positive, they also overestimated the base rate of colon cancer, the sensitivity (hit rate), and the false positive rate of the test. Windeler and Köbberling asked these physicians about probabilities and percentages. Would natural frequencies improve physicians' estimates of what a positive test tells about the presence of colon cancer? The 48 physicians in the study reported above were given the best available estimates for the base rate, sensitivity, and false positive rate, as published in Windeler and Köbberling (1986). The following is a shortened version of the full text (structured like the mammography problem in Table 1) given to the physicians. In the probability format, the information was:

> The probability that a person has colon cancer is 0.3%.
>
> If a person has colon cancer, the probability that the test is positive is 50%.
>
> If a person does *not* have colon cancer, the probability that the test is positive is 3%.
>
> What is the probability that a person who tests positive actually has colon cancer?

When one inserts these values into Bayes's rule (Equation 1), the resulting probability is 4.8%. In natural frequencies, the information was:

> 30 out of every 10,000 people have colon cancer.
>
> Of these 30 people with colon cancer, 15 will test positive.
>
> Of the remaining 9,970 people *without* colon cancer, 300 will still test positive.
>
> Imagine a group of people who test positive. How many of these will actually have colon cancer?

When the information was in the probability format, only 1 out of 24 physicians (4%) could find the Bayesian answer, or anything close to it. The median estimate was one order of magnitude higher, namely 47%. When the information was presented in natural frequencies, 16 out of 24 physicians (67%) came up with the Bayesian answer (details are in Gigerenzer, 1996b; Hoffrage & Gigerenzer, 1996).

## Wife Battering

Alan Dershowitz, the Harvard law professor who advised the defense in the first O. J. Simpson trial, claimed repeatedly that evidence of abuse and battering should not be admissible in a murder trial. In his best-seller, *Reasonable Doubts: The Criminal Justice System and the O. J. Simpson Case* (1996), Dershowitz says: "The reality is that a majority of women who are killed are killed by men with whom they have a relationship, *regardless of whether their men previously battered them*. Battery, as such, is not a good independent predictor of murder" (p. 105). Dershowitz stated on U.S. television in March 1995 that only about a tenth of 1 % of wife batterers actually murder their wives. In response to Dershowitz, I. J. Good, a distinguished professor emeritus of Statistics at the Virginia Polytechnic Institute, published an article in *Nature* to correct for the possible misunderstandings of what that statement implies for the probability that O. J. Simpson actually murdered his wife in 1994 (Good, 1995). Good's argument is that the relevant probability is not the probability that a husband murders his wife if he batters her. Instead, the relevant probability is the probability that a husband has murdered his wife if he battered her *and* if she was actually murdered by someone. More precisely, the relevant probability is not $p(G|Bat)$ but $p(G|Bat$ and $M)$, in which $G$ stands for "the husband is guilty" (that is, did the murder in 1994), *Bat* means that "the husband battered his wife," and $M$ means that "the wife was actually murdered by somebody in 1994."

My point concerns the way Good presents his argument, not the argument itself. Good presented the information in single-event probabilities and odds (rather than in natural frequencies). I will first summarize Good's argument as he made it. I hope I can demonstrate that you the reader— unless you are a trained statistician or exceptionally smart with probabilities—will have some difficulty following it. Thereafter, I will present the same argument in natural frequencies, and confusion should turn into insight. Let's see.

Good bases his calculations of $p(G|Bat$ and $M)$ on the odds version of Bayes's rule:

$$\text{posterior odds} = \text{prior odds} \times \text{likelihood ratio},$$

which, in the present case is:

$$\frac{p(G|Bat \text{ and } M)}{p(\bar{G}|Bat \text{ and } M)} = \frac{p(G|Bat)}{p(\bar{G}|Bat)} \times \frac{p(M|G \text{ and } Bat)}{p(M|\bar{G} \text{ and } Bat)} \qquad (3)$$

where $\bar{G}$ stands for "the husband is not guilty."

The following six equations (Good-1 to Good-6) show Good's method of explaining to the reader how to estimate $p(G|Bat$ and $M)$. Good starts with Dershowitz's figure of a tenth of 1%, arguing that if the husband commits the murder, the probability is at least $1/10$ that he will do it in 1994:[4]

$$p(G|Bat) > (1/10)(1/1{,}000) = 1/10{,}000 \qquad \text{(Good-1)}$$

Therefore, the prior odds (O) are:

$$O(G|Bat) > 1/9{,}999 \approx 1/10{,}000 \qquad \text{(Good-2)}$$

Furthermore, the probability of a woman being murdered given that her husband has murdered her (whether he is a batterer or not) is unity:

$$p(\text{M}|\text{G and Bat}) = p(\text{M}|\text{G}) = 1 \qquad \text{(Good-3)}$$

Because there are about 25,000 murders per year in the US population of about 250,000,000, Good estimates the probability of a woman being murdered, but not by her husband, as:

$$p(\text{M}|\bar{\text{G}} \text{ and Bat}) = p(\text{M}|(\bar{\text{G}})) \approx 1/10,000 \qquad \text{(Good 4)}$$

From Equations Good-3 and Good-4, it follows that the likelihood ratio is about 10,000/1; therefore, the posterior odds can be calculated:

$$O(\text{G}|\text{M and Bat}) > 10,000/10,000 = 1 \qquad \text{(Good-5)}$$

That is, the probability that a murdered, battered wife was killed by her husband is:

$$p(\text{G}|\text{Bat and M}) > 1/2 \qquad \text{(Good-6)}$$

Good's point is that "most members of a jury or of the public, not being familiar with elementary probability, would readily confuse this with $P(\text{G}|\text{Bat})$, and would thus be badly misled by Dershowitz's comment" (Good, 1995, p. 541). He adds that he sent a copy of this note to both Dershowitz and the Los Angeles Police Department, reminding us that Bayesian reasoning should be taught at the pre-college level.

Good's persuasive argument, I believe, could have been understood more easily by his readers and the Los Angeles Police Department if the information had been presented in natural frequencies rather than in the single-event probabilities and odds in the six equations. As with breast cancer and colon cancer, one way to represent information in natural frequencies is to start with a concrete sample of individuals divided into subclasses, in the same way it would be experienced by natural sampling. Here is a frequency version of Good's argument.

Good's Argument in Natural Frequencies

Think of 10,000 battered married women. Within one year, at least one will be murdered by her husband. Of the remaining 9,999 who are not killed by their husbands, one will be murdered by someone else. Thus we expect at least two battered women to be murdered, at least one by her husband, and one by someone else. Therefore, the probability $p(\text{G}|\text{Bat and M})$ that a murdered, battered woman was killed by her husband is at least ½.

This probability is not to be confounded with the probability that O. J. Simpson is guilty; a jury must take into account much more evidence than battering. But the probability shows that abuse-and-battering is a good predictor of the husband's (or boyfriend's) guilt, disproving Dershowitz's assertion to the contrary.

In natural frequencies, Good's argument is short and transparent. My conjecture is that more ordinary people, including employees of the Los

Angeles Police Department and jurors, could understand and communicate the argument if the information were represented in natural frequencies rather than in probabilities or odds.

In legal jargon, evidence of wife battering is probative, not prejudicial. This analysis is consistent with the impressive transcultural evidence about homicide accumulated by Daly and Wilson (1988). The typical function of wife battering seems to be to exert proprietary rights over the sexuality and reproduction of women, as well as threats against infidelity. Battering can "spill over" into killing, and killing is the tip of a huge iceberg of wife abuse.

*AIDS Counseling*

Under the headline, "A False HIV Test Caused 18 Months of Hell," the *Chicago Tribune* (3/5/93) published the following letter and response:

> Dear Ann Landers: In March 1991, I went to an anonymous testing center for a routine HIV test. In two weeks, the results came back positive.
>
> I was devastated. I was 20 years old and doomed. I became severely depressed and contemplated a variety of ways to commit suicide. After encouragement from family and friends, I decided to fight back.
>
> My doctors in Dallas told me that California had the best care for HIV patients, so I packed everything and headed west. It took three months to find a doctor I trusted. Before this physician would treat me, he insisted on running more tests. Imagine my shock when the new results came back negative. The doctor tested me again, and the results were clearly negative.
>
> I'm grateful to be healthy, but the 18 months I thought I had the virus changed my life forever. I'm begging doctors to be more careful. I also want to tell your readers to be sure and get a second opinion. I will continue to be tested for HIV every six months, but I am no longer terrified.
>
> David in Dallas
>
> Dear Dallas: Yours is truly a nightmare with a happy ending, but don't blame the doctor. It's the lab that needs to shape up. The moral of your story is this: *Get a second opinion. And a third.* Never trust a single test. Ever.
>
> Ann Landers

David does not mention what his Dallas doctors told him about the chances that he actually had the virus after the positive test, but he seems to have inferred that a positive test meant that he had the virus, period. In fact, when we studied AIDS counselors in Germany, we found that many doctors and social workers (erroneously) tell their low-risk clients that a positive HIV test implies that the virus is present (Gigerenzer, Hoffrage, & Ebert, in press). These counselors know that a single ELISA (enzyme-linked immunosorbent assay) test can produce a false positive, but they erroneously assume that the whole series of ELISA and Western blot tests would wipe out every false positive. How could a doctor have explained the actual risk to David and spared him the nightmare?

I do not have HIV statistics for Dallas, so I will use German figures for illustration. (The specific numbers are not the point here.) In Germany, the prevalence of HIV infections in heterosexual men between the ages of 20 and 30 who belong to no known risk group can be estimated as about 1 in 10,000, or 0.01%. The corresponding base rate for homosexual men is estimated at about 1.5%. The hit rate (sensitivity) of the typical test series (repeated ELISA and Western blot tests) is estimated at about 99.8%. The estimates of the false positive rate vary somewhat; a reasonable estimate seems to be 0.01% (Gigerenzer, Hoffrage, & Ebert, in press). Given these values, and assuming that David was at the time of the routine HIV test a heterosexual man with low-risk behavior, what is the probability that he actually had the virus after testing positive? If his physician had actually given David these probabilities, David nevertheless might not have understood what to conclude.

But the physician could have communicated the information in natural frequencies. He might have said, "Your situation is the following: Think of 10,000 heterosexual men like you. We expect one to be infected with the virus, and he will, with practical certainty, test positive. From the 9,999 men who are not infected, one additional individual will test positive. Thus we get two individuals who test positive, but only one of them actually has the virus. This is your situation. The chances that you actually have the virus after the positive test are about 1 in 2, or 50%." If the physician had explained the risk in this way, David might have understood that there was, as yet, no reason to contemplate suicide or to move to California.

If David were a member of a risk group, say a homosexual with a 1.5% base rate of HIV infection, the estimate would have been different. Here, the physician might have explained, "Think of 10,000 homosexual men. We expect 150 to be infected with the virus, and they all will likely test positive. From the 9,850 men who are not infected, we expect that one other will test positive. Thus we have 151 men who test positive, and 150 of these have the virus. Your chances of not having the virus are 1 out of 151, that is, less than 1%." This would not be good news, but it would still be better than leaving the doctor's office with the belief that an HIV infection is absolutely certain. David might be the lucky one, and his odds are certainly better than winning a lottery.

We do not know what risk group David was in. Whatever the statistics are, however, most people of average intelligence can understand the risk of HIV after a positive test when the numbers are represented by a counselor in natural frequencies. Not one of the 20 AIDS counselors studied by Gigerenzer, Hoffage, & Ebert (in press), however, explained his or her client's risk in natural frequencies. Except for the prevalence of HIV, all numerical information was communicated to the client in percentages.

Ann Landers's answer—don't blame the doctor, blame the lab—however, overlooks the fact that despite whatever possible reasons there may be for false positives (such as the presence of cross-reacting antibodies or blood samples being confused in the lab), a doctor should inform the patient that false positives occur, and about how frequently they occur.

## Expert Witnesses

Evidentiary problems such as the evaluation of eyewitness testimony constituted one of the first domains of probability theory (Gigerenzer et al., 1989, chap. 1). Statisticians have taken the stand as expert witnesses for almost a century now: In the Dreyfus case in the late nineteenth century in France, or more recently, in *People vs. Collins* in California (Gigerenzer et al., 1989, chap. 7; Koehler, 1992). The convictions in both cases were ultimately reversed and the statistical arguments discredited. Part of the problem seems to have been that the statistical arguments were couched not in frequencies but in probabilities which confused both the prosecution who were making the arguments and the jury and the judges who tried to understand the arguments. I will explain this point with the case of a chimney sweep who was accused of having committed a murder in Wuppertal, Germany (Schrage, n.d.).

The *Rheinische Merkur* (No. 39, 1974) reported:

> On the evening of July 20, 1972, the 40-year-old Wuppertal painter Wilhelm Fink and his 37-year-old wife Ingeborg took a walk in the woods and were attacked by a stranger. The husband was hit by three bullets in the throat and the chest, and fell down. Then the stranger attempted to rape his wife. When she defended herself and unexpectedly, the shot-down husband got back on his feet to help her, the stranger shot two bullets into the wife's head and fled.

Three days later, a forest ranger discovered 20 kilometers from the scene of the crime the car of Werner Wiegand, a 25-year-old chimney sweep who used to spend his weekends in the vicinity. The husband, who had survived, at first thought he recognized the chimney sweep in a photo. Later, he grew less certain and began to think that another suspect was the murderer. When the other suspect was found innocent, however, the prosecution came back to the chimney sweep and put him on trial. The chimney sweep had no previous convictions and denied being the murderer. The *Rheinische Merkur* described the trial:

> After the experts had testified and explained their "probability theories," the case seemed to be clear: Wiegand, despite his denial, must have been the murderer. Dr. Christian Rittner, a lecturer at the University of Bonn, evaluated the traces of blood as follows: 17.29% of German citizens share Wiegand's blood group, traces of which have been found underneath the fingernails of the murdered woman; 15.69% of Germans share [her] blood group that was also found on Wiegand's boots; based on a so-called "cross-combination" the expert subsequently calculated an overall probability of 97.3% that Wiegand "can be considered the murderer." And concerning the textile fiber traces which were found both on Wiegand's clothes and on those of the vic-

tim [. . .] Dr. Ernst Röhm from the Munich branch of the State Crime Department explained: "The probability that textile microfibers of this kind are transmitted from a human to another human who was not in contact with the victim is at most 0.06%. From this results a 99.94% certainty for Wiegand being the murderer."

Both expert witnesses agreed that, with a high probability, the chimney sweep was the murderer. These expert calculations, however, collapsed when the court discovered that the defendant was in his hometown, 100 kilometers away from the scene of the crime at the time of the crime.

So what was wrong with the expert calculations? One can dispel the confusion in court by representing the uncertainties in natural frequencies. Let us assume that the blood underneath the fingernails of the victim was indeed the blood of the murderer, that the murderer carried traces of the victim's blood (as the expert witnesses assumed), and that there were 10,000,000 men in Germany who could have committed the crime (Schrage, n.d.). Let us assume further that on one of every 100 of these men a close examination would find microscopic traces of foreign blood, that is, on 100,000 men. Of these, some 15,690 men (15.69%) will carry traces from blood that is of the victim's blood type. Of these 15,690 men, some 2,710 (17.29%) will also have the blood type that was found underneath the victim's fingernails (here, I assume independence between the two evidences). Thus, there are some 2,710 men (including the murderer) who might appear guilty based on the two pieces of blood evidence. The chimney sweep is one of these men. Therefore, given the two blood evidences the probability that the chimney sweep is the murderer is about 1 in 2,710, and not 97.3%, as the first expert witness testified.

The same frequency method can be applied to the textile traces. Let us assume that the second expert witness was correct when he said that the probability of the chimney sweep carrying the textile trace, if he were not the murderer, would be at most 0.06%. Let us assume as well that the murderer actually carries that trace. Then some 6,000 of the 10,000,000 would carry this textile trace, and only one of them would be the murderer. Thus, the probability that the chimney sweep was the murderer, given the textile fiber evidence, was about 1 in 6,000, and not 99.94%, as the second expert witness testified.

What if one combines both the blood and the textile evidences together, which seems not to have happened at the trial? In this case, one of the 2,710 men who satisfy both blood type evidences would be the murderer, and he would show the textile traces. Of the remaining innocent men, we expect one or two (0.06%) to also show the textile traces (assuming mutual independence of the three evidences). Thus, there would be two or three men who satisfy all three types of evidence. One of them is the murderer. Therefore, the probability that the chimney sweep was the murderer, given the two blood sample evidences and the textile evidence, would be between ⅓ and ½. This probability would not be beyond reasonable doubt.

*Cognitive Illusions*

Frequencies not only make everyday inferences easier, they also tend to make "cognitive illusions" of the laboratory type largely disappear. I have summarized this evidence elsewhere (Gigerenzer, 1991, 1994). One example is a cognitive illusion called "overconfidence bias." Students were given questions such as, "Which city has more inhabitants: Islamabad or Hyderabad?" They were then asked to estimate the probability (confidence) that their answer was correct. The typical result was that when students said they were 100% confident, they were correct in only about 85% of the cases. When they said they were 90% confident, they were correct in only 75% of the cases, and so on (Lichtenstein, Fischhoff, & Phillips, 1982). This discrepancy between subjective probability and objective frequency was labeled the "overconfidence bias," and human disasters of many kinds, from deadly accidents in industry to errors in the legal process, have been attributed to that "cognitive illusion." However, when we replaced the probability judgments by frequency judgments, the apparently stable cognitive illusion disappeared (Gigerenzer, Hoffrage, & Kleinbölting, 1991). We asked students after every 50 questions to estimate *how many* they got correct, and these frequency judgments no longer overestimated the actual frequencies of correct answers. In fact, they turned out to be fairly accurate, even with a tendency towards underestimation.

A second example is a medical disease problem with which Casscells, Schoenberger and Grayboys (1978) had demonstrated base rate neglect by staff and students at Harvard Medical School. Cosmides and Tooby (1996) replaced the probabilities with natural frequencies, and Bayesian responses increased from 12% (in the original probability format) to 76%. An instruction to visualize frequencies in a grid boosted the performance up to 92%. More generally, natural frequencies reduce the "base rate fallacy" in the cab problem and similar "toy" problems (Gigerenzer, 1994; Gigerenzer & Hoffrage, 1995).

A third and final example is the "Linda" problem. People read a description of Linda that suggests that she is a feminist. Thereafter, the people are asked which is more probable: (a) Linda is a bank teller; or, (b) Linda is a bank teller and active in the feminist movement. Some 80%–90% of subjects usually chose (b), a response which Tversky and Kahneman (1983) labeled the "conjunction fallacy," because the probability of a conjunction of two events (teller and feminist) cannot be larger than the probability of one of these events (teller). This "conjunction fallacy" in the Linda problem and related tasks, however, largely disappeared when people were asked for judgments of frequencies: Think of 200 women like Linda. How many of them are (a) bank tellers, (b) bank tellers and active in the feminist movement? Replacing probabilities by frequencies made conjunction violations drop from 80–90% to 0–20% (Hertwig & Gigerenzer, 1997; similar results were reported by Fiedler, 1988; Tversky & Kahneman, 1983). The effect of frequency representations and judgments on "cognitive illusions" is the strongest and most consistent "debiasing method" known today.

## Teaching Statistical Reasoning

The teaching of statistical reasoning is, like that of reading and writing, part of forming an educated citizenship. Our technological world, with its abundance of statistical information, makes the art of dealing with uncertain information particularly relevant. Reading and writing is taught to every child in modern Western democracies, but statistical thinking is not (Shaughnessy, 1992). The result has been termed "innumeracy" (Paulos, 1988). But can statistical reasoning be taught? Previous studies that attempted to teach Bayesian inference, mostly by corrective feedback, had little or no training effect (e.g., Peterson, DuCharme, & Edwards, 1968; Schaefer, 1976). This result seems to be consistent with the view that the mind does not naturally reason the Bayesian way. However, the argument developed in this chapter suggests a "natural" method of teaching: instruct people how to represent probability information in natural frequencies. Recall that students and physicians alike did not do this spontaneously, with very few exceptions (e.g., Gigerenzer & Hoffrage, 1995).

Peter Sedlmeier and I designed a tutorial program that teaches Bayesian reasoning, based on the assumption that cognitive algorithms have evolved for dealing with natural frequencies (Sedlmeier, 1997); Sedlmeier & Gigerenzer, 1998). The goal of this tutorial is to teach participants how to reason the Bayesian way when the information is represented in probabilities, as is usually the case in newspapers, medical textbooks, and other information sources. The computerized tutorial instructs participants in how to represent the probability information in terms of natural frequencies, rather than teaching them how to insert probabilities into Bayes's rule (Equation 1). The tutorial consists of two parts. In the first part, participants are shown how to translate probability information into natural frequencies, visually aided by a frequency tree (or a frequency grid); the method is illustrated by two medical problems, one of them the mammography problem. In the second part, participants solve eight other problems, with step-by-step guidance on what to do as well as step-by-step feedback. If participants have difficulties, the system provides immediate help that ensures that every participant solves all problems correctly. We conducted an evaluation study with four groups: two groups were taught how to represent probabilities in natural frequencies (visually demonstrated by a frequency tree and a frequency grid, respectively), one control group was taught how to insert probabilities into Bayes's rule using a similar computer tutorial ("rule training"), and a second control group received no training.

Sixty-two University of Chicago students participated in the study. In the rule-training group, the median number of Bayesian solutions increased from 0% (pretraining baseline) to 35% after training, and the values for the no-training control increased slightly from 0% to 5%. In the two groups that learned how to construct frequency representations by constructing frequency trees or frequency grids, the median number of Bayesian solutions increased from 0% and 5% to 80% and 70%, respectively. Thus, the immediate success of the frequency tutorials was about twice as high as that of the rule training. But did the performance last over time, or was it subject to the usual steep forgetting curve following a successful test? In a five-week follow up, the median performance of the rule-training group was down to a mere 15%. The median performance of each of the two frequency representation groups five weeks after training, however, was a strong 90%.

Thus, there is evidence that (what I take to be) the natural format of information in the environment in which humans evolved can be used to teach people how to deal with probability information. This may be good news both for instructors who plan to design pre-college curricula that teach young people how to infer risks in a technological world, and for those unfortunate souls among us charged with teaching undergraduate statistics.

## Conclusions

Information needs representation. If a representation is recurrent and stable during human evolution, one can expect that mental algorithms are designed to operate on this representation. In this chapter, I applied this argument to the understanding of human inferences under uncertainty. The thesis is that mental algorithms were designed for natural frequencies, the recurrent format of information until very recently. I have dealt with a specific class of inferences that correspond to a simple form of Bayesian inferences, in which one of several possible states is inferred from one or a few cues. Here, mental computations are simpler when information is encountered in the same form as in the environment in which our ancestors evolved, rather than in the modern form of probabilities or percentages. The evidence from a broad variety of everyday situations and laboratory experiments shows that natural frequencies can make human minds smarter.

## Notes

I would like to thank Ralph Hertwig, Ulrich Hoffrage, James S. Magnuson, Laura Martignon, and Anita Todd for their helpful comments.

   1. As we know from Stephen M. Stigler's *Law of Eponymy*, no scientific discovery is named after its original discoverer, and Bayes's rule seems to be no exception to this rule (Stigler, 1983).

   2. For a critical discussion of these interpretations see Cohen (1981), Gigerenzer (1994, 1996a), Gigerenzer and Murray (1987, chap. 5), and Lopes (1991); for a reply, see Kahneman and Tversky (1996).

   3. However, there is a price to be paid if one replaces the actual with a convenient sample size. One can no longer compute second-order probabilities (Kleiter, 1994).

4. Good possibly assumed that the average wife batterer is married less than 10 years. Good also made a second calculation assuming a value of $p(G|Bat)$ that is half as large.

## References

Barsalou, L. W., & Ross, B. H. (1986). The roles of automatic and strategic processing in sensitivity to superordinate and property frequency. *Journal of Experimental Psychology: Learning, Memory, and Cognition, 12*, 116–134.

Brase, G., Cosmides, L., & Tooby, J. (in press). Individuation, counting, and statistical inference: The role of frequency and whole object representation in judgment under uncertainty. *Journal of Experimental Psychology: General.*

Brunswik, E. (1955). Representative design and probabilistic theory in a functional psychology. *Psychological Review, 62*, 193–217.

Casscells, W., Schoenberger, A., & Grayboys, T. (1978). Interpretation by physicians of clinical laboratory results. *New England Journal of Medicine, 299*, 999–1000.

*Chicago Tribune.* (1993). A false HIV test caused 18 month of hell. March 5, 1993.

Cohen, L. J. (1981). Can human irrationality be experimentally demonstrated? *The Behavioral and Brain Sciences, 4*, 317–370.

Cosmides, L., & Tooby, J. (1996). Are humans good intuitive statisticians after all? Rethinking some conclusions from the literature on judgment under uncertainty. *Cognition, 58*, 1–73.

Daly, M. & Wilson, M. (1988). *Homicide.* New York: De Gruyter.

Daston, L. J. (1988). *Classical probability in the Enlightenment.* Princeton, NJ: Princeton University Press.

Dershowitz, A. (1996). *Reasonable doubts: The criminal justice system and the O. J. Simpson case.* New York: Simon and Schuster.

Eddy, D. M. (1982). Probabilistic reasoning in clinical medicine: Problems and opportunities. In D. Kahneman, P. Slovic, & A. Tversky (Eds.), *Judgment under uncertainty: Heuristics and biases* (pp. 249–267). Cambridge: Cambridge University Press.

Estes, W. K. (1976). The cognitive side of probability learning. *Psychological Review, 83*, 37–64.

Fiedler, K. (1988). The dependence of the conjunction fallacy on subtle linguistic factors. *Psychological Research, 50*, 123–129.

Gallistel, C. R., & Gelman, R. (1992). Preverbal and verbal counting and computation. *Cognition, 44*, 43–74.

Gigerenzer, G. (1991). How to make cognitive illusions disappear: Beyond "heuristics and biases." In W. Stroebe & M. Hewstone (Eds.), *European Review of Social Psychology.* Vol. 2 (pp. 83–115). Chichester, Eng.: Wiley.

Gigerenzer, G. (1994). Why the distinction between single-event probabilities and frequencies is relevant for psychology (and vice versa). In G. Wright & P. Ayton (Eds.), *Subjective probability* (pp. 129–162). New York: Wiley.

Gigerenzer, G. (1996a). On narrow norms and vague heuristics: A reply to Kahneman and Tversky (1996). *Psychological Review, 103*, 592–596.

Gigerenzer, G. (1996b). The psychology of good judgment: Frequency formats and simple algorithms. *Journal of Medical Decision Making, 16*, 273–280.

Gigerenzer, G., & Hoffrage, U. (1995). How to improve Bayesian reasoning without instruction: Frequency formats. *Psychological Review, 102*, 684–704.

Gigerenzer, G. & Hoffrage, U. (forthcoming). How to improve diagnostic inferences in physicians. Manuscript submitted for publication.

Gigerenzer, G., Hoffrage, U., & Ebert, A. (in press). AIDS counseling for low risk clients. *AIDS Care*.

Gigerenzer, G., Hoffrage, U., & Kleinbölting, H. (1991). Probabilistic mental models: A Brunswikian theory of confidence. *Psychological Review, 98*, 506–528.

Gigerenzer, G., & Murray, D. J. (1987). *Cognition as intuitive statistics*. Hillsdale, NJ: Erlbaum.

Gigerenzer, G., Swijtink, Z., Porter, T., Daston, L., Beatty, J., & Krüger, L. (1989). *The empire of chance: How probability changed science and everyday life*. Cambridge: Cambridge University Press.

Good, I. J. (1995). When batterer turns murderer. *Nature, 375*, 541.

Gould, S. J. (1992). *Bully for brontosaurus: Further reflections in natural history*. New York: Penguin Books.

Hacking, I. (1975). *The emergence of probability*. Cambridge: Cambridge University Press.

Hasher, L., & Zacks, R. T. (1984). Automatic processing of fundamental information. *American Psychologist, 39*, 1372–1388.

Hertwig, R., & Gigerenzer, G. (1997). The "conjunction fallacy" revisited: How intelligent inferences look like reasoning errors. Manuscript submitted for publication.

Hintzman, D. L., & Block, R. A. (1972). Repetition and memory: Evidence for a multiple trace hypothesis. *Journal of Experimental Psychology, 88*, 297–306.

Hoffrage, U., & Gigerenzer, G. (1996). The impact of information representation on Bayesian reasoning. In G. Cottrell (Ed.), *Proceedings of the Eighteenth Annual Conference of the Cognitive Science Society* (pp. 126–130). Mahwah, NJ: Erlbaum.

Jonides, J., & Jones, C. M. (1992). Direct coding for frequency of occurrence. *Journal of Experimental Psychology: Learning, Memory, and Cognition, 18*, 368–378.

Jungermann, H. (1983). The two camps on rationality. In R. W. Scholz (Ed.), *Decision making under uncertainty* (pp. 63–86). Amsterdam: Elsevier.

Kahneman, D., & Tversky, A. (1996). On the reality of cognitive illusions. *Psychological Review, 103*, 582–591.

Kahneman, D., & Tversky, A. (1972). Subjective probability: A judgment of representativeness. *Cognitive Psychology, 3*, 430–454.

Kleiter, G. D. (1994). Natural sampling: Rationality without base rates. In G. H. Fischer & D. Laming (Eds.), *Contributions to mathematical psychology, psychometrics, and methodology* (pp. 375–388). New York: Springer.

Koehler, J. J. (1992). Probabilities in the courtroom: An evaluation of the objections and polices. In D. K. Kagehiro & W. S. Laufer (Eds.), *Handbook of psychology and law* (pp. 167–184). New York: Springer.

Koehler, J. J. (1996). The base rate fallacy reconsidered: Descriptive, normative, and methodological challenges. *Behavioral and Brain Sciences, 19*, 1–53.

Lichtenstein, S., Fischhoff, B., & Phillips, L. D. (1982). Calibration of probabilities: The state of the art to 1980. In D. Kahneman, P. Slovic, & A. Tversky (Eds.), *Judgment under uncertainty: Heuristics and biases* (pp. 306–334). Cambridge: Cambridge University Press.

Lopes, L. L. (1991). The rhetoric of irrationality. *Theory and Psychology, 1*, 65–82.

Nesse, R. M., & Williams, G. C. (1995). *Why we get sick: The new science of Darwinian medicine.* New York: Vintage Books.

Paulos, J. A. (1988). *Innumeracy: Mathematical illiteracy and its consequences.* New York: Vintage Books.

Peterson, C. R., DuCharme, W. M., & Edwards, W. (1968). Sampling distributions and probability revision. *Journal of Experimental Psychology, 76*, 236–243.

Piattelli-Palmarini, M. (1994). *Inevitable illusions: How mistakes of reason rule our minds* (M. Piattelli-Palmarini & K. Botsford, Trans.). New York: Wiley.

*Rheinische Merkur.* (1974). Alibi des Schornsteinfegers: Unwahrscheinliche Wahrscheinlichkeitsrechnungen in einem Mordprozess (Alibi of a chimney sweep: Improbable probability calculations in a murder trial). Issue No. 39.

Schaefer, R. E. (1976). The evaluation of individual and aggregated subjective probability distributions. *Organizational Behavior and Human Performance, 17*, 199–210.

Schrage, G. (n.d.). Schwierigkeiten mit der stochastischen Modellbildung—zwei Beispiele aus der Praxis. [Problems with stochastic models—two examples from real life.] Unpublished manuscript.

Sedlmeier, P. (1997). BasicBayes: A tutor system for simple Bayesian inference. *Behavior Research Methods, Instruments, & Computers, 29*, 328–336.

Sedlmeier, P., & Gigerenzer, G. (1998). Teaching Bayesian reasoning in less than two hours. Manuscript submitted for publication.

Shaughnessy, J. M. (1992). Research on probability and statistics: Reflections and directions. In D. A. Grouws (Ed.), *Handbook of research on mathematical teaching and learning* (pp. 465–494). New York: Macmillan.

Shepard, R. N. (1992). The perceptual organization of colors: An adaptation to regularities of the terrestrial world? In J. H. Barkow, L. Cosmides, & J. Tooby (Eds.), *The adapted mind: Evolutionary psychology and the generation of culture* (pp. 495–532). New York: Oxford University Press.

Stigler, S. M. (1983). Who discovered Bayes's Theorem? *American Statistician, 37* (4), 290–296.

Tooby, J., & Cosmides, L. (1992). The psychological foundations of culture. In J. Barkow, L. Cosmides, & J. Tooby (Eds.), *The adapted mind: Evolutionary psychology and the generation of culture* (pp. 19–136). New York: Oxford University Press.

Tversky, A., & Kahneman, D. (1983). Extensional versus intuitive reasoning: The conjunction fallacy in probability judgment. *Psychological Review, 90*, 293–315.

Windeler, J., & Köbberling, J. (1986). Empirische Untersuchung zur Einschätzung diagnostischer Verfahren am Beispiel des Haemoccult-Tests. [An empirical study of the judgments about diagnostic procedures using the example of the Hemoccult test.] *Klinische Wochenschrift, 64*, 1106–1112.

# 2

# Social Norms and Other Minds

*The Evolutionary Roots of Higher Cognition*

DENISE DELLAROSA CUMMINS

The major issue I want to address in this chapter is this: Why did the capacity to reason evolve? The trite answer is that an intelligent organism has a definite advantage over an unintelligent one in the struggle for survival. But embedded in this trite answer is a key insight: The pressure to compete and cooperate successfully with members of one's own species (conspecifics) constituted a major force behind the evolution of reasoning capacity.

I will take it as my task in this chapter to persuade you of this particular view of the evolution of human reasoning capacity, one in which the social environment plays a leading role. The core of my argument is that fundamental components of our reasoning architecture evolved in response to pressures to reason about *dominance hierarchies*, the social organization that characterizes most social mammals. I will argue that special reasoning architecture evolved to handle problems that are repeatedly encountered by individuals living in dominance hierarchies, problems that directly impact survival rates and reproductive success. These problems include: the necessity to recognize and respond appropriately to permissions, obligations, and prohibitions; and the necessity to circumvent the constraints of the hierarchy by dint of guile, particularly through successfully forcasting others' behavior. I will argue that functional architectures evolved for solving these problems, that they emerge early in human development, and that they color our reasoning performance throughout adulthood.

### Sociality and the Brain, or What's a Mind/Brain For?

It is sometimes argued that tracing the evolution of cognition is impossible because the brain leaves no fossils. But evolution has in fact left a quite discernable record in the structures of the brain itself. The Cartesian fantasy is that mind is pure intellect, the engagement in pure thought for its own sake. But evolution doesn't work that way. Structures evolve in response to environmental demands, demands that impact on survival rates and reproductive success. As philosopher Patricia Churchland (1986) puts it, "If you root yourself to the ground, you can afford to be stupid. But if you move, you must have mechanisms for moving, and mechanisms to ensure that the movement is not utterly arbitrary and independent of what's going on outside. . . . Neurons . . . are evolution's solution to the problem of adaptive movement" (pp. 13–14).

A mind/brain, then, is for mediating the perception/action cycle. Thus, one not only expects to find brain tissue devoted to that task, but indeed, finds such tissue. Significant portions of brain tissue are devoted to solving the problem of adaptive movement (e.g., the visual cortex, the auditory cortex, the motor and sensory cortexes, and the lateral geniculate bodies). This much, I think, is relatively uncontroversial—a view that grounds the evolution of cognitive capacity in both the need to predict events in the physical environment and the need to coordinate movement with them.

But the physical environment is not alone in producing evolutionary pressures. The social environment presents a host of adaptive problems of its own. As Churchland puts it: "The pressure for nervous systems to evolve has derived . . . primarily from the need for animals successfully to predict events in their environment, *including of course events originating in other organisms*" (p. 14, italics mine).

This presumed impact of the social environment on the evolution of cognition is a more controversial issue than the impact of the physical environment, and we might ask whether there is any neurological evidence of specialization for solving problems of a social nature. The answer is incontrovertibly, Yes.

As any introductory textbook on neuroanatomy will show, the most recently evolved mammalian brain structure (the neocortex) surrounds evolutionarily older structures, just as the rind of an orange surrounds the fruit itself. These older structures, and in particular, the limbic system, are involved in processing of the most basic *socioemotional* functions: sexual behavior, aggression, and emotion.

The social environment also left a quite discernable mark on the neocortex—namely, the intimate relationship between the neural substrates involved in both processing emotion and in reasoning. Prefrontal lobe syndrome is a pattern of impaired reasoning performance that results from bilateral damage to the ventromedial prefrontal cortical lobes (Damasio, 1994). In humans, this syndrome is characterized by an impaired capacity to reason effectively about socioemotional stimuli while leaving other types of intelligent reasoning virtually untouched. Monkeys with bilateral prefrontal ablations (both ventromedial and dorsolateral) do not maintain normal social relations within their troops despite the fact that nothing in their physical appearance has changed. They show diminished self-grooming and reciprocal grooming behavior, greatly reduced affective interactions with others, diminished facial expressions and vocalizations, and sexual indifference. They can no longer relate properly to others in their troop, and others cannot relate to them. Damage to other sections of the cortex— even those resulting in paralysis—do not impair these social skills. The selective impairment of social reasoning that characterizes prefrontal lobe syndrome suggests that neural substrates exist whose primary purpose is the processing and integration of social reasoning functions.

A third neurological mark of sociality is autism, a neurodevelopmental syndrome whose most vivid impact at the cognitive level is an impaired ability to reason about the mental states of others (see Baron-Cohen, Tager-Flusberg & Cohen, 1993). As one autistic adult put it, "Other people seem to have a special sense by which they can read other people's thoughts" (Frith, Morton & Leslie, 1991, p. 436). In autism, this "mind blindness" (Baron-Cohen, 1995) makes it extremely difficult to engage in normal reciprocal social interactions. Moreover, autistic individuals typically fail reasoning tasks that require them to reason about the others' beliefs (Frith et al., 1991). Like prefrontal lobe syndrome, the selective impairment of social reasoning that characterizes autism suggests that this type of reasoning is neurologically separable from other types of reasoning.

Finally, there is the neocortex ratio. This ratio expresses the relative volume of the neocortex compared to the volume of the rest of the brain. It correlates with the mean group sizes that characterize primate species, with larger group sizes corresponding to greater neocortical volume (Dunbar, 1992, 1993). This correlation between relative neocortical volume and group size has been interpreted to mean that primates cannot maintain the cohesion and integrity of groups larger than a size fixed by the cognitive capacity of their neocortex (Dunbar, 1993). In other words, the neocortical constraint is related to the number of relationships a primate can keep track of in a complex social environment. By contrast, the neocortex ratio does *not* correlate with environmental complexity, as measured by size of foraging range area. Finally, this ratio also correlates with the prevalence of tactical deception observed across primate species, a point I shall return to later in this chapter (Byrne, 1995, pp. 219–221). As Byrne points out: "It seems more than a coincidence that the neocortical enlargement of primates correlates neatly with differences in social complexity and Machiavellian intelligence . . . Dunbar's comparison between measures of environmental and socal complexity implies that the selection pressure for this neocortical enlargement was likely a social one" (pp. 220–221).

Why all of these specialized neural structures and pathways devoted to processing socioemotional stimuli? Evolutionary theory is based on the assumption that there is a causal relationship between the adaptive problems a species repeatedly encounters during its evolution and its phenotypic structures. This leaves us with two possible explanations: Either these structures evolved specifically to solve problems of a social nature, or the structures are side effects of functions that *were* selected for. The weight of the evidence, I believe, points in the direction of the former.

## *The Pressure to Select Social Cognitive Functions*

Open any ecology text (or watch any nature film), and the problems animate organisms must solve in their natural habitats are immediately drawn in high relief: staying fed (hunting/foraging/grazing), reproducing and caring for the young, and escaping predation. A common solution to these problems will also become immediately apparent: *sociality*, that is, living among conspecifics. There are definite advantages to living in social groups. Social living yields a reduction in predator pressure through improved detection or repulsion of enemies, improved foraging and hunting efficiency, improved defense of limited resources against intruders, and improved care of offspring through communal feeding and protection. As simple examples of these functions, consider that many species have developed alarm calls for signalling the presence of predators (Cheney & Seyfarth, 1990; Sherman, 1985; Hoogland, 1983). Some species, such as elephants, brown hyenas, wild dogs, lionesses and wolves engage in communal parenting (see Wittenberger, 1981, pp. 104–109); the latter two, moreover, hunt cooperatively to maximize their success rate (Caraco & Wolf, 1975; Schaller, 1972).

But if there are advantages to living cooperatively with others of your species, there are also costs that arise from increased competition within the group for food, mates, nest sites, and other limited resources (Alcock, 1984). Again, open any ecology text (or watch any nature film), and a term that will occur soon and repeatedly is *dominance hierarchy*. In common parlance, a dominance hierarchy is a "pecking order." In functional terms, a dominance hierarchy is simply the observation that particular individuals in social groups have regular priority of access to resources—particularly reproductive resources—in competitive situations (Cheney & Seyfarth, 1990, p. 29; Clutton-Brock & Harvey, 1976, p. 215). These individuals are referred to as dominant or high-ranking, while those who have lower priority of access are called subordinate or low-ranking. In its most developed form, the dominance hierarchy is transitive, meaning that if A has priority over B, and B has priority over C, then A has priority over C, and so on. The role of dominance is most pronounced in situations characterized by high levels of resource competition, such as high population density or the onset of breeding season (Clutton-Brock & Harvey, 1976).

The dominance hierarchy is of no small importance to the evolution of species because it is intimately related to survival rates and reproductive success. Due to their greater access to resources, higher ranking individuals are less likely to die of starvation or predation than those of lower rank (Cheney & Seyfarth, 1990, pp. 33–34). In most species, there is also a direct relationship between rank and reproductive success, with higher ranking males achieving greater reproductive success than lower ranking individuals (see Bertram, 1976; Bygott, Bertram, & Hanby, 1979; Dewsbury, 1982; Clutton-Brock, 1988; Ellis, 1995; Fedigan, 1983; Hausfater, 1975; McCann, 1981; Nishida, 1983; Robinson, 1982; Silk, 1987; Tutin, 1979; de Waal, 1982; Watts & Stokes, 1971). Among primates, the relationship is even more striking because (as we shall see) dominance status is unstable; for this reason, the level of reproductive success achieved by any individual is directly related to the length of time during which the individual is high-ranking (Altmann et al., 1996).

Competing and cooperating successfully with conspecifics for limited resources, therefore, constitutes the chief problem social mammals must solve. They must solve it if they are to survive and leave viable offspring. Dominant individuals appear to solve these problems with greater ease than subordinates. If greater size were all that determined this characteristic, the story of struggle for survival in the wild would be a short one indeed—biggest wins all. But a closer look at the societies of other species, and in particular, the societies of primates, tells a very different story, one in which the evolution of greater capacity for guile and wit plays a leading role.

### Sociality, Dominance, and Primate Societies

There are two characteristics of primate dominance hierarchies that must be appreciated. First, they are not static structures; they are dynamic structures in which individuals vie for control of resources (Cheney & Seyfarth, 1990, p. 35; de Waal, 1988, 1992; Harcourt & de Waal , 1992). Lower ranking individuals attempt to engage in forbidden activities in order to secure a larger share of resources, and higher-ranking individuals defend their privileged access to resources by detecting and punishing transgressors. Second, unlike many other mammalian species, rank in chimpanzee hierarchies does *not* correlate with size of the individual; instead, acquiring and maintaining a stable high-ranking position depends on forming and maintaining alliances with individuals who will provide support during contests of rank (Harcourt, 1988; Harcourt & de Waal, 1992; Packer, 1977; Seyfarth & Cheney, 1984; Smuts, 1985). Indeed, it is in these two characteristics that social cognition looms large.

### Dominance and Reasoning about Social Norms

If you are living in a dominance hierarchy, what you are allowed to do depends in large part on your rank. Primate dominance hierarchies have been described as embodying a set of implicit "social norms" that determine, among other things, who is allowed to groom whom, sit next to whom, and mate with whom (Aruguete, 1994; Hall, 1964). In order to stay out of trouble, subordinate individuals must recognize what is *permitted* and *forbidden* given their place in the hierarchy. To maintain the status quo, high-ranking individuals must *recognize instances of cheating* and punish the transgressor forthwith. In other words, they must defend their privileged access to available resources. For example, dominant males monopolize reproductive opportunities by aggressing against or threatening to aggress against females and subordinate males who are caught socializing or consorting (Cheney & Seyfarth, 1990, p. 227). de Waal (1982) describes a dominant male whose peculiar means of punishing errant subordinates involved jumping up and down on them. At minimum, then, dominance hierarchies, as a social organization, constitute evidence that members are capable (at least) of distinguishing between what is forbidden and what is permitted under which circumstances.

As is apparent, life among low-ranking individuals is less than ideal, and it should come as no surprise that a good deal of jockeying for position occurs within these hierarchies. Changes of rank typically occur through dyadic aggression, with both members of the encounter calling for support from allies. For this reason, one's rank depends crucially on one's ability to form and maintain strong alliances based on reciprocal *obligations* (Harcourt, 1988; Harcourt & de Waal, 1992; Packer, 1977; Seyfarth & Cheney, 1984; Smuts, 1985). Vervet monkeys, for example, are more likely to respond to calls from non-kin during agonistic encounters if the caller has groomed them recently; the monkeys also form the strongest alliances with individuals who groom them most often (Cheney & Seyfarth, 1990, pp. 67–69; Seyfarth, 1976; Seyfarth & Cheney, 1984). Chimpanzees show reciprocity of supportive and retaliative interventions in aggressive encounters: The rate of intervention by individual A on behalf of B correlates with the rate of intervention by B on the behalf of A, and the rate of intervention against individual A by individual B correlates with the rate of intervention against B by A (de Waal, 1992).

Furthermore, these intervention rates indicate that alliances within some species of primates are best characterized as transactions in which each individual monitors the contribution of the other so that the collaboration may be discontinued if too large an imbalance is detected, that is, if cheating is detected. Male *Papio anubis* baboons who refuse to assist other males in abducting females are less likely to receive aid than males who assist (Alcock, 1984, p. 486). Similarly, chimpanzees retaliate against individuals who are reluctant to share food (i.e., show a low rate of food distribution relative to others) either by directly aggressing against them when they themselves request food (de Waal, 1989), or by misinforming or failing to inform them about the location of food (Woodruff & Premack, 1979). Perhaps the most well-known case is that reported by de Waal (1992), in which a subordinate male terminated his long-term alliance with an alpha male in response to the alpha male's increasingly frequent refusals to support him in contests with another male over access to estrus females. What this means is that the parties in these transactions must be capable of detecting and excluding cheaters, a particularly important point since modelling theory has shown that this capacity is necessary for reciprocity to emerge as an evolutionarily stable strategy (Axelrod, 1984; Axelrod & Hamilton, 1981; Maynard Smith, 1982; Trivers, 1971).

Even more intriguing is the fact that this appreciation of obligation structures appears to be imbued with a 'Machiavellian' sophistication in that individuals prefer to groom and support individuals of higher rank than themselves. This preference presumably is due to the fact that support from higher-ranking individuals during agonistic encounters has greater effect than support from lower-ranking individuals. For example, baboons, macaques, and vervet monkeys form matrilineal hierarchies in which a female is dominant to all of the females that are subordinate to her mother, while she is subordinate to all of the females that are dominant to her mother (Chapais, 1992; Cheney & Seyfarth, 1990; Prud'Homme & Chapais, 1993). During agonistic encounters, support is typically given to the higher-ranking females, who in turn intervene in conflicts when they themselves are dominant to the target of the aggression. By aiding higher-ranking females, lower-ranking females form strong alliances based on reciprocal obligations that enable them to move up in rank.

Field research on primate societies in the wild and in captivity clearly shows that the capacity for (at least) implicit appreciation of permission, prohibition, and obligation social norms is directly related to survival rates and reproductive success. Without at least a rudimentary capacity to recognize and respond appropriately to these structures, remaining within a social group characterized by a dominance hierarchy would be all but impossible. Further, those who are particularly adept at this type of reasoning can readily monopolize reproductive opportunities, hence passing on whatever heritable traits they possess. For example, Hall and DeVore (1965) recorded 53 complete copulations with estrus females by six adult baboon males, including one male who, individually, was the most dominant animal in the troop. Despite his greater individual dominance, this male only achieved eight copulations. His access to estrus females was effectively blocked by a coalition of three males, who, together, achieved more than twice the number of copulations of the other three males.

### Dominance and Reasoning about Other Minds

As the last example shows, the reproductive (and hence evolutionary) benefits that accrue to individuals with the cognitive wherewithal to detect, exploit, and circumvent the constraints of sheer physical dominance are enormous, and it is here that some of the most intriguing data on primate cognition are to be found. These data are concerned with the use of *deception*. The following is an example in which Belle, the only chimp who knows the location of hidden food, attempts to hide that knowledge from Rock, who is dominant to her:

Belle, accordingly stopped uncovering the food if Rock was close. She sat on it until Rock left. Rock, however, soon learned this, and when she sat in one place for more than a few seconds, he came over, shoved her aside, searched her sitting place, and got the food. Belle next stopped going all the way [to the food]. Rock, however, countered by steadily expanding the area of his search through the grass near where Belle had sat. Eventually, Belle sat farther and farther away, waiting until Rock looked in the opposite direction before she moved toward the food at all, and Rock in turn seemed to look away until Belle started to move somewhere. On some occasions Rock started to wander off, only to wheel around suddenly precisely as Belle was about to uncover some food. . . . On a few trials, she actually started off a trial by leading the group in the opposite direction from the food, and then, while Rock was engaged in his search, she doubled back rapidly and got some food. (Menzel, 1974)

This observation brings home an important point in vivid detail: The struggle for survival in chimpanzee societies is best characterized as a struggle between dominance and the outwitting of dominance, between recognizing your opponent's intentions and hiding your own. *The evolution of mind emerges from this scene as a strategic arms race in which the weaponry is ever-increasing mental capacity to represent and manipulate internal representations of the minds of others.* If you are big enough to take what you want by force, you are sure to dominate available resources—unless your subordinates are smart enough to deceive you. If you are subordinate, you must use other strategies—deception, guile, appeasement, bartering, coalition formation, friendship, kinship—to get what you need to survive.

Deceptions like these are not rare occurrences. Females and subordinate males often engage in deception in order to conceal their forbidden trysts from dominant individuals, going so far as to suppress their copulation cries. Subordinate males also hide their erections behind their hands when their courtships are interrupted by dominant males (Kummer, 1988; de Waal, 1988). Deceptions of this kind have also been observed for hiding other forbidden behaviors, such as stealing food, failing to share food, or grooming forbidden individuals (see Whiten & Byrne, 1988 for numerous examples).

Deceptions are particularly useful data because they can be analyzed in terms of "orders of intentionality," that is, they can be used to infer the minimum level of mental representation required to perpetrate the deception (Dennett, 1988). In other words, deceptions provide a way of measuring what sorts of mental states an organism is capable of. A first-order intentional system is capable of beliefs and desires that can be characterized as "x believes/wants that p." A second-order system is also capable of beliefs and desires like a first-order system, but also has beliefs and desires about its own and others' beliefs and desires. In other words, it is capable of states such as: "x wants y to believe that x is hungry;" or, "x fears that y will discover that x has a food cache." A third-order system is capable of intentional states, such as "x wants y to believe that x believes he is all alone."

Higher orders of intentionality are also possible, but become more difficult to summarize succinctly.

Note that with greater orders of intentionality, one can not only manipulate others' behavior, but others' *beliefs*. Leekam (1992), Mitchell (1986), and Byrne (1995) offer similar analyses of deception based on these distinctions. *Strategic deceptions* are attempts to manipulate behavior directly, without intending to manipulate others' beliefs. *Tactical deception* involves duping the target into believing something that is untrue, something that is to the deceiver's advantage. Finally, *intentional tactical deception* involves deliberately manipulating others' beliefs. Deceptions of this kind require insight into the beliefs of others. In its most advanced form, the deceiver recognizes not only that the deceptive act is being assessed by the target, but that the deceiver's own intentions are also likely to be scrutinized by the target (Leekam, 1992).

Are other species capable of these kinds of deceptions? Whiten and Byrne (1988; Byrne, 1995, pp. 119–145) collated and analyzed records of tactical deception contributed by numerous primatologists studying different species. They found convincing evidence of intentional deception only among the great apes, with the majority of the evidence occurring among chimpanzees.

Nature is replete with strategic deceptions, deceptions that require no mental representation at all or, at most, first-level intentionality. A simple example of deception that requires no mental representation is the hawk moth's opening of its hind wings in response to looming objects. The spots on its hind wings look strikingly similar to the eyes of a large hawk. The deception is strategic in that it is used only when something is looming (threatening). This sort of deception surely requires no capacity for mental representation, however. Tactical deceptions require at least first-order intentionality, and are common among domestic animals. Byrne (1995) uses as an example a cat who, desiring to sit in a chair currently occupied by its owner, meows at the door. The owner is duped into believing that the cat needs to go out, and gets up to open the door. The cat then claims the chair. The cat need not be capable of representing its owner's beliefs; the gambit works whether or not the cat realizes that the owner's behavior came about through the creation of a false belief. This strategic gambit requires only the capacity to have a desired goal (to go outside), to learn an association between the goal and a means (to get the owner to move toward the door by meowing), and to implement the means in service of a new goal (to lie in a chair currently occupied by the owner by getting the owner to move toward the door). Tactical deceptions like these are frequently observed among chimpanzees and baboons in the wild, less so among other species of primates (Byrne, 1995, pp. 129–130).

Deceptions that are difficult to explain *except* by attributing to the deceiver the capacity for higher order intentionality (intentional tactical deception) are harder to come by. In fact, of the small number of reports of this kind that Whiten and Byrne were able to find in their exhaustive

analysis of the primatology literature (n = 26), the overwhelming majority (n = 21) occurred among the great apes, with most of these (n = 12)
occurring among chimpanzees (Byrne, 1995, 135). The incident cited above
between Rock and Belle is one example. The first three of Rock's tactics
are not convincing cases of intentional deception, but when he feigns
distinterest and suddenly wheels around (an unusual behavior for a chimpanzee), it becomes more difficult to explain the behavior except by attributing to Rock the capacity to appreciate Belle's deceptive intentions and to
anticipate her thoughts.

One last, crucial point must be appreciated: Not only does absolute
dominance fail to correlate with size in chimpanzees and certain other species of primates, but it does not appear to correlate reliably with reproductive success (Cheney & Seyfarth, 1990, p. 34; Smuts, 1985). In one study
of chimpanzees in the Tai Forest, over 50% (7 out of 13) infants had been
sired by males outside the troop as a result of surreptitious, female-initiated
matings (Gagneux, Woodruff, & Boesch, 1997). Given the data on deception discussed in this section, this should come as no surprise. It is much
harder for an individual to dominate reproductive opportunities (or any other
resource) if competitors have the candlepower to intentionally and cleverly
deceive you. The core assumption of natural selection as a mechanism for
the evolution of species is that individual variation exists among traits in a
population. Those individuals with traits that allow them to survive better
or longer will enjoy greater reproductive success, hence propagating those
traits in the population. Given the data discussed in this section, it becomes
harder to avoid the conclusion that one such crucial trait in the evolution of
primates is an enhanced capacity to reason about social norms and other
minds *in order to thwart "natural" dominance hierarchies.*

### Domain-Specific Human Reasoning Architecture

But what does this have to do with human cognition? The answer is—quite
a bit. In fact, dominance theory, as presented in this chapter, predicts the
following: First, domain-specific reasoning strategies will be evoked when
situations for which those strategies evolved are present in the environment.
These situations are ones that require reasoning about social norms (permissions, obligations, and prohibitions) and other minds. Second, it predicts that these strategies will emerge separately—and perhaps prior to—
other types of reasoning strategies. An analysis of the data on human
reasoning supports these predictions.

#### Dominance and Reasoning about Social Norms

Consider first a phenomenon I call the *deontic effect* in human reasoning
(Cummins, 1996b, 1996c). Deontic reasoning is reasoning about rights
and obligations; that is, reasoning about what one is permitted, obligated,
or forbidden to do (Hilpinen, 1981; Manktelow & Over, 1991). Deontic

reasoning contrasts with *indicative reasoning*, which is reasoning about what is true or false. When reasoning about deontic rules (social norms), humans spontaneously adopt a violation-detection strategy: They look for cheaters or rule-breakers. In contrast, when reasoning about the truth status of statements about the world, they spontaneously adopt a confirmation-seeking strategy. This effect is apparent in the reasoning of children as young as three years of age (Cummins, 1996a; Harris & Nuñez, 1996) and has been observed in literally hundreds of experiments on adult reasoning over the course of nearly thirty years, making it one of the most reliable effects in the psychological literature (see Cummins, 1996b, 1996c, and Oaksford & Chater, 1996 for reviews of this literature).

To give a simple example of the deontic effect, consider the following hypothesis: *If a book was published in 1997, it has a recycling stamp on it.* Your job is to test whether this hypothesis is true or false. There are two books in front of you, one with a recycling stamp showing and one without. Which book's publishing date should you inspect? If you're like most people, you chose the book with the recycling stamp. Now, consider the same statement, though it is no longer an hypothesis—a law has recently been passed to ensure that books are printed on recycled paper. Books published prior to 1997 are not subject to the law. Which book's publishing date do you need to inspect? If you are like most people, you chose the book with no stamp. In other words, when reasoning about the truth or falsity of the hypothesis, you chose to inspect the case that could confirm the hypothesis. In short, you sought to discover whether the stamp and the 1997 date did, in fact, occur together. When reasoning about the social norm, you chose to inspect the case that could constitute a violation of the law. That is, you would look for possible cheating. It probably seemed perfectly obvious to you that those were the correct choices. But consider this: If you found a "1995" publishing date for the stamped book, would it have mattered? The hypothesis says nothing about the stamps appearing or not appearing for books published in other years. But had you inspected the unstamped book and found "1997," you would have clearly disproved the hypothesis. This would have provided incontrovertible proof that the hypothesis was false. Yet it did not seem necessary to you to look for potential violations of the hypothesis. This is what I call the deontic effect in human reasoning. As mentioned earlier, it has been observed in children as young as three years of age (the youngest tested so far), and persists into adulthood, regardless of overall intelligence or educational level of the reasoner. Like nonhuman primates, human primates appear "primed" to notice and respond to violations of social norms. In contrast, a violation-detection strategy is *not* evoked by other types of reasoning tasks even when the strategy is both appropriate and necessary.

Next, consider people's performance on group decision-making tasks. Weg and Smith (1993) gave subjects the opportunity to win money in transactions based on the Prisoner's Dilemma. Each subject's task was to decide whether to betray his or her collaborators in order to win a fixed amount of money, or to trust them in order to possibly win more or less than the fixed amount. Subjects showed a greater willingness to trust and a greater unwillingness to forgive betrayals of trust *than would have been predicted by rational choice theory.* Like subjects in deontic reasoning studies, these subjects seem to be particulary keen on detecting and responding to violations of social norms, whether they are explict prescriptive rules or implicit social contracts. In fact, other studies indicate that we respond more strongly to violations of reciprocity than we do to simple competitive loss alone (Rabbie, 1992).

The data so far clearly show that people are quite good at detecting and responding to implicit social norms in reasoning tasks. We are sensitive to the characteristics of the reasoning problems that cue departures from these norms, seeking out potential cheaters and responding swiftly and strongly to such transgressions. This is perfectly predicted by dominance theory, but is also predicted by other theories as well, such as social exchange theory (Cosmides, 1989; Cosmides & Tooby, 1994) and pragmatic schema theory (Cheng & Holyoak, 1985; 1989). What these other theories do not predict, however, is that human reasoning is also strongly affected by rank. Dominance theory does predict this, and there is evidence to that effect.

Researchers have found that our cognitive and emotional responses to social stimuli are mediated by consideration of social rank. Mealey and her colleagues showed subjects pictures of males with accompanying brief biographies that imparted information about the men's social status and character. The researchers found that subjects were far better at remembering low-status cheaters than high-status cheaters or non-cheaters of any rank (Mealey, Daood, & Krage, 1996). Other studies have found that increases in blood pressure associated with anger or frustration in social situations can be eliminated if the individual is given an opportunity to aggress against the person who caused his distress (target), but only if the target is of lower status than the retaliator. If the target of aggression is of higher status, however, blood pressure remains at the frustration-induced elevated level (Hokanson, 1961; Hokanson & Shetler, 1961).

Cummins (1997) tested adults on a reasoning task that described a situation in a college dormitory. In the social version of the task, reasoners were told that there was an important rule in the dormitory. The rule was *if someone was assigned to lead a study session, that person was required to tape record the session.* People who were not assigned to lead the session could record it if they wished, but they were not required to do so. The reasoners were then asked to test for compliance to the rule by choosing which study-session records to inspect. In the nonsocial version of the task, reasoners were told that someone overheard a conversation in the dormitory in which one person said to the other, "*If I am assigned to lead a study session, I always tape record the session.*" The reasoners were then asked to test the truth of the overheard statement by choosing which study-session records to inspect. In both tasks, optimal performance required looking for potential violations, that is, choosing to inspect records that indicated the person was assigned to lead a session to see if they had in fact recorded the session and choosing to inspect records that indicated the person did *not* tape record the session to find out whether they had been assigned to lead the session. But there was one additional manipulation: Half of the reasoners were told to adopt the perspective of a dormitory resident assistant (high-ranking individual) and the other half were told to adopt the perspecdtive of a student (low-ranking individual). Half of each of these groups were also told that the people they were checking on were resident assistants and the other half were told that the people they were checking on were students. Rank was found to have a clear impact on reasoning performance but only on the social version of the task: People were more likely to look for potential violations when they believed themselves to be checking on people who were lower-ranking than themselves (65%) than when they believed themselves to be checking on people who were higher-ranking (20%) or equal-ranking (RA-RA = 20%, student-student = 15%).

Finally, the effects of social dominance on reasoning emerge quite early in childhood. Transitive dominance hierarchies are evident in the interactions of children as young as three, and can be reliably reported verbally by four-year-olds, meaning that children as young as three can perform the transitive inferences that are necessary to work out these dominance relations (Smith, 1988). Yet, this skill does not transfer readily to non-social stimuli. Children in this age group can perform object-based transitive reasoning only if they are extensively drilled on the object pairs upon which the inference is to be performed (Bryant & Trabasso, 1971). Truly content-free transitive reasoning does not reliably appear until six years of age (Smith, 1998, pp. 103–104).

In summary, the human reasoning literature shows a robust deontic effect in human reasoning and a complex relationship between cheater detection and rank discrimination in human decision making. As we saw earlier, these strategies are core strategies for surviving in a primate dominance hierarchy. The early emergence of these strategies in childhood, the fact that we seem to share them with other species of primates, and the direct relationship between the capacity to use these strategies and reproductive success make it difficult to avoid the conclusion that deontic reasoning strategies are part of early-emerging, domain-specific social knowledge that is triggered when one is required to reason about which actions are permitted, obligated, or forbidden in particular circumstances. Foremost among these strategies is the need to check for violations of social norms (rule-breaking).

### Dominance and Reasoning about Other Minds in Humans

In the literature on human reasoning, reasoning about the mental states of others is called "theory of mind" reasoning. The interesting thing about theory of mind reasoning is its development in childhood. In contrast to deontic reasoning and transitive reasoning about social stimuli, both of which appear to be in place by at least three years of age (the youngest tested so far), theory of mind reasoning emerges late in development, appearing somewhere between the third to fifth year of life (depending on how it is measured).

The most common measure of theory of mind reasoning is the standard "false belief" task. In this task, a child watches while a puppet hides a toy under an object (such as a basket), and then leaves. While the first puppet is away, a second one appears, finds the toy, and hides it in a different place. The child is then asked where the first puppet will look for the toy when it returns. Four-year-olds readily solve this problem correctly, answering that the puppet will look in the original hiding place; three-year-olds, however, give different answers depending on how their beliefs are queried (Leslie, 1994; Wimmer & Perner, 1983; Zaitchik, 1991). In the standard false belief task, three-year-olds typically respond that the puppet will look in the *current* hiding place, rather than in the original hiding place (Baron-Cohen, Leslie, & Frith, 1985; Wimmer & Perner, 1983). Between the ages of three and four, therefore, something changes in the child's capacity to reason effectively about the epistemic status of others' beliefs (Gopnik & Meltzoff, 1994).

A clearer picture of the emergence of theory of mind reasoning comes from the literature on deception. Here, the young child's capacity to deceive can be analyzed in terms of levels of intentionality, just as deception among nonhuman primates can be analyzed (Leekam, 1992). Until about four years of age, children are much better saboteurs than they are deceivers. The standard paradigm involves a puppet who wants to steal a desirable object, and the child's job is to prevent the puppet from getting it. The child is required to do this either through sabotage (e.g., locking the box containing the desired object) or through deception (e.g., misleading by pointing or saying the *wrong* location of the desired object). Three-year-olds routinely succeed at sabotage but fail at deceiving, while four- and five-year-olds routinely succeed at both tasks (Perner, 1991). As my earlier discussion of deception and orders of intentionality showed, sabotage requires at most first-order intentionality, but intentional deception requires the type of insight into other's mental states that only higher-order intentionality can afford. Somewhere between the ages of three and four, children become capable of second- and third-order intentional reasoning.

To bring this point home more clearly, consider the following study by Roth (1990, cited in Leekam, 1992). The child watches while a puppet named Rina hides some chocolate in a box. Another puppet, Yosi, asks Rina where the chocolate is, and Rina says it is in the dog house. When asked where Yosi thought the chocolate was, the majority of five-year-olds and three-year-olds said in the dog house. But when asked where Rina (who hid and therefore knows where the chocolate really is) thought the chocolate was, the majority of five-year-olds said the box while the majority of three-year-olds said the dog house. The younger children seemed to have difficulty managing these many-layered representations, losing track of or failing to fully appreciate that the liar knows the truth but intends to mislead.

There are two further characteristics of theory of mind reasoning that are important to dominance theory. The first is that there is a monotonic relation between the number of older siblings a child has and the child's performance on theory of mind reasoning tasks (Jenkins & Astington, 1996; Lewis, Freeman, Kyriakidou, Maridaki-Kassotaki, & Berridge, in press; Perner, Ruffman, & Leekam, 1994; Ruffman, Perner, Naito, Parkin, & Clements, 1996). This relationship has perplexed researchers, but the most common explanation advanced for it is that older siblings' superior meta-cognitive skills make them better able to both teach or assist younger siblings in the acquisition of social knowledge, as well as to provide ample opportunity for younger siblings to learn about mental representations through pretend play and the like (Ruffman et al., 1996). But this conundrum is just as easily (perhaps more easily) explained through dominance theory. As any parent knows, siblings spend an enormous amount of time competing with each other for resources, attention, and so on. We even have a special term for it—sibling rivalry. Younger siblings are smaller and less knowledgable than their older siblings, putting them at a distinct disadvantage. Having older siblings would, therefore, make one more highly motivated to develop whatever latent potential one has for representing the mental states of others: I can compete or cooperate more successfully with you if I can successfully predict what you are likely to do, likely to want me to do, or likely to believe.

This might lead the reader to conclude that social norm and theory of mind reasoning are simply learned during the first few years of life. No special-purpose neural-cognitive machinery is needed to explain its emergence. But this conclusion is inconsistent with the following second important characteristic. Autistics typically fail false belief tasks, while mentally retarded children of equal mental age typically pass them. Autistics also fail tasks that require deception while simultaneously succeeding at tasks that require sabotage (Sodian & Frith, 1992), and perform normally on tasks requiring pictorial and mechanical reasoning (Baron-Cohen, Leslie, & Frith, 1986; Leslie & Thaiss, 1992). This pattern of selective intellectual impairment implies that theory of mind reasoning is dependent on distinct neurological substrates that are absent or damaged in this subset of the population.

In summary, the developmental and adult literatures on human reasoning show quite clearly that some reasoning capacities emerge earlier than others. Children can reason transitively about social dominance relations long before they can reason transitively about other stimuli. Children can also represent and reason effectively about social norms long before they can reason effectively about others' beliefs. In other words, the reasoning capacities that emerge earliest in development are those that we have in common with other primates. Those that emerge late, such as reasoning about belief, are more recent evolutionary accomplishments, and it is with respect to these latter capacities that the great apes diverge most significantly from other primates, and humans from the great apes. Dominance theory provides a unifying explanation for the diverse and perplexing reasoning patterns that have been reported in these literatures.

## Closing Comments

In developing dominance theory, I drew heavily on scientific observations of reasoning performance among adults, children, and nonhuman primates. In a sense, I could have picked up a newspaper, a novel, a movie, or a history book just as easily, or randomly sampled the great works of art and literature from any era of human civilization. These samplings would have been replete with stories of struggles for, with, or against dominance. Tragic love stories, plays, and operas have been spun from the struggles of young females, who, desired by alpha males, instead prefer young subordinate males who often come from rival clans or families of unequal social rank. Historical novels and plays have been written about the strife that ensues when reigning monarchs and barons (alpha males) covet each other's territory.

Even a look at human history shows quite unequivocally that humans have the unfortunate tendency to organize themselves into dominance hierarchies at both local and global levels. A monarchy, with its social stratification of power and status, is a dominance hierarchy. Indeed, much of human history is a careful record of intrigues and wars aimed at gaining or limiting domination of territory and resources. When one talks of Somalian warlords who get priority of access to western aid packages, one is talking about a dominance hierarchy in which alpha males with strong alliances monopolize available food resources. Street gangs typically organize themselves into dominance hierarchies in which the entire group submits to the wishes of a single, dominant individual. Research on children's social interactions has shown that children as young as three years of age organize themselves into dominance hierarchies. The ubiquitous dominance of males over females in nearly all primate species (the Bonobo chimpanzees being a notable exception) is what we call "male authority" and sexism in our own species. And, finally, a careful analysis of birth order and openness to scientific discovery by Sulloway (1996) shows that grappling with dominance structures within the family impacts even our very personalities, with first-borns (dominant siblings) seeking to maintain the status quo through rigid conformity, and later-borns (subordinates) seeking to rebel against those constraints.

In fact, telling primates (human or otherwise) that their reasoning architectures evolved in large part to solve problems of dominance is a little like telling fish that their gills evolved in large part to solve the problem of oxygen intake from water. The struggle for survival through competition and cooperation with members of one's own species is as old as life itself. If the data on social norm and theory of mind reasoning show us anything, it is that the winners are most likely to be those with the capacity to exploit or route the constraints of the dominance hierarchy. If one were to guess at which problems cognition evolved to solve, one would be hard pressed to come up with a better candidate than dominance.

## Note

I would like to thank Colin Allen and Robert Cummins for helpful comments on a previous version of this manuscript. Correspondence regarding this paper should be addressed to the author at: Department of Psychology, 6000 J Street, California State University, Sacramento, CA 98519–6007, or to dcummins@saclink. csus.edu.

## References

Alcock, J. (1984). *Animal behavior: an evolutionary approach.* Sunderland, MA: Sinauer Assoc.

Altmann, J., Alberts, S. C., Haines, S. A., Dubach, J., Muruth, P., Coote, T., Geffen, E., Cheesman, D. J., Mututua, R. A., Saiyalel, S. N., Wayne, R. K., Lacy, R. C., & Bruford, M. W. (1996). Behavior predicts genetic structure in a wilde primate group. *Proceedings of the National Academy of Sciences, 93,* 5795–5801.

Aruguete, M. (1994). Cognition, tradition, and the explanation of social behavior in nonhuman primates, [Review of *Social processes and mental abilities in nonhuman primates*]. *American Journal of Primatology, 33,* 71–74.

Axelrod, R. (1984). *The evolution of cooperation.* New York: Basic Books.

Axelrod, R., & Hamilton, W. D. (1981). The evolution of cooperation. *Science, 211,* 1390–1396.

Baron-Cohen, S. (1995). *Mindblindness: An essay on autism and theory of mind.* Cambridge, MA: MIT Press.

Baron-Cohen, S., Leslie, A. M., & Frith, U. (1985). Does the autistic child have a "theory of mind?" *Cognition, 21,* 37–46.

Baron-Cohen, S., Leslie, A. M., & Frith, U. (1986). Mechanical, behavioural and intentional understanding of picture stories in autistic children. *British Journal of Developmental Psychology, 4,* 113–125.

Baron-Cohen, S., Tager-Flusberg, H., & Cohen, D. (Eds.). (1993). *Understanding other minds: Perspectives from autism.* Oxford: Oxford University Press.

Bertram, B. C. R. (1976). Kin selection in lions and evolution. In P. P. G. Bateson & R. A. Hinde (Eds.), *Growing points in ethology* (pp. 281–302). Cambridge: Cambridge University Press.

Bryant, P. E., & Trabasso, T. (1971). Transitive inference and memory in young children. *Nature, 240,* 456–458.

Bygott, J. D., Bertram, B. C. R., & Hanby, J. P. (1979). Males lions in large coalitions gain reproductive advantage. *Nature, 282,* 839–841.

Byrne, R. (1995). *The thinking ape: Evolutionary origins of intelligence.* Oxford: Oxford University Press.

Caraco, T., & Wolf, L. L. (1975). Ecological determinants of groups sizes of foraging lions. *American Naturalist, 109,* 343–352.

Chapais, B. (1992). Role of alliances in the social inheritance of rank among female primates. In A. Harcourt & F. B. M De Waal (Eds.), *Coalitions and alliances in humans and other animals* (pp. 29–60). Oxford: Oxford University Press.

Cheney, D. L., & Seyfarth, R. M. (1990). *How monkeys see the world*. Chicago: University of Chicago Press.

Cheng, P. W., & Holyoak, K. J. (1985). Pragmatic reasoning schemas. *Cognitive Psychology, 17*, 391–416.

Cheng, P. W., & Holyoak, K. J. (1989). On the natural selection of reasoning theories, *Cognition, 33*, 285–313.

Churchland, P. S. (1986). *Neurophilosophy*. Cambridge, MA: Bradford/MIT Press.

Clutton-Brock, T. H. (1988). Reproductive success. In T. H. Clutton-Brock (Ed.), *Reproductive success*. Chicago: University of Chicago Press.

Clutton-Brock, T. H., & Harvey, P. H. (1976). Evolutionary rules and primate societies. In P. P. G. Bateson & R. A. Hinde (Eds.), *Growing points in ethology* (pp.195–238). Cambridge: Cambridge University Press.

Cosmides, L. (1989). The logic of social exchange: Has natural selection shaped how humans reason? Studies with the Wason selection task. *Cognition, 31*, 187–276.

Cosmides, L., & Tooby, J. (1994). Beyond intuition and instinct blindness: Toward an evolutionarily rigorous cognitive science. *Cognition, 50*, 41–77.

Cummins, D. D. (1996a). Evidence of deontic reasoning in 3- and 4-year-olds. *Memory & Cognition, 24*, 823–829.

Cummins, D. D. (1996b). Evidence for the innateness of deontic reasoning. *Mind & Language, 11*, 160–190.

Cummins, D. D. (1996c). Dominance hierarchies and the evolution of human reasoning. *Minds & Machines, 6*, 463–480.

Cummins, D. D. (1997). *Cheater detection is modified by social rank*. Paper presented at the Human Behavior and Evolution Society meeting, University of Arizona, Tucson, June 1997.

Damasio, A. R. (1994). *Descartes error: Emotion, reason, and the human brain*. New York: Grosset/Putnam.

Dennett, D. C. (1988). The intentional stance in theory and practice. In R. W. Byrne & A. Whiten (Eds.), *Machiavellian intelligence* (pp. 180–202). Oxford: Oxford University Press.

Dewsbury, D. A. (1982). Dominance rank, copulatory behavior and differential reproduction. *Quarterly Review of Biology, 57*, 135–159.

Dunbar, R. I. M. (1992). Neocortex size as a constraint on the behavioral ecology of primates. *Journal of Human Evolution, 20*, 469–493.

Dunbar, R. I. M. (1993). Coevolution of neocortical size, group size, and language in humans. *Behavioral and Brain Sciences, 16*, 681–735.

Ellis, L. (1995). Dominance and reproductive success among nonhuman animals: A cross-species comparison. *Ethology & Sociobiology, 16*, 257–333.

Fedigan, L. (1983). Dominance and reproductive success in primates. *Yearbook of Physical Anthropology, 26*, 91–129.

Frith, U., Morton, J., & Leslie, A. M. (1991). The cognitive basis of a biological disorder: Autism. *Trends in Neuroscience, 14*, 433–438.

Gagneux, P., Woodruff, D. S., & Boesch, C. (1997). Furtive mating in female chimpanzees. *Nature, 387*, 358–369.

Gopnik, A., & Meltzoff, A. N. (1994). Minds, bodies and persons: Young children's understanding of the self and others as reflected in imitation and "theory of mind" research. In S. Parker & R. Mitchell (Eds.), *Origins of a theory of mind*. Hillsdale, NJ: Erlbaum.

Hall, K. R. L. (1964). Aggression in monkey and ape societies. In J. Carthy & F. Ebling (Eds.), *The natural history of aggression* (pp. 51–64). London: Academic Press.

Hall, K. R. L., & DeVore, I. (1965). Baboon social behavior. In I. DeVore (Ed.), *Primate behaviour* (pp. 53–110). New York: Holt, Rinehart, & Winston.

Harcourt, A. H. (1988). Alliances in contests and social intelligence. In R. W. Byrne & A. Whiten (Eds.), *Machiavellian intelligence* (pp. 131–152). Oxford: Oxford University Press.

Harcourt, A. H., & De Waal, F. B. M. (Eds.). (1992). *Coalitions and alliances in humans and other animals*. Oxford: Oxford University Press.

Harris, P. L., & Nuñez, M. (1996). Understanding of permission rules by preschool children. *Child Development, 67,* 1572–1591.

Hausfater, G. (1975). Dominance and reproduction in baboons (*Papio Cynocephalus*): A quantitative analysis. *Contributions in Primatology, 7,* 1–150.

Hilpinen, R. (1981). *New studies in deontic logic*. Boston: Reidel/Kluwer.

Hokanson, J. E. (1961). The effect of frustration and anxiety on overt aggression. *Journal of Abnormal and Social Psychology, 62,* 346–351.

Hokanson, J. E., & Shetler, S. (1961). The effect of overt aggression on physiological arousal. *Journal of Abnormal and Social Psychology, 63,* 446–448.

Hoogland, J. L. (1983). Nepotism and alarm-calling in the black-tailed prairie dog (*Cynomys ludovicianus*). *Animal Behavior, 31,* 472–479.

Jenkins, J., & Astington, J. W. (1996). Cognitive factors and family structure associated with theory of mind development in young children. *Developmental Psychology, 32,* 70–78.

Kummer, H. (1988). Tripartite relations in hamadryas baboons. In R. W. Byrne & A. Whiten (Eds.), *Machiavellian intelligence* (pp. 113–121). Oxford: Oxford University Press.

Leekam, S. R. (1992). Believing and deceiving: Steps to becoming a good liar. In S. J. Ceci, M. D. Leichtman, & M. E. Putnick (Eds.), *Cognitive and social factors in early deception* (pp. 47–62). Hillsdale, NJ: Erlbaum.

Leslie, A. M. (1994). Pretending and believing: Issues in the theory of ToMM. *Cognition, 50,* 211–238.

Leslie, A. M., & Thaiss, L. (1992). Domain specificity in conceptual development: Neuropsychological evidence from autism. *Cognition, 43,* 225–251.

Lewis, C., Freeman, N., Kyriakidou, C., Maridaki-Kassotaki, K., & Berridge, D. (in press). Social influences on false belief access: Specific contagion or general apprenticeship? *Child Development*.

Manktelow, K. I., & Over, D. E. (1991). Social roles and utilities in reasoning with deontic conditionals. *Cognition, 39,* 85–105.

Maynard Smith, J. (1982). *Evolution and the theory of games*. Cambridge: Cambridge University Press.

McCann, T. S. (1981). Aggression and sexual activity of male southern elephant seals (*Mirounga Leonina*). *Journal of Zoology, 195,* 295–310.

Mealey, L., Daood, C., & Krage, M. (1996). Enhanced memory for faces of cheaters. *Ethology and Sociobiology, 17,* 119–128.

Menzel, E. W. (1974). A group of chimpanzees in a 1-acre field: Leadership and communication. In A. M. Schrier & F. Stollnitz (Eds.), *Behavior of nonhuman primates* (pp. 83–153). New York: Academic Press.

Mitchell, R. W. (1986). A framework for discussing deception. In R. W. Mitchell & N. S. Thompson (Eds.), *Deception: Perspectives on human and nonhuman deceit* (pp. 3–40). New York: SUNY Press.

Nishida, T. (1983). Alpha status and agonistic alliance in wild chimpanzees (*Pan Troglodytes Schweinfurthii*). *Primates, 24,* 318–336.

Oaksford, M., & Chater, N. (1994). A rational analysis of the selection task as optimal data selection. *Psychological Review, 101,* 608–631.

Packer, C. (1977). Reciprocal altruism in olive baboons. *Nature, 265,* 441–443.

Perner, J. (1991). *Understanding the representational mind.* Cambridge, MA: MIT Press.

Perner, J., Ruthman, T., & Leekam, S. R. (1994). Theory of mind is contagious: You catch it from your sibs. *Child Development, 65,* 1228–1238.

Prud'Homme, J., & Chapais, B. (1993). Aggressive interventions and matrilineal dominance relations in semifree-ranging barbary macaques. *Primates, 34,* 271–283.

Rabbie, J. M. (1992). The effect of intragroup cooperation and intergroup competition on in-group and out-group hostility. In F. de Waal & A. H. Harcourt (Eds.), *Coalitions and alliances in humans and other animals* (pp. 175–208). Oxford: Oxford University Press.

Robinson, J. G. (1982). Intrasexual competition and mate choice in primates. *American Journal of Primatology, 1* (Suppl.), 131–144.

Ruffman, T., Perner, J., Naito, M., Parkin, L., & Clements, W. C. (1996). *Older (but not younger) siblings facilitate false belief understanding.* Unpublished manuscript, University of Sussex.

Schaller, G. B. (1972). *The Serengeti lion.* Chicago: University of Chicago Press.

Seyfarth, R. M. (1976). Social relationships among adult female monkeys. *Animal Behavior, 24,* 917–938.

Seyfarth, R. M., & Cheney, D. L. (1984). Grooming, alliances, and reciprocal altruism in vervet monkeys. *Nature, 308,* 541–543.

Sherman, P. W. (1985). Alarm calls of Belding's ground squirrels to aerial predators: Nepotism or self-preservation? *Behavior, Ecology, and Sociobiology, 17,* 313–323.

Silk, J. B. (1987). Social behavior in evolutionary perspective. In B. B. Smuts, D. L. Cheney, R. M. Seyfarth, R. W. Wrangham, & T. T. Struhsaker (Eds.), *Primate societies* (pp. 318–329). Chicago: University of Chicago Press.

Smith, P. K. (1988). The cognitive demands of children's social interactions with peers. In R. W. Byrne & A. Whiten (Eds.), *Machiavellian intelligence* (pp. 94–110). Oxford: Oxford University Press.

Smuts, B. (1985). *Sex and friendship in baboons.* Hawthorne: Aldine Press.

Sodian, B., & Frith, U. (1992). Deception and sabotage in autistic, retarded, and normal children. *Journal of Child Psychology and Psychiatry and Allied Disciplines, 37,* 591–605.

Sulloway, F. (1996). *Born to rebel.* New York: Pantheon.

Trivers, R. L. (1971). The evolution of reciprocal altruism. *Quarterly Review of Biology, 46,* 35–57.

Tutin, C. E. G. (1979). Mating patterns and reproductive strategies in a community of wild chimpanzees (*Pan Troglodytes Schweinfurtü*). *Behavioral Ecology and Sociobiology, 6,* 29–38.

de Waal, F. (1982). *Chimpanzee politics.* Baltimore: Johns Hopkins University Press.

de Waal, F. (1988). Chimpanzee politics. In R. W. Byrne & A. Whiten (Eds.), *Machiavellian intelligence* (pp. 122–131). Oxford: Oxford University Press.

de Waal, F. (1989). Food sharing and reciprocal obligations among chimpanzees. *Journal of Human Evolution, 18,* 433–459.

de Waal, F. (1992). Coalitions as part of reciprocal relations in the Arnhem chimpanzee colony. In A. H. Harcourt & F. de Waal (Eds.), *Coalitions and alliances in humans and other animals* (pp. 233–258). Oxford: Oxford University Press.

Watts, C. R., & Stokes, A. W. (1971). The social order of turkeys. *Scientific American, 224,* 112–118.

Weg, E., & Smith, V. (1993). On the failure to induce meager offers in ultimatum games. *Journal of Economic Psychology, 14,* 17–32.

Whiten, A., & Byrne, R. W. (1988). The manipulation of attention in primate tactical deception. In R. W. Byrne & A. Whiten (Eds.), *Machiavellian intelligence* (pp. 211–224). Oxford: Oxford University Press.

Wimmer, H., & Perner, J. (1983). Beliefs about beliefs: Representation and constraining function of wrong beliefs in young children's understanding of deception. *Cognition, 13,* 103–128.

Wittenberger, J. F. (1981). *Animal social behavior.* Boston: Duxbury Press.

Woodruff, G., & Premack, D. (1979). Intentional communication in the chimpanzee: The development of deception, *Cognition, 7,* 333–362.

Zaitchik, D. (1991). Is only seeing really believing? Sources of true beliefs in the false belief task. *Cognitive Development, 6,* 91–103.

# 3

# Building a Cognitive Creature from a Set of Primitives

*Evolutionary and Developmental Insights*

MARC HAUSER & SUSAN CAREY

[A]nthropology and psychology cannot be seen as truly independent disciplines. The centerpiece of anthropological theory is the centerpiece of psychological theory: a description of the reliably developing architecture of the human mind, a collection of cognitive adaptations. These evolved problem solvers are the engine that link mind, culture and world. Domain-specific performance is the signature of these evolved mechanisms, a signature that can lead us to a comprehensive mapping of the human mind.

(COSMIDES & TOOBY, 1994)

From an evolutionary perspective, it would be extremely surprising to find a nonhuman animal lacking in computational specializations. Simply take a mental walk through your average zoo or natural history museum. Consider bats and dolphins that use biosonar to see the world auditorily, honey bees that can detect polarized light, snakes that can see into the infrared, songbirds that can simultaneously tap into two independent sound sources to sing their glorious courtship melodies, fish that can detect electric pulses, and both vertebrates and invertebrates that can generate their own light sources as advertisements for mating or defensive ploys against predators. These are indeed marvelous specializations, and they illustrate the power of natural selection to fine tune an organism's neural machinery for computational tasks that allow it either to solve species-typical ecological problems, or to capitalize on species-typical ecological opportunities (Darwin 1859, 1871; Dawkins, 1986).

Yet, it is unfortunate that the causes and consequences of such variation in design features often go unnoticed in research on human cognition. Just as in the case of nonhuman animals, it would be extremely surprising if it turned out that humans lacked unique, species-typical, computational abilities. One such species-specific specialization that we may be quite confident about underlies the human ability to learn, produce, and comprehend language. Human language is the most powerful form of natural communicative expression in the animal kingdom (see synthetic pieces by Bickerton, 1990; Chomsky, 1986; Lieberman, 1984; Pinker, 1994). Indeed, it is unlikely that the human capacity for language is a single computational ability; presumably many different computational specializations serve language learning and use. Thinking about language in terms of species-typical adaptations raises research questions and provides research opportunities. Two related research questions immediately come to mind: What are the evolutionary roots of the human language capacity; and, what are the relations among computational specializations for other cognitive tasks and those that underly language? Research opportunities derive from framing these questions in a comparative context.

The research program we advocate seeks the basic cognitive building blocks for human language. Just as neuropsychologists seek functional dissociations as evidence for computational specializations, and developmental psychologists seek developmental dissociations as evidence for the building blocks of cognition, so studies of nonhuman populations are ideally suited to test hypotheses about the special features of a given cognitive process. That is, in establishing how and why species differ in cognitive functioning, we obtain evidence relevant to the identification of the necessary and sufficient prerequisites to carry out a particular cognitive task.

Evolutionarily minded psychologists often claim that the time machine for relevant selection pressures on human cognitive algorithms need only be pushed back to the Plio-pleistocene period of hominid existence, the period called the "Environment of Evolutionary Adaptedness" (EEA) (see essays in Barkow et al., 1992). This general perspective is puzzling. As we demonstrate here, the roots of many important cognitive specializations are found early in primate evolution, if not before.

Only humans develop a communicative system that is characteristic of all human languages. We do not know, however, which components of the learning mechanism that support language acquisition are part of the species-specific learning device, and which are computational devices that evolved prior to the evolution of the hominid branch of the phylogenetic tree. The strategy, then, is to look at certain key features of language (e.g., as we describe below, concepts of number, object, and agency) to ask whether they are part of the language acquisition device. Two sorts of evidence will ultimately come to bear on this problem: 1) Are such abilities or representations available prelinguistically in human infants?; and, 2) Are such abilities or representations available to nonlinguistic primates, or even non-primates? We seek cognitive processes that babies or our primate cousins lack, as well as those they share in common with older humans. The end product of this research program, far in the future, would be a clearly articulated set of computations that both prevents nonhuman animals or young infants from acquiring a natural language and facilitates language acquisition in normally developing humans (Hauser, 1996).

In order to make use of the comparative approach so familiar to biologists (Harvey & Pagel, 1991; Ridley, 1983), we must be aware that similarity in the expression of a trait can arise from at least two different processes during species comparison. On the one hand, two species can express the same trait because both have inherited the trait from a common ancestor. Here, we speak of the shared trait as a homology. The five-digit hand that we see in humans and chimpanzees is, for example, a case of homology because the common ancestor of these two species almost certainly expressed this particular morphological structure. In contrast, two distantly related species can express the same trait because individuals from each species confront a common ecological problem in which selection has favored the same solution. This provides evidence of convergent evolution, and in this case, we speak of the shared trait as a homoplasy. For example, in songbirds and humans, the young go through a period of vocal development during which elements of the adult repertoire are produced in a primitive form, clearly influenced by auditory experience (Marler, 1970; Locke, 1993). This developmental trait, called babbling, is a homoplasy because songbirds and humans do not share a common ancestor that babbled. And yet, the structure, function, and significance of babbling in these two distantly related taxonomic groups are similar.

The distinction between homology and homoplasy is important. It provides us with important guidelines to select species for comparison. Moreover, it tells us that comparative studies require investigation into both taxonomically distal and proximal organisms. Such in-depth analyses into the tree of life allow us to learn from both cases in which computational abilities differ between two species and from cases in which computational abilities are similar.

If the comparative approach advocated is to succeed, we will require rigorous comparative methods. Studies of comparative cognition can be crudely divided into two categories. On the one hand are studies using highly controlled and sophisticated training techniques to examine, under captive conditions, what animals are capable of learning. Thus, for example, operant procedures have been used to explore the nature of nonhuman animal categorization processes and the structure of their conceptual representations (reviewed in Herrnstein, 1991; Thompson, 1995). Similarly, researchers working with apes and dolphins have taught individuals to use either formal sign language or an artificial language to attempt to uncover some of the constraints on language acquisition (Premack, 1986; Premack &

Premack, 1994b; reviewed in Roitblat et al., 1993). On the other hand are studies carried out under more naturalistic conditions, using a combination of observational and experimental techniques. For example, field and laboratory playback experiments have explored the putative meaning of nonhuman primate vocalizations, in addition to the cognitive processes underlying the implementation of such vocalizations (Cheney & Seyfarth, 1990; Gouzoules et al., 1984; Evans & Marler, 1995; reviewed in Hauser, 1996).

Both approaches have their merits (e.g., controls over stimulus presentation, ecologically relevant tests in the species-typical environment), but both use methods almost never used in studies of human cognition. This leads to the problem articulated by Macphail (1982, 1987, 1994), who claims that comparative analyses are doomed to failure in the absence of comparative methods that could be used across species. The danger, Macphail warns, is that, by using different methodological approaches, one may be vulnerable to criticism that interspecific differences are driven by method differences and interspecific similarities may sometimes be spurious. This problem is most salient in animal/human comparative work, but the points apply in comparisons among nonhuman species as well.

Over the past two years, we have begun a comparative research program of human infant and nonhuman primate cognition that derives its power from the implementation of one experimental technique—the preferential looking time paradigm. The use of comparable methods to address cognitive processing across humans and nonhumans is, of course, not completely novel. There has been extensive work on animals from a Piagetian perspective, using the methods Piaget developed for studying sensorimotor development in human infants (see Antinucci, 1989, for a review). Work by Adele Diamond (1988) on the neurocognitive constraints on object permanence tasks in human infants and rhesus macaques is an elegant testimony to what can be learned when the same methods are deployed across species. Both the Piagetian techniques and Diamond's work depend upon the reaching abilities of babies and primates, and are, we believe, somewhat more limited than the preferential looking time procedure, especially in the range of topics and species that can be explored.

We begin by briefly describing the general logic of the preferential looking time paradigm. We then turn to a discussion of two broad classes of cognitive primitives that we are currently investigating from a comparative perspective. These two cognitive domains, concepts of objects and number, on the one hand, and agency, on the other, were selected because they appear to recruit nonlinguistic concepts, but are fundamentally important to our capacity for linguistic processing. Thus, they seem ideal domains from which to begin an exploration of the computational primitives subserving language from an evolutionary point of view.

A simple entry into the logic of the looking time procedure (see Spelke 1985 for a detailed discussion) is to consider what happens to adults when they sit and watch a magic show. Consider a classic example: a magician samples a random person from an audience, placing him in an opaque box with feet emerging at one end and head emerging at the other end. The magician draws his trusty saw, shows the audience that it is real, and then proceeds to saw the body in half. Having finished this seemingly gruesome task, he first separates the two halves, walks in between them, and then brings them back together. The presumably petrified audience member then walks out of the box, intact, and with no signs of blood or asymmetries in the way in which he was reassembled. Of course there are no signs of blood or body asymmetries. It was a trick. The body was never split in half. And yet, for all of our knowledge, we sit in awe, looking intensely, looking for the trick that violated our expectations. But our expectations as human adults need not be the same as or even similar to those of the developing human infant or more anciently evolved nonhuman.

Armed with this logic, cognitive developmentalists have established the power of the preferential looking time technique in asking—sans language— what human infants know about the world, especially in its physical, mathematical, and psychological aspects (Baillargeon & DeVos, 1991; Baillargeon, 1994; Leslie, 1982; Leslie & Keeble, 1987; Spelke, 1991, 1994; Spelke et al., 1995; Wynn, 1992, 1996). In general, the technique starts with either a series of familiarization or habituation trials designed to remove the effects of novelty on the subject's attention to displayed events. Subsequently, the subject is presented with test events that are either consistent or inconsistent with the constraints provided by physical, mathematical, or psychological principles (i.e., from a normal adult's perspective; the terms "expected" and "unexpected," as well as "possible" and "impossible," are also used in a similar fashion). Thus, for example, in order for a coffee cup to serve as a functional container for coffee, it must have a solid base with no perforations in areas where coffee is likely to rest. Knowing this, human adults would certainly be surprised (i.e., have their expectations violated) to see coffee remain inside a cup with a quarter-sized hole in its base. We would not, however, be surprised to see a 2″ × 2″ block of wood remain in the cup because it is larger than the hole and is a solid object. But is a human infant born with such expectations? If not, what kinds of experience are critically involved in acquiring the relevant knowledge? And of equal interest, if such knowledge is innately specified, did we inherit it from our primate relatives?

*Object and Number Primitives*

In the psychological literature, the object and number concepts of nonlinguistic creatures are usually studied separately, often with distinct methodologies. Explorations of the infant's or animal's concept of physical objects are often placed within a Piagetian framework (e.g., Antinucci, 1989; Piaget, 1952), or within the framework of studies of physical reasoning that probe appreciation of contact causality, the solidity of objects, support relations among objects, etc. (e.g., Baillargeon, 1994; Leslie, 1994, Spelke, 1994). Work on concepts of number, in contrast, focuses mainly on the representation of integers. The animal literature consists largely of conditioning studies that require discrimination of different numerical values (e.g., Boysen & Capaldi, 1993; Meck & Church, 1983). There are also a few studies of addition and subtraction (e.g., Boysen, 1993), as well as studies of symbolic representation of integers (e.g., Boysen, 1993; Matsuzawa, 1985; Rumbaugh & Washburn, 1993; Pepperberg, 1987). The infant literature consists largely of studies of habituation to different numerical values (e.g., Antell & Keating, 1983; Starkey & Cooper, 1980; Strauss & Curtis, 1981; Wynn, 1996), and studies of arithmetical abilities that exploit the preferential looking procedures described above (e.g., Koechlin et al., in press; Simon et al., 1995; Wynn, 1992, 1996).

Upon reflection, it seems clear that nonlinguistic object and number concepts must be studied together. Consider, first, our representation of integers—our procedures for enumeration. We cannot simply count what is in a room. Before we begin to count. We must decide what to count; we must individuate the entities in the room (where one entity stops and another begins), and, we must recognize, when we look away from and return to a portion of the room, which entities are the same ones as those we have counted before. In other words, any enumeration procedure requires individuated entities as its input. The concepts that provide criteria for individuation and numerical identity (sameness in the sense of "same one") are called *sortals* in the philosophical literature. In experiments in which objects are being counted, questions arise about the sortals under which the objects are being individuated.

Next consider object permanence. All studies of object permanence are, in part, studies of criteria for numerical identity—they involve the capacity to establish a representation of an individual, tracing this individual through time and through loss of perceptual contact. When we use the term "object permanence" to describe the baby's knowledge, we presuppose that he/she recognizes that the object retrieved from behind the barrier is the same one as the one that was hidden.

Thus, the exploration of the capacities of animals and infants to represent sortals is central to our understanding of the evolutionary and ontogenetic histories of both concepts, object and number. We will argue below that the relation between these concepts is even closer: what has been taken as evidence for counting by infants actually may not be: instead, evidence reflects criteria for individuation and identity of physical objects, as well as a capacity to build short term memory representations of small numbers of individual objects.

In this section, we first explore the expression of number and sortal concepts in human language, the acquisition of sortal concepts and numerical concepts in human infants. We then present data from nonhuman primates that bear on the evolutionary history of the distinct primitives revealed in the human infant studies. We end by speculating on the evolutionary and ontogenetic sources of the uniquely human count system.

### The Expression of Number and Sortal Concepts in Human Language

Not all languages have a counting sequence that expresses natural numbers. Nonetheless, numerical concepts are fundamental to all human languages. Number is universally reflected in grammaticized contrasts, the most important numerical primitive being the concept, one. Number is typically grammatically marked on both nouns and verbs, usually reflecting the basic distinction between one/many (singular/plural), or sometimes reflecting three distinctions, one/two/many. In addition, noun quantifiers express numerical concepts. In the distinction, an/another/few/many, "an" picks out one, and "another" picks out a numerically distinct individual. Few/many/some all express subtly different contrasts from one. Finally, all languages have a grammatical particle that expresses numerical identity, sameness in the sense of same one.

"One" must be applied to an individuated entity. Thus, languages must represent concepts which pick out individuals, the sortals mentioned above. Sortals have been extensively studied in the philosophical literature on logic and semantics (Wiggins, 1967, 1980; Hirsch, 1992; see Macnamara, 1982; Xu & Carey, 1996, for discussion of sortal concepts within the context of psychological studies of concepts). In languages with a count/mass distinction, sortal concepts are expressed by count nouns, which is why they are called "count nouns," so named because they provide the criteria for individuation and numerical identity that enable entities to be counted.

Thus, number is reflected in language in three different ways: explicitly, in counting sequences ("one, two, three," and so on); grammatically, in number markers on nouns and verbs and in the quantifier systems; and, in the criteria for individuation and identity embodied in the sortal concepts the language lexicalizes. In the following sections, we ask which, if any, of the representational resources language uses to express numerical concepts are available to prelinguistic infants and nonhuman primates.

### Object as a Primitive Sortal, the Quantifiers One/Another: Evidence from Human Infants

Piaget was the first to attempt to bring empirical data to bear on the question of whether human infants have a representation of objects that exists apart from themselves, apart from their own actions upon them, and apart from their perceptual contact with them. In his famous studies of object permanence, Piaget found that infants younger than eight months will not retrieve an object placed under or behind a barrier. He believed his finding revealed that infants did not represent the object's continued existence. Indeed, Piaget argued that even when infants succeed in this basic object permanence task, they do not yet represent objects as enduring through space/time, for they continue to display surprising failures in object search tasks, such as the A not B error. If infants eight- to eleven-months-old see an object disappear in location A, they will search in location A to retrieve it. Subsequently, if the object is hidden in location B, the infant will search again in location A. Thus, Piaget concluded that the eight-month-olds' success reflects not an appreciation of object permanence, but instead a generalization: search where you see something disappear, and something interesting will happen. Piaget argued that it is not until infants can reason about invisible displacements of objects (Stage 6 of the object permanence sequence; 18 months) that we can be certain that they represent object permanence. Piaget saw this achievement as part of the transition to symbolic thought, part of the transition to language.

Piaget's position differs from Spelke's nativist proposal that spatiotemporal continuity is one of the core principles that determines which entities in the world actually are objects (a metaphysical claim). In Spelke's view, this property of object does not have to be constructed over time; it is part of the set of innate principles that determines what infants take to be an object in the first place (an epistemological claim). Spelke offers data from the looking time methods described in the introduction in support of her position. For example, Baillargeon, Spelke, and Wasserman (1985) and their colleagues habituated infants to a screen that rotated 180 degrees in front of them. The screen rotated toward and away from the infants. After habituation, a solid rectangular block was placed in the path of the screen's rotation, such that it was occluded from the infants' view as the screen rotated towards it. In possible events, the screen stopped when it hit the object behind it and then rotated back toward the infant (now traversing 135 degrees rather than 180 degrees). In impossible events, the screen rotated the full 180 degrees, apparently rotating through the object that was behind it. Infants as young as three and a half months remain habituated when viewing the possible events, but they dishabituate to the impossible events (Baillargeon, 1987). This phenomenon shows that 1) Infants know that the object continues to exist behind the screen. 2) Infants know that one solid object cannot pass through the space occupied by another solid object. Thus, besides demonstrating knowledge of object permanence, these data suggest that young infants also know that two objects cannot be in the same place at the same time (see also Spelke et al., 1995).

Many other experiments using the looking time methods support the conclusion that very young infants understand object permanence. Here, two more experiments are briefly described, chosen because they illuminate the relationship between object permanence and spatiotemporal criteria for individuation and numerical identity of objects. The experiments also show that prelinguistic infants' representations are quantified by one and another.

The first experiment shows that infants do not merely expect objects to continue to exist through time when out of view. Infants also interpret apparent evidence for spatiotemporal discontinuity as evidence for two numerically distinct objects. Spelke et al. (1995) showed four and a half-month-old infants two screens, from which objects emerged as in Figure 3.1. The

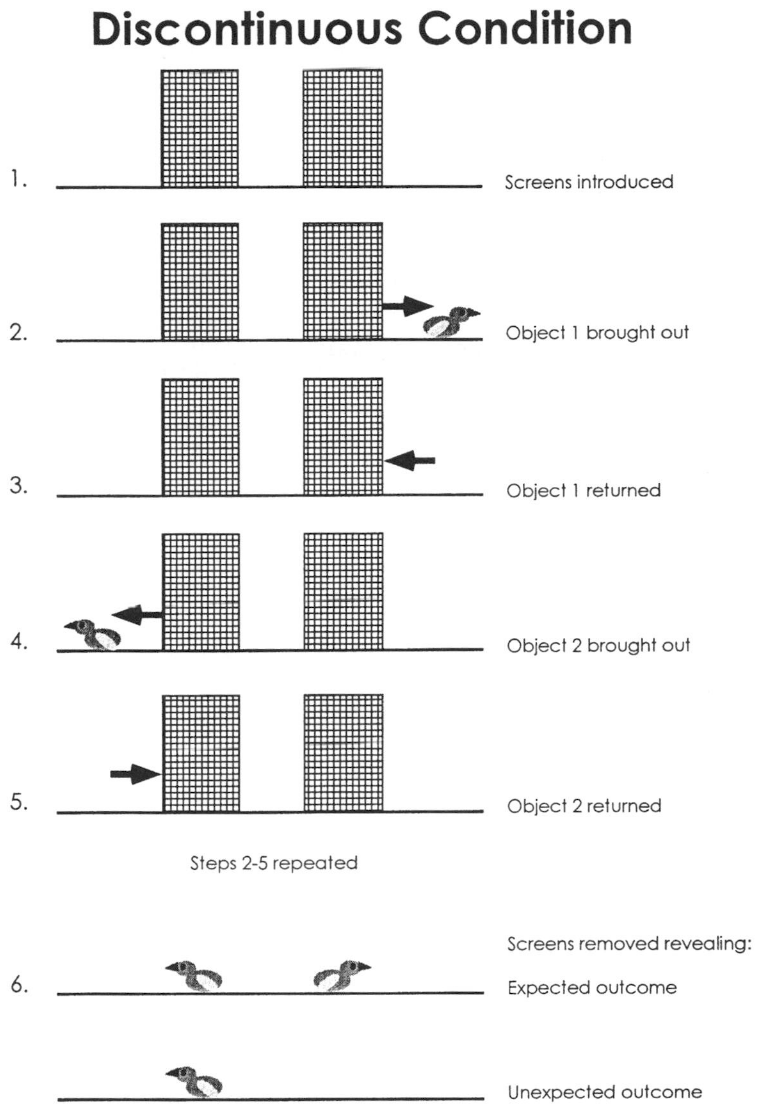

# Discontinuous Condition

1. — Screens introduced

2. — Object 1 brought out

3. — Object 1 returned

4. — Object 2 brought out

5. — Object 2 returned

Steps 2-5 repeated

Screens removed revealing:

6. — Expected outcome

— Unexpected outcome

*Figure 3.1   Experimental procedure to test whether infants use spatiotem-poral discontinuity to infer the existence of two distinct objects in an event.*

objects were never visible together; their appearances were timed so that the movements would be consistent with a single object going back and forth behind the two screens. However, no object ever appeared in the space between the screens. Rather, one object emerged from the left edge of the left screen and then returned behind that screen. After a suitable delay, a second object emerged from the right edge of the right screen and then returned behind it. When shown such movements, adults draw the inference that there must be two numerically distinct objects involved in this display, for objects trace spatiotemporally continuous paths—one object cannot get from point A to point B without tracing some continuous trajectory between the points. Spelke's infants made the same inference. If the screens were removed and only one object was revealed, they were surprised, as shown by longer looking at outcomes of one object than at the expected outcome of two objects. Control experiments established that infants were indeed analyzing the path of motion, and not, for example, expecting two objects just because there were two screens. Specifically, if an object appeared between the screens as it apparently went back and forth, emerging as before from either side then the infants expected an object (see Xu & Carey, 1996, for a replication with ten-month-olds). These data show:

1. Infants know that objects continue to exist when they are invisible behind barriers.
2. Infants distinguish one object from two numerically distinct but physically similar objects (i.e., they have criteria for object individuation and numerical identity, and they distinguish one object from another object.
3. Infants use spatiotemporal criteria for object individuation; if there is no spatiotemporally continuous path between successive appearances of what could be one or more objects, they establish representations of at least two numerically distinct objects.

Like the experiment outlined above, Wynn's (1992, 1996) studies of infants' abilities to add and subtract (see chapter 4) provide further, conclusive evidence that infants represent object permanence, and that spatiotemporal criteria determine object individuation and numerical identity. Wynn showed four and a half-month-old infants an object, a Mickey Mouse doll, placed on a stage. She then occluded the doll from the infants' view by raising a screen, introducing at the same time a second doll behind the screen, but withdrawing an empty hand from behind the screen. Then, she lowered the screen, revealing either the possible outcome of two objects, or the impossible outcome of one object or of three objects. Infants looked longer at the unexpected outcomes than at the expected outcome. Wynn also carried out a subtraction version of this study, beginning with two objects on the stage, occluding them with a screen, removing one from behind the screen, and, upon lowering the screen, revealing either the possible outcome of one object or the impossible outcome of two objects. Again, four and a half-month-olds looked longer at the unexpected outcome. Wynn interpreted these studies to show that infants can add one plus one to yield precisely two, and that they can subtract one from two to yield one. Before considering exactly how infants represent number, the implications of Wynn's studies for infant representations of objects are as follows:

1. Infants represent objects as continuing to exist behind invisible barriers.
2. Infants distinguish two numerically distinct but physically similar dolls from one doll (i.e., infants have criteria for individuation and numerical identity, and they distinguish one object from another object).
3. Infants' criteria for individuation and numerical identity of objects are spatiotemporal, including principles such as one object cannot be in two places at the same time.

Contrary to Piaget's position that the sortal concept, object, is built up slowly over the first two years of human life, we conclude that the concept is most likely an innate primitive of the human conceptual system that serves to guide how experience shapes the development of physical knowledge. It is certainly available by two and a half to three months, well before it is expressed in natural languages. Also, the prelinguistic infants' representational resources include the basic quantifiers one and another. These two aspects of numerical representation, although central to human language, articulate infants' representations of the world prior to language production or comprehension. Of course, this provides only weak evidence that these quantificational devices did not evolve along with the computational resources that underlie the uniquely human linguistic capacity; they may, instead, be expressed earlier in development than other components of a uniquely human computational system for language. To address this question, we turn to animal studies.

### Object as a Primitive Sortal, the Quantifiers One/Another: Evidence from Nonhuman Primates

There is a long tradition of Piagetian studies of object permanence in nonhuman animals (for studies on dogs and cats, see Dore & Dumas, 1987; Gruber et al., 1971; for studies on primates, see Antinucci, 1989). Across a wide range of species, the search behavior characteristic of Piaget's Stage 4 of object permanence has been observed; and, across a wide range of primate species, Stage 5 has been well confirmed. Primates as evolutionarily distant from people as tufted capuchin monkeys, and primates as evolutionarily close as gorillas and chimpanzees, search for objects hidden under covers. They do not make the A not B error, and they perform as well as human infants of fifteen to eighteen months of age. There is also evidence that apes solve Stage 6 problems, although the success of monkeys at this level is more hotly contested (Natale & Antinucci, 1989).

Success at Piaget's Stage 5 tasks is underscored by Adele Diamond's studies comparing rhesus and human infants on the delayed response task used in animal frontal function studies. Goldman-Rakic and Diamond noted the similarity between this task and Piaget's object permanence task (objects are hidden in one of two or more wells, a delay is introduced, and then the animal/baby is provided an opportunity to retrieve the object). Diamond showed that the development of delayed response success in two- to four-month-old rhesus monkeys (including A not B errors and developmental increases in the delays that can be tolerated) is mirrored, in parametric detail, by parallel development in the same tasks performed by human infants between seven and nine months of age (see Diamond, 1988, 1991).

Object permanence requires the establishment of a representation of an individual that can be tracked through space and time. Given the evidence that prelinguistic infants as young as four months use spatiotemporal criteria for object individuation, we expected that primates from many branches of the evolutionary tree would also rely on such criteria for individuation and identity in tasks such as Spelke et al.'s (1985) and Wynn's (1992, 1996). Indeed, this result is anticipated by some of Tinklepaugh's observations in the 1920s (Tinklepaugh, 1929). Rhesus monkeys were presented with two pieces of food hidden in a given location. The experimenter surreptitiously removed one of them, so when the monkeys uncovered the food, they found only one piece. Tinklepaugh reports that they were surprised, and that the number of reaches into the well was determined by the number of objects (one or two) the monkey saw placed there.

Before we could pursue these results, we faced a serious methodological challenge. Could we use the looking time methods with nonhuman primates? In the wild? In the laboratory? Would monkeys be curious about the magic tricks we show infants? Would they sit still and look at the outcomes? We believed these first studies to be as important for methodological considerations as for the scientific questions about criteria for individuation and numerical identity for objects.

Our first studies were of wild rhesus monkeys (*Macaca mulatta*) living on the island of Cayo Santiago, Puerto Rico. We carried out three studies based on Wynn's addition and subtraction experiments (Hauser et al., 1996). Our method was to catch the attention of a passing adult monkey, to turn the video camera on him or her to record looking times, and to show the monkey an event that either did or did not involve a magic trick. We made a box, open on the top, with a removable screen that covered the front. Our stimuli were bright purple eggplants, clearly food and of great interest to the monkeys; but the eggplants were unfamiliar food, so the monkeys were somewhat wary.

The first question we needed to answer was whether the monkeys would sit through the whole show, so our first shows were short. Unlike the infant methodology, in which looking times of both possible and impossible outcomes are recorded and often accompanied by within-subject baseline data for each infant, our first experiment with rhesus monkeys involved a single trial. Figure 3.2 shows the three trial types. Twenty-four monkeys saw T1 trials, in which they were shown the empty box, the screen was put in place, and one eggplant was withdrawn from the experimenter's apron and placed in the box. The experimenter's empty hand was shown to the

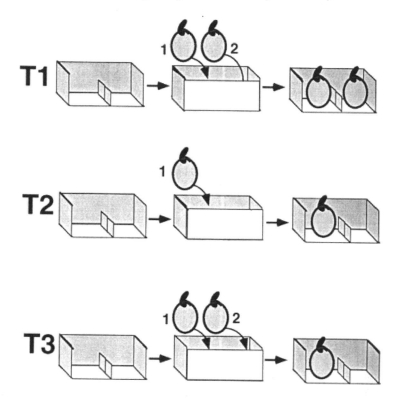

*Figure 3.2  Test trials to procedure to assess whether rhesus monkeys represent the addition of one object and then another object into a box as two objects in a box.*

monkey, and then a second eggplant was withdrawn from the experimenter's apron and placed in the box. The screen was then removed, revealing the expected outcome of two eggplants in the box. Twenty-four monkeys watched T2 trials, identical to T1 trials, except that in these trials only one eggplant was deposited in the box, and, when the screen was removed, the expected outcome of one eggplant in the box was revealed. Both T1 and T2 were possible outcome trials. Finally, 13 monkeys were shown T3 trials in which eggplants were placed in the box as in the T1 trials (i.e., 1 + 1), but the outcome was just a single eggplant, as in the T2 trials. The magic trick was pulled off by placing one eggplant into a hidden pouch on the backside of the screen. Thus, T3 was the only trial type with an impossible outcome. Looking times were recorded for a fixed ten seconds after the screen was removed.

Like human babies, the monkeys looked longer at the impossible outcomes of the T3 trials than at the possible outcomes of either the T1 trials or the T2 trials (mean = 2.4 sec). Thus, as expected, adult rhesus monkeys distinguish one object from two numerically distinct but physically similar

objects, and they maintain representations of objects they see disappear behind barriers.

These results were confirmed in a second series of experiments in which
adult monkeys were shown to tolerate longer events. These experiments consisted of within-monkey comparisons of two baseline trials, followed by either T1 (n = 15), T2 (n = 12), or T3 (n = 12). In the baseline trials, no arithmetical operations were performed; for example, monkeys were shown one
trial of a single eggplant being placed in the box in full view and one trial of
two eggplants being placed, simultaneously, in the box in full view. These trials
(orders counterbalanced across monkeys, of course) served to familiarize the
monkeys with outcomes of both one and two eggplants in the box, but gave
no information as to how many to expect in the test trials. Figure 3.3 shows
the results. Monkeys looked markedly less on the second familiarization trial
than on the first, and they maintained short looking times on each of the
possible outcome trials (T1 and T2). On the impossible outcome trials (T3),
monkeys looked markedly longer than on the possible outcome trials, and also
markedly longer than on the second of the familiarization trials. Thus, in both
of these addition (1 + 1 = 2 or 1) studies, wild rhesus monkeys demonstrated
surprise, in the form of long looking times, at impossible outcomes.

A third study in Hauser et al., 1996 compared looking times of two
subtraction events (2 − 1 = 1, possible outcome; 2 − 1 = 2, impossible outcome). Whereas the magnitude of the looking time differences was not as
striking as in the two addition studies, the monkeys did look longer at the
impossible outcomes than at the possible outcomes. They also looked longer
at the impossible outcomes than at the outcomes of the second of the two
familiarization trials (although this difference was significant only on non-
parametric measures).

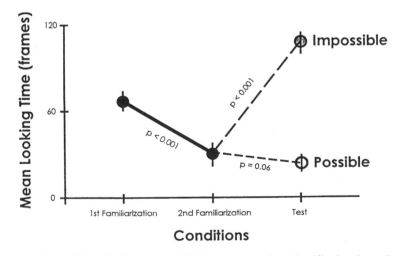

*Figure 3.3   Rhesus looking times (30 frames/second) to familiarization trials,
possible outcomes (T1, T2) and impossible outcomes (T3).*

Methodologically, these studies establish that it is possible to use the looking time measures for studies of primate representations, even in the wild. Theoretically, they confirm the findings from Piagetian studies of object permanence that rhesus monkeys establish representations of objects, and track them through time, even when the objects are out of view. The results add to this literature the finding that, like human infants, rhesus monkeys distinguish between one object and two numerically distinct objects. The monkeys represent at least one sortal concept, object, and quantifiers such as one and another. These studies leave many questions open, of course, including the precise nature of the representations underlying performance on these tasks. The rest of this section concerns the search for data that constrain our hypotheses about the nature of such representations in primates, including prelinguistic human infants.

Emboldened by our findings on rhesus monkeys, we set out to establish whether the looking time procedure could be used to explore the representational systems of primates far more evolutionarily distant from human beings, than are rhesus monkeys. Our next subjects were small, New World monkeys called cotton-top tamarins (*Saguinus oedipus oedipus*), but studying them posed new methodological challenges. Our sample was a colony of eight adult and two sub-adult tamarins in four family groups, housed in the Primate Cognitive Neuroscience Laboratory at Harvard University. We needed to establish an experimental set up in which we could carry out looking time experiments, and since there are only 10 subjects, we could not afford to lose subjects due to inattention. With so few subjects, we could not use the between-subjects designs of the rhesus monkey studies in the wild. Furthermore, if we were to carry out a series of studies on related issues, we would have to establish that repeated testing with similar magic tricks did not lead to decreased interest in the relevant stimuli or classes of events. These studies are of theoretical interest as well because there have been few studies of object permanence with nonhuman primates more evolutionarily distant from humans than rhesus (see Antinucci, 1989, for a review).

In the experimental setup we devised, subjects are never physically handled. They are lured from their home cage to a 1' × 1' × 1' Plexiglas transport box with a small piece of food (individuals move willingly into the transport box, and thus arrive in our testing rooms without stress). From the transport box, they move readily into a Plexiglas test box, the sides and back of which are opaque, and the front panel of which is transparent. The monkeys observe the magic tricks through the front panel. Located toward the base of the front panel is an opening through which monkeys can be given food to help ensure that they maintain interest in the events unfolding before them.

Because subjects have been repeatedly tested in the Plexiglas box, they have learned to sit quietly, without jumping, for 15–20 minutes; this is ample time to conduct the present experiments. All experiments are videotaped so looking times can be accurately assessed by raters who are blind to the experimental condition the monkeys are in. Our first experiments were four one plus one addition studies (Uller, 1997), two of which we briefly describe below. The stimuli were small stacks of Froot Loops (small colorful rings of sweet cereal), and after every few trials in which looking times were recorded, the monkeys were given a Froot Loop to eat. Intense interest in these treats helped maintain the monkeys' cooperation through experimental sessions that included both baseline trials and two test trials (one with a possible outcome, and one with an impossible outcome).

For the first study, we constructed a smaller version of the test box used in the rhesus studies described above, because tamarins are much smaller than rhesus, and our stimuli were columns of Froot Loops rather than eggplants. Each monkey participated in an experimental session consisting of six trials—four baseline trials and two test trials. The baseline trials served both to familiarize the monkeys with the objects being placed in the box, and to familiarize them with the screen being removed to reveal the objects. The baseline trials also established whether the monkeys had an intrinsic preference for displays of one object or two objects. There was no magic in the baseline trials. One-object baseline trials consisted of one object being lowered into the box and revealed when the screen was removed; two-object baseline trials consisted of two objects being lowered into the box simultaneously, with two objects being revealed upon removal of the screen. The two test trials were identical to T1 (1 + 1 = 2, possible outcome) and T3 (1 + 1 = 1, impossible outcome) trials shown in Figure 3.2. Order of outcomes was counterbalanced across subjects.

Eight monkeys completed the experiment. Not surprisingly, given their interest in these stimuli, they had a baseline preference for displays of two objects (Mean = 4.21 s) over displays of one object (Mean = 2.27 s); seven of the eight looked longer at two objects than at one object during the four baseline trials. In sharp contrast, during the test trials, the monkeys looked longer at the outcomes of one object (the impossible outcome; Mean = 2.13 s) than at the outcomes of two objects (the possible outcome; Mean = 1.55 s); seven of the eight looked longer at the impossible outcomes than at the possible outcome. The interaction between looking time preference (one object vs. two objects) and trial type (baseline, test) was significant ($F$,1,7 = 44.054, p < .0001).

Like rhesus monkeys, cotton-top tamarins also look longer at the impossible outcomes of a 1 + 1 = 2 or 1 addition task. Tamarins individuate objects and track them through time, even when the objects are out of sight. However, these studies, by themselves, do not show that rhesus and tamarin monkeys expect 1 + 1 to be precisely two. They are consistent with many other possible interpretations. For example, a possible interpretation that has never been ruled out holds that the monkeys (and the infants) are not tracking numerically distinct objects at all. Perhaps they are simply sensitive to the amount of stuff, the amount of Froot Loops in these studies, the amount of eggplant in the wild rhesus studies, and the amount of Mickey Mouse stuff in Wynn's studies. Under this interpretation, the unexpected outcomes in the 1 + 1 = 2 or 1 studies are unexpected because there is less stuff than the subject expected, not because there are fewer items.

Our second study tested this alternative hypothesis in a 1 + 1 = 2 or big 1 study. The outcomes of the test trials were either the expected outcome of two Froot Loop columns or a single, large Froot Loop column, twice the height of the single columns. If the monkeys are tracking amount of Froot Loop stuff or surface area of the stimuli, then both of these outcomes are possible. Looking times should simply reflect whatever baseline preferences monkeys have between these two stimuli. However, if monkeys are tracking the number of objects, they should be surprised at the unexpected outcome of one larger object. The design for this study mirrored that for the previous study; there were four baseline trials that familiarized the monkeys with the two types of stimuli; one or two objects were placed into the box, and baseline line preferences were established. No magic tricks were performed during the baseline trials. In the test trials, the objects were lowered, one at a time, into the box (as in the T3 trials of Figure 3.2), and the outcomes were either two objects (possible outcome) or one large object (impossible outcome). Each monkey had two test trials; order (possible outcome first, impossible outcome first) was counterbalanced across monkeys.

Nine of the ten monkeys completed all six trials. The baseline preference was for displays of two objects; eight of the nine monkeys looked longer at the two-object displays (Mean = 2.1 s) than at the displays of a single large object (Mean = 1.3 s). This preference was reversed in the test trials; seven of the nine monkeys looked longer at the impossible outcome of one big object (Mean = 2.4 s) than at the expected outcome of two objects (Mean = 1.5 s). Apparently, monkeys are tracking individuated objects in these studies, not amount of stuff, or perceived surface area.

Just as in the studies with wild rhesus monkeys, these tamarin studies make several important methodological points. The looking time methodology yields interpretable results from monkeys that are as evolutionarily distant from humans as cotton-top tamarins. Further, with similar methods and materials, it is possible to run a series of looking time experiments on the same small population of animals, keeping 80–90% of the subjects on task through each of four experiments, and yielding interpretable findings throughout (see Uller et al., in preparation, for a description of the whole series).

These experiments show that like rhesus monkeys and preverbal human infants, cotton-top tamarins represent the sortal object, with spatiotemporal criteria for individuation and numerical identity. In addition, the representational resources of these two species, like those of prelinguistic infants, include the basic quantifiers one/another. These two aspects of numerical representation, so central to human language, are part of the human primate heritage and did not evolve along with the computational resources that underly the uniquely human linguistic capacity.

The Representation of Number by Human Infants

We've discussed the infant and primate addition/subtraction studies as they bore on nonlinguistic representations of object (object permanence, principles of individuation, and numerical identity for objects) and on nonlinguistic representations of basic quantifiers such as one/another. We argued that these are cognitive building blocks that emerged early in primate evolution, if not before. Next, we turn to the infant addition/subtraction studies as they bear on the question of prelinguistic infants' representation of number, especially the representation of the first three natural integers, one, two, and three (Wynn, chapter 4, this volume).

Simple habituation experiments provide ample evidence that young infants, even neonates, are sensitive to numerical distinctions among sets of one, two, and three entities (e.g., dots: Antell & Keating, 1983; sets of varied objects: Starkey & Cooper, 1980; continuously moving figures: van Loosbroek & Smitsman, 1990; jumps of a doll: Wynn, 1996). In such studies, infants are habituated to arrays of a given set size (e.g., two entities), which are then shown to dishabituate to arrays of a different set size (e.g., one or three entities). Wynn's addition and subtraction studies confirm that prelinguistic infants discriminate among sets of one, two, and three objects. Additionally, infants know some of the numerical relations among the sets, for they have been shown to succeed at $1 + 1$, $2 - 1$, $2 + 1$, and $3 - 1$ tasks (Koechlin et al., in press; Simon et al., 1995; Uller, 1997; Wynn, 1992, 1996).

The results presented so far leave open the nature of the representations underlying infants' performance. What these representations might be, and the senses in which they may or may not be "genuinely numerical" is a source of intense debate. In order to engage this debate, one must distinguish between classes of models that may underlie performance to attempt to bring data to bear on which, if any, underlie infant performance. We know of three serious proposals for infant representation of number that could account for their successes in the studies cited above.

In the Numeron List Model, Gelman and Gallistel (1978) proposed that infants establish numerical representations through a counting procedure. According to the proposal, there is an innate, mentally represented list of symbols called "numerons," for instance, !, @, +, %, $ (Of course, we do not know how such symbols would actually be written in the mind). Entities to be counted are put in one-to-one correspondence with items on this list, always proceeding in the same order through the list. The number of items in the set being counted is represented by the last item on the list reached, and its numerical values are determined by the ordinal position of that item in the list. For example, in the above list, "@" represents two, because "@" is the second item of the list.

In the Accumulator Model, Meck and Church (1983) proposed that animals represent number with a magnitude that is an analog of number. The idea is simple—suppose that the nervous system has both the equivalent of a pulse generator that generates activity at a constant rate, and a gate that can open to allow energy through to an accumulator that registers how much energy has been let through. When the animal is in a counting mode, the gate is opened for a fixed amount of time (say 200 ms) for each item to be counted. The total energy accumulated will then be an analog representation of number. This system works as if length were used to represent number. For example, "—" would be a representation of one, "——" a representation of two, "———" a representation of three, and so on (see Gallistel, 1990, for a summary of evidence for the accumulator model).

In the Object File Model (Uller 1997; Simon et al., 1995), evidence suggests that infants may be establishing a mental model of the objects in an array. That is, they may be constructing an imagistic representation of the stage floor, the screen, and the objects behind the screen, creating one object-file (Kahneman & Triesman, 1984) for each object behind the screen. Such a model represents number, for example, the number two, in virtue of being an instantiation of:

$$(\exists x)(\exists y)((object(x) \ \& \ object(y)) \ \& \ x \neq y \ \& \ \forall z(object(z) \rightarrow (z = x) \ V \ (z = y)))$$

In English, this formula states that there is an entity and another entity numerically distinct from it, that each entity is an object, and there is no other object. This sentence is logically equivalent to, "There are exactly two objects," but note that, in such a representation, there is no single symbol for two, not "2," or "@," or "——," or any other. This model exploits no representational resources other than those demonstrated in the previous sections—object sortals and the capacity to distinguish one from another.

Besides differing in the nature of integer representation, the three proposals differ in the process underlying discrepancy detection between the formed representation of introduced objects and removed objects behind the screen and the representation of the resultant display after the screen is removed. Take a 1 + 1 = 2 or 1 event as an example. In the two integer symbolic models, the results of two counts are compared—the symbol for the number of objects resulting from adding operations (e.g., "@" or "——") is compared to the symbol resulting from a count of the objects in the outcome array ("@" or "——" in possible outcomes, versus "!" or "—" in impossible outcomes). According to the object file proposal, a representation that consists of two object-files (constructed during the addition portion of the event) is compared to a representation of two object-files (possible outcome) or one object-file (impossible outcome) by means of a process that detects one to one correspondence between the object files in the two representations.

These three proposals for nonlinguistic representational systems for number are genuinely different from each other. The first two (the numeron list model and the accumulator model) embody distinct symbols for each integer, but differ in the nature of the symbols they use. In the numeron list model, each symbol bears a discrete and arbitrary relation to the number it represents. In the accumulator model, in contrast, an analog representational system exploits the fact that the symbols are magnitudes linearly related to the numbers they represent. Furthermore, as previously noted in discussion of the object file model, there is no distinct symbol that represents each integer at all. In this model, there is nothing that corresponds to counting in terms of a set of symbols, whether arbitrary (numerons) or analog (states of the accumulator). Natural languages exploit the numeron list system, so, we are particularly interested in evidence that this may be the representational mechanism that underlies the representation of number by prelinguistic infants and animals.

Uller et al. (1997, under review) present several arguments that favor the object file model as the model which underlies performance on the infant addition and subtraction experiments. The main argument is empirical: several experimental manipulations that might be expected to influence the robustness of mental models of the objects in arrays but not a symbolic representation of the number of individuals, such as "@" or "——," are shown to affect performance of infants in the addition studies. To give just one example, the timing of the screen's placement on the stage, relative to the placement of the objects behind it, determines success in a $1 + 1 = 2$ or 1 addition study. The classic Wynn study (1992), and all its replications (Koehaene et al., in press; Simon et al., 1995; Wynn, 1996) use an "object first design". The first object (1) is placed on the stage, the screen is introduced, and then the second object (+ 1) is introduced behind the screen. Infants as young as four months of age succeed in this design. Uller et al. (under review) contrasted this design with a "screen first" design in which the screen is placed on an empty stage, one object (1) is introduced behind it, and then a second (+ 1) is introduced behind it. Both of these designs simply require incrementing the counting mechanism twice, yielding a representation of two ("@" or "——"), and holding this symbol in memory until the screen is removed. In other words, these two experimental designs should be equivalent in difficulty.

If we make some reasonable assumptions about the factors that might influence the robustness of mental models, then it seems likely that the "object first" design will be markedly easier than the "screen first" design. These assumptions are: 1) a mental model of an object actually seen on the stage is more robust than one constructed in imagery; and, 2) each update of a mental model in imagery decreases robustness of the model. The "object first" condition begins with a representation of one object on the stage constructed from perception and requires only one update in imagery; the "screen first" condition requires that the representation of the first object on the stage is constructed in imagery, and requires two updates in imagery. Indeed, infants succeed in "object first" tasks by age four to five months, but in comparable "screen first" tasks they do not succeed until 10-months of age (Uller et al., under review). Note that in the rhesus and tamarin studies reviewed earlier, the monkeys succeeded in the more difficult "screen first" design.

Other considerations favor the object file model as well, not the least of which is the finding of a sharp limit on the numerosities infants represent. Simple habituation experiments with infants, as well as the addition/subtraction studies, have shown that infants represent the numerical values of one, two, and three, but in general fail to discriminate among higher numerosities. There is no such limit on the accumulator model or the numeron list model. This limit is, however, predicted by the object-file model, based on the assumption that there is a limit to parallel individuation of three object-files in short term memory (see Trick & Pylyshyn, 1994).

In sum, we suggest that the weight of evidence currently available supports the proposal that the representation of number underlying infants' successes and failures in the addition/subtraction experiments and habituation studies, consists of mental models of the objects in arrays. These representations are numerical insofar as they require that the infant have criteria for numerical identity. A representation that instantiates ∃x etc is logically equivalent to "there are two objects," because comparisons among models are on the basis of one to one correspondences among object-files. However, they fall short of symbolic representations of number, because there is no unique symbol for each integer, and there is no counting process defined over them.

The upshot of this argument is that there is no evidence for a prelinguistic representational system of the same structure as natural language count sequences, such as "1, 2, 3, 4, 5 . . .". There is no evidence from the infant studies that such a system is an antecedently available representational system, available to be exploited in the learning of language. The difficulty children experience when learning to count (Wynn, 1992; chapter 4, this volume) lends further credence to this conclusion.

### The Representation of Number by Nonhuman Primates

There is a long history of studies of animal representation of number (see Boysen & Capaldi, 1993, for a recent review of this large literature). These studies have been of several types. Some have required animals to learn to make responses contingent on some number of stimuli or some number of previous responses. Others have required animals to choose the larger or smaller of two stimuli, differing only in number of individuals. And recently, there have been several studies of primates' (chimpanzees, rhesus monkeys, and one nonprimate, an African grey parrot) abilities to learn explicit symbols for integers, usually, zero or one through six, but sometimes up through eight or nine (Matsuzawa, 1985; Pepperberg, 1994; Boysen, 1993, 1996; Rumbaugh & Washburn, 1993). All of these studies require extensive training, up to several years. The degree of training involved has led some commentators (e.g., Davis & Perusse, 1988) to speculate that number is not a salient dimension of animals' experience of the world, and although they can be induced to encode number of objects or actions, they do not do so spontaneously. Others (e.g., Gallistel, 1990) dispute this claim, arguing that number, at least in some ethologically relevant contexts such as foraging for food, is automatically encoded. The looking time studies with cotton-top tamarin and rhesus monkeys reviewed earlier bear on this debate. Clearly, animals of both species automatically encode the difference between one versus two entities with no training whatsoever required.

The literature contains other demonstrations of nonhuman primate addition skills. Boysen (1993, 1996) reviews her studies of the chimpanzee, Sheba, who had been previously trained to match Arabic numerals (1–4) with numbers of objects. In the first addition study, Sheba went to one location, noted the number of oranges placed there (e.g., two), went to a second location and noted the number of oranges placed there (e.g., one), and then went to a third location and indicated the sum by pointing to one of four cards (one, two, three, or four). The next studies dispensed with the oranges; Sheba went to the first location, looked at a card with an Arabic numeral (e.g., 1), went to the second location and looked at a card with an Arabic numeral (e.g., 3), and then went to the third location and pointed to the card that depicted the sum.

Rumbaugh and Washburn (1993) summarize another series of chimpanzee addition studies. Chimpanzees were presented with two sets of two trays of candies, for example, three and four in one set, and two and six in the other. The chimpanzees could choose one of the sets of trays, and were allowed to eat the candies from the selected set. The only incentive to add or enumerate the total number of candies in one set was to get the larger amount. The chimpanzees learned to do this. A variety of control experiments ruled out strategies such as taking the set with the largest single number of candies (e.g., the side with the tray with six candies in the above example), or avoiding the side with the smallest single number of candies.

In parallel with the infant studies, the important question in all of the animal studies concerns the nature of the mental representations of number that subserve these abilities. We argued earlier in favor of the position that representations of individual objects in the array underlie success on the infant addition and subtraction studies; that is, we favored the object-file model. To date, there are no relevant data that would bear on deciding between classes of models of the representations subserving the monkey $1 + 1 = 2$ or 1 studies. The object-file model is a possibility, but an alternative possibility is that the monkeys are spontaneously counting over some symbolic representation of number (as in the numeron model or the accumulator model).

It is important to note that some of the other primate addition studies are also consistent with the object-file model. Boysen's original addition studies with Sheba are an example, assuming that four is within the limits of primate capacities for parallel individuation (see Trick & Pylyshyn, 1994 for data that establish that the human limit is as high as four). Consider, first, the oranges version of the study. Upon encountering the first set of oranges, Sheba could have constructed a model containing an object-file for each orange, and she could have updated this model by adding the number of object-files that corresponded to the number of oranges she encountered second. To choose the correct Arabic numeral, she would have had to learn to associate a representation with one open object-file with "1", two open object-files with "2", and so on. This same association would allow her to solve the purely symbolic version of the task with the same strategy. That is, upon encountering the first numeral ("2") she would set up a memory representation with two open object-files, and would update it by adding the number of object-files depicted by the second numeral ("1"), yielding a model with a total of three object-files open. She would then indicate the correct Arabic numeral as in the version of the task that used oranges. Of course, it is also possible that Sheba's mental representations of one, two, three, and four may have been symbolic—accumulator representations or numeron representations. The importance of the fact that Sheba had been taught external symbolic representations of number, for example, written numerals, will be discussed below. For now, we wish only to stress that Sheba's achievements in these studies leave open the nature of the mental representations of number mapped onto those symbols.

Although the original addition experiments with Sheba are consistent with the object-file model of numerical representation, it is also clear that primates must have additional resources for number representation. They must, because they succeed in representing numbers that exceed the limit on parallel individuation, which in humans is somewhere between three and five. There is no reason to believe that nonhuman primates would have a greater capacity for parallel individuation than humans. For example, in other experiments, Sheba learned Arabic numerals up to nine, and also demonstrated knowledge of the ordinal relations among all pairs of numerals from zero to nine. Squirrel monkeys, a New World primate species, also have this latter ability (Rumbaugh & Washburn, 1993). And in Rumbaugh's addition experiments, chimpanzees summed to eight or nine (Rumbaugh & Washburn, 1993). These numbers exceed the memory limitations on concurrently opened object-files, and implicate some other mental representational system for number.

We now turn to whether that system is likely to be the numeron list model or some analog system, such as the accumulator model suggested by Meck and Church (1983). Recall that the primary distinction made in our discussion of the representation of number by human infants was that the numeron list model consists of a mentally represented list of arbitrary, discrete, symbols and a counting procedure that deploys them. In contrast, the analog model consists of magnitude representations and a procedure for establishing magnitudes that is proportional to the number of items to be enumerated.

The argument we would make concerning the nature of primate non-linguistic representation of number is parallel to that made by Wynn (1992, 1995) concerning the nature of infant nonlinguistic representations of number (see chapter 4, this volume). Wynn rejects the numeron list model for infant representation of number based on an ease of learning argument. Note first that explicit linguistic representations, "1, 2, 3, 4, 5, and so on" are a list of numerals. The only difference between the explicit numeral list representations of natural language and the posited nonlinguistic numeron list model is that numerons are mentally represented symbols or symbols in the language of thought. Wynn argues that if nonlinguistic number representation consists of a list of numerons, then learning to count in a natural language should be easy. Once children have identified the list in English (1, 2, 3, 4, etc.) that serves the purpose of the numeron list (!, @, +, %, etc.), they should demonstrate an understanding of how each of the English numerals functions in representing number. In her toddler counting experiments, Wynn showed that between the ages of two and a half and three and a half, children can recite the count sequence, usually to 10. They can also "count" in the sense that they can enumerate a set of items by tagging each one, reciting the count sequence in order, and respecting one to one correspondence (see Gelman & Gallistel, 1978, 1986 for extensive studies of early counting). Importantly, Wynn also showed that children as young as two and a half know that "one" refers to the number one, and that "two, three, four, five" all contrast with one and refer to numbers bigger than one. That is, they have identified the list as representing some aspects of number. Most crucially, Wynn showed that for a full year between ages two and a half and three and a half, children don't know to which number "2," "3," or "4" refers. Wynn argues that this state of affairs is inconsistent with the proposal that the underlying nonlinguistic representation of number is the numeron list model. If it were, all that the children would need to do to understand how natural languages represent number would be to establish which list in natural languages functions as does the numeron list (see also Carey, 1995).

We read the literature on teaching symbolic representations of number to nonhuman primates to support a parallel argument. There are four series of attempts to teach primates symbols for number; all involve chimpanzees (see Thomas, 1992; Matsuzawa, 1985; Boysen, 1993; Rumbaugh & Washburn, 1993, for accounts of these experiments). Each of these series of studies yields rich and fascinating information concerning chimpanzee representation of number, but it is beyond the scope of this chapter to plumb all of the findings. Here we wish to make three points. First, it is extremely difficult to teach chimpanzees symbols for numbers. In studies by Thomas it took chimpanzees 500,000 trials to learn binary symbols for one through seven. In Matsuzawa's studies, it took chimpanzees 95 hours of continuous training to learn Arabic numeral representations of one through six (compared to much less time to learn a comparable number of object labels or color labels). Chimpanzees in Boysen's studies took several years of daily training. Second, we are convinced that Boysen's chimpanzees, and Rumbaugh's, had learned to count by using a numeral list system. If the reader is not convinced that these studies have yet demonstrated such computation, then this just strengthens the point we wish to make. Third, when one looks at the details of what is necessary to put this skill together, it is extremely unlikely that the chimpanzees are merely learning an explicit symbolic representational system, structured identically to their nonlinguistic representational system for number.

To illustrate these points, consider Boysen's studies. Boysen taught Sheba and two other chimpanzees, Darrell and Kermit, a symbol system for number through several steps. First, they were trained to make explicit one to one correspondences, putting one object into each of six egg carton compartments. Then, they were taught to match sets of one, two, or three objects with cards with one, two, or three dots. Then, the cards with one, two, or three dots were replaced with cards with the symbols 1, 2, and 3. Numerals four and higher were taught directly as correspondences between the numeral and arrays of the relevant number of objects. Each new skill needed extensive training. After having learned to point to the correct numeral when shown a variety of arrays, new training was required for the chimpanzees to point to the correct array when shown a numeral. Still more training was needed for the chimpanzees to learn to construct arrays of one, two, three, or four spools when shown one of the numerals (Sheba did not master this as well as Darrell, even though on most tasks she was the star pupil). More telling, even after two years of practice in these number-numeral correspondences, two of the three chimpanzees failed to learn the serial order relations among the numerals 1–5 (Sheba succeeded; Darrell and Kermit failed). The chimpanzees who initially failed the task eventually succeeded following another year of being trained to pick the smaller numeral as well as the larger one. Sheba spontaneously invented manual tagging (touching objects one at a time while enumerating them) to help to establish number/numeral correspondences between arrays and numerals four or greater, and she eventually mastered the numerals up to nine, including the ordinal relations among them. That is, after being trained to pick the larger of two numerals from a subset of the numerals in her repertoire, she generalized to pick the larger numeral from the pairs she'd never been trained on, doing so on the first exposure to the pairs. The end performance of these chimpanzees is very impressive indeed.

Two striking points emerge from these studies. First, the chimpanzees ultimately achieved significant mastery of an explicit numeral representational system for number. Second, given the extensive training required (not unlike that of preschool children, who also work at it for months before they can use a list of numerals to represent number), it appears that this is a new representational capacity being constructed, not simply an explicit expression of a numeron list structure antecedently available. Given that chimpanzees can learn explicit representations of numbers beyond the range of parallel individuation, it seems likely that one antecedently available representational system for number may be something like the analog accumulator model proposed by Meck and Church (1983).

In sum, we read the animal number literature to be consistent with the claim that the numeron list system of representation of integers (widely but not universally expressed in natural languages) is a human cultural construction. It is not the representational system that underlies human infant appreciation of small numbers (here, we favor the object-file model), nor is it the representational system that underlies nonhuman primate representations of either small or larger numbers (here, we favor the accumulator model, and leave open the possibility that the object-file model is also available for the primates to draw upon in these tasks). Of course, if analog representations of number are available widely in the animal kingdom, from rats to chimpanzees, it is very likely that these systems are part of the building blocks of human cognition as well. However, so far there is no evidence that human infants can exploit these systems.

### Specific Object Sortals: Evidence from Prelinguistic Human Infants

We argued that prelinguistic infants and nonlinguistic primates represent at least one sortal concept, object, which provides spatiotemporal criteria for individuation and identity. But human adults use other types of information to establish individuals and to trace identity through time, specifically, property information and membership in kinds more specific than physical object. An example of the use of property information follows: If we see a large, red cup on a window sill, and later we see a small, green cup there, we infer that two numerically distinct cups were on the sill, even though we have no spatiotemporal evidence to that effect (i.e., we didn't see both cups at once in different locations). With respect to kind information, adult individuation and numerical identity depend upon sortals more specific than physical object (Hirsch, 1982; Macnamara, 1987; Wiggins, 1980). When a person, Joe Schmoe, dies, Joe ceases to exist, even though Joe's body still exists, at least for a while. The sortal person provides the criteria for identity of the entity referred to by "Joe Schmoe;" the sortal body provides different criteria for identity.

Recent data suggest that young infants represent only the sortal object and no more specific sortals such as book, bottle, car, person, dog, ball, and so on. That is, infants represent only spatiotemporal criteria for individuation and identity, and not criteria that specify more specific kinds. Consider the event depicted in Figure 3.4. An adult who witnesses a truck emerge from behind and then disappear again behind the screen, and who then witnesses a duck emerge from behind and then disappear behind the screen, would infer that there are at least two objects behind the screen— a truck and a duck. That adult would make this inference in the absence of any spatiotemporal evidence for two distinct objects, not having seen two at once or any suggestion of a discontinuous path through space and time. Adults trace identity relative to sortals such as "truck" and "duck," knowing well that trucks do not turn into ducks.

Xu and Carey (1996) have carried out four experiments based on this design, finding that ten-month-old infants are not surprised at the unexpected outcome of only one object, even when the objects involved are highly familiar objects such as bottles, balls, cups, and books. By twelve months of age, infants make the adult inference, showing surprise at the unexpected outcome of a single outcome.

# Property/Kind Condition

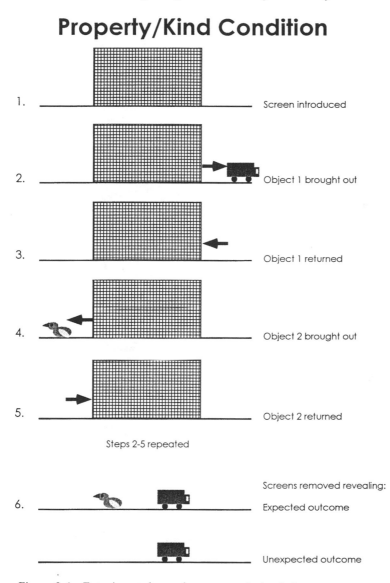

1. ——————— Screen introduced

2. ——————— Object 1 brought out

3. ——————— Object 1 returned

4. ——————— Object 2 brought out

5. ——————— Object 2 returned

Steps 2-5 repeated

Screens removed revealing:

6. ——————— Expected outcome

——————— Unexpected outcome

*Figure 3.4   Experimental procedure to test whether infants use property or kind information to infer the existence of two distinct objects in an event.*

Xu and Carey (under review) found convergent evidence for the emergence of sortals more specific than object between the ages of ten and twelve months. They habituated infants to the display found in Figure 3.5. Adults see this display as a duck standing on top of a truck. That is, adults use the kind difference between a yellow rubber duck and a red metal truck to parse this display into two distinct individual objects, even in the absence of spatio-temporal evidence of the two objects moving independently of each other.

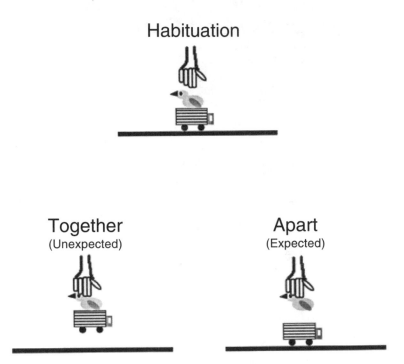

*Figure 3.5   Experimental procedure to test whether infants use property or kind information to segregate an ambiguous display in two distinct objects.*

In the infant test trials, the experimenter's hand reached down and picked up the duck by its head; in the unexpected outcomes, the single duck/truck rose as one piece; in the expected outcomes, just the duck was lifted by the hand. Ten-month-olds were not surprised at the unexpected outcome; twelve-month-olds, like adults, were, as revealed by longer looking when the duck/truck was raised as a single object.

Xu and Carey (1996; under review) interpret these results to show that before twelve months of age, infants use only the spatiotemporal criteria provided by the sortal object when establishing representations of distinct objects in their mental models of the world. By twelve months, infants have constructed more specific sortals, such as cup, bottle, truck, ball, book, duck, and so on.

We are not claiming that young infants cannot represent properties of objects. Indeed, very young infants can be habituated to different exemplars of dogs, tigers, or vehicles, and they will dishabituate if shown an exemplar of a new category (e.g., Cohen & Younger, 1983; Quinn & Eimas, 1993). Young infants clearly recognize bottles, cups, books, toy trucks, toy ducks, and balls, for they know some object specific functions for them (which ones to roll, which ones to drink from, etc.). Similarly, young infants clearly recognize examples of person, for they expect people to move by themselves and to be able to interact causally without contact (see the section "Agency as a Primitive" later in t his chapter). Young infants also recognize particular people, such as their mothers. But none of these phenomena show that infants represent concepts like "a bottle, a book, a cup, or Mama," specific sortals or proper names that provide criteria of individuation and identity. One could both recognize examples of objects which exemplify cuphood, or Mamaness, and have particular expectancies about objects with such properties, without representing Mama as a single enduring individual, or representing cup as a distinct sortal from book. Xu & Carey's results suggest that prior to age twelve months or so, such is the human infant's representational system.

It is significant that infants begin to comprehend and produce object names at about ten to twelve months of age, the age at which they begin to use the differences between cups and elephants to individuate objects. In two different studies of highly familiar objects (bottle, ball, book, cup) Xu and Carey (1996) found that comprehension of the words for these objects predicted the small number of ten-month-olds who could use these contrasts for object individuation. That is, infants do not seem to learn words for bottlehood; they begin to learn words such as "bottle" just when they show evidence of sortal concepts (e.g., bottle) that provide criteria for individuation and numerical identity.

These data raise a question on which primate data could bear. In human development, the construction of sortals more specific than object is contemporaneous with the earliest stages of language comprehension. Possibly, then, the capacity to represent concepts with the logical force of count nouns is part of the human species' specific linguistic capacity. If so, we would not expect other primates to represent sortals for object kinds. Alternatively, the capacity to represent sortals more specific than object may be part of an evolutionarily ancient adaptation that predates the emergence of human linguistic representational capacity. Therefore, we would expect other primates to behave as twelve-month-olds behave in tasks such as Xu and Carey's tasks.

### Specific Object Sortals: Evidence from Nonhuman Primates

The question at hand is not whether primates distinguish among categories of things—conspecifics from other animals, food from rocks, et cetera. Of course they do. The question is whether such categorical distinctions provide criteria for individuation and numerical identity of objects as the animal creates representations of the objects in its environment. Do primates, unlike young infants, take the difference between a cup and a tray to signal a difference between two numerically distinct individuals? At present, there are almost no data that bear on this question.

It is important to see which data *do not* decide this question, even though they may be suggestive. Tinklepaugh (1929), in the study cited in the section on a primitive sortals included trials in which his monkeys saw the experimenter hide a piece of banana. When the monkeys moved to re-trieve the food, they found only a piece of lettuce. They searched for the banana, and showed great displeasure. Tinklepaugh concludes (and we agree) that the monkeys search patterns were guided by a representation of the hidden object. That is, they set up a representation of an object with certain properties (banana properties) and when they failed to find a match to that representation, they were disappointed. This observation shows that the monkeys can bind properties in an object-file, once it is opened. It does not, however, tell what properties guide the opening of the file. All that we can conclude is that Tinklepaugh's monkeys had spatiotemporal informa-tion that enable them to open the object-with-banana-properties file; they saw the object placed in the container.

Arguing along the same lines, when the monkeys looked for the ob-ject-with-banana-properties, but found the lettuce, their reaction suggests that they detected a difference, but not necessarily. When the lettuce was hidden, and the banana was found, Tinklepaugh saw no evidence of sur-prise, or search for the lettuce; the monkeys happily ate the banana. Thus, the search for object-with-banana-properties may reflect extreme disappoint-ment in not finding a match to the hidden object. In such a case, the dis-covered lettuce is simply irrelevant.

What is needed is a design like Xu and Carey's (1996), in which pat-terns of looking time establish either how many objects the animal thinks are hidden behind a screen (Figure 3.4) or how many objects comprise an ambiguous display such as that of Figure 3.5, in which only property or kind information licenses the animal to open two distinct object-files. We have carried out two relevant studies, and the results we have to report to date are extremely preliminary. Our intent is simply to make the logic of the question we are asking clear.

The first study (Uller, Hauser, & Carey, in preparation) was based on Xu and Carey's (under review; see Figure 3.5) and involved tamarins. Stimuli consisted of a piece of monkey chow resting on a marshmallow; both types of food were highly familiar to the monkeys. The monkeys were shown two trials of the composite stimuli, with a hand perched above, ready to grasp the chow. Looking times were 6.8 seconds and 4.6 seconds, showing en-coding and increasing boredom with these arrays. Next, the test trials were presented: the hand grasped the chow and either lifted the chow alone (ex-pected event), or lifted the composite chow/marshmallow (unexpected event). There is absolutely no effect on looking times due to the contrast between expected (3.79 sec.) versus unexpected (3. 81 sec.) outcomes in the test trials. These data are similar to those of the ten-month-olds in Xu and Carey's study; they provide no evidence that tamarins use the distinc-tion between monkey chow and marshmallows to parse this ambiguous stimulus into two objects.

Before we conclude that tamarins do not use property/kind differences in object individuation, we need to show that the method is sensitive. To do this, we need to show that the tamarins will look longer at the unexpected outcome if given spatiotemporal evidence that the chow is a separate object from the marshmallow. This could be done by the monkeys moving the chow laterally off the marshmallow, before each of the two familiarization trials. In this case, the tamarins should look longer at the unexpected outcome of the whole chow/marshmallow coming up when the chow is lifted from above. If this control works, we will need to generalize the failure of the property/kind condition to different pairs of objects. Food does sometimes stick together, after all. Such studies are underway. Still, to date, the only data available suggest that tamarins, like ten-month-old human infants, do not use property/kind differences between objects for the purpose of object individuation.

Free-ranging rhesus monkeys present a different story (Uller, Hauser, & Carey, in press). Using a modified version of Xu & Carey's (in press) design (Figure 3.4) we tested twenty-four monkeys from the Cayo Santiago, Puerto Rico, population. Each monkey was familiarized with two occurrences of one object (an orange carrot) emerging from one side of a screen, alternating with two occurrences of another object (a yellow piece of squash) emerging from the other side of the screen. After this familiarization, the screen was removed, revealing either the expected outcome of two objects, or the unexpected outcome of one object. Each monkey saw two test trials (one expected, one unexpected) with order of outcome counterbalanced across monkeys. Overall, the monkeys looked longer at the unexpected outcome of one object (3.8 sec.) than at the expected outcome of two objects (3.1 sec.), but this difference was not significant. However, there was an interaction between trial number and outcome, as well as a main effect of trial number. The monkeys looked much less on the second test trial than the first, no matter what the outcome. If just the first trials are analyzed (12 monkeys saw the unexpected outcome on the first trial; 12 saw the expected outcome on the first trial), the looking time difference favoring the unexpected outcome is significant. That is, on the trials on which we still had the monkeys' attention, they looked longer at the unexpected outcome of one object than at the expected outcome of two objects. They apparently used the differences between the carrot and the squash to establish representations of two numerically distinct objects.

These data, if confirmed in further studies, suggest that the capacity for individuation based on property or kind differences, as well as on the basis of spatiotemporal properties, does not emerge only when the fully evolved human language faculty is present. At least one nonhuman primate species, evolutionarily more distant from humans than are the apes, also has this capacity.

Conclusions: Ontogenetic and Evolutionary Building Blocks
for Number Representations

Early in primate evolution (and probably earlier), and early in the conceptual history of the child, several of the building blocks for a representation of number are firmly in place. Those discussed in this section include criteria for individuation and numerical identity (the sortal object, more specific sortals like cup and carrot, and quantifiers such as one and another). Furthermore, there are conceptual abilities we did not dwell upon, but which are equally important, such as the capacity to construct one to one correspondences and the capacity to represent serial order relations (see Boysen, 1993, 1996; Rumbaugh & Washburn, 1993). Finally, there is no doubt that animals and infants are sensitive to numerical distinctions among sets of objects; that is, they represent number as one dimension of their experience of the world. These include representations of small numerosities (perhaps in the form of one, two, or three object-files held in parallel in short term memory) and representations of larger numerosities (perhaps in the form of an analog representational system such as the accumulator model). All of these aspects of representations of number are prior, both evolutionarily and ontogenetically, to the linguistic expression of numerical concepts in the lexicon or syntax of natural languages.

We argued that the representation of the integers in terms of a list of numerals or numerons (mentally represented numerals), is most likely a human cultural construction. Mastering the representation requires months or years of training, both by human children and by chimpanzees, suggesting that it is importantly different from the prelinguistic representations of numbers available to both infants and animals. The object-file and accumulator models are importantly different from the numeron list model in just the required senses.

It is possible that this construction was made possible by human language. It is important to note that the process by which children master the numeral representational system for language differs from that by which chimpanzees have mastered those aspects of it (Boysen, 1993; Rumbaugh & Washburn, 1993). Human children learn the list of numerals, and the counting procedure, well before they map any of the numerals beyond "1" onto the numbers they represent. They then laboriously learn what "2" means, and then "3." By the time they have learned what "4" means, they have induced the principle by which the whole list represents number, and they immediately know what all the numbers in their count sequence mean (Wynn, 1992). To date, no animal has been shown to make this induction, to be capable of learning an arbitrarily long list of numerons (many children can count to 10 or 20 before they know what "2" means). Although human language may be necessary both for the original construction of a symbolic numeron representational system for number and for the mastery of the system through the process that normally developing children attain, chimpanzees at least can also master many important parts of the system.

In sum, we have so far found no evidence for any aspect of object/ number representations that is part of the human specialization for language. Some representations that we looked for clearly predate language capacities; others may require the language faculty, even though it does not come freely to the child simply because of the human specialization for language learning. We turn now to our second case study within the research program we advocate—a study of some of the building blocks of the human concepts of agency that are universally expressed in human language.

## Agency as a Primitive

> Viewing Agents as transmitters of information, and not just FORCE, heralds the beginnings of the capacity to solve the problems created by the fact that in the real world Agents' behavior is determined by cognitive properties. The solution to this problem hinges on understanding how meaning enters into the causation of behavior. The social intelligence that now dominates this planet is the result of the evolution of neural mechanisms that rapidly find this solution. (Leslie, 1994)

### Theoretical Issues

In the previous section we discussed a number of issues relevant to the emergence of an organism's understanding of objects and numerosity. We now turn to a topic that, in many ways, is conceptually allied with the previous discussion. In particular, we explore the notion of object agency by detailing, developmentally and evolutionarily, how individuals come to understand the principles underlying object motion, including what causes the objects to move, as well as the consequences of their movements with respect to other objects in the environment. The conceptual unification with the previous section, therefore, lies in the fact that the problem of agency is intimately tied to the object concept (e.g., Baldwin, 1995; Hornsby, 1995). This section extends, however, the problem of how individuals individuate objects through time to how they integrate their understanding of objects into a more dynamic physical and social world. For example, does a human infant or nonhuman primate know that when a snake moves toward Marc Hauser, Marc will move, even if the snake hasn't contacted him? And do human infants and nonhuman primates know that if Marc Hauser eats cheese, but avoids snakes, Marc is likely to approach the cheese, but not the snake when presented with a choice between the two? Clearly, responding appropriately to snakes and cheese is of functional significance to both the human infant and the nonhuman primate. But responding appropriately in such situations is different from an ability to understand why such responses would be expected, or an ability to predict others' responses in comparable situations. Understanding the reasons why an agent moves and acts the way it does raises several profound problems in cognitive science and philosophy (Bermudez et al., 1995; Heil & Mele, 1995), problems that would take us too far from the more narrow goals of this chapter. Thus, we restrict our discussion to a subset of topics in which research on nonhuman and human primates has blossomed into some relevant, empirical fruits—the mechanics of object motion, including the principles guiding self-propelled movement and goal-directed behavior. Though we concentrate on these components of object agency (see Gelman, 1990; Leslie, 1994; Premack, 1990; Premack & Premack, 1994), we will briefly discuss how they relate to a third, critically important component: a metarepresentional capacity that enables the individual, as agent, to think about its own thinking and the thinking of other agents—to have a theory of mind (e.g., Baron-Cohen, 1995; Premack & Woodruff, 1978; Whiten, 1991). Ultimately, we believe that this third component is where the most fundamental differences between human and nonhuman primates are likely to be uncovered. More succinctly, this is where humans will leave nonhuman primates in their cognitive dust.

To set up our discussion, consider the following scene from Disney's animated film, "Aladdin." At one point, Aladdin finds himself trapped in a cave with the monkey, Abu. From behind a pile of gold coins and jewels, the magic carpet emerges, accidentally frightening Aladdin and Abu. Abu swipes at the carpet while Aladdin yells. The next scene is a spectacular feat of animation. The carpet (a swatch of red cloth with gold tassles at each corner) walks away, virtual shoulders and head drooped down, dejected and depressed. Aladdin then reassures the carpet with his kind words, at which point the carpet zips over and embraces both Aladdin and Abu with his tassled arms.

The reader may cry out, "Oh come now! Certainly this is excessive anthropomorphism." Yes, indeed it is. And it works because the Disney animators have given life to the carpet by making it move on its own, with actions that are all too reminiscent of our own actions in similar contexts (e.g., when Abu swipes and makes contact with the carpet, it moves away). In essence, Disney has gotten us to empathize with a carpet! But this is a profound move, and one to which we readily fall victim. We do fall victim and empathize because we are primed, perhaps innately so, to take an intentional stance (Allen, 1995; Dennett, 1987, 1995) toward a wide array of moving objects, especially ones that appear to have the capacity to exert force and to cause other objects to respond or respond to them. Given certain kinds of motion, together with certain kinds of physical attributes, we are readily willing to assign intentions, goals, desires, and so on to objects that are clearly animate as well as to those that merely appear to be animate because of those motions. But it is unclear, at present, whether nonhuman animals would make similar attributions in such contexts.

As the description above captures, our lexicon is filled with words that express important features of object agency (Talmy, 1988; see philosophical discussions in Heil & Mele, 1995). Thus, we talk of "things" being the result of, happening because of, hindering others from moving, and so on. And we make use of such linguistic tools even in situations when the underlying mechanisms are ambiguous or concealed (e.g., the rain extinguished the fire, the wind prevented the sail boat from advancing). However, as we suggested for the case of object and number primitives, we, together with researchers such as Leslie and Premack, would like to explore whether creatures lacking the expressive power of language understand some of the causes and consequences of object motion as one integral component of object agency.

In the comparative analysis that follows, we take as a starting point Leslie's (1994) theoretical perspective on object agency. For Leslie, infants come equipped with the ability to infer the underlying mechanics of object agency from events in the world. Their earliest inferences, therefore, relate to object mechanics, the fact that objects can function as agents. Leslie makes an explicit distinction between Agent and animate: "Most objects that are Agents are animate and certainly all the objects that ever, in the course of evolution, contributed to the adaptation of our cognitive systems for dealing with Agency were animate. Nevertheless, I assume that the notion of animateness is external to Ageny and proprietary to the biological domain" (121). For Leslie, the notion of force differs from "energy." Whereas energy refers to the kinds of mechanical forces in the environment, force refers to the cognitive representation of mechanical events in the environment. The emergence of these different modules or systems does not represent a stage-shift in the traditional Piagetian sense. This first level of understanding is called the child's Theory of Body mechanism (ToBY). Evidence for ToBY comes from studies showing, for example, that infants between 3 and 4 months understand launching events (e.g., Hume's billiard balls, Michotte's launching sequences) in the sense that a moving object must physically contact a stationary object to cause the latter to move—simple contact mechanics. What is somewhat confusing in Leslie's treatment, however, is the distinction between an agent as a mere cause and agent as an object with an internal source for self-propelled motion. Thus, in the launching paradigm (see below), when a ball rolls in from offstage, strikes a stationary ball, and causes the latter to move, the perceptual input is deficient, failing to provide the viewer with sufficient information to establish whether the first moving ball was self-propelled or not. This distinction is an important one with respect to the psychological notion of agent, given that it appears to depend on animate objects that can move on their own.

The domain-specific module that is selectively involved in making sense of physical objects (i.e., ToBY) is followed, developmentally, by the emergence of a second module that functionally locks onto psychological objects, specifically objects with actions that are interpreted as goal-directed and based on propositional attitudes. This module is called the Theory of Mind Mechanism (ToMM), and it consists of two subsystems, one dedicated to assessing goal-directed actions and self-generated motion (ToMM-1), and the second concerned with how mental states drive behavior relative to some goal (ToMM-2). Thus, a child with ToMM-1 attributes goal-directedness and self-generated motion to entities it deems as agents. In contrast, a child with ToMM-2 attributes full-blown intentional states (beliefs, desires) to entities it deems agents, including itself. As mentioned in the previous paragraphs, our focus is on ToBy and ToMM-1. It

is worth pointing out here, however—a stage setter for our conclusion—
that the intellectual tie breaker between humans and nonhumans is likely
to lie within the power of ToMM-2.

Premack and Premack (1994a, 1995), using the same kind of logic as
Leslie, have argued that object motion inherently carries information about
the internal causes of motion. Although they say little about the role of
animacy in this attribution, they contend that certain patterns of object
motion carry information about social relationships and the relative value
(e.g., ownership, property rights) of objects. Thus, for example, objects that
are self-propelled differ fundamentally from those that require an external
force to move. Self-propelled objects have the potential to engage in or avoid
interactions. Furthermore, self-propelled objects that repeatedly pursue a
single path differ from those that engage in more variable paths, the latter
appearing perceptually to be more intentionally motivated (Figure 3.6). In
other words, whereas repeated action implies that there is a goal, such repetition must be accompanied by a tinge of variability if intentional properties are to be attributed. Last, the pattern of motion can be used to infer
whether two or more objects are engaged in cooperative or competitive
interactions. For instance, imagine a large circle, C, sitting in front of a small
circle, c. If a square, S, moves toward c, and C moves in front, blocking
contact by S, we might readily interpret this as C defending c, or C helping
c against S. In sum, the Premacks have suggested that during development
particular patterns of motion may provide the intial perceptual input upon
which human infants build theories of moral agency.

In the following sections, we take the theoretical framework outlined
by Leslie (1994), together with some of the insights by Premack and
Premack (1994a, 1995), to examine the emergence, in both nonhuman
primates and human infants, of ToBY and ToMM-1. Unlike the work reviewed above on object identity and numerosity, the empirical database is
much thinner for object agency, and this is especially the case for nonhuman primates. Thus, for example, there are no experiments specifically testing the features of ToBY in nonhuman primates. Consequently, we both
discuss potentially relevant data on causal reasoning in nonhuman primates
and suggest possible experiments.

Evidence of ToBY in Human Infants

The French experimental psychologist, Michotte (1962), claimed that in
human adults, causality is perceptually plucked from observations of spatiotemporal patterns of interactions. In contrast, Piaget (1955) argued that
the ability to understand causality emerges late in development, and is largely
the result of the infant's growing experiences with sensorimotor action
patterns that lead to specific consequences (e.g., using his or her hands to
pick up objects). As mentioned above, the Piagetian emphasis on action
to display knowledge may cover up important domains of understanding.
To better understand how infants perceive causal events between objects,

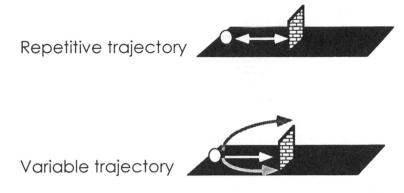

Repetitive trajectory

Variable trajectory

*Figure 3.6    Schematic illustrations of two types of object motion. See text for details.*

Leslie (see also, Golinkoff & Kerr, 1978; Keil, 1979; Lesser, 1977) conducted a series of preferential looking time experiments. In the first study, four and a half to eight month-old infants were exposed to a set of six action sequences, each sequence characterized by a specific form of object motion (Figure 3.7). The first sequence (a) represents Hume's billiard ball launching effect. Here, a red box moves towards a stationary green box, and upon contact, the green box immediately moves off. Adults perceive this sequence as: red box caused green box to move. In contrast, in sequences (b), and especially (c), we don't perceive the movement by the red box as being causally related to the movement of the green box. In fact, we perceive the movement by the green box to be self-generated—the green box is self-propelled. A test session involved first habituating the infants to a particular sequence. Having been habituated to one sequence, they were then tested on a different sequence in which looking times were evaluated for evidence of dishabituation. Overall, both young and old infants consistently habituated to repeated presentations of the first test sequence. The paired sequence leading to the most statistically significant dishabituation was direct launching → no prior movement. That is, when infants first saw a highly probable launching event, they were apparently surprised when the previously stationary object moved on its own. The other pairings produced intermediate levels of dishabituation. These results suggest that spatiotemporal properties of movement patterns are both salient to young infants and organize their perception of events.

Leslie's results also raise several questions. First, as Leslie notes, it is not clear whether the infants perceive the presented sequences as a single movement as opposed to a temporally structured sequence of movement events. This distinction is critical to the interpretation of the infant's pattern of habituation and dishabituation. Second, it seems somewhat surprising that infants showed such significant dishabituation to the direct launching → no prior movement pairing. Specifically, it is unclear why infants

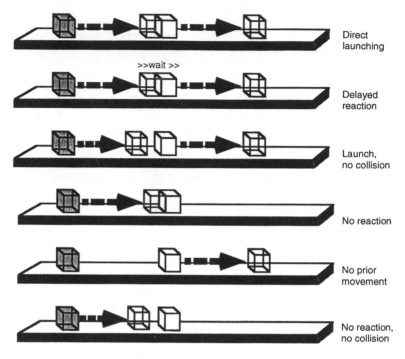

*Figure 3.7    Schematic illustration of launching events. Adapted from Leslie (1984).*

appear to make the assumption that because red box launches green box, green box is incapable of self-generated motion. More importantly, two other pairings would seem to represent much more ambiguous and unexpected cases: (i) direct launching → delayed reaction, and (ii) direct launching → no reaction. In both the delayed and no reaction conditions, the red box moves toward the stationary green box, exactly as it did in the habituation series with direct launching. But now, instead of seeing the green box move off, it either stays in place for a short period of time and then moves, or it remains in place. Given that infants learned during the habituation series that the red box is capable of displacing the green box upon contact, delayed reaction or no reaction should be extremely surprising.

To more carefully assess the infant's capacity to perceive causal events, and to address some of the aforementioned methodological problems, Leslie and Keeble (1987) carried out a modified version of Leslie's original launching experiments. The general idea in this version was to distinguish between perception of mere spatiotemporal associations as opposed to cause-effect interactions. To do this, one group of infants was habituated to the direct launching event, whereas a second group was habituated to a delayed reaction event. Both groups were then tested with their respective habituation sequence, but temporally reversed. For example, one group is habituated to the red box directly launching the green box and is then tested with the green box directly launching the red box. A third group served as a control, receiving the same habituation and test sequence (i.e., no direction reversal). Results showed that the control group did not dishabituate in the test trial. In contrast, both the delayed reaction and direct launching groups dishabituated, with looking times significantly longer in the test trial than during the last habituation trial. Moreover, the magnitude of dishabituation was significantly greater in the direct launching group. Leslie and Keeble argue that because spatiotemporal patterns were controlled, the infants' response was largely dictated by the causal properties of the visual events.

### Causal Reasoning and ToBY in Nonhuman Primates

Under natural conditions, monkeys and apes do all sorts of things that would seem to suggest that they understand the requisite sequence of events required to bring about particular effects. For example, chimpanzees termite fish by first removing all of the side branches from a long thin branch, and then inserting the remaining pole into a termite mound, waiting for the termites to climb out and up, providing the chimpanzees with easy access. In West Africa, members of one chimpanzee population have figured out that if they strip bark off the thorny Kapok tree, they can use the bark as sandals for their feet and as seats for their rear ends, thereby allowing them to more readily enjoy the process of extracting and eating fruits from the tree. A problem with interpreting these cases as evidence of causal reasoning is that observational learning may have provided all but the inventor of the tool with the requisite steps to achieve the targeted solution. For the inventor, however, some of these cases cannot be accounted for by trial and error alone, and thus some level of causal reasoning must have been involved. Is there any experimental evidence for causal reasoning in nonhuman primates, or for understanding that moving objects can be functionally responsible for effecting the "behavior" of other objects? We begin by saying a few words about research on causal reasoning because it is relevant to the problem of how nonhuman primates perceive the relationship between objects, actions and events, or consequences. We then describe some preliminary experiments on object motion and contact, using the looking time procedure with cotton-top tamarins.

In contrast to a majority of research with apes who were trained on an artificial or sign language, Premack's (1976, 1986) research program focused on the kinds of conceptual representations that an organism would require in order to acquire a language that was not only structured like human language, but was as expressive as well. As Premack has mused, if chickens had syntax, they would have nothing interesting to say. In this sense, the theoretical spirit of Premack's approach is exactly analogous to the one that we have been advocating; his methods were, however, different from those employed by developmental psychologists working on human infants. In one apparently quite difficult task, even Premack's star chimpanzee, Sarah, failed, and before the final trial could be run, she "lost sphincter control and ran screaming about the cage" (Premack & Premack 1994b, 359). One of Premack's first experiments on causal reasoning involved presenting chimpanzees with photographs of an apple, then a cut apple, and finally, three objects: knife, pencil, container of water. The subject's task was to identify the object in the final photograph that was responsible for transforming a whole apple into a cut apple. Only language-trained chimpanzees passed this kind of test (e.g., choosing the knife as the causal agent that connects an apple to a cut apple), and they did so with both familiar and unfamiliar objects. Other causal reasoning tests, of varying difficulty involving static images and video sequences of human action sequences, were administered. Again, only the language-trained chimpanzees passed with any degree of success. Upon seeing a fire, they were able to attribute the appropriate action for a human being (getting a bucket of water), ruling out inappropriate actions.

From a comparative perspective, Premack's experiments, and those conducted by other research teams (e.g., studies of problem solving and tool use, Visalberghi & Fragaszy, 1991) share one problem in common—training. Thus, even though Premack and his colleagues ran comparable experiments on human children (see Premack & Premack, 1994), the children either received no training, or different sorts of training (e.g., in some experiments, they were explicitly told what particular object tokens stand for, something that obviously cannot be done with chimpanzees). As pointed out in the introduction to this book, given differences in procedure, we cannot be sure whether the difficiencies exhibited by monkeys and apes reflect problems of performance or ability.

Experiments on physical causality by Antinucci and his colleagues (see essays in Antinucci, 1989), as well as experiments in our own lab (e.g., Hauser, in press, Hauser et al., 1996), both involve procedures that more closely approximate those used by developmentalists working with human infants, and generally involve minimal training. In particular, based on experiments by Willatts (1984, 1990) with human children (see Spinozzi & Poti, 1989 for similar work), we have conducted a means-end relational experiment with the tamarins. Subjects are required to first assess which of two possible pieces of cloth on a tray will give access to a small piece of food. Located *on* one piece of cloth is a food reward, whereas the food reward is displaced *off* to a side of the other cloth. When the tray is pushed forward, subjects are allowed to pull only one cloth; because they are only allowed one choice, this is a forward planning task. To succeed, subjects are required to understand the concept of "On versus Off" in one condition and the concept of "Connectedness" in a second condition (see Figure 3.8 for a sample of trials). For both conditions, the tamarins also had to understand that the cloth can support and bring the food forward if pulled. Subjects readily solved this problem, pulling the appropriate cloth (means) to obtain the food (end). Impressively, in one condition, they were presented with a choice between an inaccessible, but very large piece of food,

TEST CHAMBER

openings for tamarin hands; subject can only reach same-side cloth through each opening.

Tray with cloth sand food. First presentation is at a level that clearly shows cloths and gap, but subjects can't reach cloths. Second presentation is at level where subjects can reach through the openings and pull cloth.

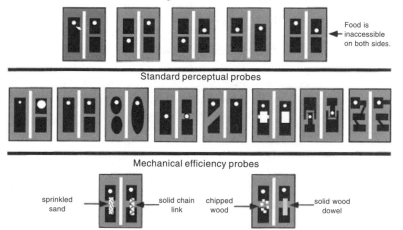

Initial training set for Connectedness

Food is inaccessible on both sides.

Standard perceptual probes

Mechanical efficiency probes

sprinkled sand        solid chain link        chipped wood        solid wood dowel

*Figure 3.8  Experimental set-up for means-end task (top). Cloths are in black, food pellets in white. A sample of conditions used to test tamarins' understanding of the concept CONNECTEDNESS (bottom).*

as opposed to an accessible, but very small piece of food. Although subjects initially stumbled on this condition, being "drawn" toward the large piece, all nine tamarins were able to inhibit this response successfully by pulling the cloth with the small piece of food. Given this success, the tamarins, and other monkeys as well (Spinozzi & Poti, 1989), appear to have some understanding of physical causality; they understand that action on one object can causally effect the location of a second object.

Though Leslie-type causality experiments have yet to be conducted, looking time experiments are currently underway that enable us to explore the parameter space of ToBY in cotton-top tamarins (Schecter & Hauser, in prep). As one example, we have implemented the design used by Spelke (1991) to test whether infants understand the relation between object motion and the presence or absence of physical barriers. Thus, as illustrated in Figure 3.9, subjects are habituated to a ball rolling down a slightly inclined ramp toward a terminal wall. Having habituated, subjects are shown the same ramp, but now a new wall has been placed approximately two-thirds of the way down the ramp toward the terminal wall. In the possible condition, the display is shown, and then all but the starting position of the ball at the top of the ramp is occluded. The ball is launched, and when the occluder is removed, the ball is at rest next to the first wall. The impossible condition is identical to the possible condition, except that the ball is seen at rest next to the terminal wall once the occluder is removed; it is impossible because the ball appears to have moved through a solid wall. In the control conditions for this experiment, the displays are the same, but now the ball is dropped from above rather than rolled. Here, there are no impossible trials. Infants as young as six months look longer at the impossible condition (i.e., ball rolled), but maintain habituation to the possible condition where the ball is rolled, as well as both test conditions where the ball is dropped.

We have run nine tamarins on this condition (half started with the horizontal ball movement and half with the vertical). For the horizontal test, subjects looked significantly longer in the impossible condition than in the possible condition, but looking time in the impossible condition did

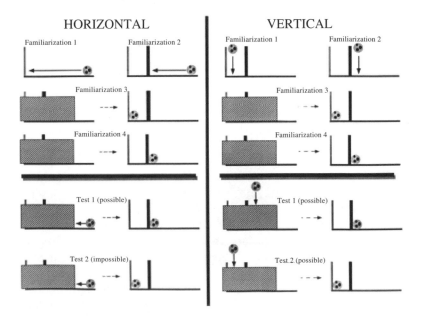

*Figure 3.9   Familiarization and test trials for experiment on tamarins' understanding of object motion and solidity constraints. The left panel shows conditions involving horizontal object motion, whereas the right panel shows conditions for vertical motion.*

not increase significantly above the final familiarization trial. For the vertical tests, there were no changes in looking time from the final familiarization trial. If we adhere to the standard statistical approach to looking time experiments, then the tamarins would appear to have failed this test: they did not show an increase in looking time to the impossible condition above the final familiarization trial. However, if we take the combined results from all the test trials, subjects did look longer at the one impossible condition, thereby suggesting that they detected a significant difference. The failure to show a significant increase above the familiarization trial may indicate overall boredom with the display. We are now in the process of altering the design of this experiment in an attempt to increase the saliency of the display. Having rerun this particular condition, we plan on setting up a tamarin version of Leslie's launching experiments, in addition to some of the motion-contact experiments recently published by Baillargeon and her colleagues (Baillargeon, 1995; Kotovsky & Baillargeon, in press).

### Evidence of ToMM-1 in Human Infants

The kinds of causal events tested by Leslie and colleagues involve, generally speaking, inanimate objects. Animate objects may or may not follow similar patterns of interaction. Consider direct launching. If Susan is standing still, and Marc runs toward her at full speed, arms positioned straight out, he will almost certainly displace Susan if he makes contact. In this situation, we would certainly make the inference that Marc caused Susan to move. But now imagine a visually similar situation, labelled "launch-no collision" in Figure 3.8. Here, Marc runs toward Susan, stops a bit short, and Susan immediately moves off. Even more dramatically, Marc stands still, yells at Susan, and Susan moves away from Marc. And, just to push this one step further, Susan sees Jack the Ripper about 100 meters away, facing the opposite direction. Susan runs like a bat out of hell in the opposite direction. Although there is no contact in these situations, Susan's movement is not at all surprising. Thus, whereas one animate object can cause another to move in the absence of contact, contact is necessary in explanations of motion of most inanimate objects (barring artifacts with motors, springs, or batteries inside).

To determine when such expectations emerge during human development, Spelke and colleagues (1995) conducted an experiment with six-month-old infants. Two sequences were contrasted. One sequence involved two large and distinctively colored boxes moving on wheels, and the other sequence involved two human adults. Following familiarizations, infants watched as one moving object (inanimate or animate) contacted or failed to contact the stationary object, but in both cases, the stationary object then moved off. Only in the case of the inanimate object sequences did infants dishabituate when the moving object failed to make contact but nonetheless appeared to launch the stationary object. Spelke and colleagues conclude that human infants form different expectations about animate and inanimate objects, expecting inanimate but not animate objects to fall within the constraints of a contact principle (i.e., no action at a distance). Although this conclusion is reasonable, there is a slightly different interpretation of the infants' response. Rather than specifically attending to motion and contact, infants form different expectations about animate and inanimate objects with regard to their capacity for self-propelled motion. Thus, when an inanimate object stops short of another, and the stationary object moves off on its own, it is surprising because inanimate objects are not expected to move on their own; the fact that the objects failed to make contact is not what the infants are responding to. In contrast, people, as animate objects, do move independently of other objects in the environment. Nonetheless, the design of this experiment is beautifully simple. It can be readily modified to more carefully explore the human infant's understanding of animate objects, in addition to exploring whether, and to what extent, nonhuman primates distinguish between animate and inanimate objects. We turn to this final problem in the next section.

### Evidence of ToMM-1 in Nonhuman Primates

To determine whether nonhuman primates have ToMM-1, and to explore whether the looking time methodology can be brought to bear on this issue, we designed an experiment to determine what factors influence nonhuman primates' expectations about potential changes in an object's spatial location. Experiments were conducted on cotton-top tamarins (Hauser, in press).

The testing apparatus consisted of a two-chambered box, separated by an opaque partition with a hole (Figure 3.10). The tamarins were first familiarized with the box, and in particular, were exposed to the center partition and the fact that objects can pass from one side of the chamber to the other by means of the hole. Tamarins were allowed to cross from one side of the chamber to the other. They also observed a human hand moving a piece of food from one side to the other. They never observed any of the test objects crossing through the partition. In condition one, we compared the tamarins' response to a live mouse (self-propelled and animate) and a mouse-sized cluster of Froot Loops (non-self-propelled, no motion, and inanimate). Tamarins have seen mice, and they are often given Froot Loops as a food reward; see Table 3.1 for the experiment's overall design.

Following familiarization trials that involve seeing each object in either chamber one or two, two test trials were run. During test trials, an object was placed in one chamber. A screen was lowered for approximately ten seconds and then removed, revealing the object in either the same chamber or the opposite chamber. If the tamarins form expectations about objects based on their capacity for self-generated motion, then they should be surprised (look longer) to find the Froot Loop cluster in the opposite chamber from which it was originally placed. They should not, however, be surprised to see the live mouse in either the same or different chamber. Looking time results (Figure 3.11) appear to support this prediction; all

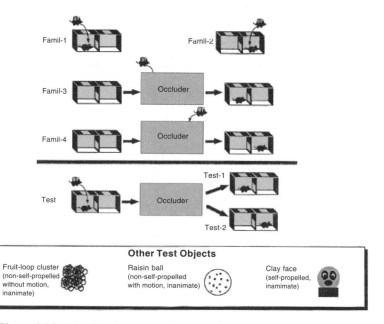

*Figure 3.10  Familiarization and test trials for experiment on tamarins'
understanding of self-propelled motion and animacy.*

subjects showed habituation across familiarization trials, and they only
showed dishabituation (i.e., a revival in looking time) when the Froot Loop
cluster appeared in a different chamber from its original position. These
results show that the tamarins form different expectations about the potential
spatial location of objects that move, are animate, and are self-propelled
(i.e., a live mouse), on the one hand, and objects that have none of these
features (i.e., a cluster of Froot Loops), on the other.

But this study leaves open the question of which features are critically
involved in the tamarins' differential response. For example, the results
presented fail to address the issue of self-propelled motion—at a much simpler level, the mouse moves and the Froot Loop cluster does not. To assess
whether motion alone accounts for the results, we ran a third condition: a
bright yellow clay ball with raisins embedded on its surface was rolled into

*Table 3.1  Stimuli Used in Tamarin Test of Self-propelled Motion*

| Object | Features | Animate? |
|---|---|---|
| live mouse | self-propelled | animate |
| Froot Loop cluster | nonself-propelled, no motion | inanimate |
| raisin ball | nonself-propelled, moved by experimenter | inanimate |
| clay face | self-propelled | inanimate |

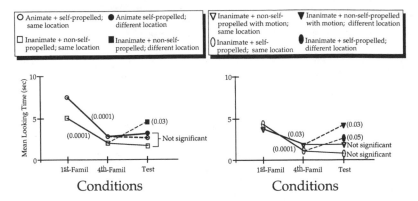

*Figure 3.11   Looking time (seconds) results from experiments on tamarins' understanding of self-propelled motion and animacy.*

one chamber by the experimenter. In this display, the tamarins saw an object with motion, but the source of energy for this object's motion was generated from an external source (i.e., the experimenter). In test trials, the raisin ball was rolled into one chamber and then, as it came to a complete resting position, the occluder was raised, blocking the chamber from the tamarin's view. When the occluder was lowered, the raisin ball was seen at rest in either the same or the opposite chamber. Based on looking time analyses, the tamarins appeared to form the same sorts of expectations about the position of the raisin ball as they did for the Froot Loops. They looked longer when the raisin ball appeared in a different chamber than when it appeared in the same chamber. These results suggest that the tamarins' expectations about the potential location of an object is not strictly determined by whether it moves or not.

The tamarins may, however, have taken a simple snapshot of the final portion of the display, right before the occluder was placed in position. That is, they created an image of the raisin ball at rest. Thus, if they form the expectation that objects at rest prior to occlusion are unlikely to appear in a different location, then this would explain the results obtained. In an attempt to rule out this hypothesis, we ran a final condition: a colorful clay face with an embedded magnet was moved ("magically") by a second magnet located below the chamber. In test trials, subjects first saw the clay face lowered into one chamber where it remained at rest for one second and then began to move, exploring the chamber in much the same way that the mouse explored the chamber. Consequently, because the clay face moved on its own from a resting position, it appeared to be self-propelled. Results showed, however, that the tamarins responded to the clay face in the same way that they responded to the Froot Loops and raisin ball. They looked longer when it appeared in a different chamber than when it appeared in the same chamber.

The different patterns of looking time obtained for the live mouse and the clay face cannot be explained as a difference in self-propelled motion. Both objects moved on their own. Surprisingly, then, tamarins appear to set up expectations in this particular paradigm that are more firmly rooted in a conceptual framework that handles the animate-inanimate distinction than expectations that involve objects that are either self-propelled or not.

Can it be that tamarins have an understanding of animacy, using this understanding to generate predictions about objects in the world? Perhaps, but there are alternative explanations that must be examined. For example, though both the mouse and clay face were self-propelled, there may have been subtle differences in motion, perhaps related to an assessment of biological motion (Johansson, 1973). Although little work has been conducted on the perception of biological motion by nonhuman animals, experiments by Blake (1993) on domestic cats suggest that they are capable of discriminating biological motion from nonbiological motion, using Johansson's classic light-point displays (see Cutting, 1978). This attribution may be related to certain key features, such as the presence or absence of moving limbs (arms and legs for the mouse, nothing for the clay face), changes in head position corresponding to changes in direction, and so on. Further, the specific pattern of motion may be relevant to the expectation set up. As pointed out in our discussion of theoretical issues, Premack and Premack (1994b) have suggested, for example, that there is a fundamental difference in motion trajectories between objects that are merely goal-directed and those that have an intention to reach a goal. Specifically, a motorized robot may have the goal of reaching a wall on the opposite side of the room in the same way that a human child might have such a goal. If a barrier is placed in between the robot and the opposing wall of the room, the robot (a not-so-smart-one) will move straight toward the barrier, bump into it, move back and repeat this pattern over and over and over again (for discussion of robotic motion and goals, see McFarland, 1995). In contrast, we would expect a human child to show more variation, perhaps bumping into the barrier at first, but then trying different trajectories to circumvent the problem. Thus, intentional creatures are likely to show greater variability in their movements.

These ideas can readily be implemented into the general design of our experiment. Specifically, the same clay figure could be made to move back and forth from a position at the center of a chamber to the partition, with its "eyes and nose" facing the partition on each go. This would, we suggest, set up the expectation that the clay face object "wants" to go through the partition. In contrast, we could turn the clay face around and have it go into the wall on the opposite side of the partition. This would potentially set up the expectation that the clay face is trying to avoid the partition, or at least not approach it.

On a different level, other features of the object could be changed. Thus, several properties of a live mouse make it different from the clay face. The mouse has fur, breathes, has moving eyes, head, limbs, and so on. Each of these features could be explored independently and in combination. Thus, for example, what expectations do the tamarins form when they see an unconscious mouse (e.g., one that has been anesthetized, doesn't move, but still shows signs of breathing), a stuffed mouse, a wind-up toy mouse with moving limbs, and so on. We are currently running these kinds of experiments in an attempt to more carefully examine the claim that tamarins, as well as other species, have a concept of animacy which they use to guide their expectations about objects in the world. As in our studies of object identity, and number, the experiments designed here for the tamarins can readily be run on human infants.

### The Beginnings of ToMM-2: Some Empirical Routes into the Problem

Although we have steered clear of issues relevant to the theory of mind (i.e., Leslie's ToMM-2), the empirical literature on human children is vast (Carruthers & Smith 1996; Gopnik & Meltzoff 1997), and there is a fledgling literature on nonhuman primates (Cheney & Seyfarth, 1990; Povinelli et al., 1990, 1991; Povinelli & Eddy, 1996; see critiques by Heyes, 1993). Thus far tests of macaques have failed to provide evidence that individuals base their responses on mental state attribution, thus leading Cheney and Seyfarth (1990) to conclude that there is no evidence for a theory of mind in monkeys. Chimpanzees may, however, represent a different case. In an experiment that was identical to one run on rhesus monkeys (Povinelli et al., 1990), Povinelli and colleagues (1991) ran an experiment with chimpanzees in which they were required to distinguish between a knowledgeable human observer who knew where food was concealed (i.e., because he remained in the room when the food was concealed) and an ignorant human observer who did not know where the food was concealed (i.e., he was out of the room at the time when food was concealed). Although none of the chimpanzees succeeded immediately at this task, after several hundred trials they did, and were then able to generalize to new conditions. In a more recent and extensive set of experiments (Povinelli & Eddy, 1996), however, results convincingly show that young chimpanzees fail to understand that seeing is knowing, a cognitive ability that seems to be necessary to develop a theory of mind in humans (e.g., Baron-Cohen, 1995). Thus, for example, many autistic children never understand the fact that a person's gaze is highly informative in terms of what that person knows.

Unfortunately, to repeat our broken record, the techniques used on humans and nonhuman primates for testing ToMM-2 differ, therefore making interspecific comparisons difficult. In other words, the nonhuman primate failures may reflect a difference in performance, not ability. The general procedure discussed in the section on evidence of TOMM-1 in nonhuman primates, however, could be tweaked to look more deeply into what tamarins and human infants expect vis-à-vis the potential intentions of other creatures.

Consider the possibility of a nonverbal "false belief test" (Wimmer & Perner, 1983), one that can take advantage of the looking time procedure (see Premack & Premack, 1994a for a similar suggestion) to capture the nonhuman primate's expectations. We have one strong empirical reason to think that this might work, methodologically that is. A recent experiment by Clements and Perner (1994) has shown that although children do not pass the linguistic version of the false belief test until approximately three and a half to four years of age, they do pass the same test at about two and a half years if, instead of asking about their beliefs, you simply look at their eyes to study their expectations. In the classic false belief test, a child witnesses a puppet show with two characters, Sally and Anne. Sally takes a ball and places it in a basket and then leaves the room. While she is gone, Anne removes the ball from the basket and places it in a box. When Sally returns, the child is asked "Where will Sally search for the ball?" children under the age of four years typically say "the box" whereas older children say "the basket." What Clements and Perner discovered, however, is that the younger children *first* looked toward the basket and *then* said "the box." There is a sense, then, in which young children implicitly generate the appropriate expectation; but when required to explicitly state their expectation with language, something goes wrong. At least this is the intriguing hypothesis put forward by Clements and Perner.

The general idea behind our looking time version of a false belief test is that an organism who understands the causal factors underlying belief states (their own and others) will recognize the fact that, in the absence of certain kinds of knowledge, individuals may form false beliefs (i.e., believe that p, when in fact, the current state of affairs indicates not-p). We have developed a nonverbal false belief test for nonhuman primates and have begun to collect pilot data with the cotton-top tamarins. In general, since we believe that ToMM-2 represents the crucial cognitive dividing line between humans and nonhumans, we expect the tamarins (and other nonhuman primates as well) to fail the test we are about to propose. Nonetheless, it is worth running to convince ourselves, and others, that the difference lies in ability, not performance.

The general logic underlying the experiment is to first set up an agent with explicit desires (goals) during familiarization, and then to present a situation in which the agent either pursues an action that is consistent with the prior goals, or fails to do so. In particular, an Experimenter stands between a tamarin located in a test box and a human (Agent) seated in a chair behind a table. The Experimenter holds an apple, tears off a piece, and gives it to the Agent, who consumes it. This is repeated, establishing, minimally, an association between apple and Agent. In the next familiarization condition, the Experimenter waves the apple from side to side in front of the Agent, as the Agent attempts to grab the apple; the Agent stretches, but cannot reach the apple. This step is designed to set up the goal or desire of the Agent and the fact that the Experimenter doesn't always give the apple to the Agent. The next familiarization consists of showing the tamarin that both a red box on the right and a green box on the left are empty and that, when an apple is placed in the red box, the green box remains empty, whereas the red box contains the apple. This familiarization is conducted in the absence of the Agent. The final familiarization involves placing an apple in the red box and an apple in the green box; both placements are conducted in such a way that the Agent and tamarin subject see where the apple has gone. The Agent stretches forward and touches either the red or green box. Upon touching the box, the Experimenter reaches in and gives the Agent a piece.

Now the first test. The red and green box are placed on opposite sides of a stage in front of the Agent, and both the Agent and the tamarin are allowed to see that the boxes are empty. The Experimenter then shows the Agent an apple, and places it into the green box. The Experimenter then steps back, and the Agent either stretches and touches the green box with the apple (expected) or stretches and touches the empty red box (unexpected). We predict that if tamarins set up expectations based on goals, or even more simply, the strength of association, then they should look longer when the Agent touches the empty box. This test does not yet show whether the tamarins exhibit belief-desire psychology.

Now the critical step. Rerun the last test, but before allowing the Agent to touch a box, introduce a screen, occluding the Agent's view of the two boxes. While the screen is in place, the Experimenter removes the apple from the green box and places it into the red box. Next, remove the screen to allow the Agent to touch one box. Here, if the Agent touches the red box, the tamarins should be surprised (again, look longer), but if and only if they know that their knowledge differs from the Agent's knowledge. We do not have data yet, but stay tuned.

## Conclusions

We have had three goals. First, in studies of nonhuman primates, we advocate the use of the looking time methodology that has proved so fruitful in the study of human infants. We have shown that this method yields interpretable data both in the case of wild, free-ranging, rhesus monkeys and in the case of a laboratory population of cotton-top tamarins. Second, we advocate a broad program of research into the computational building blocks of human language, seeking their evolutionary and developmental history. Finally, we have presented very preliminary results from our earliest studies that use the looking time methodology in the service of this research program. To our surprise, we have found, so far, no evidence for knowledge revealed by the looking time methods in human infants that is missing in adult monkeys. Rather, we have hints of the opposite: tamarins and rhesus succeed at the more difficult screen-first addition studies, whereas eight-month-old human infants fail; and, rhesus succeed in using property/kind information in object individuation, whereas ten-month-old humans fail. Such results both cry out for developmental studies in monkeys, and suggest that comparative studies afford the possibility of bringing new data to bear on the mechanisms underlying changes in human infant cognitive development.

Clearly, this work is still very much in its infancy. But the feasability and fruitfulness of the research program we advocate is not, to our minds at least, in doubt.

## Note

Correspondence should be addressed to either Dr. Marc Hauser, Departments of Psychology and Anthropology, Program in Neurosciences, Harvard University, 33 Kirkland St., Cambridge, MA, 02138, or Dr. Susan Carey, Department of Psychology, New York University, New York, NY 10003.

## References

Allen, C. (1995). Intentionality: Natural and artificial. In H. L. Roitblat & J.-A. Meyer (Eds.), *Comparative approaches to cognitive science* (pp. 93–110). Cambridge, MA: MIT Press.

Antell, S., & Keating, D. (1983). Perception of numerical invariance in neonates. *Child Development, 54,* 695–701.

Antinucci, F. (1989). *Cognitive structure and development in nonhuman primates.* Hillsdale, NJ: Erlbaum.

Baillargeon, R. (1994). A model of physical reasoning in infancy. In C. Rovee-Collier & L. Lipsitt (Eds.), *Advances in infancy research, Vol. 9* (pp. 114–139). Norwood, NJ: Ablex.

Baillargeon, R., & DeVos, J. (1991). Object permanence in young infants: Further evidence. *Child Development, 62,* 1227–1246.

Baillargeon, R., Spelke, E., & Wasserman, S. (1985). Object permanence in five month old infants. *Cognition, 20,* 191–208.

Baldwin, T. (1995). Objectivity, causality, and agency. In J. L. Bermudez, A. Marcel, & N. Eilan (Eds.), *The body and the self* (pp. 107–126). Cambridge, MA: MIT Press.

Barkow, J., Cosmides, L., & Tooby, J. (1992). *The adapted mind.* Oxford: Oxford University Press.

Baron-Cohen, S. (1995). *Mindblindness.* Cambridge, MA: MIT Press.

Bickerton, D. (1990). *Species and language.* Chicago: University of Chicago Press.

Blake, R. (1993). Cats perceive biological motion. *Psychological Science, 4,* 54–57.

Boysen, S. T. (1993). Counting in chimpanzees: nonhuman principles and emergent properties of number. In Boysen S. T., & Capaldi E. J. (Eds.), *The development of numerical competence* (pp. 39–59). Hillsdale, NJ: Erlbaum.

Boysen, S. T. (1996). "More is less": The distribution of rule-governed resource distribution in chimpanzees. In Russon, A. E., Bard, K. A., & Parker, S. T. (Eds.), *Reaching into thought: The minds of the great apes* (pp. 177–189). Cambridge: Cambridge University Press.

Boysen, S. T., & Bernston G. G. (1989). Numerical competence in a chimpanzee. *Journal of Comparative Psychology 103,* 23–31.

Boysen, S. T., & Capaldi, E. J. (1993). *The development of numerical competence: Animal and human models.* Hillsdale, NJ: Erlbaum.

Carruthers, P., & Smith, P. K. (1996). *Theories of theories of mind.* Cambridge: Cambridge University Press.

Cheney, D. L., & Seyfarth, R. M. (1990). *How monkeys see the world: Inside the mind of another species.* Chicago: Chicago University Press.

Chomsky, N. (1986). *Knowledge of language: Its nature, origin, and use.* New York: Praeger.

Clements, W. A., & Perner, J. (1994). Implicit understanding of belief. *Cognitive Development, 9,* 377–395.

Cohen, L. B., & Younger, B. (1983). Perceptual categorization in the infant. In E. K. Scholnick (Ed.), *New Trends in Conceptual Representation.* Hillsdale, NJ: Erlbaum.

Cosmides, L., & Tooby, J. (1994). Beyond intuition and instinct blindness: Toward an evolutionarily rigorous cognitive science. *Cognition, 50,* 41–77.

Cosmides, L., & Tooby, J. (1994). Origins of domain specificity: The evolution of functional organization. In L. A. Hirschfeld & S. A. Gelman (Eds.), *Mapping the mind: Domain specificity in cognition and culture* (pp. 85–116). New York: Cambridge University Press.

Cutting, J. (1978). A program to generate synthetic walkers as dynamic point-light displays. *Behavioral Research Methods and Instrumentation, 10,* 91–94.

Darwin, C. (1859). *On the origin of species.* London: John Murray.

Darwin, C. (1871). *The descent of man and selection in relation to sex.* London: John Murray.

Darwin, C. (1872). *The expression of the emotions in man and animals.* London: John Murray.

Davis, H., & Perusse, R. (1988). Numerical competence in animals: Definitional issues, current evidence, and new research agenda. *Behavioral and Brain Sciences, 11,* 561–615.

Dawkins, R. (1986). *The blind watchmaker.* New York: W. W. Norton.

Dennett, D. (1987). *The intentional stance.* Cambridge, MA: MIT Press.

Dennett, D. (1995). Do animals have beliefs? In H. L. Roitblat & J.-A. Meyer (Ed.), *Comparative approaches to cognitive science* (pp. 111–118). Cambridge, MA: MIT Press.

Diamond, A. (1988). Differences between adult and infant cognition: Is the crucial variable presence or absence of language? In L. Weiskrantz (Ed.), *Thought without language* (pp. 337–370). Oxford: Clarendon Press.

Diamond, A. (1991). Neuropsychological insights into the meaning of the object concept development. In S. Carey & R. Gelman (Eds.), *The epigenesis of mind* (pp. 112–134). Hillsdale, NJ: Erlbaum.

Dore, F. Y., & Dumas, C. (1987). Psychology of animal cognition: Piagetian studies. *Psychology Bulletin, 102,* 219–233.

Eimas, P., & Quinn, P. (1994). Studies on the formation of perceptually based basic-level categories in young infants. *Child Development, 65,* 903–917.

Evans, C. S., & Marler, P. (1995). Language and communication: Parallels and contrasts. In H. L. Roitblat & J.-A. Meyer (Eds.), *Comparative approaches to cognitive science* (pp. 341–382). Cambridge, MA: MIT Press.

Gallistel, C. R. (1990). *The organization of learning.* Cambridge, MA: MIT Press.

Gelman, R. (1990). First principles organize attention to and learning about relevant data: number and the animate-inanimate distinction as examples. *Cognitive Science, 14,* 79–106.

Gellman, R., & Gallistel, C. R. (1978/1986). *The child's understanding of number*. Cambridge, MA: Harvard University Press.

Gelman, S. A., Coley, J. D., & Gottfried, G. M. (1994). Essentialist beliefs in children: The acquisition of concepts and theories. In L. A. Hirschfeld & S. A. Gelman (Eds.), *Mapping the mind: Domain specificity in cognition and culture* (pp. 341–366). New York: Cambridge University Press.

Golinkoff, R. M., & Kerr, J. L. (1978). Infant's perception of semantically defined action role changes in filmed events. *Merrill-Palmer Quarterly, 24,* 53–61.

Gopnik, A., & Meltzoff, A. (1997). *Words, thoughts, and theories*. Cambridge, MA: MIT Press.

Gouzoules, S., Gouzoules, H., & Marler, P. (1984). Rhesus monkey (*Macaca mulatta*) screams: representational signalling in the recruitment of agonistic aid. *Animal Behaviour, 32,* 182–193.

Gruber, H. E., Girgus, J. S., & Banuazizi, A. (1971). The development of object permanence in the cat. *Developmental Psychology, 4,* 9–15.

Harvey, P., H., & Pagel, M. D. (1991). *The comparative method in evolutionary biology*. Oxford: Oxford University Press.

Hauser, M. D. (1996). *The evolution of communication*. Cambridge, MA: Bradford Books/MIT Press.

Hauser, M. D., MacNeilage, P., & Ware, M. (1996). Numerical representations in primates. *Proceedings of the National Academy of Sciences, 93,* 1514–1517.

Hauser, M. D. (in press). Expectations about object motion and destination: Experiments with a nonhuman primate. *Developmental Science*.

Heil, J., & Mele, A. (1995). *Mental causation*. Oxford: Clarendon Press.

Herrnstein, R. J. (1991). Levels of categorization. In G. M. Edelman, W. E. Gall, & W. M. Cowan (Eds.), *Signal and sense* (pp. 385–413). Hillsdale, NJ: Wiley-Liss.

Heyes, C. (1993). Anecdotes, training, trapping and triangulating: Do animals attribute mental states? *Animal Behaviour, 46,* 177–188.

Hirsch, E. (1982). *The concept of identity*. New Haven: Yale Univeristy Press.

Hornsby, J. (1995). Agency and causal explanation. In J. Heil & A. Mele (Eds.), *Mental causation* (pp. 161–188). Oxford: Clarendon Press.

Huttenlocher, J., Jordan, N., & Levine, S. (1994). A mental model for early arithmetic. *Journal of Experimental Psychology: General. 123* (3), 284–296.

Johansson, G. (1973). Visual perception of biological motion and a model for its analysis. *Perception and Psychophysics, 14,* 201–211.

Kahneman, D., Treisman, A., & Gibbs, B. (1992). The reviewing of object files: Object specific integration of information. *Cognitive Psychology, 24,* 175–219.

Keil, F. (1979). The development of the young child's ability to anticipate the outcomes of simple causal events. *Child Development, 50,* 455–362.

Koechlin, E., Dehaene, S., & Mehler, J. (in press). Numerical transformations in five month old infants. *Cognition*.

Kotovsky, L., & Baillargeon, R. (in press). Calibration-based reasoning about collision events in 11 month-old infants. *Cognition*.

Leslie, A. M. (1982). The perception of causality in infants. *Perception, 11,* 173–186.

Leslie, A. M. (1984). Spatiotemporal continuity and the perception of causality in infants. *Perception, 13,* 287–305.

Leslie, A. M. (1994). ToMM, ToBY, and Agency: Core architecture and domain specificity. In L. A. Hirschfeld & S. A. Gelman (Eds.), *Mapping the mind:*

*Domain specificity in cognition and culture* (pp. 119–148). New York: Cambridge University Press.

Leslie, A. M., & Keeble, S. (1987). Do six-month old infants perceive causality? *Cognition, 25,* 265–288.

Lesser, H. (1977). The growth of perceived causality in children. *Journal of Genetic Psychology, 130,* 145–152.

Lieberman, P. (1984). *The biology and evolution of language.* Cambridge, MA: Harvard University Press.

Locke, J. (1993). *The path to spoken language.* Cambridge, MA: Harvard University Press.

Macnamara, J. (1982). *Names for things.* Cambridge, MA: MIT Press.

Macphail, E. M. (1982). *Brain and intelligence in vertebrates.* Oxford: Clarendon Press.

Macphail, E. (1987). The comparative psychology of intelligence. *Behavioral and Brain Sciences, 10,* 645–695.

Macphail, E. M. (1994). *The neuroscience of animal intelligence.* New York: Columbia University Press.

Mandler, J. (1988). How to build a baby: On the development of an accessible representational system. *Cognitive Development, 3,* 113–136.

Mandler, J. (1992). How to build a baby: II. Conceptual primitives. *Psychological Review, 99,* 587–604.

Marler, P. (1970). Birdsong and speech development: Could there be parallels? *American Scientist, 58,* 669–673.

Matsuzawa, T. (1985). Use of numbers by a chimpanzee. *Nature, 315,* 57–59.

McFarland, D. (1995). Opportunity versus goals in robots, animals, and people. In H. L. Roitblat & J.-A. Meyer (Eds.), *Comparative Approaches to Cognitive Science* (pp. 415–434). Cambridge, MA: MIT Press.

Meck, W. H., & Church, R. M. (1983). A mode control model of counting and timing processes. *Journal of Experimental Psychology: Animal Behavior Processes, 9,* 320–334.

Michotte, A. (1962). *The perception of causality.* Andover, MA: Methuen.

Natale, F., & Antinucci, F. (1989). Stage 6 object-concept and representation. In F. Antinucci (Ed.), *Cognitive structure and development in nonhuman primates* (pp. 97–112). Hillsdale, NJ: Erlbaum.

Pepperberg, I. M. (1994). Numerical competence in an African gray parrot (*Psittacus erithacus*). *Journal of Comparative Psychology, 108,* 36–44.

Piaget, J. (1952). *The origins of intelligence in children.* New York: International University Press.

Piaget, J. (1955). *The child's construction of reality.* London: Routledge and Kegan Paul.

Pinker, S. (1994). *The language instinct.* New York: William Morrow.

Povinelli, D. J., & Eddy, T. J. (1996). What young chimpanzees know about seeing. *Monographs of the Society for Research in Child Development, 61* (2).

Povinelli, D. J., Nelson, K. E., & Boysen, S. T. (1990). Inferences about guessing and knowing by chimpanzees (*Pan troglodytes*). *Journal of Comparative Psychology, 104,* 203–210.

Povinelli, D. J., Parks, K. A., & Novak, M. A. (1991). Do rhesus monkeys (*Macaca mulatta*) attribute knowledge and ignorance to others? *Journal of Comparative Psychology, 105,* 318–325.

Premack, D. (1976). *Intelligence in ape and man.* Hillsdale, NJ: Erlbaum.

Premack, D. (1986). *Gavagai!* Cambridge, MA: MIT Press.

Premack, D. (1990). The infant's theory of self-propelled objects. *Cognition, 36,* 1–16.

Premack, D., & Dasser, V. (1991). Perceptual origins and conceptual evidence for theory of mind in apes and children. In A. Whiten (Ed.), *Natural Theories of Mind* (pp. 253–266). Oxford: Basil Blackwell.

Premack, D., & Premack, A. J. (1994a). Origins of human social competence. In M. Gazzaniga (Ed.), *The cognitive neurosciences* (pp. 205–218). Cambridge, MA: MIT Press.

Premack, D., &Premack, A. J. (1994b). Levels of causal understanding in chimpanzees and children. *Cognition, 50,* 347–362.

Premack, D., & Premack, A. J. (1995). Intention as psychological cause. In D. Sperber, D. Premack, & A. J. Premack (Eds.), *Causal cognition: A multidisciplinary debate* (pp. 85–199). Oxford: Clarendon Press.

Premack, D., & Woodruff, G. (1978). Does the chimpanzee have a theory of mind? *Behavioral and Brain Sciences, 4,* 515–526.

Quinn, P., & Eimas, P. (1993). Evidence for representations of perceptually similar natural categories by 3- and 4-month-old infants. *Perception, 22* (4), 463–475.

Ridley, M. (1983). *The explanation of organic diversity.* Oxford: Clarendon Press.

Roitblat, H. L., Herman, L. M., & Nachtigall, P. E. (1993). *Language and communication. Comparative perspective.* Hillsdale, NJ: Erlbaum.

Rumbaugh D. M., & Washburn D. A. (1993). Counting by chimpanzees and ordinality judgements by macaques in video-formatted tasks. In S. T. Boysen & E. J. Capaldi (Eds.), *The development of numerical competence. Animal and human models.* Hillsdale, NJ: Erlbaum.

Savage-Rumbaugh, E. S., Murphy, J., Sevcik, R. A., Brakke, K. E., Williams, S. L., & Rumbaugh, D. M. (1993). Language comprehension in ape and child. *Monographs of the Society for Research in Child Development, 58,* 1–221.

Simon T., Hespos, S., & Rochat, P. (1995). Do infants understand simple arithmetic? A replication of Wynn (1992). *Cognitive Development, 10,* 253–269.

Spelke, E. S. (1985). Preferential looking methods as tools for the study of cognition in infancy. In G. Gottlieb & N. Krasnegor (Eds.), *Measurement of audition and vision in the first year of post-natal life* (pp. 323–364). Hillsdale, NJ: Erlbaum.

Spelke, E. S. (1991). Physical knowledge in infancy: Reflections on Piaget's theory. In S. Carey & R. Gelman (Eds.), *The epigenesis of mind: Essays on biology and cognition* (pp. 37–61). Hillsdale, NJ: Erlbaum.

Spelke, E. S. (1994). Initial knowledge: six suggestions. *Cognition, 50,* 431–445.

Spelke, E. S., Vishton, P., & von Hofsten, C. (1995). Object perception, object-directed action, and physical knowledge in infancy. In M. Gazzaniga (Ed.), *The cognitive neurosciences* (pp. 165–179). Cambridge, MA: MIT Press.

Spelke, E. S., Phillips, A., & Woodward, A. L. (1995). Infants' knowledge of object motion and human action. In D. Sperber, D. Premack, & A. Premack (Eds.), *Causal cognition* (pp. 44–76). Oxford: Clarendon Press.

Spinozzi, G., & Poti, P. (1989). Causality I: The support problem. In F. Antinucci (Ed.), *Cognitive structure and development in nonhuman primates* (pp. 113–120). Hillsdale, NJ: Erlbaum.

Starkey, P. (1992). The early development of numerical reasoning. *Cognition, 43,* 93–126.

Starkey, P., & Cooper, R. (1980). Perception of numbers by human infants. *Science, 210,* 1033–1035.

Strauss, M. & Curtis, L. (1981). Infant perception of numerosity. *Child Development, 52,* 1146–1152.

Talmy, L. (1988). Force dynamics in language and cognition. *Cognitive Science, 12,* 49–100.

Thomas, R. K. (1992). Conceptual use of number: Ecological perspectives and psychological processes. In T. Nishida, W. C. McGrew, P. Marler, M. Pickford, & F. B. M. de Waal (Eds.), *Topics in primatology, vol. 1: Human origins* (pp. 305–314). Tokyo: Tokyo University Press.

Thompson, R. K. R. (1995). Natural and relational concepts in animals. In H. L. Roitblat & J.-A. Meyer (Eds.), *Comparative approaches to cognitive science* (pp. 175–224). Cambridge, MA: MIT Press.

Trick, L., & Pylyshyn, Z. (1994). Why are small and large numbers enumerated differently? A limited capacity preattentive stage in vision. *Psychological Review, 101,* 80–102.

Uller, C. (1997). *Origins of numerical concepts: A comparative study of human infants and nonhuman primates.* Cambridge, MA: MIT Press.

Uller, C., Carey, S., Huntley-Fenner, G., & Klatt, L. (under review). What representations might underlie infant numerical knowledge. *Cognitive Development.*

Uller, C., Carey, S., & Hauser, M. (in press). Is language needed for constructing sortal concepts? A study with nonhuman primates. *Proceedings of the 21st Annual Boston University Conference on Language Development.*

Van Loosbroek, E., & Smitsman, A. (1990). Visual perception of numerosity in infancy. *Developmental Psychology, 26,* 916–922.

Visalberghi, E., & Fragaszy, D. (1991). Do monkeys ape? In S. T. Parker & K. R. Gibson (Eds.), *"Language" and intelligence in monkeys and apes* (pp. 247–273). Cambridge, MA: Cambridge University Press.

Whiten, A. (1991). *Natural theories of mind.* Cambridge, MA: Basil Blackwell.

Wiggins, D. (1980). *Sameness and substance.* Cambridge, MA: Harvard University Press.

Willatts, P. (1984). The Stage-IV infant's solution of problems requiring the use of supports. *Infant Behavior and Development, 7,* 125–134.

Willatts, P. (1990). Development of problem-solving strategies in infancy. In D. F. Bjorklund (Ed.), *Children's strategies: Contemporary views of cognitive development* (pp. 143–182). Hillsdale, NJ: Erlbaum.

Wimmer, H., & Perner, J. (1983). Beliefs about beliefs: Representation and constraining function of wrong beliefs in young children's understanding of deception. *Cognition, 13,* 103–128.

Wynn, K. (1992). Addition and subtraction by human infants. *Nature, 358,* 749–750.

Wynn, K. (1995). Origin of numerical knowledge. *Mathematical Cognition, 1,* 36–60.

Wynn, K. (1996). Infants' individuation and enumeration of actions. *Psychological Science, 7,* 164–169.

Xu, F., & Carey, S. (1996). Infants' metaphysics: the case of numerical identity. *Cognitive Psychology, 30,* 111–153.

Xu, F., & Carey, S. (under review). Property-kind distinctions in infancy.

# 4

# An Evolved Capacity for Number

KAREN WYNN

The elegant and complex system of formal mathematics that we have developed over the course of several thousand years is unique to the human species. No other animal possesses such knowledge. Nonetheless, the origins of this knowledge may be found in a core basis of numerical competence that we share with many other species. In this chapter, I will suggest that humans possess a mental "number mechanism," designed through natural selection, with which we represent and reason about number. I shall first review empirical evidence showing numerical competence in both human infants and nonhuman animals; that is, evidence that numerical abilities exist independently of the acquisition of language and of exposure to culturally transmitted mathematical knowledge. Next, I shall present a possible model of the mental structure of this "number mechanism," and then discuss the evolutionary advantages to having such abilities. Finally, I will discuss limitations of this mechanism that have implications for the acquisition of further mathematical knowledge.

## Numerical Competence in Nonhuman Animals and Human Infants

### Numerical Abilities in Human Infants

Human infants are able to represent and reason about number. Many studies have shown that infants can distinguish between different small numbers of objects. When repeatedly presented with ("habituated to") displays containing a given number of objects, infants will then look longer when presented with displays containing a new number of objects. This pattern of looking is found even when non-numerical aspects of the displays, such as the configuration of the items, the overall area taken up by the objects, the density of item placement, and so on are all controlled for (e.g., Antell & Keating, 1983; Starkey & Cooper, 1980; Strauss & Curtis, 1981; van Loosbroek & Smitsman, 1990). Using this general methodology, infants can discriminate two from three items, and in some studies, three from four (Strauss & Curtis, 1981) or even four from five (van Loosbroek & Smitsman, 1990). Items that infants enumerated in these studies range from points of light (e.g., Starkey & Cooper, 1980), to photographs of actual household objects (Starkey, Spelke & Gelman, 1990), to computer-generated "random checkerboard" patterns (van Loosbroek & Smitsman, 1990).

Infants are also able to enumerate punctate sounds in a sequence, and are able to recognize a numerical correspondence across sets of different kinds of entities (Starkey, Spelke & Gelman, 1990). In one experiment, infants were habituated to photographs of either two or three household objects. In the test phase, they were presented with test trials in which a black disk on the display stage emitted two drumbeats, and trials in which the disk emitted three drumbeats. Infants looked at the disk longer when it emitted the same number of drumbeats as the number of items in the photographs to which they had been habituated.

Finally, infants can enumerate physical actions presented sequentially. In two experiments, we habituated six-month-olds to the jumping activity of a puppet (Wynn, 1996). In the first experiment, one group of infants was repeatedly presented with trials in which the puppet jumped twice, pausing briefly between the jumps, and then stood motionless. Another group of infants was presented with trials in which the puppet jumped three times, again pausing between jumps, and stood motionless at the end of the sequence. Infants' looking time to the motionless puppet was measured at the end of each trial. Infants were shown these trials until their looking time dropped to half of its initial levels, at which point they were considered to be habituated. Following this habituation, both groups of infants were presented with novel two- and three-jump test trials, and again their looking time was measured. Infants looked significantly longer on trials containing the number of jumps other than what they had been habituated to; that is, the infants habituated to two jumps looked longer on trials when the puppet jumped three times, and vice versa, showing that the infants were able to enumerate the jumps in the sequences (see Figure 4.1a).[1]

In the second experiment of Wynn (1996), we asked whether infants could discriminate between two- and three-jump sequences, only this time, the puppet remained in constant motion throughout each sequence—between jumps, the puppet's head wagged from side to side in an exaggerated fashion. In such a sequence, one cannot identify the individual actions of the puppet through a low-level perceptual analysis (e.g., on the basis of the presence or absence of motion), but must analyze the pattern of motion in the sequence. Indeed, there is more than one way to pick out distinct actions in such a sequence—for example, one might pick out and count individual jumps as distinct from head-wagging, or one might pick out and count the repetitions of the repeating pattern of "jumping-followed-by-head-wagging." The extraction of discrete actions from a continuous sequence of motion is a cognitive imposition. Nonetheless, in this experiment infants again looked significantly longer at the puppet on the new-number test trials (see Figure 4.1b), showing that they were able both to parse the puppet's continuous sequence of motion into distinct segments on the basis of the structure of motion in the sequence, and to enumerate these segments. Thus, infants can enumerate complex, cognitively determined individuals.

Visual items, sounds, and physical actions are all very different kinds of entities. The visual items or patterns presented to infants in the above studies endure together through time and occupy different locations in space; thus, to identify the boundaries of an individual item requires primarily an analysis of spatial information. Sounds, in contrast, are not defined in terms of spatial extent; rather, they occur at different points in time and endure only temporarily. Thus, to identify the boundaries of a sound requires primarily an analysis of temporal information. Finally, actions consist of internally structured patterns of motion that unfold over time, so identification of their boundaries entails an integration of both spatial and temporal information. The fact that infants can enumerate entities with such distinct properties, presented either simultaneously or sequentially, and presented in different perceptual modalities, indicates that they possess abstract, generalizable representations of these small numbers.

Furthermore, infants are able to reason about the numbers they can represent. They are not only able to discriminate between different numbers of entities, but have procedures for manipulating their representation of the number of items in a given situation to yield an updated numerical representation as the situation changes. This was shown in a series of experiments (Wynn, 1992a). In these experiments, infants were shown a small collection of objects. They then saw an object added to or removed from the collection. The resulting collection of objects shown to infants was either numerically consistent with the addition or subtraction, or it was inconsistent. Because we know that infants look longer at outcomes that violate their expectations if they can compute the number of objects that should result, they should therefore look longer at inconsistent outcomes than consistent ones.

In the first experiment, one group of five-month-old infants was shown an addition situation in which one object was added to another identical object, while another group was shown a subtraction situation in which one object was removed from a collection of two objects. Infants in the "one plus one" group saw one item placed into a display case. A screen then rotated up to hide the item, and a second item was brought into the display and placed out of sight behind the screen, alongside the first (see Figure 4.2a). The "two minus one" group saw two items initially placed into the display. The screen rotated up to hide them; then, one item was removed from behind the screen and taken out of the display (see Figure 4.2b). For both groups of infants, the screen then dropped

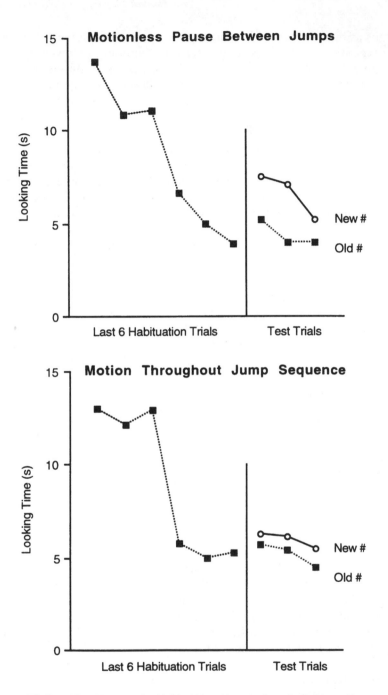

*Figure 4.1  Six-month-olds' looking times on last six habituation trials and on old- and novel-number test trial jump sequences in Wynn (1996), with (a) sequences with motionless inter-jump intervals; and (b) sequences in which the puppet was in continuous motion (Courtesy of Psychological Science).*

to reveal either one or two items, and infants' looking times to these outcomes were recorded.

Pretest trials that presented infants with displays of one and two items revealed no significant preference for one number over the other, and no significant preference between the two groups. But there was a significant difference between the looking patterns of the two groups on the test trials; infants in the "one plus one" group looked longer at a one-item than at a two-item result, while infants in the "two minus one" situation looked longer at a two-item than at a one-item result (Figure 4.3).

In another experiment, infants were shown one item added to another as were the "one plus one" group above, but in this case the final number of objects revealed was either two or three. Again, infants looked significantly longer at the inconsistent outcome, in this case looking longer at the outcome of three objects than at the outcome of two objects (Figure 4.4). Pretest trials revealed no baseline preference to look at three items over two items.

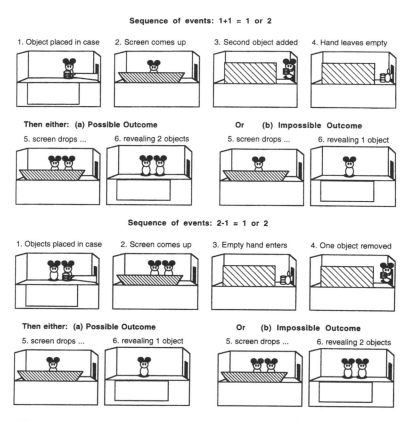

*Figure 4.2.   Sequence of events shown to 5-month-olds in Wynn (1992), Experiments 1 and 2 (courtesy of Nature).*

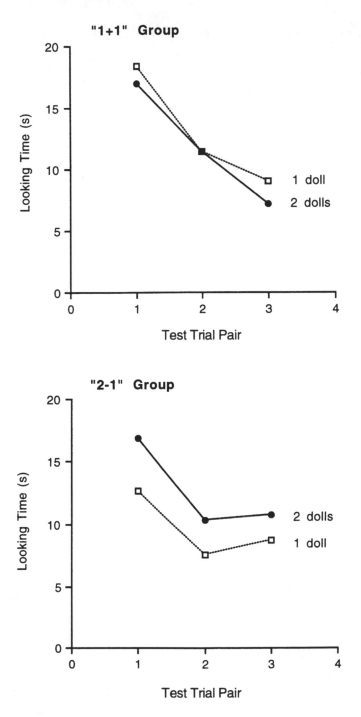

*Figure 4.3. Five-month-olds' looking times to outcomes of 1 doll and 2 dolls following "1+1" versus "2-1" event sequences in Wynn (1992).*

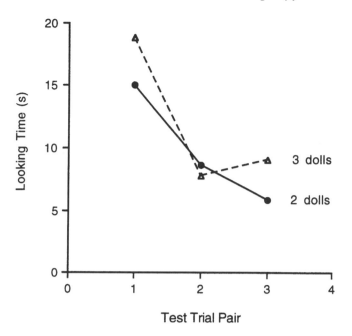

*Figure 4.4. Five-month-olds' looking to 2 versus 3 objects, following a "1+1" sequence of events in Wynn (1992).*

These results show that five-month-old infants are not only able to identify and represent a number of objects present in a display, but they are able to update these representations in accordance with real-world events, to infer the numerical results of these events. The results also show that infants understand the numerical relationships between the numbers they can represent; they understand that one more than one makes two and that one less than two makes one.[2] These results are robust; they have been replicated both in my own and in other laboratories, using different stimuli and with variations in the procedure (e.g., Baillargeon, 1994; Koechlin, Dehaene & Mehler, in press; Moore, 1997; Simon, Hespos, & Rochat, 1995; Uller, Carey, Huntley-Fenner, & Klatt, 1994; Wynn, 1995).

The early age—five months—at which infants exhibit this competence precludes its linguistic or cultural transmission. Furthermore, although infants of this age can grasp an object if it is placed in their hands or (often) if it is put directly in front of them, they are typically unable to let go of an object voluntarily (due to the persistence of the grasping reflex, e.g., Diamond, 1991). Therefor, infants could not have attained such knowledge as a result of performing collectings and segregatings of objects themselves and observing the results (e.g., as suggested by Kitcher, 1984). These facts suggest that this knowledge is part of infants' built-in repertoire of cognitive competence.

### Numerical Abilities in Nonhuman Animals

Not only humans, but many different warm blooded vertebrate species, both avian and mammalian, are able to represent number and engage in numerical reasoning. Extensive reviews of these abilities are available elsewhere (e.g., Davis & Perusse, 1988; Gallistel, 1990), and I will limit myself here to a few examples.

Rats, for example, can be trained to press a minimum, specific number of times on a particular lever before pressing a single time on a second lever for a reward. The number of presses required has been varied, from as few as four to as many as 24. Furthermore, the rats' responses are clearly based on the number of presses they give rather than on the duration of lever-pressing activity. When trained to press the first lever for a certain duration, rats will press for an added proportion of the trained time in order to be sure that they have met the requirement; but when trained to press a certain number of times, they will press a certain extra, constant number of presses, independent of the required number (Mechner & Guevrekian, 1962). Similar abilities have also been shown in pigeons, with a somewhat different task (Rilling, 1967; Rilling & McDiarmid, 1965).

In addition to enumerating their own actions, rats have also shown an ability to enumerate sequentially encountered items in the external world. In one experiment, rats were trained to turn down the third, fourth, or fifth tunnel encountered in a maze. Once trained, the rats carried this over to new mazes with novel spatial configurations in which the distance between the tunnels changed from trial to trial, and in which a corner had to be turned before the rewarded tunnel was reached (Davis & Bradford, 1986). Given this, the rats could not simply have been running for a fixed length of time before turning down a tunnel, or determining the extent to which they felt fatigued by the run. Rather, they must have been encoding the numerosity of the tunnels in order to succeed at the task.

Birds have shown similar abilities. For example, canaries were trained to select an object based on its ordinal position in an array (Pastore, 1961). Their task was to walk along a runway with 10 cubicles spaced irregularly along it, and, stop at whichever cubicle held, for example, the fifth aspirin. Each cubicle contained between zero and two aspirins; the number in a given cubicle varied from trial to trial. The distance between cubicles, the number of aspirins per cubicle, and the ordinal position of the cubicle containing the nth aspirin all varied from trial to trial. The birds, therefor, could not have been responding in terms of distance traveled or extent of fatigue, nor could they have been basing their response on the completion of some kind of rhythmic pattern. They must have been responding on the basis of the ordinal position of the aspirin.

Animals can also discriminate different numerosities of simultaneously presented objects. In one study, a raccoon was taught to choose the Plexiglas box that contained three items when it was presented with an array of three to five boxes, each of which contained from one to five items (Davis, 1984).

Nonnumerical cues such as size, stimulus density, odor, and location of target box were controlled for, and the raccoon continued to respond correctly when the trained items were replaced with novel items. In an especially intriguing series of studies, Pepperberg (1987) trained an African Gray Parrot, Alex, to squawk the appropriate number word (in English) when presented with up to five objects. Alex's responses generalized to novel objects. Most interestingly, when presented with a tray that contained two different kinds of objects, for example two keys and three corks, Alex was able to answer correctly any of three questions: "How many?" (correct answer: five); "How many key?" (correct answer: two); and, "How many cork?" (correct answer: three).

At least primates, and possibly other animals, are also able to appreciate numerical relationships between numerosities and to compute the results of additions and subtractions. In one study, Church and Meck (1984) trained rats both to press a lever on the left whenever they were presented with two sounds or two light flashes, and to press a lever on the right when presented with four sounds or four light flashes. The experimenters then presented the rats with a sound and a light flash that occurred simultaneously, followed by another sound/light flash pairing (thus there were four stimuli in all). In this situation, the rats pressed the left lever, showing that they had computed that there were 4 stimuli altogether.

Perhaps the most sophisticated computation ability shown in primates was revealed in an experiment in which Boysen and Berntson (1989) taught a female chimpanzee to associate the Arabic numerals "0" through "4" with their respective numerosities. Without further training, she was able to choose the numeral representing the sum of oranges hidden in two different locations. Most impressively, when the collections of oranges in the two locations were each replaced with a card with an Arabic numeral printed on it, she was able, without further training, to pick out the Arabic numeral representing the sum of these numerals. Chimpanzees are not alone in their ability to determine the results of additions and even subtractions of items; Hauser and Carey (chapter 3) describe in detail numerous studies showing addition and subtraction abilities in rhesus monkeys and cotton-top tamarins.

The studies reviewed above show that both human infants and nonhuman animals are able to enumerate collections of items. For both, the specific perceptual properties of the items to be counted do not matter for enumeration purposes: animals and infants can enumerate different kinds of entities, including physical objects, actions, and sounds, which share little to nothing in the way of perceptual attributes. The mode of presentation of items to be counted, likewise, does not seem to be important to the enumeration process; infants and animals can enumerate items presented simultaneously, items presented sequentially, items presented visually, and items presented aurally (as of yet it is an open question whether they can enumerate items presented tactually). Not only can animals and infants enumerate entities, they can also engage in true numerical reasoning—they appreciate the relationships between these numerical values, and they can compute the results of numerical changes made to a situation. All these facts suggest the existence of a mental mechanism or process that specializes in the tasks of representing and reasoning about number.

## A Mechanism for Representing and Reasoning about Number

The "accumulator model" is a model of such a mental mechanism, originally proposed to account for numerical competence in rats (Meck & Church, 1983). More recently, it has also been proposed as the basis for human infants' and adults' nonverbal numerical competence (Gallistel & Gelman, 1991, 1992; Wynn, 1990a, 1992c). There are a number of similarities in rats' ability to determine number and their ability to measure temporal duration. To account for these similarities, Meck and Church (1983) proposed that a single mechanism underlies both abilities, and expanded a model for measurement of temporal intervals (developed by Gibbon, 1981) to incorporate a counting component. Briefly, their proposed mechanism works as follows: at a constant rate, a pacemaker puts out pulses of energy that can be passed into an accumulator by the closing of a mode switch (see Figure 4.5). In its timing mode, the switch closes at the beginning of the temporal interval being timed and remains closed for its duration, passing energy into the accumulator continuously at a constant rate. Thus, the amount of energy in the accumulator varies in direct proportion to the length of the timed duration. The fullness of the accumulator after it times some duration can be compared with fullness values previously stored in memory to determine whether the just-timed duration is longer, shorter, or the same as a duration associated with some event. In its counting mode, when an entity is experienced that is to be counted, the switch closes for a brief, fixed interval and then opens again. Thus, when counting, the accumulator fills up in equal-sized increments, one increment for each entity counted; and its final fullness value varies in direct proportion to the number of entities so counted. This mechanism contains numerous accumulators and switches, so that the animal can count different sets of events and measure several durations simultaneously.

Evidence for functional similarity between rats' timing processes and their counting processes comes from several experiments (see Meck & Church, 1983). First of all, methamphetamine increases rats' perceptions of duration and of numerosity by exactly the same factor, suggesting that the same mechanism is affected in both cases. This effect could be explained on the model by the drug causing an increase in the rate of pulse generation by the pacemaker, leading to a proportionate increase in the final value of the accumulator, regardless of the mode in which it was operating. Second, both numerical and duration discriminations transfer to novel stimuli with the same strength when rats trained on auditory stimuli were then tested on mixed auditory and cutaneous stimuli. Finally, Meck and Church experimentally tested the prediction that a count yielding the same final ac-

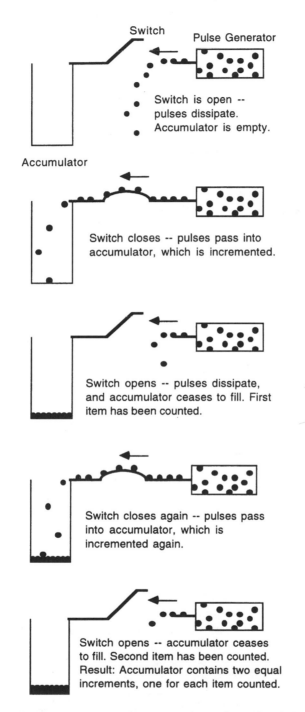

*Figure 4.5. Schematic diagram of the states of the Meck & Church (1983) accumulator mechanism as it enumerates two items. The resulting fullness level of the accumulator is the mental representation for two (courtesy of* Current Directions in Psychological Science*).*

cumulator value as a previously trained duration would be responded to as if it were that duration. If an animal's decision (e.g., to press or not to press a lever) based on comparing the accumulator's current fullness value with a previously stored value, one might expect the animal to respond whenever the current value matches the stored value, regardless of whether it resulted from a timing or a counting process. This prediction was confirmed—when rats were trained to respond to a specific duration of continuous sound, they immediately generalized their response, when presented with the number of one-second sound segments calculated to fill up the accumulator, in its counting mode, to the same level as that for the duration on which the rats were initially trained. This transfer was equally strong in the other direction as well, from number to duration. Meck and Church concluded, on the basis of all of these data, that the same mechanism underlies both counting and timing processes, at least in rats.

It is the entire fullness of the accumulator, comprised of all the increments together, that represents the numerosity of the items counted. This means that magnitude information is inherently embodied in the structure of the representations, themselves magnitude values—the fullness values of the accumulator. Thus, the relationships between the representations exactly reproduce the relationships between the quantities they represent. For example, three is one more than two, and the accumulator mechanism's representation for three (the magnitude of fullness of the accumulator) is one more increment than the representation for two. Eight is four times as large as two, and the accumulator's representation for eight is four times as large as the representation for two. The structures of the numerical symbols on this system are compositional—they can be decomposed to reveal numerical information (see also Wynn, 1992c).

Consider the information implicit in a system such as this. A comparison of any two symbols will indicate whether the represented numerosities are the same or different. The symbols also carry, by virtue of their structure, information on whether one of the represented numbers is larger or smaller than the other, and by how much. If animals and infants possess such a representation of numerosity, they will be able both to determine more-than/less-than relations and to compute the results of additions and subtractions, if they have appropriate procedures for operating over these representations to extract such information.

For example, addition could be achieved by concatenating two (or more) representations, or, more specifically, by either transferring the contents of two accumulators into an empty third accumulator, or dumping the contents of one of the accumulators into the other. A more-than/less-than/equal-to comparison of two accumulators, A and B, could be achieved by simultaneously dumping out one increment from A and one from B, checking both A and B to see if either is empty, 'dumping' another increment from each, checking each again, and so on. If A and B become empty at the same check, the two numbers are equal. If not, the accumulator that becomes empty first represented the smaller number. The difference between the two values would be indicated by the remaining fullness value of the non-empty accumulator.[3] To avoid loss of the initial values in the above operations, the mechanism could initially create "working copies," say A' and B', upon which to carry out the operations.

Nonetheless, the accumulator model has serious weaknesses as well. Most notably, because of inherent variability in the rate at which the pacemaker generates pulses, and in the amount of time the switch closes for each increment, the exact fullness of the accumulator after counting a given number of items will vary from count to count. There will be a mean fullness value for each number, with the actual resulting fullness from counts of a given number being normally distributed about this mean. The variance of this distribution increases with increasing numerosity due to the additive nature of the physical variability of the accumulator's functioning. Because of this, larger numbers will be more easily confused with each other than smaller numbers of the same difference in magnitude, since higher counts will have a greater variability than smaller ones. Indeed, experiments with human infants (e.g., Starkey & Cooper, 1980; van Loosbroek & Smitsman, 1990) and with animals (e.g., Mechner & Guevrekian, 1962; Rilling, 1967) show that larger numbers are more difficult to distinguish from each other.

Similarly, numerical computations requiring several iterations of pouring or copying of values will yield less precise results than simpler computations, again because of the additive nature of the variability. But there have not yet been studies experimentally showing this, and such studies will be difficult to do, in part because we do not know how different numerical computations are actually performed. Therefore, we do not know which ones are the more complex ones.

## Evolutionary Considerations

### Adaptive Benefits of Numerical Abilities

Why would the ability to quantify discrete numbers of entities, and the ability to engage in numerical reasoning, be beneficial? If this capacity results from a specific mental mechanism dedicated to determining and reasoning about number, then it surely arose through natural selection, and must have conferred some adaptive benefits in our evolutionary history. What might these adaptive benefits be?

Gallistel (1990) reviews evidence that animals can determine rate of food return (calculated as number of food encounters per unit of time, multiplied by average amount of food observed or obtained per encounter), noting that "the adaptive value of being able to estimate rate of return is obvious." The suggestion is that the capacity to count evolved because it allowed animals to calculate the rate of food return of different locations. This, in turn, dictates choice of optimal habitat and foraging grounds.

Another possibility, not inconsistent with the above, proposed by Wynn and Bloom (1992), is that enumerative capacities evolved because they help animals to track sets of objects, typically other animals, over time and space. Animals move—they frequently disappear behind other objects, and re-emerge at a later time. Multiple objects pose a special problem for tracking and individuating processes; if they are not easily distinguishable on perceptual grounds, the capacity to determine their numerosity may play an essential role in tracking them. For instance, imagine being a rabbit chased by three coyotes that are shifting in position, moving behind trees and brush, and so on. Knowing that there are three of them, and being able to enumerate those currently visible, will govern your behavior in obvious ways. In situations such as this, a sensitivity to numerosity might be essential to continued survival.

Enumeration and object tracking are distinct abilities. In many instances of object tracking, even with multiple objects, sensitivity to number is neither necessary nor sufficient. If one has two cats, Watson and Wolfgang, it is not necessary to count in order to determine if both are in the house; one simply has to determine if Watson is in the house and if Wolfgang is in the house. Further, in the rabbit example above, knowing how many coyotes are chasing you is not sufficient for tracking them. If one of the three disappears behind some brush, and a fourth appears from another direction, you will be fooled into thinking the set of objects has not changed—unless you have the additional ability to track individual entities.

But precisely because the ability to determine number does not reduce to tracking individuals, the former can be invaluable when the latter is difficult or impossible, as it might be if all of the coyotes look alike to you, and you are too busy running from them to watch their every move. If you know that three coyotes are chasing you, you don't have to track the individual coyotes to know that one is missing if you now look back and see only two. Thus, a need to keep track of groups of homogeneous objects may have created enough selective pressure for a sensitivity to numerosity to evolve.

## Issues of the Evolutionary Development of Numerical Abilities

The fact that a wide range of humans and other vertebrate species possess similar numerical abilities suggests that these abilities may have developed far back in our evolutionary history, at a point prior to the branching off of these different species. However, this is not the only possible explanation for why these species possess similar abilities. Numerical competence may have developed independently in different species, as an easily instantiated biological solution to a common problem space. In order to discriminate between these different possibilities, we will need to study in more detail the exact nature and limits of these abilities in different species. If we were to find, for example, nonadaptive similarities in the numerical capacities of both bird and mammalian species, this would suggest that numerical competence did not evolve independently in birds and mammals.

The accumulator mechanism described above is not a mechanism solely for number; it is also capable of representing duration. This raises the question of the developmental relationship between the ability to measure number and the ability to measure duration. It is likely that the mechanism initially evolved for one of these purposes, and was later co-opted to perform the other function as well. It would need relatively minor modification to extend its function from one to both abilities. If temporal measurement were initially selected for, the additional ability to enumerate could be achieved by building in the capacity to close and open the switch repeatedly and for the same duration each time (perhaps achieved by simply closing and opening the switch as rapidly as physically possible, thus preventing the need to actually measure the duration of closing of the switch to assure sameness of duration from one closing to another). Alternatively, if it was the enumerative capacity that was initially selected for, the ability to measure temporal duration could later be achieved by adapting the switch so it could remain closed for longer periods, opening immediately upon the cessation of the event being timed.

It is difficult to discriminate between these two possibilities at present. Evidence for one or the other of these alternatives might be gained from a thorough study of the timing and counting abilities of many species. If one evolved prior to the other, it is possible that not all of the descendants of the group with the first ability developed the second. For example, if the ability to measure duration is more widespread (belonging to all vertebrates, say), and the ability to measure number is only found in a subgroup of this (say, all warm blooded vertebrates), this would suggest that duration measurement evolved prior to number measurement.

## Why Is Learning Mathematics So Difficult?

Above, I have presented evidence that human infants, along with a range of warm blooded vertebrates, are able to represent number and to reason about different numbers of entities in their environments. I have also described a model of the mental mechanism that may underlie these abilities, a mechanism that is dedicated to measuring and reasoning about number in one mode, and duration in another. I have suggested that such a mechanism may have evolved through the process of natural selection.

But to suggest that we innately possess a mechanism dedicated to representing and reasoning about number clearly does not imply that all of our mathematical knowledge arises directly from this mental number mechanism. In particular, some aspects of numerical learning will require other, more general, conceptual resources to master, because there are many limitations to the accumulator mechanism.

First, the accumulator is capable of representing discrete numbers of individual entities encountered in the environment. It cannot represent any numbers other than positive integers. Numbers such as zero, the negative integers, fractions, irrational numbers, imaginary numbers, and so on, are kinds of numerical entities that the accumulator is intrinsically incapable of representing. The ability of the human mind to grasp these kinds of entities, then, must arise from more general cognitive capacities. For example, reflection on the structure of the positive integers (whose representation is supported by the accumulator) may be extended, through processes of analogical reasoning (see Gentner, 1983), in the "opposite" direction to yield negative integers (for discussion of how the development of understanding fractions as numbers is achieved, see Gelman, Cohen & Hartnett, 1989).

Second, the accumulator mechanism does not represent mathematical concepts other than specific numerical values, such as infinity, prime number, and cube root. All it gives rise to are specific numerical values themselves. The emergence of mathematical concepts beyond these values must result from other cognitive capacities. For example, the application of language's inherent iterative structure to the number naming system may have led to the concept of numerical infinity (see Bloom, 1994).

Third, while infants and animals are able to perform additions and subtractions on the numerical representations produced by their enumeration mechanism, there are some operations that the mechanism cannot support due to functional limits on its computational powers. Just which operations infants and animals can and cannot perform is an empirical question; we do not know yet which operations place computational burdens too great for the system to accomplish. Some candidate operations might, however, be division, determining square or cube roots, and integrating or taking derivatives. Once again, the development of these mathematical operations must result from a general cognitive capacity to reason about and manipulate symbols.

Finally, even acquiring the linguistic counting system of a child's culture goes significantly beyond the abilities granted by infants' enumeration mechanism. Studies show that learning the counting system of their language is a difficult process for young children, one which, once achieved, grants them greater powers of numerical reasoning (Wynn, 1990b, 1992b). In a longitudinal study, I presented two- and three-year-olds with tasks that required an understanding of linguistic counting for optimal performance. In the "give-a-number" task, children were asked to give a puppet (Big Bird) between one and six animals from a pile of toy animals. In the "point-to-x" task, children were first shown pairs of pictures, each containing a different number of items, and then were asked to point to the picture with a specific number of items, for numbers ranging from one to six.

In both tasks, when they were asked to give more than one animal, or to point to a picture of more than one object, children at younger ages did not count the items when responding. This does not mean that they never answered correctly—children were often able to respond correctly when asked for smaller numbers, one, two, and sometimes three, suggesting that they had been able to map the meanings of these smaller number words to their corresponding numerosities by enumerating collections with their innate enumeration mechanism and hearing the appropriate number word applied to the collection. This would not work consistently, though, for larger numbers. The inherent variability in the accumulator mechanism would yield "fuzzy" representations for larger collections, making it difficult to map a number word onto its precise numerosity.

It is clear that younger children's responses were based on the application of their innate enumeration mechanism, not on linguistic counting. In follow-up questions in the "give-a-number" task, the younger children showed no understanding of how the act of counting the items related to the number of items there were when they were asked to count the items they had given to Big Bird in order to make sure they'd given the number asked for. They did tend to count the items when asked to do so, but if they came up with an incorrect number, they either did not appear to recognize the discrepancy (e.g., "One, two, three—that's five!" said a boy who was counting out three items he'd given when asked for five), or appeared utterly stymied as to how to remedy the discrepancy. Many children spontaneously devised the "remedy" of revising the ordered list of counting words in their counting (e.g., a child who was asked for five and gave three, and then asked to "count to make sure there are five," counted the items as follows: "one, two . . . [long pause of apparent consternation while looking at the remaining uncounted object] five!" [Pointing to the last object] "It's five!"). Other children rearranged the items they'd given (one child who had given two objects when asked for three exchanged the places of the two objects saying, "Now there's three," upon being asked to "fix it so there's three"). Still others added more items to those they had given the puppet, even when their initial mistake had been to give too many (e.g., a child asked to give three items gave a handful that contained six; when asked to count and make sure there were three items, and subsequently, after counting them correctly, to "fix it so there's three," he gathered several additional animals and placed them, together with his original six, in front of Big Bird). All these strategies suggest that, although the younger children had some understanding of how to *count*, they did not understand how counting determines *number*.

This was in marked contrast to their behavior a few months later, when they were able to succeed at larger numbers (e.g., five and six) as well as the smaller numbers, by using counting systematically to get the correct answer. Children typically achieved this competence roughly at the age of three and a half, though there was great individual variation. Most interestingly, once children achieved this competence, their strategy also changed when asked for the smaller numbers that they had previously been successful on. Despite having successfully used their enumeration mechanism to identify the correct number, they now rejected this strategy in favor of counting. Because of children's difficulties with coordinating their pointing with their vocalizing, this actually led to an increase in erroneous responses for these small numbers. This shift from a previously successful strategy to a somewhat less successful one is powerful evidence both of a fundamental shift in children's conception of the task, and of the role of counting in determining numerosity. It also highlights the impressive representational advantage conferred by acquisition of a linguistic counting system. Such acquisition allows equally precise representations of all positive integer values, regardless of their size.

One achievement unique to the human species is the development of cultural knowledge that is elaborated and enriched over many successive generations. The formal system of mathematics, the historical development of which can be traced back for thousands of years, is an excellent example of this kind of knowledge. More work needs to be done to clarify just how our unlearned core of numerical competence, one which we hold in common with other species, interacts with other cognitive capacities to allow the development of this elegant and complex system.

## Notes

I am grateful to Paul Bloom for very helpful comments on an earlier version of this paper. This work was supported by an NICHD FIRST award to the author. Correspondence should be addressed to the author at: The Department of Psychology, University of Arizona, Tucson, AZ 85721. E-mail should be sent to: wynn@u.arizona.edu.

1. The habituation and test jump sequences were structured to rule out the possibility that infants might respond on the basis of the tempo of jumps or overall duration of the jump sequences.

2. See Wynn (in preparation) for discussion of why these abilities in infants cannot be explained in terms of the more general capacity to track individual objects.

3. My purpose in describing how these computations might be acheived is to show that they are possible within the accumulator model, not to make definitive claims of how the animal or infant actually makes such computations; there are other procedures within the accumulator model that could also subserve addition, subtraction, comparison of two values, and the like.

## References

Antell, S., & Keating, D. P. (1983). Perception of numerical invariance in neonates. *Child Development, 54,* 695–701.

Baillargeon, R. (1994). Physical reasoning in young infants: Seeking explanations for impossible events. *British Journal of Developmental Psychology, 12,* 9–33.

Bloom, P. (1994). Generativity within language and other cognitive domains. *Cognition, 51,* 177–189.

Boysen, S. T., & Berntson, G. G. (1989). Numerical competence in a chimpanzee (*Pan troglodytes*). *Journal of Comparative Psychology, 103,* 23–31.

Church, R. M., & Meck, W. H. (1984). The numerical attribute of stimuli. In H. Roitblatt, T. G. Bever, & H. S. Terrence (Eds.), *Animal cognition*. Hillsdale, NJ: Erlbaum.

Davis, H. (1984). Discrimination of the number three by a raccoon (*Procyon lotor*). *Animal Learning and Behavior, 12*, 409–413.

Davis, H., & Bradford, S. A. (1986). Counting behavior by rats in a simulated natural environment. *Ethology, 73*, 265–280.

Davis, H., & Perusse, R. (1988). Numerical competence in animals: Definitional issues, current evidence and a new research agenda. *Behavioral and Brain Sciences, 11*, 561–615.

Diamond, A. (1991). Neuropsychological insights into the meaning of object concept development. In S. Carey & R. Gelman (Eds.), *The epigenesis of mind: Essays on biology and cognition* (pp. 67–110). Hillsdale, NJ: Erlbaum.

Gallistel, C. R. (1990). *The organization of learning.* Cambridge, MA: MIT Press.

Gallistel, C. R., & Gelman, R. (1991). The preverbal counting process. In W. E. Kesson, A. Ortony, & F. I. M. Craik (Eds.), *Thoughts, memories, and emotions: Essays in honor of George Mandler.* Hillsdale, NJ: Erlbaum.

Gallistel, C. R., & Gelman, R. (1992). Preverbal and verbal counting and computation. *Cognition, 44*, 43–74.

Gelman, R., Cohen, M., & Hartnett, P. (1989). To know mathematics is to go beyond the belief that "Fractions are not numbers." *Proceedings of Psychology of Mathematics Education*, vol. 11 of the North American Chapter of the International Group of Psychology.

Gentner, D. (1983). Structure-mapping: A theoretical framework for analogy. *Cognitive Science, 7*, 155–170.

Gibbon, J. (1981). On the form and location of the psychometric bisection function for time. *Journal of Mathematical Psychology, 24*, 58–87.

Kitcher, P. (1984). *The nature of mathematical knowledge.* Oxford: Oxford University Press.

Koechlin, E., Dehaene, S., & Mehler, J. (in press). Numerical transformations in five-month-old human infants. *Mathematical Cognition.*

Mechner, F. M., & Guevrekian, L. (1962). Effects of deprivation upon counting and timing in rats. *Journal of the Experimental Analysis of Behavior, 5*, 463–466.

Meck, W. H., & Church, R. M. (1983). A mode control model of counting and timing processes. *Journal of Experimental Psychology: Animal Behavior Processes, 9*, 320–334.

Moore, D. S. (1997). *Infant mathematical skills? A conceptual replication and consideration of interpretation.* Poster presented at the Biennial Meeting of the Society for Research in Child Development, Washington, DC, April.

Pastore, N. (1961). Number sense and "counting" ability in the canary. *Zietschrift fur Tierpsychologie, 18*, 561–573.

Pepperberg, I. M. (1987). Evidence for conceptual quantitative abilities in the African Grey Parrot: Labeling of cardinal sets. *Ethology, 75*, 37–61.

Platt, J. R., & Johnson, D. M. (1971). Localization of position within a homogeneous behavior chain: Effects of error contingencies. *Learning and Motivation, 2*, 386–414.

Rilling, M. E. (1967). Number of responses as a stimulus in fixed interval and fixed ratio schedules. *Journal of Comparative and Physiological Psychology, 63*, 60–65.

Rilling, M. E., & McDiarmid, C. (1965). Signal detection in fixed ratio schedules. *Science, 148*, 526–527.

Simon, T. J., Hespos, S. J., & Rochat, P. (1995). Do infants understand simple arithmetic? A replication of Wynn (1992). *Cognitive Development, 10*, 253–269.

Starkey, P., & Cooper, R. G., Jr. (1980). Perception of numbers by human infants. *Science, 210,* 1033–1035.

Starkey, P., Spelke, E. S., & Gelman, R. (1990). Numerical abstraction by human infants. *Cognition, 36,* 97–128.

Strauss, M. S., & Curtis, L. E. (1981). Infant perception of numerosity. *Child Development, 52,* 1146–1152.

Uller, M. C., Carey, S., Huntley-Fenner, G. N., & Klatt, L. (1994). *The representations underlying infant addition.* Unpublished manuscript.

van Loosbroek, E., & Smitsman, A. W. (1990). Visual perception of numerosity in infancy. *Developmental Psychology, 26,* 916–922.

Wynn, K. (1990a). *Development of counting and the concept of number.* Massachusetts Institute of Technology. Unpublished doctoral dissertation.

Wynn, K. (1990b). Children's understanding of counting. *Cognition, 36,* 155–193.

Wynn, K. (1992a). Addition and subtraction by human infants. *Nature, 358,* 749–750.

Wynn, K. (1992b). Children's acquisition of the number words and the counting system. *Cognitive Psychology, 24,* 220–251.

Wynn, K. (1992c). Evidence against empiricist accounts of the origins of numerical knowledge. *Mind & Language, 7,* 315–332.

Wynn, K. (1995). Origins of numerical knowledge. *Mathematical Cognition, 1,* 35–60.

Wynn, K. (1996). Infants' individuation and enumeration of sequential actions. *Psychological Science, 7,* 164–169.

Wynn, K., & Bloom, P. (1992). The origins of psychological axioms of arithmetic and geometry. *Mind & Language, 7,* 409–416.

# 5

# Cognitive Ethology
## *The Minds of Children and Animals*

CAROLYN A. RISTAU

"And *what* is that?" said the Queen (pointing to Alice).

(LEWIS CARROLL, ALICE IN WONDERLAND)

Indeed, trying to comprehend how one individual understands another—how one conceptualizes another—is a central problem in understanding animal cognition, or children's or even human adults'.

I will first confront the problem of how children come to attribute minds to others, for eventually they do. Then I will ask if any aspect of children's development of understanding is applicable to the understanding various species of animals may grow to have of another.

Selected evidence will be noted. Throughout, I will suggest methods to explore these issues in children and animals. Finally, implications for the evolution of mind will be discussed.

### *How Children (and Some Animals?) Come to Attribute Mind to Others*

A child or another primate, mammal, bird, and many other species must, upon encountering an object, determine what sort of object it is, particularly with respect to their behavior towards it. Minimally, is it to be approached, avoided, circumnavigated while going somewhere else or is it simply to be sensed at a distance? Although one observes behaviors, they are at least a partial reflection of the organism's understanding of the object.

For some species, under some conditions not readily specifiable, something more happens: the organism attempts to determine more precise characteristics of the object. Among the circumstances provoking such evaluations is the motivational state of the creature. If hungry, for example, the organism is likely to be concerned about whether the object is edible. The object's physical characteristics—hardness, weight, sharpness, and so forth—are likely to be of concern either if the organism is about to interact with it . . . or, as in the case of sufficiently mature humans, the organism has both the inclination and ability to muse about those attributes.

It seems likely that many species determine whether the object is alive, or more specifically, animate. This determination does not involve all the properties contained in the concept as held by adult humans. Minimal characteristics of animacy for humans would seem to include some notion of self-movement and capacity for interactions; these provide good starting points for exploring "animacy" as it may be understood by young children and other species.

Given that the object is animate, two problems immediately arise: a) What does/can an organism find out about the creature? b) How is it done?

We adult humans may garner information about a person's past history, current status, and identity through the use of language. We are also able to assess, imperfect though it may be, a person's current mental states, including intentions or purposes in an encounter. As human children, we presumably were able to determine less and probably were interested in less.

As children, we did not have a vast array of experiences nor the ability to reason at long length nor theoretical psychological concepts to guide our understanding of others and to conjecture about another's mental states and intentions.

What capacities do children and animals bring to bear upon their understanding of others' minds? In this chapter I make the case that such knowledge arises through the interaction of innate constraints, highly specialized innate abilities and interactions with the environment. The constraints predispose selective attention to certain aspects of the environment. The specialized abilities allow knowledge that is not attainable through processes of logical reasoning. Guided by these constraints and abilities, an animal or child interacts with the environment, learning, reasoning, and eventually knowing something of the minds of others.

### From the Beginning: What Does an Organism Learn about Objects and Events?

We should reasonably assume that an organism learns what it needs to learn or what is important to learn at each stage of its existence. Stimulus salience and the functional significance of an object to an organism help determine the organism's selective attention and memory. These proclivities can be detected by studying the organism's apparent "mistakes" and biases, including emphasis on different sense modalities among species and on biologically significant information, for instance, spatial information.

In this next section, I will consider looming, one example of salience common to many species. Then, I will examine how biased learning can occur in Pavlovian conditioning, apparently depending on the organism's motivational state; these effects are usually termed "biological constraints" on learning. Next, I will look to mistakes in various cognitive tasks that reveal an organism's bias in attending to specific classes of stimuli or aspects of the situation. I will also offer several examples in which spatial information provides a particularly powerful biasing effect in attention and memory. Finally, I will note the importance of an object's function in characterizing that object to an organism.

For just about all visual species, it is biologically important to be aware that an object is *looming*; that is, a form is rapidly magnifying in the visual field, a situation that generally signals an impending impact. Evidence from infants as young as two or three weeks of age indicates that they are sensitive to looming stimuli. The infants typically blink their eyes, stiffen, and cry as if sensing a coming collision. Other species, exposed to similar forms (e.g., a rapidly increasing shadow on a screen) act in analogous ways: crabs flatten, frogs jump, and monkeys leap (Schiff, 1965; Yonas, 1981).

In addition to cross species tendencies to respond similarly to biologically significant stimuli, different species and individuals of different ages may find diverse aspects of an object or event to be particularly salient. Garcia and Koelling's classic work (1966) showed us that, depending on the kind of reinforcement that followed, rats learned about different stimulus characteristics in a classical conditioning paradigm. In some conditions, the rats were given an electric shock while drinking "bright, noisy, tasty" water or shortly thereafter. Such water had a sweet taste and was presented simultaneously with "bright" light and a sound. In other cases, instead of being shocked, the rats were made ill by drugs or radiation. If they had been shocked, the rats learned to be fearful of only the light and sound that had accompanied drinking the water. If they had been made (apparently) nauseous, they learned to fear the taste of the water, and they would not drink the same saccharine flavored water used in training. Yet, these rats readily drank "bright, noisy" water. Most contemporary researchers interpret this phenomenon as an example of "belongingness," a type of "biological constraint on learning." The rats are evolutionarily prepared to associate illness with taste. Presumably gastric distress and taste/olfaction are innately linked through the feeding system that is specialized to rely primarily on olfactory and taste cues available during the rats' nocturnal foraging. In a related experiment, quail that rely on visual cues in their grain foraging learned to fear a visual cue, color, when it was paired with illness (Wilcoxin, Dragoin, & Kral, 1971).

Sometimes, the alerting reactions of an organism give us insight into the nature of the stimulus it is expecting. Thus, Holland's work (1977, 1980) indicates how, by behavioral means (i.e., ethological cues), observers can determine if rats are expecting a tone to sound or a light to flash, either signaling the arrival or delivery of food. The rats awaiting the signal reared up on their hind legs and/or moved toward the feeder if they had been trained with a light. They showed an increase in overall activity if they had been trained with a tone.

An organism's initial mistakes or predispositions in a learning task can also reveal its proclivities to be more interested in certain aspects of the environment over others. We can, in fact, consider that such information is giving us an insight into the organism's structure of mind, revealing which stimuli it is predisposed to attend to, and how it is predisposed to interpret those stimuli.

Indeed, cognitive psychologists in particular recognize the importance of analyzing the nature of "mistakes" made by humans in problem solving, decision making, and other conceptual tasks (e.g., Tversky & Kahneman, 1974, 1981). For example, in estimating probabilities that certain events will occur, humans show an "anchoring effect." They bias their guesses depending on an existing probability estimate, even when they know that the estimate has been chosen randomly. Seeing that the spin of a roulette wheel establishes the first guess, they are nevertheless influenced to make their estimate high if the random choice was high, or low if it was low. Likewise, the "availability" heuristic strongly influences human behavior to such an extent that evaluations of traits or estimates of events depend upon the relative availability of relevant information, how readily the information can be recalled, or how graphic the information's associated image is. Subjects usually guess that "r" occurs more frequently as a word's first letter than as a third letter, even when the reverse is true. Subjects do this because we seem to store words, in part, by their initial acoustic sound, making it easier to think of a word beginning with *r* than a word having *r* as a third letter. Though these predispositions produce errors in the special laboratory circumstances in which they are investigated, they are useful heuristic processes to deal with the time and information constraints of the world in which we need to interact. We typically do not have unlimited access to information nor do we have the time to think carefully through many possibilities. The heuristics that lead to errors by the subjects lead to successful management of everyday life. Given the similar evolutionary pressures on rather rapid decision-making by nonhuman animals, it is likely that we will find many of these same proclivities in most animal species as well. For them, the probabilities might entail choosing the foraging area that is frequented both by more tasty prey and by fewer predators who will compete to eat the same prey, or even them.

Spatial biases are also common "mistakes" and are widespread among various species. In the early phases of discrimination learning, many species show a mistaken "position preference"; that is, they tend to choose repeatedly a certain spatial location rather than rely on the correct (often visual) discriminative cue. It is interesting to note here as well how important visual cues are to the human species, the designers of the experiments. Yet, in most of the discrimination experiments, the animals, typically rats or pigeons, are being rewarded with food. Particularly with these creatures, food is likely to be relocated in a previous location; hence, it is reasonable for the subjects to be biased toward choosing a particular place in space.

Space is so important in the lives of animals and humans, even outside the domain of food location, that it is reasonable to expect its strong influence in an organism's focus of attention, the structure of its memory systems, and perhaps even in its communication systems. One would likewise expect a significant portion of brain anatomy to be devoted to its comprehension, analysis, and memory storage. Evidence supports all of these suppositions.

Beginning with neuroanatomical considerations, the considerably sized structure, the hippocampus and/or surrounding tissues, have been implicated in the ability to store spatial memories, in particular those involved in the retention of spatial locations (O'Keefe, 1993). Particular "place cells" fire in the rat hippocampus when the rat is in a specific location in a maze (O'Keefe & Dostrovsky, 1971). A different cell fires for each different general location. In one experiment, a particular place cell was apparently associated with the location of the food reward. This cell continued to fire when the rat was in the place where food ought to be, irrespective of whether food was available in the trial. Furthermore, the place cell fired correctly even when the maze was rotated so that the rat's starting point in the maze changed and the direction it needed to turn to reach the food reward changed (the food was so placed that it always bore the same relation to certain nearby cues with a curtain arranged to obliterate room cues) (O'Keefe and Black, 1978).

Other brain structures are also importantly implicated in spatial memory. Recently, the cerebellum, long thought to be involved primarily with balance and coordination of movement, has been shown to be involved in cognitive processes, particularly those concerned with space.

The tendency to rely on spatial location as a very significant, remembered aspect of the environment and events provides the basis for "the method of loci," an age-old mnemonic device. Using this device, the memorizer strives to associate each item in a list to be remembered with a particular location, perhaps in a room or along a walk. To recall the items, the memorizer then walks through the locations, either physically or figuratively. Given the importance of spatial location in the life of organisms, particularly with respect to location of food and homesite, it is noteworthy that a "mere" insect, the honeybee, has evolved a communication system sophisticated enough to indicate to another bee the distance and direction of food.

Spatial location also figures importantly in the cognitive biases of other species. Consider the various "language" experiments on ape and other species. Although these projects have, for the most part, lost important opportunities to analyze initial mistakes made in "word" learning by the animals, we can find some relevant information (Ristau & Robbins, 1982; Ristau, 1996). We know, for instance, that although the chimpanzees Sherman and Austin tended to associate a lexigram (a colored geometric symbol) with a spatial location, the experimenters intended the lexigram to "mean" a specific tool (Savage-Rumbaugh et al., 1978; discussed in Ristau & Robbins, 1982 and Ristau, 1996).

Other biases or tendencies to selective attention also operate. Another chimpanzee, Washoe, was being taught the sign language for "flower" when presented with a flower. Instead, she seemed to associate the hand sign with "odor," generalizing its usage to pipe tobacco and kitchen fumes (Gardner & Gardner, 1969), and suggesting the importance of olfactory cues to a chimpanzee.

When the previously mentioned apes, Sherman and Austin, did learn the correct use of the lexigrams to mean specific tools, the most effective method of training was a "functional" one rather than a mere association/ labeling one. Seeing the experimenter use the tool, then using the tool themselves to open containers with food, while employing the lexigram to request the tool was essentially the functional method used (Savage-Rumbaugh, op. cit., Ristau & Robbins, op. cit., Ristau, 1996). And Washoe and other young chimpanzees who learned hand signs are reported to have most readily learned the signs for manipulable events/objects (e.g., "on" as used to turn a light switch on and off; "open" as used to open jars, etc.). The same emphasis on function seems to be important in a young child's early understanding of words. Piaget said it most succinctly: to a child, "a hole is to dig" (Piaget & Inhelder, 1969; see also Bruner, 1964).[1] The young child's earliest use of "mama" is considered by most linguists to be holophrastic— a term that means the presence of mama, mama's milk, her warmth all at once. Interpreted from the approach I am suggesting, it is the mother's functions (with respect to the infant) through which the infant forms the understanding of "Mama." These functions are known to the young child through the child's inter*action*: suckling, sensing temperature, and receiving kinesthetic feedback from being held by the mother. The young child incorporates her own bodily actions and sensations into her schema, or loosely interpreted, mental representation of the concept or word.

Note how I am not characterizing the "turning on" of lights or "opening" of doors merely as actions or movements. I think the critical matter is not that the child or chimp is making movements in the process of word learning. Rather, these movements are intrinsic to the meaning of the "word;" they indicate the essential function of the word with which they are associated.

I shall return to this theme repeatedly. I suggest that many understandings of the world, particularly for prelinguistic humans, and presumably for nonhuman animals, are very much *functionally* defined. Many things and many events appear to be understood based on the functions they serve, especially with respect to the organism.

## What Does an Organism Understand about Inanimate Objects?

Let us first consider studies of children's understanding of inanimate objects. Object permanence, conservation of mass, volume, and number as well as other attributes have been researched first by Piaget, and then by others (e.g., Gelman & Gallistel, 1978; Carey, 1987). Piagetian developmental concepts and methods have also been used by primatologists (e.g., Chevalier-Skolnikoff, 1974), though not without considerable controversy over the interpretation of the results.

Let us consider in some detail the phenomenon of object permanence, whereby an object, after it is no longer immediately present (e.g., if it is covered and thus out of sight) is still considered to exist. Let us examine this phenomenon from the vantage point of the usefulness of object permanence in the animal's or young child's understanding of its world. In other words, let us examine this phenomenon from both an ecological and a functional perspective.

Experimental studies with dogs and cats provide evidence that these animals can achieve object permanence (Dore & Dumas, 1987). However, these results are clearly not readily obtained in all circumstances nor for all species. For example, informal observations with a considerable number of species of dogs indicate, contrary to our intuitions, that dogs that have been shown a toy in which they evince interest do not then search for it when it is hidden before their eyes underneath a blanket or other object (D. Ingle, pers. comm.). They do not even search when there is an obvious lump in the blanket. Yet, in more natural ecological conditions, dogs and other predatory species need to have some object permanence in order to continue searching for prey they are following. Apropos of this problem, human infants as young as four months are reported to show surprise and spend longer time periods looking when a moving object goes behind an obstruction and then either reappears at the other side at the "wrong" time (given its speed and direction) or simply doesn't reappear (Gelman & Kit-Fong, 1996): This capacity occurs long before a child is deemed to achieve object permanence in standard Piagetian tests. Piagetians consider that full object permanence is achieved at about 18 months of age, but more recent research suggests much younger children have these abilities (e.g., Spelke et al., as discussed in chapter 3).

Why do we see these discrepancies in results? In part, testing circumstances vary among the dogs in what appear to be biologically significant ways. When a predator pursues prey, the "object" is moving, in fact moving autonomously, and the predator is actively engaged in pursuit. Standard tests for object permanency, however, typically use stationary objects or objects moved slowly from one location to another nearby location by the experimenter. A similar critique can be made for the differential infant responding in the "obstruction of moving object" versus standard object permanence tests.[2] The fact that the critical difference may lie in the movement of the object may have particular significance because movement, particularly autonomous movement, appears to be one of the very important characteristics distinguishing children's designation of objects that are "alive" versus "not-alive" objects (see later discussion). More simply, it may be the case, as Piaget himself suggested, that a falling or moving object so strongly engages the child's attention that the child continues to remain engaged even for a while after the object is not in view.

We should also consider the nature of the abilities involved in the various instances of infant's "object permanence." Are these capacities the same in different circumstances, or are they substantially different from the array of component abilities inherent in what we term "adult human object permanence?" What of the nature of object permanence in other species? The data suggest a cognitive model for understanding object permanence that is designed for predation. An organism may thus exhibit object permanence a "predator-prey" domain, but could not be considered to have that appreciation in other domains or abstractly (see modularity approaches as discussed by Fodor, 1983; Rozin, 1976). The "predator-prey" domain may, in fact, be more properly construed as the domain of "animate/alive" versus "not animate/not alive." Whatever the proper specification of the domain (*if*, indeed, this is the most appropriate conceptualization) in Rozin's words, the organisms do not have "access to the cognitive unconscious," nor do they have the understanding operable in another domain; the understanding has not been made conscious.

It may also be that "object permanence" is simply too sophisticated a concept for the abilities described. Some animals when strongly engaged may be able to predict the "directedness" of biologically important ("alive") objects when they are motivated to do so. The human infant may have this ability more generally, not needing to be engaged in predatory pursuit to expect a temporarily obstructed moving object to reappear. As previously noted, Piaget considered that the infant's attention could be captured by a moving or falling object, so he treated the child's abilities under such conditions differently from those exhibited in the standard (stationary) "object permanence" tests. Perhaps biological relevance could be manipulated in "object permanence" tests with dogs. The "toy" could, in some conditions, simulate a moving prey object for a hungry species of hunting dog, for example. The prey could also be merely a stationary "toy" in others.

It is also possible that for many species, "object permanence," or whatever else the capacity should be termed, is so closely tied to a domain-specific ability that many other characteristics/stimuli associated with the phenomenon in natural ecological circumstances are influencing outcomes in the confines of the laboratory experiment. For example, for at least some species of dogs, perhaps the substrate under which the "toy" or other object of interest is hidden is of particular importance. A dog may search for an object hidden under dirt while ignoring objects under other coverings. By standard tests, the dogs would not be judged to have "object permanence" in the latter condition. Perhaps, hiding done by the dog rather than hiding done by the experimenter is a significant variable. In short, for objects that are not moving rapidly (i.e., are not "prey"), the dog may expect that hidden objects ("bones") were placed by the dog himself under dirt. Nothing of interest ought to be under a piece of cloth. Species may differ in these regards, and past learning may overcome these tendencies. Strong odors may overcome these tendencies for a hungry dog. Experiments with birds that cache seeds (marsh tits and chickadees) have shown that hiding done by the birds rather than by the experimenter does indeed influence the birds' accuracy in remembering the storage sites (Shettleworth & Krebs, 1986).

It is also possible that the dog's apparent disinclination to uncover a toy hidden by the experimenter may be due to social relationships. A human is usually dominant over a dog. The dominant human hides a bone or interesting object and, understandably, the dog is hesitant to take that bone (suggestion by C. Allen, ed.; see also D. Cummins, this volume). To explore this possibility, one could manipulate the situation so as to facilitate the dog's "permission" to take the bone. For example, the object used could be the dog's own toy, or the human could leave after hiding the bone.

The social interaction inherent in an "object permanence" test could be yet more complex as suggested by work of Miklosi and Csányi (1997). Their results from dogs, children, and college students, suggest the paradigm is being construed as a "game" with rules to follow. The game is "look behind each of the barriers" . . . this is done even in the condition when *no* object is hidden.

Object permanence must also be involved when a parent bird or other species continues to search for lost offspring that are unseen and unheard during the searching. In my own field experiments with plovers, a type of shorebird, a parent may continue to search for 15 minutes or longer after we have turned off a loudspeaker projecting chick distress calls. In this case, the immediate so-called "object," was a sound.

When investigating "naturalistic object permanence," the use of a biological perspective might be more fruitful than the typical variations employed by most experimental psychologists. Likewise, comparisons should be made to the laboratory learning literature. For example, the "delayed match to sample" laboratory procedure *may* be properly analogous to the disappearance and subsequent reappearance of a prey insect under a leaf. In the delay procedure, the subject is presented with a "sample" object and then, after a delay, presented with either a single object or a pair of objects. The subject then has to choose the one similar to the sample (or inhibit response to the incorrect choice when only one object is available). It may be relevant to note that the "sample" in these studies is typically associated with food reward (if matched appropriately). Are the experimenters thereby evoking a "prey object permanence" module (if such exists)? Would presenting a moving sample produce positive matches more readily and in more species, especially if the choice were located in an appropriate position along the path of the moving sample? Does the response required of the dog indicate its choice affect outcomes. Might biting at the choice produce more correct responses than pressing a panel in another location with its nose or paw? Does the use of stimuli that more closely resemble typical prey result in better performance?

Alternatively, when displaying stationary presentations, are we making the task much more difficult by setting the sample and the choice(s) in different locations? Previous research using looking time measures has shown that infants of four months can individuate two similar objects placed in different locations (see chapter 3 by Hauser and Carey and chapter 4 by Wynn, this volume). It is likely that animals and infants given the "delayed match to sample" procedure are simultaneously facing the unintended task of object individuation as well. Placing the sample and choices in the same location might reveal more rapid learning of the "match to sample" and toleration of longer delay times. Note also that when we compare organisms' successes on a "delayed match to sample" task and the standard "object permanence" task, we are contrasting results achieved, typically, after hundreds of trials to results attained after only a few trials).

There is yet another perspective. Should we be using the term "object permanence" at all? Are we actually exploring the animal's or young infant's understanding of the continued "existence" of an object? We surely cannot mean that the entire world disappears for a very young infant when she turns her head or blinks her eyes. The infant of any age is not surprised to find that the rest of the world is still there when she turns her head back again. Neither is she surprised when she either crawls past or is carried past an obstruction and the rest of the world reappears at the other side (S. Larson, pers. comm.). Perhaps a more accurate description of most tests of object permanence is that they are assessments of both the child's developing ability to maintain attention to objects and the child's comprehension of the physics of objects. Actual object permanence might better be construed, as suggested by Spelke (1994), an innate given, present in the infant's (and probably most animals') first perceptions of objects (see previous discussion of Spelke's work in chapter 3, this volume).

We may still ask why this characteristic of an object is a "primitive." It is possible that evolutionary pressures such as those arising from predator-prey interactions may have been an important impetus to such early development of object constancy. Still speculating, we can further expand Spelke's idea to suggest that humans and most animals may be constructed to assume stability and constancy, not disappearance and change. In other words, they should detect deviations from the assumed (i.e., detect change). Many constructions of at least the vertebrate nervous system support this interpretation. Change in retinal stimulation is required to maintain neural responding. Habituation to sensory input in other modalities—auditory, olfactory, pressure—also occurs rapidly. We even assume constancy when viewing rapidly changing stimuli (Grime, 1995 as reported by Dennett, 1996).

In summary, I have explored the concept of "object permanence," particularly as it functions for animals in the natural environment, taking predator-prey interactions as one example. Looking time and time spent searching can function as measures in lab and field studies of animals and nonverbal children. I questioned why tests that use moving stimuli suggest earlier acquisition of "object permanence" than do tests with stationary stimuli. A few possible interpretations of these results are: a "predator-prey" domain-specific ability has been engaged; moving stimuli capture attention better than do stationary ones; or, per Spelke, "object permanence" is a primitive given for children (and probably for most animals). I then suggest that these seemingly disparate views may be intertwined in the evolutionary development of object permanence. Finally, I suggest that in most studies that appear to be relevant to object permanence, we are instead exploring the infants' or animals' understanding of the physics of objects, as well as characteristics of the organisms' attention and memory. In all, exploring animals' and infants' understandings of the physical world from an evolutionary and ethological vantage point can suggest radically different ways both to conceptualize these understandings and to investigate them experimentally.

## What Does an Organism Understand about Animate Objects?

First, how do we know that an organism considers another organism to be animate? The classic work on this subject is Piaget's. In his view, children less than 10 years old overattribute characteristics of animacy. They interpret many physical phenomena in terms of intentional states in the inanimate objects involved. Indeed, all of us have probably witnessed a child of three years or so engaged in an interaction such as the following: a child collides with a table corner, then he angrily hits the table while scolding it for hurting him. Piaget considers that *intentional causation* is a child's earlier interpretation of causation, while *mechanical causation* is a much later understanding. These interpretations, though providing an important framework for much research, have undergone revision in contemporary developmental psychology studies.

In fascinating work by Carey (1987), children's understandings of "alive" have been examined, using a variety of methods. The essential phenomenon is that children overattribute the quality of being "alive," judging many nonliving things to be alive. Piaget and others, in particular, Laurendeau and Pinard (1962), describe about five stages in the development of the meaning of "alive" to the child. Initially, the child appears to have no concept, making random judgements about what is and is not alive; then, "alive" is exemplified by activity of any sort; finally, "alive" is exemplified by autonomous movement only. Carey (1987), by more precise analysis of children's responses, shows that although movement is a major criterion for being "alive," it is not the only one. Sometimes anthropomorphic similarities are used to justify a judgement of "alive;" a child judges and describes a table as "alive" because it has legs. The child's growing general biological knowledge helps it to more correctly label things as alive or not. Sometimes the child, especially an older one of about 10 years, appears to interpret the experimenter's question differently in terms of intent, using the "alive-not alive" distinction to mean, for example, alive-dead, real-imaginary, real object-photo, or existent-extinct. In her studies, Carey also distinguishes between a concept the child may have and the word onto which the concept may be mapped. For the arguments of the present chapter, I wish to emphasize Carey's stress on activity, particularly autonomous activity, in the young child's notion of "alive." Second, the importance (to a child and to an animal) of conceptualizations that overlap only partially with our human adult concept of "alive."

Thus far, this discussion has concerned children who have at least minimal linguistic competence, but how do we explore nonverbal infants' and animals' understandings? (See chapter 3, this volume, for discussion of infant primates' understanding of animate motion).

We might expect an organism not only to investigate some inanimate object, but also to attempt to communicate with, or to escape from, an animate object. Yet, it is also true that an effective fail-safe or default mechanism for a prey animal in an uncertain situation would be to react as though the unknown object were alive, possibly predacious, especially if the object had even a few characteristics of an animate being. Thus, it would be a sensible evolutionary adaptation for a prey to flee or to engage in antipredator behaviors if it encountered a rolling rock. Indeed, in pilot studies, I have observed that a piping plover, on its first interaction with a moving cardboard box (on a radio controlled miniature dune buggy) in the general region of its nest/young, initially gave a broken wing display to the box, much as the plover does to a human intruder or to natural predators. Note how, in these instances, the significant determination might have been whether the encountered object was predacious rather than "alive." The plover's behaviors suggest a time honored kind of experimentation used by the early ethologists and developed by comparative psychologists: create artificial models, in this case of animate objects, and by adding and deleting characteristics, determine which are most salient to the organism.

Such experiments may lead us to understand what characteristics provoke parenting, antipredator, or predacious responses, but they do not necessarily answer the question of which sort of objects an organism considers to be animate. Perhaps the question is wrong. There is no good reason to think that many organisms, or even young infants for that matter, need to have a concept of animate. Nor, lacking a "concept," must they be able to separate animate objects from inanimate. Organisms *do* need to know the biological significance of the object, whether it is safe or dangerous, whether it is food, whether it is a parent, an offspring, or a potential mate. All of these matter at different times of organisms' existences. This raises a theme I shall repeat. The most appropriate question to ask about the understanding of an animal or young child may be a biologically based, functional one. What is the object likely to do to and for the child/animal? How is the child/animal to interact with it?

One way a child interacts with at least some animate creatures is by imitation. Meltzoff (1995) studied imitation 18-month-old children. As discussed later in more detail, the children had the opportunity first to observe adult humans who had a specific goal with a toy (e.g., pulling apart a dumbbell), and second, to see a similar goal-directed action by a mechanical device. The device contained a pair of pincers that pulled at the dumbbell ends just as the human's fingers did. It did not, however, look "robot-like." The children spontaneously imitated the human, but would not imitate the mechanical device.

What, or who, precisely are the children choosing to imitate? We know that they do imitate their parents, but can we specify the model's characteristics that inspire imitation? Special bonding with the model may facilitate imitation, but such bonding is not required; these children imitated an unknown human experimenter. Would a very good model of a dog serve as a model? What about a well-known figure from children's television, such as Big Bird from Sesame Street, or a robot that looked more humanoid or that gave the child treats? In short, it makes good survival sense for a child in the real world to imitate parents, kin, and friends who are concerned with the wellbeing of the child. Of course, in the real world those creatures are humans.

To summarize, in trying to investigate what an organism considers to be animate, I noted the child's tendencies to attribute animacy and mental states even to inanimate objects. Explorations of children's linguistic understanding of "alive" (Carey, 1987) reveal that they use a highly varied set of criteria, although autonomous movement is prime among them. Nonlinguistic studies emphasize the biological significance of animate objects in the organism's understanding—it seems more important to know how to respond to and interact with an animate object than to be concerned about criteria for animacy versus inanimacy. A fail-safe mechanism for most species would be to interact with an unknown object as though it were animate, and probably predacious. Meltzoff's (1995) work on selective imitation by children suggests the model available for imitation needs to have certain characteristics—we know little as yet about such characteristics except that children imitate a human adult (an animate and friendly creature) and do not imitate a specific mechanical device. The use of models with variable characteristics pertaining to animacy and biological significance promises to be a fruitful means to explore these problems. Engagement with the models could be evaluated by such measures as looking time, following, natural classes of interaction (e.g., attempts to mate or flee), and by tendencies to imitate.

## *What Purposes Might Another Have?*

Folk psychological ideas have been applied to the behavior of human adults, children, and animals, not without controversy (e.g. Michel, 1991; Stich, 1991), but not without heuristic value either. Most useful, at least for the study of animals, has been the application of a restricted set of terms, in particular, those of "belief/desire" intentional terms (Ristau, 1983) that have been the concern of numerous philosophers as well (Bennett, Dennett, Searle among others). Since the use of mentalistic terms such as "want" and "belief" when studying animals still provokes great controversy among comparative and experimental psychologists, in the interest of promoting constructive communication, I strongly encourage all those who might become unduly upset to consider my use of these terms merely as heuristic devices. To do so is not my stance, but it is a possible one.

As I have previously discussed, I think the notion of a "purpose" or "wanting" is a biologically potent one (Ristau, 1988). Other intentional terms such as "guess" and "hope" are far more difficult to apply to animals' cognizing. In fact, such terms are so difficult, perhaps even impossible, that I will, for the present, ignore them. But for an organism to "want to do something," or in proper intentional idiom "to want it to be that case that" has its roots in evolution; it is a viable comparative concept, a viable ontogenetic one.

Developmentally, many needs of infants, human and otherwise, are carefully "programmed." A hungry infant of mammalian species typically manages to get to a nipple. The stimulated mother or the stimulated nipple, via hormonal intercession, such as oxytocin, squirts milk into the infant's mouth. Gradually, the reflexive hold is loosened, and the developing child, with the same biological "want," has a variety of means to obtain a variety of foods. Eventually language aids the process as well. If we grant that looking at animals' cognizing from an intentional stance might be fruitful, how do we as scientists determine which purposes another species, or even an infant, might have? A concern that has been raised is that belief/desire theory drastically underdetermines an organism's belief and/or desire (i.e., a belief-desire pair and the associated behavior admits of too many possibilities). To help constrain the possibilities, Bennett (1991) stresses the importance of the environment. Instead of a triad, he proposes grounding the possibilities in a "environment-belief-desire-behavior" quadrangle. The "environment" is the stimulus characteristics or the contexts of the behaviors.

I think there is another approach which is also useful. It may well be the case that for many organisms there either are a restricted number of possible purposes. At the very least, we can progress to understand the animals by dealing with a restricted number.

When viewed from this perspective, W. J. Smith's (1977) work analyzing the kinds of messages found in the signaling systems of diverse species, including birds and mammals, presaged this concern. Smith determined that there were a limited number of messages, including identity of species, of sex, and, for many species, of the individual. Many messages were concerned with the probability and nature of the vocalizer's behavioral tendencies (e.g., locomotion, approach, flight, aggression); some were, in a sense, imperative (e.g., approach if you are an unmated female). One can thus consider very many of these to be expressive of "purposes" (what the signaler wants or intends to do), in some general sense. The purposes are, for the most part, intentions with respect to the communicator or with respect to the recipient of the signal.

In some cases, the term "purpose" may be too complicated and not necessary to describe the understandings involved. "Behavioral tendencies" would be the term preferred by W. J. Smith in the foregoing analysis, particularly because tendencies are more readily tied to observable behaviors. In other cases, an alternative to claiming to understand another's "purpose" in some situations is, instead, to understand another's direction of movement. Such knowledge appears to be quite primitive, both ontogenetically and evolutionarily (recall discussion of an infants' "surprise" when a temporarily obstructed moving object reappears at the wrong time). A later ontogenetic and evolutionary development is the recognition that there is an endpoint or goal to the movement and that another can have an *intended* direction and endpoint. This last idea seems to be the same as the notion of "directedness" that Tomasello and Call (1997) suggest suffices to describe the understandings apes and monkeys may have of another.

Some experiments have investigated human infants' understanding of purpose. In one study, human infants about 18 months old seem to understand a human adult's purpose while manipulating objects, even if the adult is thwarted and does not accomplish the apparent goal (Meltzoff, 1995). In the experiments, some infants watched adults perform simple procedures with each of five toys (e.g., a disk with a hole that fits over a post; two blocks that could be pulled off a bar that connects them, etc.). Others saw the adults try but fail to perform a procedure, and still others saw the adults handle the toys, but not attempt the procedures. The rest of the infants saw the toys, but saw no demonstration of any sort. The children spontaneously imitated the adults' *intended* goal action, whether the adult had accomplished it or not (average of 76% and 80% of the times, respectively). In only 20% and 24% of the respective occasions did the children produce the procedures if they had seen either an adult randomly manipulate the toy or no adult with the toy at all. This technique of studying spontaneous imitation may also be used to reveal an animal's understanding of a goal. Such investigations have been attempted with primates and other species, though the ability to imitate goal-directed behavior may be limited to certain primates and birds (e.g., gray parrots as studied by Moore, 1996). Songs, however, are readily imitated by conspecifics such as whales and many *species* of birds.

To summarize briefly, the study of animal purposes is likely to be a promising direction of research because animals need to perform goal-directed behavior to survive. Changes to increase flexibility, voluntary control, and any forethought constitute gradations in the development of full-fledged, conscious, planned, intentional purposes sometimes held by human beings.

### "Here's Lookin' at You, Kid"

Creatures, all of us, are very much concerned with whether another's goals/purposes involve ourselves. We need not even conceptualize the problem with terms like "self." As the first step to understand another's possible interest in us, we and many other creatures are built both to be extremely capable of detecting eyes and to be very sensitive to the direction in which the eyes are gazing. In particular, we are very adept at determining whether another's eyes are gazing toward ourselves. If the eyes are not looking our way, then, as an automatic response, we and other organisms turn our eyes to the target of another's gaze (Baron-Cohen, 1994; Baron-Cohen, Tager-Flusberg & Cohen, 1993).

These sensitivities to eye direction are part of what Gopnik and Meltzoff (1997) have termed nature's innate solution to the problem of "Other Minds" or, more accurately, to the *content* of other minds. Infants come to know much about the contents of another's mind not through philosophizing, but, according to Gopnik, through early imitation. The approach has been termed "kinesthetic-visual matching." As described by Mitchell, Parker, and Boccia (1994), it "serves as a foundation for role reversal, empathy, perspective taking and theory of mind." I shall deal briefly with these matters later. Actually, easy detectability of eyes is even more primitive than the abilities called for by Gopnik.

What precisely can be learned by monitoring another's gaze; at what age and in what species can the learning take place? Butterworth has studied this problem with young human children (1991) and others have conducted research with birds and nonhuman primates. Let us begin with some of the most basic questions.

### Does an Organism Monitor Another's Gaze toward Itself?

Is an organism particularly attentive and responsive to another's eye gaze towards itself?

For human infants and adults, and indeed for many species, eye gaze directed to oneself can have powerful emotional effects. A nursing infant may either fret if its mother breaks eye contact, or it may nip the nipple providing milk. In a tense situation, such as the presence of a stranger, an older infant may burst into tears until reestablishing eye contact with its mother. For humans past puberty, a certain sort of gaze across a crowded room can be a most effective form of invitation.

A potential predator gazing toward prey can cause the prey to engage in prolonged defensive behavior; the same predator not looking toward the prey provokes a much more minimal reponse. Relevant experimental data derive from hognose snakes. These snakes take longer to recover from "death feigning" when an intruder, one meter away, looks directly at them, than when the intruder averts his eyes. The snakes feign death an even shorter time if the human intruder leaves (Burghardt, 1991; Burghardt & Greene, 1988). The entire process leading to quiescent death feigning can be quite elaborate, including writhing, anal discharges, a bloody mouth with the tongue hanging out, and rolling over. A less elaborate display, termed "tonic immobility," has also been shown in lab experiments with chickens (Gallup, Cummings, & Nash, 1972) and anoles (Hennig, 1977) to be more prolonged in the presence of an intruder who stares at the animal as compared to behavior when the intruder is not looking at the animal.

## Does an Organism Monitor Another's Gaze to a Target Other Than Oneself?

We humans are considered to be extremely capable of detecting eyes and their direction of gaze, particularly if that gaze is directed towards ourselves. If the eyes are looking elsewhere, we automatically turn our gaze to the target of another's gaze. Are other species similarly capable?

## What Do We Know of the Sensitivity of Other Species to the Direction of Another's Gaze?

The role of gaze in anti-predator behaviors of a ground-nesting shorebird, the piping plover, was studied in field experiments (Ristau, 1991). In this work, differently dressed intruders walked along the beach on a path parallel to the dunes where the plovers nested. The paths were at considerable distances from the dunes, ranging from about 15 to 25 meters. One intruder consistently scanned the dunes (and hence the nest region) while walking. The other, instead, scanned the ocean.

Before each trial began, a parent bird was on the nest. It left as the intruder walked along the beach, staying away from the nest longer when the intruder who gazed toward its nest walked by than when the intruder who looked away from the nest walked by. Time off the nest is here considered to be a measure of the bird's arousal. A calm bird of this species or one who is minimally agitated, remains seated on the nest. It should be noted, also, that the bird had available cues other than gaze direction, for example orientation of the head and upper torso, so that eye gaze may not have been the (only) relevant cue. Also, since the intruder began walking while the parent sat on the nest, the human therefore did, at some point, look in the direction of both the bird and nest. However, the start point was far away from bird and nest, some 125 to 150 meters or more.

Data gathered during other experiments with piping plovers indicate additional behaviors dependent upon the intruder's direction of gaze and/ or movement (Ristau, 1991). The birds often perform broken-wing displays as a human intruder approaches their nest or young. In the display, the birds lean to the side and drag their wings along the ground, often vocalizing raucously. Before beginning such a display, the birds will walk away from the nest and sometimes fly to another location. When the plovers' locations of display were examined, we found that in all available cases, the plovers not only flew to be closer to the intruder, but in *85% of the cases flew to be closer to the center of the intruder's visual field*. Note that the birds could have used information from direction of the intruder's movement and general body orientation, as well as direction of eye gaze, to choose locations for display. The data do support an interpretation that plovers detect and respond to the direction of an intruder's gaze (or behaviors typically associated with gaze direction) even when that gaze is directed to a target other than themselves (i.e., their nest).

Other species are also reported to have the capacity to follow another's gaze. Evidence derives from observations in the wild, particularly of primates, including some species of monkeys. Observations of some captive and home-reared chimpanzees also provide data. For example, Plooij (1978) noted that chimps in the wild followed his gaze as well as gazes of their conspecifics. Those who have home-reared or captive chimpanzees report that the apes follow humans' gaze to targets.

Since, as with the plover studies, there are typically multiple cues to the direction in which an organism is gazing (e.g., head and torso direction), a well controlled lab experiment in which head direction and eye direction can be separately manipulated is useful. Povinelli had five to six year-old chimpanzees each observe a human who looked to a location above and behind the chimpanzee. In one condition, the human moved both eyes and head, while in the other, the human kept his head still and moved his eyes. Both situations were adequate to provoke the chimpanzee to look where the human was looking, approximately equally in both conditions.

The situation is slightly different with monkeys. There are numerous instances of monkeys in the wild being reported to follow the gaze of another. However, in one well controlled laboratory study of monkeys, specifically capuchin moneys (Anderson, Sallaberry, & Barbier, 1995), the monkeys were not able to use human eye direction to select successfully the one of two containers baited with food. Other cues, such as touching the baited container, were effective. Yet in another laboratory study, monkeys did at least respond to direction of eye gaze by changing their own eye gaze direction (Tomasello & Colleagues, 1996, pers. comm). In this study, two rhesus monkeys were seated facing each other, while the experimenter was up in an observation tower, facing the back of one monkey. When one monkey looked, the other turned and followed its gaze.

### What Precisely Can Be Learned Through Monitoring Another's Gaze; At What Age?

Butterworth and his colleagues have studied this problem with young human children, ranging in age from 6 months to 18 months, a period encompassing, as he sees it, three stages in the development of joint visual attention (Butterworth, 1991; Butterworth & Cochran, 1980; Butterworth & Jarrett, 1980). He and others suggest that this ability enables a "meeting of the minds" in the same object.

In the experiments, mother and infant are seated face to face in the center of a room with an undistracting environment. Pairs of identical objects are placed at various positions to the left and right of the room. The mother is instructed to interact with her child and then, when signaled, to turn, silently and without pointing, to look at a designated object. The entire episode is videotaped for later analysis.

At six months old, babies look to the correct side of the room, but cannot tell which of two identical targets on that side the mother is looking at. Basically, they are accurate in locating the object if it is closest to Mom as they scan away from her. Furthermore, for babies to localize, the targets need to be within their own visual field, not behind the babies. It's not that the infants cannot turn; they do, for instance, to localize a noise. It could be interesting to explore more fully the infants' comprehension of the space behind them. Would they turn to see the source of a squirt of water, a beam of light in a dusty, darkened room where the particles in the air are lit by that beam, or later merely to a beam shining on a few objects along its path, or to follow a moving object which mother continues to watch as it begins within the infants frontal gaze and then moves behind the infant? Would the size or nature of the object influence the infants' gaze?

Continuing the developmental story, at 12 months, infants *begin* to localize objects correctly, whether first or second along the scan path away from the mother, so long as the target is stationary. They still do not search for objects behind them, even if their visual field is devoid of objects.

By 18 months, babies are equally correct whether the object is first or second along their scan line away from mother. Now they will search behind them if there is nothing in front of them (i.e., objects in view grab their attention; they *cannot* successfully *inhibit* attention to them).

We might also ask what feature of eye gaze is necessary for joint visual attention? Eye movements are not, for correct orientation occurs even with sunglasses on the "model" (Butterworth, 1996). Of course, even the youngest infant has been exposed to the simultaneous cues of eye movements, head turning, and often upper torso turns, so it is reasonable that any one of these cues might serve to direct the infant's attention. Also, sunglasses do not provide conflicting information to the infant; if anything, they may accentuate the position of the eye region. It could be interesting to investigate the infant's ability to rely on direction of pupil gaze when it conflicts with the direction the head is turned.

We should also recognize, as the philosopher Gordon (1992, 1995) cautions, that the seemingly simple task of joint gaze is more complicated than it first appears. Our determination of the "target" of another's gaze very much depends upon what is *salient* to us in the other's line of gaze. In Butterworth's experiments, the experimental rooms were so barren and devoid of objects that there was little to compete for salience other than the presumably interesting object chosen by the researchers. Salience depends upon our biases and interests unless we are sophisticated enough to make adjustments for the others' biases. For the youngest organisms, it may be that simple heuristics, like the item that is closest to the model in the model's line of gaze are dominant over other possibilities. I do not know, but I would surmise that, for even younger infants, objects closest to the infant have dominance.

In brief, the stages in the infant's capacity to develop joint visual attention suggest cognitive aspects of this task not otherwise obvious. The fact that a young infant selectively turns to acoustic stimuli behind itself, but does not do so when mother gazes at an object behind the infant, also suggests a certain isolation of the acoustic and visual systems from each other, even developmentally. The stages in developing human, joint visual attention and the separation of visual and acoustic sytems likewise suggests that one should investigate the possibililty among species of different sensory systems supporting differential cognitive capacities. A case in point is the superiority in rats of some olfactory-based learning over learning that relies on visual information (Eichenbaum & Otto, 1993).

### Can Strategic Use of Directed Gaze Be Used to Achieve Social Goals and Deception?

More advanced than joint visual attention to an object is the primate's apparent voluntary and strategic use of directed gaze. Consider the following example:

> Subadult male ME attacks one of the young juveniles who screams repeatedly, pursuing ME while screaming (this is common when aid has just been successfully solicited). Adult male HL and several other adults run over the hill into view, giving aggressive pantgrunt calls; ME, seeing them coming, stands on hindlegs and stares into the distance across the valley. HL and the newcomers stop and look in this direction; they do not threaten or attack ME. No predator or baboon troop can be seen through 10 X 40 binoculars. (Example No. 73, Byrne & Whiten, 1985, chacma baboons)

Chimpanzees have been reported to use directed gaze apparently to avoid an altercation. As reported by Frans de Waal, one of two interacting chimpanzees looked studiously at the ground. The potential aggressor did likewise, and soon the tensions abated sufficiently so that a grooming episode began, further alleviating the stress (1982).

### Does an Organism Understand What Is Required for Another to See?

Being able to use information dependent upon another's eye gaze does *not*, however, also imply that the organism understands much of what is required for another individual to see. Thus, young chimpanzees who used the direction in which a human trainer looked in order to choose a goody-filled box rather than an empty one, nevertheless did not remove a neckerchief tied around the eyes of the human in that context (Povinelli & Eddy, 1996). But these data continue to support a notion that eye direction, and the typically associated direction of head and torso, are primitive information givers. To realize that the eyes are needed for the other to gather information (e.g., the location of the goodies) requires a different and more advanced kind of understanding.

Relation of Directed Gaze to Social Referencing—I Wanna Go Where You Go, Do What You Do, and I'll Be Happy.

Eye gaze also plays an important role in "social referencing." Broadly defined, social referencing is the process whereby an individual checks another's facial expression, including direction of attention, to obtain information.

Social referencing can help a juvenile, a rhesus monkey in the following example, to determine its emotional response in an ambiguous situation. I refer to an observation, similar to others reported in the literature, in which I stood before a caged rhesus monkey mother and her juvenile offspring. The mother stared directly at me, bared her teeth in a grimace, and screamed. The young monkey looked repeatedly and rapidly back and forth between me and its mother, and then also stared at me and screamed, apparently taking the cue for its behavior from the mother.

Other relevant work investigates how it is that wild monkeys are frightened of snakes, but lab-reared monkeys are not (Cook & Mineka, 1989). In a videotaped sequence used in the experiment, an adult monkey, seeing a live snake, shrieked, fear-grimaced, and otherwise behaved as frightened monkeys do. The subjects, lab-reared monkeys, viewed the videotaped model, apparently reacting either to a snake or to a bouquet of artificial flowers. The subjects, who had not previously been exposed to either snakes or flowers, learned to respond with fright to the snake, but not to the flowers. Without this experience, the monkeys did not respond fearfully to a videotaped or live snake. Thus, in this episode, innate predispositions caused the naive monkeys to learn to be afraid of snakes but not flowers. It would be of interest to specify, if possible, the particular characteristics of the snake and flowers that caused the subject monkeys to behave as they did. For example, does the feared object need to resemble a live snake very exactly, or are characteristics such as movement the critical ones?

Experiments with human children as young as nine-months-old also demonstrate the process of social referencing. The babies observed an adult human looking inside each of two boxes, saying, "yuk," with a look of disgust when looking inside one, and smiling delightedly (apparently) at the contents of the other. The nine-month-olds, but not seven-month-olds, selectively and happily played with the toys that had provoked smiles and did not choose to play with the others (Gopnik & Meltzoff, 1997).

Some consider that at least some of these situations require that the "learner" have an understanding about the other's belief. But it is not clear that the cognition involved in the above imitating requires such an assumption. An understanding about the other's belief *may* sometimes be involved. It behooves us scientists to devise, if possible, methods to determine what is involved in each instance.

As do some other investigators (e.g., Gopnik, Meltzoff, Parker, Boccia, & Mitchell), I believe that innate, hardwired phenomena are importantly responsible for at least some of the effects just described. Some aspects may be similar to the process of "social facilitation" or "social contagion." An example common to many species, even humans, is that of a well-fed organism who begins to eat again when other conspecifics do.

In some circumstances, the process might better be termed "mood contagion," though this is a label, not an explanation. When distress spreads among group members, it may be that merely experiencing another's distress itself causes distress. That is not likely to be the explanation for all emotions; experiencing another's anger, for example, might cause one to be frightened rather than angry. *How* do we differentiate experimentally between these two possibilities, social/mood contagion versus social referencing. In fact, there is probably a gradation of possibilities, rather than just these two. An emotional response that results from a reasoned, logical appraisal of the situation is yet another alternative.

The case of the young monkey looking between both me and its mother is probably more advanced than mere mood contagion. To test this, one could devise a live situation with two intruders unknown to the infant. One of the intruders would be an ally or comfortable, familiar creature to the mother, and the other would be a stranger. Observing the infant's behavior would reveal whether it simply becomes generally fearful or copies the mother's response to each individual.

Some factors that could influence the potency of social referencing include: the social relationship between the observer and the referenced "other;" the emotional or motivational state and interest/attention of the observer (e.g., if hungry, the observer might well be more likely to learn and react as the other does when selecting food); the novelty of the situation; and, the past history of the observer in similar situations.

An adaptive function of social facilitation and social referencing is creating a similar "mood" or affect among members of a conspecific group, and facilitating coordination and integration of similar behaviors in the group. Again, akin to precise imitation with visual-kinesthetic matching, social facilitation helps solve the problem of knowing other minds by putting everyone into the *same mind*.

## Other Forms of Mind Reading

In addition to being in the same mind, an organism can be acutely responsive to the needs of another. Mothers of many species are "wired up" to be very responsive to their offspring. Thus, when a baby cries, a listener, especially a female, and more especially a female who has already had offspring, becomes somewhat disconcerted and distressed.[3] Such results were obtained in experiments conducted in an office job setting from acoustic playbacks of infants' crying. Ongoing work was disrupted as described. In short, the human is motivated to act to stop the crying. Nursing mothers are programmed physiologically in other ways. For many new mothers, *any* baby's cries will provoke a milk ejection reflex, though gradually, the stimuli that elicit the response become more restricted.

Attunement to a rhythm can synchronize behaviors. An interacting, vocalizing human mother and baby develop a rhythmic pattern of turn-taking. Rhythmic attunement is a part of many successful social interactions. Some interactions are intimate, like love-making or dancing; others are less intimate, such as walking or otherwise locomoting together. Sharing a rhythm, we know that we can tell very rapidly when our mate is "out of sorts," whereas we may not be so readily able to detect moods in someone else. I do not think it is a case necessarily of using a longer list of experiences to reason from; it is something we determine unconsciously, and then simply "know." If pressed, we can sometimes introspect sufficiently to describe a set of subtle behaviors that reflect the different mood.

The importance of a special bond arises repeatedly in issues of development. Studies of turn-taking and attunement in early social/communicative interactions between a mother and child have been conducted by Stern and colleagues (1985). Inadequately "bonded" mother-infant pairs show poorer development of these various skills. It has been argued that bonding between the researcher and subject is important even in the artificial "language learning" of apes (Ristau & Robbins, 1982; Ristau 1996, in press), and in the special abilities that human-reared apes may possess. Some researchers have suggested that a positive relationship between researcher and subject likewise has impacts on the results obtained in typical experimental psychology laboratory studies (Sechzer, 1983). (Some effects may be obvious—a rat who is gently placed in the experimental apparatus may be less fearful, and therefore may perform better, than a rat who is handled roughly). In other studies, some songbirds (e.g., zebra finches) have been shown to learn selectively the songs of their fathers, even though they are naturally exposed to many other songs as well (Immelmann, 1969; Bohner, 1983, 1990; Clayton, 1987; for evidence suggesting learning from two or more models, see Williams, 1990). Of course, in a satisfactory analysis of the phenomenon, one must take account of the relative frequency and duration of exposure to different songs, the loudness of each, the age of the juvenile when exposed to the song, and so on, rather than blithely attributing the process to a special "bond." By the same token, in the natural environment, in this and other circumstances for learning or communication, a special "bond" could insure the presence of many facilitatory factors.

### How Do We Read Another's Mind?

As adults, we may engage in highly complex, cognitive tasks in which we imagine ourselves in the other's situation, drawing on similar past experiences to re-create the emotions and beliefs the other may have. We fine-tune our analogies by trying to take account of t he other's motivations and past history, probably different from our own. Things are somewhat easier if we are in the presence of the other, because we then have "ethological signals" to guide us. And finally, we can simply ask.

By re-creating the other's mental state, we experience it and see what it is like. How might an infant or child attain this experience? As previously noted (p. 226), Gopnik and Meltzoff (1994, 1997) and others have suggested that nature's way of solving the philosophical problem of the knowledge of other minds may be by visual-kinesthetic matching or imitation. Or, also reasonably, and especially as the infant develops, social input aids the process (Barresi & Moore, 1996).

Might other species, primates in particular, also share some of these abilities? The human infants' imitative abilities described by Meltzoff and Moore (1983) have not been tested for in other species. This might be accomplished through the use of a videotaped example, either of an actual conspecific's behavior or a computer modification of a real image.

It is also of interest to ask which facial expressions an infant or young child imitates. Any expression at all? A set? If so, which? Are there some expressions to which the infant will react emotionally, rather than imitate?

Further, why should imitating a facial expression allow the imitator to experience the associated emotion? I have noted that such a capacity facilitates coordination and integration of group activities, insofar as all members are in similar mind states: if there is food available, eat it; if danger lurks, the entire group should be made aware of it to act appropriately. Given these advantages, it is plausible for such an ability to evolve, if it could.

There is a modicum of evidence that supports the "facial feedback hypothesis," suggesting that adult humans who "put on a happy face" (i.e., put on a simulated smile by carefully following motoric instructions) tend to be in better moods than those who "put on a sad face." Each subject also recalls more mood-relevant memories; brain activity is also heightened in the areas typically active during positive moods (Ekman, 1994). In order to control for cognitive factors that might produce the positive mood if the person were aware he was smiling, scientists had the subjects perform a task that induced a smile (e.g., holding a pen between their teeth) as contrasted to performing a task that did not induce a smile (holding the pen between their lips) (Strack, Martin, & Stepper, 1988). The effect is not powerful enough to lift severe depression, nor does it seem likely to succeed as an effective means of psychotherapy. It does, however, at least suggest that imitators of emotional facial expressions may be entering the associated mind state of the model.

The flip side of this phenomenon is suggested by old studies of group meetings in which people who held similar opinions, as determined by discussion and later votes on the issues, tended to assume similar postures around the table, for example leaning on an elbow, and so on. This is not to say that these postures reveal various cognitive states. Rather, this suggests that the sharing of mind states is an interactive process whereby one tends to imitate the stance and perhaps facial expression of one who shares a similar view. Conversely, the act of imitating, at least of facial expressions, facilitates experiencing similar mind states.

These ideas are, of course, highly speculative.

*Theories!*

How do the previous views compare with more precisely formulated current theories concerning the same issues? There have been many detailed discussions of these issues, and I refer the interested reader to Gordon (1986, 1992) and Gopnik & Meltzoff (1994; 1997). Most reviews actually concern themselves with the slightly older child, in particular the child in important cognitive transitions between the ages of three, to four-five years.

The essential problem with which these theories attempt to deal is the asymmetry of first person and third person point of view. The child must come to understand both that another may hold a belief different from her own, and that a belief may be contrary to fact. It is at about age four or five that these important steps seem to occur.

The by now classic task used to assess the child's understanding is some variant of the "false belief" test. Much has already been written about optimal ways to assess the child's understanding: what the child comprehends and can express verbally, and what she expresses behaviorally but possibly not verbally (Perner, 1991). Given the differences that exist, one cannot overemphasize the importance of using several convergent methods to assess comprehension in children and animals. With children, difficulty comprehending verbal instructions may confuse the nature of the task; nonhumans cannot even have that problem. Eye glances of both children and other species can be recorded, but, as will be discussed later, this is more complicated information than it seems.

In the original version of the "false belief" test, a child is given a "Smarties" box (a box of popular British chocolate candy similar to M&M's). The experimenter asks, "What's in the box," and the child responds, "Smarties." However, upon opening it, she sees that there are pencils inside. Then the adult asks what the child's friend, or a puppet, will say is in the box. Three-year-olds by and large answer, "Pencils," while four- and five-year-olds tend to say, "Smarties." Some theorists interpret this to mean the four- or five-year-old has an understanding of "false belief" that the three-year-old does not have. The three-year-old instead is interpreted to assume that everyone shares her mental state, knowing the box has pencils.

The major interpretations of the behaviors just described have been termed "situation theory" (Perner, 1991), "simulation" theory (Gordon, 1986, 1992), and "theory theory" (Gopnik, in press). According to situation theory, the child thinks about the situation. She literally puts herself in the place of the other. In so doing, she keeps thinking in terms of "facts," but she flags different sets of facts as embedded in alternative points of view. Another child, to a four-year-old, does not have a "model" of the world, but a point of view instead.

In simulation theory, information about what others are thinking comes from mental models that represent the world, rather than facts about the world. Finally, theory theory or "theory formation theory" claims that the child's knowledge of mind, and an adult's too, has some characteristics of a scientific theory, both with respect to the status of the claims, and the methods by which claims are changed and evidence is sought and weighed.

Karmiloff-Smith (1992) offers a "theory of representation redescription" that emphasizes the radically new cognitive structures that can emerge when the developing organism is able to take a third person view of himself and his mental states, rather than merely having views of the external world or others' activities (see Tomasello & Call, 1997).

Precisely which aspects of the abilities described by the various theories are unique to humans is very controversial. Tomasello and Call, for example, very reasonably decline to pose the question for primates species as: "Does species X attribute mental states to others?" or, "Does species Y have a theory of mind?" Instead, they subdivide their analysis to determine whether an organism understands in another its behavior and perception, its intentions and attention, and, its knowledge. They conclude that no nonhuman primates understand their conspecifics' behavior intentionally or mentally, though some apes raised by humans may present a special case of achieving abilities not otherwise observed. The approach of Tomasello and Call seems an appropriate one to be applied to the youngest human children as well, though eventually humans do achieve more sophisticated comprehension.

In addition to differences in theoretical interpretations of experimental results, there are other interesting complications that pertain to differences between the beliefs the children appear to have based on their looking behavior versus those beliefs based on their verbal replies. In another version of the false belief test (Perner, 1991), Sam the Mouse (puppet) leaves his cheese in box A. After he leaves the room, his Mom moves it to box B. Sam returns and says he will go get the cheese. Each child is asked, "Where will Sam go?" A videocamera records the reactions of the children.

In this paradigm, children are likely to look at one of the two boxes. Four-year-olds look to box A, where Sam originally left the cheese. Eighty percent of three-year-olds look to box A; but when asked, most say box B. In fact, 50% of the three-year-olds look at the right box and say the wrong answer. How can we understand the understanding of the three-year-old?

It may be that the looking behavior should be subjected to a finer-grained analysis. Certain kinds of looking, possibly more similar to a direct gaze, may be associated with verbally stating the correct answer or voluntarily pointing to the correct location. Other looking may be associated with puzzlement, much like the longer looking times infants are reported to have when witnessing "surprising" events, such as a moving body passing behind an obstruction and coming out at the "wrong" place. A detailed video analysis of the children's looking behavior may reveal associated ethological cues about the more precise nature of the gaze (e.g., possible frowns associated with puzzlement, or more shifting of gaze in those cases when the wrong answer is given).

Is there any way in which a variant of a false belief test can be devised for nonhumans? The "linguistically" trained apes offer some glimmer of hope. One could have such an ape watch a videotaped sequence. In the sequence Sam, a known conspecific or human, places a treat in location A and leaves. Then, during Sam's absence, the treat is moved. The experimenter asks the ape "Where Sam?" With sufficient training (under simpler conditions) to choose a picture of Sam's location, an ape might possibly be able to comprehend and perform this "false belief" task, indicating which position Sam chose to investigate. (See also Hauser and Carey's chapter in this volume for a description of a nonverbal false belief task that they have begun to use with monkeys, specifically cotton top tamarins.)

*Future Directions*

### Interactions of Philosophers and Scientists

Issues such as understanding another's mind, intentions, or any cognitive processes are of interest to both scientists and philosophers. Both disciplines benefit from interaction. The scientist may grow both to recognize the sometimes hidden assumptions underlying experimental work and to consider more thoroughly the concepts being investigated, while the philosopher may make a more useful contribution by the constraints imposed from new empirical findings that he is otherwise unlikely to know. Similarly, scientists need interaction within their discipline. Laboratory psychologists interested in learning, and ethologists studying cognition and behavior in field settings, are interested in the same phenomena, but they keep their distance from each other both theoretically and spatially, seldom attending the same conferences. Researchers of infants and animals are coming to recognize their common ground, both with respect to the methodological problems of dealing with nonverbal organisms, and with the theoretical problems of attempting to understand cognition that is likely to be very different from the more familiar adult human cognition.

### Study of Animals in Their Natural Habitat

More scientists, perhaps philosophers too, should observe and study the natural lives of animals, particularly from a cognitive point of view. With such experience, we are more likely to appreciate the complex problems that animals routinely solve in their daily existence. More controlled experiments can then be conducted, in the field or in the laboratory, to further analyze the organisms' capacities.

### Specific Areas of Interest

As suggested in this manuscript, spatial understanding appears to play a prominent role in the cognitive systems of animals and humans. We find spatial concepts and information exerting strong influences in the conceptual structures that organize thinking, in information conveyed in animal communication (e.g., bees, vervet monkeys), in the metaphors in human languages (Lakoff, 1987), in biases in attention and memory. Continued study of the role of spatial information in the evolution of communication and problem solving is like to be very fruitful.

The importance of gaze in social interactions has been emphasized in numerous researchers' work, particularly in Baron-Cohen's system of increasing complexity of innate mechanisms, such as detecting gaze directed towards oneself, towards objects, the capacity to share attention to an object with another being, and finally some species' capacity to attribute mental states to another. More thorough investigations of these capacities should be conducted among species.

### Methodologies

It seems fruitful to continue using looking time measures in both children and animals, in both laboratory and more natural settings. These measures have been used to suggest both the organism's surprise at improbable events and its choice in a discrimination problem or other tasks. I suggest that at least some discrepancies in results obtained with looking time and motor responses (e.g., reaching) may be resolved by a finer-grained analysis of expressions that accompany the looking. Videotape is often essential in such microbehavioral analyses.

Time spent searching and proximity measures can be useful measures with animals in the field. An example is the plovers' reaction under various conditions to acoustic playback of chick distress calls (Ristau, in prep).

In the laboratory, more subtle measures would be helpful to reveal the child's or even the animal's understanding. For example, a task with three alternatives rather than two would permit a researcher to examine the subject's first and second choices. The first choice might perhaps be dominated by an emotional response or a place preference, but once the subject discovers his mistake, the second choice could indicate incipient knowledge.

### Functional Approach to Cognition

In considering possible building blocks of cognitive capacities and the kinds of capacities that might readily be molded by evolutionary forces, it seems plausible that the cognitive units should be functional units, some perhaps very task specific, some less so. We recognize that the visual system has dedicated circuitry; likewise we recognize very specialized capacities in smaller brained creatures such as insects. The human may be understood to have many more such circuits or "modules" of understandings. Each domain or module might then be composed of very many of these "modules." Examples of such "modules" might be the attention detecting mechanism described by Baron-Cohen (1994). The essential part of this idea is the emphasis on the *functional* aspect. Not every "module" needs to be functional; the visual system's detection of movement and of color are also basic building blocks.

Considering cognitive capacities from a functional point of view, and attempting to understand that function from a biological, niche-specific point of view, should provide some insight into the differences in cognitive capacities between species.

Other basic cognitive capacities are more general, perhaps even arising first as a general, rather than a domain-specific capacity. Particularly significant is the capacity for inhibition. As discussed, it is this capacity that may underlie young children's difficulty in object permanence tasks when the object is moved from position A to B but they continue to choose position A. The inability to inhibit emotional responding to permit a more cognitive evaluation of a situation is likewise apparent in many studies of young children and of the "linguistic-trained apes" (see discussion in Ristau, 1988; 1996).

A functional emphasis is also useful in attempts to understand the meanings of animal communication signals. Thus, we might expect a signal to indicate not only that the communicator or another is moving, but also that it intends to move and the function of moving. A function might be to approach with affiliative or aggressive intent, to flee, or to be vacillating between two possibilities among many others.

*Summary and Conclusions*

I considered the problem of how children come to attribute minds to others, and how we might investigate whether animals do also. First, I asked what any organism learns about objects and events, noting that innate constraints predispose selective attention and interpretations. An example of such a constraint includes the phenomenon of "belongingness," whereby certain classes of stimuli are much more readily associated with each other than are others. Another example is the emphasis given to spatial information by many species. Yet another example is the importance of "functional" definitions in the understandings of children and animals. Many objects and events appear to be understood based on the function each serves.

Next I briefly considered children's understanding of inanimate objects, examining in particular the phenomenon of "object permanence." I suggested that the function the object serves to the organism and the nature of the organism's interaction with the object may influence the perceived "permanence" of the object to the organism.

In attempting to explore what children understand about animate objects, I examined research on the developing child's concept of "alive," and research on imitation. These studies suggested the importance of innate predispositions.

Given that an object is animate, I next considered how an organism comes to understand the "purposes" an animate creature might have. Again, at least for children, there seems to be an innate bias to attribute purposes or intentions to others. Note that the notion of some intentions may also be considered more broadly in terms of the "functions" that one serves with respect to the other organism.

I then tried to examine the rudimentary capacities that might be necessary precursors to the ability to understand another's goals or purposes, particularly purposes involving oneself. Primary is the ability to detect another's direction of eye gaze: whether the other is gazing towards oneself; and, if not, what is the other's target of gaze? I examine evidence, including field research indicating that a shorebird, the piping plover, can discriminate between a human intruder who looks towards its nest area and one who does not (Ristau, 1991). Some of the data from monkeys and apes indicate that they can look to the direction that a conspecific, or in some cases, a human, is looking.

Studies with human infants explore the development of the capacity to follow the direction of another's (mother's) gaze (Butterworth, 1991). This capacity is intrinsic to the ability to develop joint visual attention to the same object or event. In other words, this capacity is intrinsic to forming the basis for sharing and communicating about that object or event.

Do at least some species that have a capacity for joint visual attention also have the capacity to voluntarily control their own eye gaze to manipulate the attention of another in order to gain some personal advantage? Field data from baboons and chimpanzees suggest this is so. Last, does an organism who can engage in joint visual attention necessarily also understand what is required for another to see? Here the data, at least from chimpanzees, is negative. In one experiment, chimpanzees who had experienced blindfolds themselves did not remove a blindfold from the eyes of a human model when it would have been advantageous to do so (Povinelli & Eddy, 1996, in press).

The capacity for joint visual attention is also a prerequisite for social referencing, the ability of an individual to gather information in an ambiguous situation from the reaction of another, in particular the emotional reaction of another to an object of shared attention. This can strongly determine the individual's own reaction and is probably especially important to understand the emotional responding of young children and animals. There also appear to be other mechanisms by which interacting individuals adopt similar mind states and/or "read each other's minds." It may also be the case that organisms have evolved to be particularly adept at "reading" the minds of certain, but not all, other individuals. Mammalian mothers appear to be especially sensitive to responding to their infants' needs. Humans seem particularly able to determine the moods of their mates, or perhaps, the moods of anyone with whom they are bonded and spend much time.

Finally, I asked more generally by what processes human children and adults and other species "read each other's minds." I suggested, as have others, that part of the process, especially for the youngest children and perhaps some animal species, is visual-kinesthetic matching or imitation. By entering into a similar mind state, some knowledge is gained of the content of the "other's" mind. I then briefly considered some of the current theories being explored about how somewhat older children, especially those ranging from four years and above come to attribute mind and mind states to others.

## Notes

I thank the editors for their constructive comments on earlier drafts of the manuscript and Lila Braine and Sue Larson for helpful discussions.

1. Note that a different criticism of standard tests is also likely to be influencing the results, though not directly pertinent to the present discussion. The young child may be unable to inhibit a dominant response. Thus, in the "A-not-B-effect," the child continues to search where it has searched many times before for a hidden toy (in position A, where the toy was first placed) not in position B (where the child saw the experimenter place the toy). The ability to inhibit a dominant response is thought to require full maturation of the frontal lobes, which does not occur during the child's first year of life (Diamond, 1988).

2. There are recent, interesting neurophysiological data which bear on this point. D'Amasio, using functional MRI scans of adult human brain activity, notes a likely distinction between systems that handle conceptual categories versus the brain areas most involved with the words for those categories. He suggests that natural selection may have created a heightened sensitivity to certain kinds of conceptual categories, such as familiar faces, places, tools, animals, and foods. Most pertinent to the present discussion, the MRI findings of active brain areas may reflect the different ways people learn to identify objects: usually by *seeing* animals (hence the importance of the occipital lobe and visual association areas) and by looking at, holding, and *using* tools. Thus we may speculate that, for at least some categories of objects (e.g., tools), something about the activity or functional use of the objects may be importantly involved in the neurophysiological basis of the concept of the object (Bower, 1996).

3. Infants respond this way as well, crying in response to the sound of another infant crying. This response has been variously interpreted as mood contagion, reflexive behavior, or empathy, depending on the theoretical bent of the researcher.

## References

Anderson, J. R., Sallaberry, P., & Barbier, H. (1995). Use of experimenter-given cues during object-choice tasks by capuchin monkeys. *Animal Behaviour, 49,* 201–208.

Astington, J., Harris, P., & Olson, D., Eds. (1988). *Developing theories of mind.* Cambridge: Cambridge University Press.

Baron-Cohen, S., Tager-Flusberg, H., & Cohen, D. (1993). *Understanding other minds.* Cambridge: Cambridge University Press.

Baron-Cohen, Simon. (1994). *Mindblindedness.* Cambridge, MA: MIT Press.

Barresi, J., & Moore, C. (1996). Intentional relations and social understanding. *Behavioral and Brain Sciences, 19,* 107–122, 142–154.

Bohner, J. (1983). Song learning in the zebra finch (*Taeniopgygia guttatta*): Selectivity in the choice of a tutor and accuracy of song copies. *Animal Behaviour, 31,* 231–237.

Bohner, J. (1990). Early acquisition of a song in the zebra finch (*Taeniopgygia guttatta*). *Animal Behaviour, 39,* 369–374.

Bower, B. (1996). Creatures in the brain. *Science News, 149,* 234. (April 13, 1996).

Bruner, J. S. (1964). The course of cognitive growth. *American Psychologist, 19,* 1–15.

Burghardt, G. M. (1991). The cognitive ethology of reptiles: A snake with two heads and horned snakes that play dead. In C. A. Ristau (Ed.), *Cognitive ethology: The minds of other animals* (pp. 53–90). Hillsdale NJ: Erlbaum.

Burghardt, G. M., & Green, H. W. (1988). Predator simulation and duration of death feigning in neonate hognose snakes. *Animal Behaviour, 36,* 1842–1844.

Butterworth, G. E. (1996). Paper presented to the International Conference on Infant Studies. Providence, RI.

Butterworth, G. E. (1991). The ontogeny and phylogeny of joint visual attention. In Whiten, A. (Ed.), *Natural Theories of Mind* (pp. 223–232). Cambridge, MA: Blackwell.

Butterworth, G. E., & Cochran, E. (1980). Towards a mechanism of joint visual attention in human infancy. *International Journal of Behavioural Development, 19,* 253–272.

Butterworth, G. E., & Jarrett, N. (1980). *The geometry of pre-verbal communication.* Paper presented at the annual conference of the Developmental Psychology Section of the British Psychological Society, Edinburgh.

Byrne, R. W., & Whiten, A. (1985). Tactical deception of familiar individuals in baboons (*Papio ursinus*). *Animal Behaviour 33,* 669–673.

Carey, S. (1987). *Conceptual change in childhood.* Cambridge, MA: MIT Press.

Carroll, L. (1941). *Through the looking glass.* New York: Heritage Press.

Chevalier-Skolnikoff, S. (1974). A Piagetian model for describing and comparing socialization in monkey, ape and human infants. In S. Chevalier-Skolnikoff & F. E. Poirier (Eds.), *Primate bio-social development: Biological, social, and ecological determinants* (pp. 159–187). New York: Garland.

Clayton, N. S. (1987). Song tutor choice in zebra finches. *Animal Behaviour, 35,* 714–721.

Cook, M., & Mineka, S. (1989). Observational conditioning of fear to fear-relevant versus fear-irrelevant stimuli in rhesus monkeys. *Journal of Abnormal Psychology, 98,* 448–459.

de Waal, F. B. M. (1982). *Chimpanzee politics: Power and sex among apes.* New York: Harper & Row.

Dennett, D. C. (1996). Talk to the Society for Philosophy and Psychology. San Francisco State Univ., June 1996.

Diamond, A. (1988). The abilities and neural mechanisms underlying A-not-B performance. *Child Development, 59,* 523–527.

Dore, F. Y., & Dumas, C. (1987). Psychology of animal cognition: Piagetian studies. *Psychological Bulletin, 102,* 219–233.

Eichenbaum, H., & Otto, T. (1993). Odor-guided learning and memory in rats: Is it "special"? *Trends in Neuroscience, 16*(1)(175), 22–24.

Ekman, P., & Davidson, R. J. (1993). Voluntary smiling changes regional brain activity. *Psychological Science, 4,* 342–345.

Fodor, J. (1983). *The modularity of mind.* Cambridge, MA: MIT Press.

Gallup, G. G., Jr., Cummings, W. H., & Nash, R. F. (1972). The experiments as an independent variable in studies of animal hypnosis in chickens. *Animal Behaviour, 20,* 166–169.

Garcia, J., & Koelling, R. A. (1966). The relation of cue to consequence in avoidance learning. *Psychonomic Science*, 121–122.

Gardner, R. A., & Gardner, B. T. (1969). Teaching sign language to a chimpanzee. *Science*, *165*, 664–672.

Gelman, R., & Kit-Fong, T. (Eds.) (1996). *Perceptual and cognitive development*. San Diego: Academic Press.

Gelman, R., & Gallistel, R. C. (1978). *The child's understanding of number*. Cambridge, MA: Harvard University Press.

Gopnik, A. (1996). The scientist as child. *Philosophy of Science*, *63*, 485–514.

Gopnik, A., & Meltzoff, A. N. (1994). Minds, bodies and persons: Young children's understanding of the self and others as reflected in imitation and "theory of mind" research. In S. T. Parker, & R. W. Mitchell, & M. L. Boccia (Eds.), *Self-awareness in animals and humans: Developmental perspectives* (pp. 166–186). New York: Cambridge University Press.

Gopnik, A., & Meltzoff, A. N. (1997). *Words, thoughts and theories*. Cambridge, MA: Bradford, MIT Press.

Gordon, R. M. (1986/1995). Folk psychology as simulation. *Mind and Language*, *1*, 156–71. In M. Davies & T. Stone, *Folk Psychology: The theory of mind debate*, Blackwell.

Gordon, R. M. (1992). The simulation theory: Objections and misconceptions. *Mind and Language*, *7*, 87–103.

Gordon, R. M. (1995). Paper presented to the annual conference of the American Philosophical Association, New York.

Hennig, C. W. (1977). Effects of simulated predation on tonic immobility in Anolis Carolinensis: The role of eye contact. *Bulletin of the Psychonomic Society*, *9*, 239–242.

Holland, P. C. (1977). Conditioned stimulus as a determinant of the form for the Pavlovian conditioned response. *Journal of Experimental Psychology: Animal Behavior Processes*, *3*, 77–104.

Holland, P. C. (1980). Influence of visual conditioned stimulus characteristics on the form of Pavlovian appetitive conditioned responding in rats. *Journal of Experimental Psychology: Animal Behavior Processes*, *6*, 81–97.

Immelmann, K. (1969). Song development in the zebra finch and other estrilid finches. In R. A. Hinde (Ed.), *Bird vocalizations* (pp. 61–74). Cambridge: Cambridge University Press.

Karmiloff-Smith, A. (1992). *Beyond Modularity: A developmental perspective on cognitive science*. Cambridge, MA: MIT Press.

Lakoff, G. (1987). *Women, fire and dangerous things: What categories reveal about the mind*. Chicago: University of Chicago Press.

Laurendeau, M., & Pinard, A. (1962). *Causal thinking in the child: A genetic and experimental approach*. New York: International Universities Press.

Meltzoff, A. N. (1995). Understanding the intentions of others: Re-enactment of intended acts by 18-month-old children. *Developmental Psychology*, *31* (5), 838–850.

Meltzoff, A. N., & Moore, M. K. (1983). Newborn infants imitate adult facial gestures. *Child Development*, *54*, 702–709.

Michel, G. F. (1991). Human psychology and the minds of other animals. In Ristau, C. A. (Ed.), *Cognitive ethology: The minds of other animals* (pp. 253–270). Hillside, NJ: Erlbaum.

Miklosi, A., & Csányi, V. (1997). Papers presented at the Satellite Meeting of the XXVth International Ethological Congress: Cognitive Ethology: Practice and Interpretation. Budapest, Hungary.

Mineka, S., & Cook, M. (1993). Mechanisms involved in the observational conditioning of fear. *Journal of Experimental Psych: General, 122*(I), 23–28.

Mitchell, R. W., Parker, S. T., & Boccia, M. L. (1994). Responses to Povinelli, D. (1993), "Reconstructing the Evolution of Mind," *American Psychologist*, 1993, *48*, 493–509. (Responses in *American Psychologist*, 1994, pp. 759–762.)

Moore, B. R. (1996). The evolution of imitative learning. In C. M. Heyes & B. G. Galef, Jr. (Eds.), *Social learning in animals: The roots of culture* (pp. 245–265). San Diego, CA: Academic Press.

O'Keefe, J. (1993). Hippocampus, theta, and spatial memory. *Current Opinion in Neurobiology, 3*, 917–924.

O'Keefe, J., & Black, A. H. (1978). Single unit and lesion experiments on the sensory inputs to the hippocampal cognitive map. In L. Weiskrantz (Ed.), *Functions of the septo-hippocampal system. Ciba Foundation Symposium* 58. Amsterdam: Elsevier.

O'Keefe, J., & Dostrovsky, J. (1971). The hippocampus as a spatial map: Preliminary evidence from unit activity in the freely-moving rat. *Brain Research, 34*, 171–175.

Parker, S. T., Mitchell, R. W., & Boccia, M. L. (Eds.), *Self-awareness in animals and humans*. Cambridge: Cambridge University Press.

Perner, J. (1991). *Understanding the representational mind*. Cambridge, MA: Bradford Books/MIT Press.

Piaget, J., & Inhelder, B. (1969). *The psychology of the child*. New York: Basic Books.

Plooij, F. X. (1978). Some basics traits of language in wild chimpanzees. In A. Lock (Ed.), *Action, gestures and symbol* (pp. 11–131). London: Academic Press.

Povinelli, D. J., & Eddy, T. J. (1996 in press). Chimpanzees: Joint Visual Attention. *Psychological Science*.

Povinelli, D. J., & Eddy, T. J. (1996). What young chimpanzees know about seeing. *Monographs of the Society for Research in Child Development*. Serial No. 247, *61:3*.

Povinelli, D. J., Nelson, K. E., & Boysen, S. T. (1990). Inferences about guessing and knowing by chimpanzees. *Journal of Comparative Psychology, 105*, 318–325.

Ristau, C. A. (1983). Intentionalist plovers or just dumb birds? (Commentary on Dennett, D. C. Intentional systems in cognitive ethology: The 'Panglossian paradigm' defended). *Behavioral and Brain Sciences, 6*, 373–375.

Ristau, C. A. (1988). Thinking, communicating, and deceiving: Means to master the social environment. In G. Greenberg & E. Tobach (Eds.), *Evolution of social behavior and integrative levels*. T. C. Schneirla Conference Series. Hillsdale, NJ: Erlbaum.

Ristau, C. A. (1991). Aspects of the cognitive ethology of an injury-feigning bird, the piping plover. In Ristau, C. A. (Ed.), *Cognitive ethology the minds of other animals* (pp. 91–126). Hillsdale, NJ: Erlbaum.

Ristau, C. A. (1996). Animal language and cognition projects. In Lock, A. & C. R. Peters (Eds), *Handbook of human symbolic evolution* (pp. 644–685). London: Oxford University Press.

Ristau, C. A., & Robbins, D. (1982). Language in the Great Apes: A critical review. In J. S. Rosenblatt, R. A. Hinde, C. Beer, & M. C. Busnel (Eds.), *Advances in the study of behavior*, vol. 12, (pp. 142–255). New York: Academic Press.

Rozin, P. (1976). The evolution of intelligence and access to the cognitive unconscious. In E. Stellar & Sprague, J. M. (Eds.), *Progress in psychobiology and physiological psychology*, vol. 6. New York: Academic Press.

Savage-Rumbaugh, E. S., Rumbaugh, D. M., & Boysen, S. (1978). Linguistically mediated tool use and exchange by chimpanzees. *Behavioral and Brain Science*, *1*: 555–557.

Schiff, W. (1965). Perception of impending collision. *Psychological Monographs* *79*, 1–26.

Sechzer, J. A. (1983). Discussion. In Sechzer, J. A. (Ed.), *The role of animals in biomedical research*, vol. 406. Annals of the New York Academy of Sciences. New York: New York Academy of Sciences.

Shettleworth, S. J., & Krebs, J. R. (1986). Stored and encountered seeds: A comparision of two spatial tasks in marsh tits and chickadees. *Journal of Experimental Psychology: Animal Behavior Processes*, *12*, 248–257.

Smith, W. J. (1977). *The behavior of communicating*. Cambridge, MA: Harvard University Press.

Spelke, E. S. (1994). Initial knowledge: Six suggestions. *Cognition*, *50*, 431–445.

Stern, Daniel N. (1985). *The interpersonal world of the infant: A view from psychoanalysis and developmental psychology*. New York: Basic Books.

Stich, S. (1991). *From folk psychology to cognitive sciences*. Cambridge, MA: MIT Press.

Strack, F., Martin, L. L., & Stepper, S. (1988). Inhibiting and facilitating conditions of the human smile: A nonobtrusive test of the facial feedback hypothesis. *Journal of Personality and Social Psychology*, *54*, 768–777.

Tomasello, M., & Call, J. (1994). Social cognition of monkeys and apes. *Yearbook of Physical Anthropology*, *37*, 273–305.

Tomasello, M., & Call, J. (1997). *Primate Cognition*. New York: Oxford University Press.

Tversky, A., & Kahneman, D. (1974). Judgment under uncertainty: Heuristic and biases. *Science*, *125*, 1124–1131.

Tversky, A., & Kahneman, D. (1981). The framing of decisions and the psychology of choice. *Science*, *211*, 453–458.

Whiten, A., & Byrne, R. W. (1988). The manipulation of attention in primate tactical deception. In R. W. Byrne & A. Whiten (Eds.), *Machiavellian intelligence: Social expertise and the evolution of intellect in monkeys, apes and humans* (pp. 211–223). Oxford: Oxford University Press.

Whiten, A., & Byrne, R. W. (1988). Tactical deception in primates. *The Behavioral and Brain Sciences*, *11*, 233–244.

Whiten, A. (Ed.). (1991). *Natural theories of mind: Evolution, development and simulation of everyday mindreading*. Oxford: Oxford University Press.

Wilcoxin, H. C., Dragoin, W. B., & Kral, P. A. (1971). Illness-induced aversions in rat and quail: Relative salience of visual and gustatory cues. *Science*, *171*, 826–828.

Williams, H. (1990). Models for song learning in the zebra finch: Fathers or others? *Animal Behavior*, *39*, 745–757.

Yonas, A. (1981). Infants' response to optical information for collision. In R. N. Aslin, J. R. Alberts, & M. R. Petersen (Eds.), *Development of Perception* (pp. 313–314). New York: Academic Press.

# 6

# Playing with Play
## *What Can We Learn about Cognition, Negotiation, and Evolution?*

MARC BEKOFF

Jethro (a dog) runs toward Rosie (another dog), stops immediately in front of her, crouches on his forelimbs (bows), wags his tail, barks, immediately lunges at her, bites her scruff, shakes his head rapidly from side-to-side, works his way around to her backside and mounts her, jumps off, does a rapid bow, lunges at her side, slams her with his hips, leaps up and bites her neck, and runs away. Rosie takes wild pursuit of Jethro, leaps on his back, bites his muzzle and then his scruff, and shakes her head rapidly from side-to-side. They then wrestle with one another and part, only for a few minutes. Jethro walks slowly over to Rosie, extends his paw toward her head, and nips at her ears. Rosie gets up and jumps on Jethro's back, bites him, and grasps him around his waist. They then fall to the ground and wrestle with their mouths.

This description of a play encounter between two dogs (it could be between other canids, felids, nonhuman primates, or humans) shows that when they engage in social play, they perform behavior patterns that are used in other contexts, such as aggression, reproduction, and predation. They, and other animals, including humans, also use actions that are important to initiate and maintain play, in this case "bows." Social play in nonhuman animals (hereafter animals) is usually a cooperative turn-taking venture, and an important question arises, namely: "How do animals negotiate cooperative agreements?" I will consider this and other questions in this essay, for the study of animal play provides access into animals' minds.

Available data strongly suggest that play-soliciting actions seem to be used to communicate to others that actions such as biting, biting and shaking of the head from side-to-side, and mounting, are to be taken as play and not as aggression, predation, or reproduction. On this view, bows are performed when the signaler wants to communicate a specific message about her desires or beliefs. While we cannot be sure that two dogs, for example, are engaging in first- or second-order intentional behavior (Dennett, 1983), some data do suggest this possibility. For example, suppose we wanted to know why Rosie permitted Jethro to nip at her ears. One explanation may be that Rosie believes Jethro is playing. And perhaps Jethro believes that Rosie believes that Jethro is playing. Providing answers to questions such as these is one of the challenges of research in animal cognition.

The category of behavior called social play has challenged students of animal and human behavior for a long period of time (van Hooff, 1973; Bekoff & Byers, 1981; Fagen, 1981, 1993; Burghardt, 1988, 1998; Rosenberg, 1990; Bekoff & Allen, 1992; Jamieson & Bekoff, 1993; Allen & Bekoff, 1994, 1997; Bekoff, 1995a, 1995b; Pellegrini, 1995; Bekoff & Jamieson, 1996). For some, social play was written off as a behavior that was not worth studying, while for others, the difficulty of studying social play in a rigorous manner prompted them to claim that while it was worth studying, a sufficiently "scientific" study of social play could never be done. Others, recognizing that social play behavior was interesting and fun to study, embarked on a challenging journey that has yielded valuable data concerned with the following questions: Why do animals perform behavior patterns that are unique to social play? Why do they perform sequences of behavior that incorporate actions from many different contexts? How do animals negotiate cooperation and agreements to participate in social play? How do they develop socially and learn rules of social interaction? and, How do they ask permission to engage in social play? It also has become at least a little less unorthodox to speculate on the existence of a humorous or comic dimension in the natural lives of animals, and the possible evolutionary implications of such a dimension (R. Fagen, personal comm., April 27, 1995; Burghardt, 1998). For example, we can ask how animals' obvious enjoyment of engaging in social play and their persistent efforts to lure others to play influences the development and evolution of this behavioral phenotype.

The tractability of social play as an evolved phenotype also makes it attractive to those interested in learning more about nonhuman and human cognition (Pellegrini, 1995). Understanding activities such as play may also be important to develop new research that deals with comparative approaches to cognition, including building androids (Caudill, 1992, p. 5). The broad comparative study of social play also lends itself nicely to Tinbergen's (1951/1989, 1963) suggestions that ethology should be concerned with (at least) the evolution, adaptation, causation, and development of behavior (Jamieson & Bekoff, 1993; Burghardt [1997] suggests adding a fifth category to Tinbergen's, namely, private experience), and it is clear that careful studies of social play do inform these areas. Studies of social play also cross disciplinary boundaries. Those interested in social play come from various academic areas (e.g., zoology, psychology, anthropology, computer science, cognitive science, medicine, philosophy, and sociology) and consider questions that deal with topics such as evolution, ecology, development, social communication, neurobiology, and cognition. For example, many scientific researchers provide data essential to understand social play within the context of the natural history of a species, with respect to evolutionary and development contexts, or with respect to individual differences within a species. These accounts, while useful and stimulating, can be pretty dry and unexciting to those interested in larger questions about, say, possible relationships between play and cognition. Philosophers and others not locked into science usually are more willing to talk about animals' beliefs and desires and how these sorts of attributions help us to explain the existence of play in an animal's behavioral repertoire. While I am a fan of dry and laborious analyses of social play, I also am a proponent of letting one's hair down to entertain challenging ideas that will stimulate further research. Animals obviously enjoy playing, and perhaps researchers' enjoyment of studying play will result in our learning more about animal cognition and the evolution of cognition. Lorenz (1996, p. 219) stresses the necessity for "a playful interest in animals," and notes how this attitude was prevalent among early ethologists.

In this chapter, I consider how analyses of mammalian social play (hereafter play) inform inquiries into the evolution of cognitive mechanisms. Play has been described in most mammals in which its possible existence has been investigated (Fagen, 1981, chapter 3). Some of the most elaborate and complex forms of play occur among the social carnivores (wild and domestic cats, wolves, coyotes, domestic dogs, bears) and nonhuman primates, animals with highly developed cerebral cortices and relatively high encephalization quotients (Bekoff & Byers, 1981; Fagen, 1981; the encephalization quotient is the ratio of actual brain size to brain size expected from the regression equation for the relationship between brain size and body size; see Jerison, 1973). Perhaps it is a combination of these neural factors and possibly other variables that have played a significant role in the ability of individuals to engage in play—to have the cognitive skills to negotiate cooperative agreements; to ask for permission to engage in a specific activity; to encapsulate one's behavior within a pretend context; and perhaps, even to make mental attributions to others. With the goal of learning more about how studies of animal cognition can inform studies of human cognition, mammalian play is a good behavioral phenotype on which to concentrate. When animals play, they typically perform behavior patterns that are used in other contexts (e.g., predation, aggression, or reproduction), and yet these behavior patterns take on a different meaning when encapsulated in the context of play. For example, when Jethro bit Rosie and shook his head rapidly from side-to-side, he did not continue to the point of eliciting submissive behavior from her. Nor did she squeal and roll over submissively or run away. He also did not attempt to copulate with her when he mounted her from behind, and she did not try to shake him off of her back.

How important is it to negotiate play and to agree that play is the name of the game? Very much so. When animals play, behavior patterns are for the most part "borrowed" from other contexts, and individuals need to be able to tell one another that they do not want to eat, fight, or mate with the other individual(s); rather, they want to play with them. In most species in which play has been observed, specific actions have evolved to initiate ("I want to play with you") or to maintain ("I still want to play with you regardless of what I just did to you or regardless of what I am going to do to you") play. These actions seem to function in negotiations between participants, the result of which is that they foster an agreement to engage in play rather than to partake in aggression or predation, for example. There is no solid evidence that animals invite others to play and then exploit them (Bekoff, 1978). Furthermore, self-handicapping (e.g., Altmann, 1962; Watson & Croft, 1996) and role reversals have also been observed, in which, for example, dominant individuals allow themselves to be dominated only in the context of play.

In considering how play is initiated and maintained, I will discuss in varying depth issues, including: the sorts of information that are shared during play; what cognitive psychologists who study humans can learn from cognitive ethologists who study other animals; and, what play can tell us about the emergence of mind in animals. Pretend play, in which an individual creates an imaginary situation or distorts reality, has attracted the attention of many researchers interested in the development of human behavior (see Leslie, 1987; Perner, 1993, for a detailed discussion of the different sorts of pretend play), and pretend play also seems to occur in nonhumans. Dogs and cats often chase their tails and bite them as if the tails were prey or competitor. They also frequently attempt to kill their food bowl or mate with it. Some dominant animals also engage in self-handicapping or role-reversing during play, in which they seem to pretend that they are not really dominant, perhaps to get others who would otherwise not play with them to play with them (it is rare for the self-handicapping individual to then attempt to dominate his partner; Watson & Croft, 1996).

While there are few data concerned with the evolutionary precursors to social pretend play in human children (for further discussion see Mitchell, 1990; Jensvold & Fouts, 1993), it may be the case that when a wolf is playing with another wolf, using behavior patterns typically used in sexual or predatory encounters, she is thinking about mating or eating her partner and pretending to do so, although the end result of the interaction—play and not killing or mating—does not, however, allow this explanation to be made with any degree of certainty. Requiring that the individual is thinking about the activity in which he or she is pretending to engage is not a criterion that is applied to human children, and there is no reason to require it in the case of animals (in which its occurrence could not be discovered by direct questioning. Perhaps neurobiological analyses in nonhumans and humans would help us along here by showing that similar EEG patterns are produced (multiply realized) in play and in what are deemed to be real instances of mating, preying, or fighting.

Before looking at the data, one point needs to be addressed. Useful analyses of play requires phrases that some deride as being anthropomorphic (animals enjoy playing; they gain pleasure from playing; they want to play; they believe that others want to play with them). Critics hold that words such as "wants," "believes," or "intends" apply solely to humans. While some categorically dismiss any analyses of animal behavior that use anthropomorphic terms, others believe that careful use of anthropomorphism can be useful to study animal behavior and animal minds (for discussion, see Burghardt, 1991; Bekoff & Allen, 1997). I believe that detailed comparative analyses of play can be useful to inform questions about the evolution of animal minds. Do individuals have beliefs; do they have desires; do they make attributions of intentions to others; do they represent internal states of others; what is the content of their mental states? It seems clear that without a cognitive vocabulary, it would be impossible to discuss play in any useful way (Mitchell, 1990; Jamieson & Bekoff, 1993; Bekoff, 1995a). When most animals play, they use specific signals to signal their intentions—their desire to play and their beliefs that if they perform a particular behavior, then play will occur—and they also perform behavior patterns that are typically performed in other contexts, but whose meaning is changed in the context of play. The richness and diversity of play can only be captured by using mental terms. A detailed consideration of some selected aspects of mammalian play can inform philosophers about important issues in philosophy of mind, including: naturalistic (and other) accounts of intentionality, representation, and communication. Such a consideration could, perhaps, cause philosophers to refine some of their ideas as well.

### What Is Social Play?

From early serious efforts to come to terms with social play (play) behavior, a number of definitions were offered (Bekoff & Byers, 1981; Fagen, 1981; Martin & Caro, 1985), and these definitions provided the framework for numerous comparative and evolutionary studies. Presently, it is difficult to pick up a journal that deals with the comparative study of animal behavior without finding at least one article that concerns itself with the structure or function of play (predominantly in mammals). While play is easy to recognize, there does not seem to be any stipulative definition that would apply to all instances of what is called "social play" in the diverse species in which the activity has been observed. However, the lack of a rigorous definition need not be an impediment to conduct solid research; to require a rigorous definition prior to empirical research may unreasonably require possession of knowledge that must first be gained by empirical research (Allen & Bekoff, 1994).

To get the ball rolling, I will use a general definition that has weathered the years (Bekoff & Byers, 1981, 300): "Hal is all motor activity performed postnatally that *appears* (my emphasis) to be purposeless, in which motor patterns from other contexts may often be used in modified forms and altered temporal sequencing. If the activity is directed toward another living being is called social play." (Martin & Caro, 1985, p. 65, provide a slightly modified version of this definition.) Note that this is a positive definition. Play is defined in terms of what it is, not in terms of what it is not. For years, it was trendy to refer to play as being not aggression, not predation, and not reproduction, but these sorts of definitions proved to be of little or no value to those who were interested to learn more about play. Note also that the definition centers on the structure of play sequences—what animals do when they play—and not on possible functions of play. Suffice it to say here: functional accounts of play, while yielding interesting comparative information, would really muddy the definitional waters. Analyses of the possible play functions have resulted in unconsolidated mixes of speculations (R. Fagen, personal comm.), and it is unlikely that there is one single reason why all animals play. There seem to be many possible, not mutually exclusive, functions of play (e.g., socialization, physical training, cognitive development, energy regulation) depending on the species being studied, perhaps the ages and sexes of the participants, and the location in which they are playing. Discussion along these lines goes beyond the bounds of this essay (for reviews, see Bekoff & Byers, 1981; Fagen, 1981; Martin & Caro, 1985; Burghardt, 1988, 1998). Furthermore, functional accounts of play that appeal to possible benefits and costs of playing are fraught with difficulties (as are most discussions of function in terms of potential benefits and costs) (see Allen & Bekoff, 1995a). With respect to play, both short-term and long-term benefits and costs need to be considered; and the necessity to account for benefits and costs over long periods of time for individuals of long-lived species in which play is a notable activity is not an exercise that would be recommended to nontenured professors!

Despite its easy-to-recognize features, play has been a very difficult behavioral phenotype with which to deal rigorously. While there are very few people who would claim that animals do not engage in this easily recognizable activity, broad comparative analyses of play are still forthcoming, although the database has greatly increased over the past five years (Burghardt, 1998). Not only does play between species vary in structure (behavior patterns used and their temporal sequencing), but there also are marked individual differences within species that make generalizations difficult and tenuous. This variability can be the result of numerous factors, including: the ages of the participants, their sexes, their relative social ranks, their experience with one another as play partners, their energy levels, their level of physical (aerobic and anaerobic) fitness, food abundance, how permissive their caretakers are, and where they are playing. Indeed, it is the flexibility and versatility of play that makes it a good candidate for comparative and evolutionary cognitive studies. As Allen (1997) has noted: "Behavioral flexibility is relevant to mentalistic attributions because it is connected to an organism's monitoring of its own performance. An organism that cannot detect when its states misrepresent its environment will be limited to adjusting its behavior only when the proximal causes of those states are removed." Indeed, behavioral flexibility (and communication) and an individual's ability to adjust to variations in environmental situations are the main criteria to which Griffin (1992) appeals in his discussions of consciousness in many nonhuman animals. I will not take on issues of animal consciousness here, for this sort of endeavor would both take us far afield of where I want to go, and would probably prove a journey with little or no direction because of all of the problems associated with dealing with consciousness in animals (including humans). However, I will appeal to the behavioral flexibility that is apparent in the play of many mammals to discuss different aspects of how animals initiate and maintain play, and how these patterns of behavior are useful to learn about the cognitive abilities of animals and the evolution of cognition.

### Play Signals and Intentional Behavior: Do Animals Negotiate Agreements?

> [C]ooperation merely depends upon the behaviour of one animal serving as a stimulus that elicits a certain response from the other. (Pearce, 1987, p. 261)

> Levels of cooperation in play of juvenile primates may exceed those predicted by simple evolutionary arguments. (Fagen, 1993, p. 192)

In order to discuss whether or not certain actions (hereafter called play signals) serve to communicate an individual's desire to engage in play—"If I perform this action I believe that play will occur or will continue"—a number of other questions loom and beg to be studied. Do animals make plans for the future? What is represented in the heads of animals who desire to play or who are engaged in play? Do individuals desire to play with others? Do individuals believe that if they perform a particular behavior pattern then others will play with them? Do animals make attributions of mind to others? Do animals negotiate agreements when they want to play or want to continue to engage in play? Do beliefs lead to other beliefs, not only to behavioral responses?

Asking whether or not animals are able to negotiate agreements seems to be the sort of question that could land someone in very hot water, especially when skeptics about animal minds are the audience (see quotation by Pearce, 1987, above). Some skeptics might ask: "How in the world could an animal negotiate anything in the absence of language?" Others might be very concerned with the use of anthropomorphic language, while others might be concerned about the use of unscientific, folk psychological explanations. Some skeptics might also be concerned about the difficulty of making claims about the content of animals' mental states. Still others might be concerned about the assumption that animals have any mental states at all. (The fact that there are many reasonable humans who seem unable to negotiate agreements doesn't seem to bother such skeptics in the least.)

While some of the issues raised by skeptics deserve serious consideration, a full discussion is beyond the scope of this essay (see Bekoff & Allen, 1994, 1997; Allen & Bekoff, 1995b, and references therein). The point here seems to be a simple one. In some (perhaps most) instances of play, I have argued (Bekoff, 1978, 1995a), based on empirical data, that the participants need to cooperate and to negotiate agreements so that they can cooperate in ongoing play. And, after they agree to play, there seem to be social regulations and social obligations to maintain the play mood. Furthermore, there are data that suggest that animals often seek permission to play with another animal by performing behavior patterns that indicate that play and not another activity is desired. For example, in the self-handicapping (e.g., inhibited biting or clawing; Steiner, 1971; Watson & Croft, 1996) and role-reversing (being chased rather than chasing) in which dominant animals engage to get more subordinate individuals to play, the dominant individuals seek permission to engage in play with animals who might otherwise avoid interaction with them. The end result is that the two individuals agree to cooperate, with self-handicapping and role-reversing being a means to negotiate this agreement. These data are important to consider in discussions of the evolution of cognition, for they tell us that certain cognitive abilities must be present even before an individual has the linguistic sophistication of a human. Let's look at some data in more detail.

### The Dance of Play: Initiating, Maintaining, and Agreeing to Play

Because play is composed of actions that are also used in other contexts, an individual needs to be able to communicate to potential play partners that he is not trying to dominate them, eat them, or mate with them. Rather, he is trying to play with them. Behavioral observations of many animals who engage in play suggest that they desire to do so and believe that their thoughts of the future—how the individuals to whom their intentions are directed would be likely to behave—would be realized if they clearly communicated their desires to play, using signals that, in some cases, seem to have evolved specifically to communicate play intention (for further discussion see Tomassello et al., 1985; Tanner & Byrne, 1993; Bekoff, 1995b). In this view, play is seen as a cooperative enterprise, the result of negotiations that allow play to occur and decrease the likelihood that aggression or predation will ensue. While other animals might also cooperate, including those for whom we are hard-pressed to grant the presence of sophisticated cognitive abilities (e.g., cleaning fish), the flexibility of play and the ease with which even two strange animals are able to play after only brief introductions to one another, lead to the conclusion that interactions between players are not merely the result of (somewhat hard-wired and inflexible) coevolved systems but the result, instead, of ongoing negotiations that require careful assessments throughout an encounter. It seems to be the flexibility of play that is important to allow animals to negotiate the desired outcome. (Given the state of knowledge concerning animals for whom we are reluctant to grant the presence of sophisticated cognitive abilities, it might be premature to write them off as not having well-developed cognitive skills that are used for different types of negotiations.)

Do animals cooperate in play, and how do they agree on or negotiate what it is they are going to do? To begin to answer these questions, let's consider in more detail the question of whether or not signals that appear to be used to communicate play-intention (play-soliciting signals) to other individuals could foster the cooperation among participants that is necessary for play to occur. Such play-soliciting signals seem to transmit messages such as: "what follows is play;" "this is still play despite what just happened or is going to happen;" or, "let's play again, wasn't it fun" (Bekoff, 1995a). Supporting evidence concerning the importance of play signals that allow cooperative social play to occur comes from studies in which it is shown that play-soliciting signals show little variability in form or temporal characteristics and that they are used almost solely in the context of play. For example, one action that is commonly observed in the context of social play in canids (and some other mammals) is the highly stereotyped "bow." In certain canids, the bow seems to function to permit recipients to engage (or to continue to engage) in social play (Bekoff, 1977, 1995a). Also, the first bows that very young canids have been observed to perform are highly stereotyped, though learning seems to be relatively unimportant in their development. These features of bows can be related to the fact that when engaging in social play, canids typically use action patterns that are also used in other contexts such as predatory behavior, agonistic encounters, or mating, contexts in which misinterpretation of play intention could be injurious.

How are agreements reached in the context of social play? How is turn-taking by individuals accomplished? In most species in which play has been described, play-soliciting signals appear to foster some sort of cooperation between players so that each responds to the other in a way both consistent with play and different from the responses that the same actions would elicit in other contexts (Bekoff, 1975, 1978); play-soliciting signals provide aid to the interpretation of other signals by the receiver (Hailman, 1977, p. 266). In coyotes, the response to a threat gesture that is preceded by a play signal or one that preceded follows a play threat signal that had been performed in the beginning of an interaction, is different from the response to threat in the absence of any preceding play signal (Bekoff, 1975). The play signal somehow altered the meaning of a threat signal by establishing (or maintaining) a "play atmosphere." Unfortunately, there have been no other similar quantitative analyses, but observations of play in diverse species support the idea that play signals can, and do, serve to establish a social context that both allows play to occur and alters the significance of behavior patterns that are borrowed from other contexts and used in social play (see below).

Some other characteristics of bows and also some of the properties of play support a cognitive explanation of play, and can be used to inform questions about their use for initiating and maintaining social play. For example, bows themselves occur throughout play sequences, but usually at the beginning or toward the middle of playful encounters. Intentional explanations of the way in which bows are used in ongoing play are helpful to understand how animals negotiate agreements, especially because of the apparent flexibility of how bows are used. In a detailed analysis of the form and duration of bows (Bekoff, 1977), it has been shown that bows are highly stereotyped and that bows are always less variable when performed at the beginning, rather than in the middle of, ongoing play sequences. These data have been used to argue that bows are important in the initiation of play. Other observations also support this idea. For example, one dominant female coyote pup was successful in initiating chase play with her subordinate brother in only 1 of 40 (2.5%) occasions, her lone success occurring on the only occasion when she had signaled previously with a bow (Bekoff, 1975). There may be more variability for bows performed during play bouts when compared with bows performed at the beginning of play sequences due to: (1) fatigue, (2) the fact that animals are performing them from a wide variety of preceding postures; or (3) because there is less of a need to communicate that "this is still play" than there is when trying to initiate a new interaction. Data for distinguishing among these three possible explanations do not currently exist.

Play signals are also used to maintain social play in situations in which the performance of a specific behavior during a play bout could be misinterpreted. This is of interest because it suggests that an individual knows, first, what he is going to do next, and second, the possible effect his behavior will have on the recipient. In a recent study (Bekoff, 1995a), I hypothesized that if bites accompanied by rapid side-to-side head shaking (or other behavior patterns typically used in other contexts, such as aggression or predation) could be or were misread by the recipient, then the animal who performed the potentially misinterpretable actions might have to communicate to its partner that the actions were performed in the context of play, not meant to be taken as aggressive or predatory moves. In this view, bows would not occur randomly in play sequences; the play atmosphere would be reinforced and maintained by performing bows immediately before or after actions that could be misinterpreted. These ideas had not previously been analyzed empirically. I found that bow distribution during play that involves these actions is not random; instead, they tend to occur immediately before or after a potentially misinterpretable action (for descriptions, see Bekoff, 1974, 1995a; Hill & Bekoff, 1977). The bows seem to serve as a form of punctuation that clarifies the meaning of other actions that follow or precede them. In addition to sending the message, "I want to play," when they are performed at the beginning of play, bows performed in a different context, namely during play, might also carry the message, "I want to play despite what I am going to do or just did—I still want to play," when there might be a problem sharing this information between the interacting animals.

Species differences have also been found that can be interpreted, using known variations in the early social development of these canids (Bekoff, 1974; see also Feddersen-Petersen, 1991). The interspecific differences are also related to the questions about how individuals monitor their own behavior—what they might know about themselves and others. For example, infant coyotes are much more aggressive and engage in significantly more rank-related dominance fights than either the infant (or adult) dogs or the infant wolves that have been studied. During the course of my study, no consistent dominance relations have been established in either the dogs or the wolves, and there have been no large individual differences among the play patterns that were analyzed in this study. Play in coyotes typically is observed only after dominance relationships have been established in paired interactions. Coyotes appear to need to make a greater attempt to maintain a play atmosphere, and indeed, they seem also to need to communicate their play intentions before play begins more clearly than do either dogs or wolves. (Bekoff, 1975, 1977). Indeed, as mentioned above, one dominant female coyote pup successfully initiated chase play with her subordinate brother in only 1 of 40 occasions, and was successful only when she had signaled previously with a play bow (Bekoff, 1975). Furthermore, subordinate coyote infants are more solicitous and perform more play signals later in play bouts. These data suggest that bows are not nonrandomly repeated merely when individuals want to increase their range of movement or stretch their muscles. However, because the head of the bowing individual is usually below that of the recipient, bowing may place the individual in a non-threatening (self-handicapping) posture. Self-handicapping may be explained by an individual's assessing a situation and deciding what she has to do to enable play to continue. It also suggests that one is aware of how others will interpret her behavior (e.g., Watson & Croft, 1996). Tanner and Byrne (1993) observed a captive, female lowland gorilla concealing her play face, concluding that the gorilla was aware of her spontaneous facial expression and the consequence it entailed, namely that play would follow within a few seconds.

In summary, detailed data and careful observations of a wide variety of animals lead to the conclusion that play-soliciting signals appear to foster cooperation between players so that each responds to the other in a way that is consistent with play and different from the responses the same actions would elicit in other contexts (see Thompson, 1996 for a comprehensive list of play solicitation behaviors in primates, rodents, insectivores, carnivores and ungulates). It is important to remember, too, that cues other than those provided by visible actions may also be important in the play solicitation (Fagen, 1981). In his analysis of play, captive common marmosets (Callithrix jacchus), Chalmers (1980) identified what he called "play markers" (e.g., the play-face), behavior patterns that always appear playful—their existence is considered sufficient but not necessary to regard behavior as playful. He also found that animals were more persistent in bouts with markers, and bouts with markers lasted longer than bouts without markers. Play markers have also been observed in pigs (Newberry, Wood-Gush, & Hall, 1988). The information shared by use of play signals or play markers concerns the readiness of an individual or individuals to engage in play. Play can be a risky affair (Fagen, 1981; Caro, 1995), but it is also an important activity for young and old animals alike; by using play signals, individuals can engage in and enjoy the activity. Perhaps it is the case that playing has benefits that are important for developing organisms as well as adults, making it unlikely that animals will use play signals to deceive others (Bekoff, 1978).

## Information Sharing and Theories of Mind:
## The Usefulness of Comparative Evidence

Studying play in animals, perhaps even in ants (Darwin, 1871), is useful to inform ideas about the evolution of cognition. With respect to the evolution of cognition and ideas about evolutionary continuity, and perhaps questions of homology with respect to structure and function (see Atz, 1970), the question, "How might information between senders and recipients be shared?", lends itself nicely to comparative evolutionary studies (despite Ingold's [1988] claim that animals have no thoughts whatsoever and are mindless communicators). For example, it is possible that the recipient shares the intentions (beliefs, desires) of the sender, based on the recipient's own prior experiences of situations in which she performed bows. Do available data suggest that some animals who engage in play have a theory of mind—can they and do they make attributions of mental states to others? While I realize that I am now stepping out on to thin ice, I want to pursue this discussion in some more depth, for I believe that there are data—some of which have been discussed here—that allow a tentative answer of "yes" to these questions.

In an essay on human behavior that has yet to find its way into comparative ethological circles, Gopnik (1993) has argued that "certain kinds of information that comes, literally, from inside ourselves is coded in the same way as information that comes observing the behavior of others. There is a fundamental cross-modal representational system that connects self and other" (p. 274). Gopnik (see also Meltzoff & Gopnik, 1993) claims that others' body movements are mapped onto one's own kinesthetic sensations, based on prior experience of the observer. She supports her claims with discussions of imitation in human newborns that can occur spontaneously at birth. For example, Gopnik wants to know if there is an equivalence between the acts that infants see others do and the acts they perform themselves, positing that "there is a very primitive and foundational 'body scheme' that allows the infant to unify the seen acts of others and their own felt acts into one framework" (Gopnik, 1993, p. 276). If by "primitive and foundational," Gopnik means phylogenetically old, then there should be some examples, or at least precursors, of this ability in other animals. Gopnik and her colleague, Andrew Meltzoff, also consider the possibility that there is "an innate mapping from certain kinds of perceptions of our own internal states. . . . In particular, we innately map the body movements of others onto our own kinesthetic sensations. This initial bridge between the inside and the outside, the self and other, underlies our later conviction that all mental states are things both we and others share" (Gopnik, 1993, p. 275). Flanagan (1992) also is interested in ways in which mental states can be shared, introducing the notion of a "mental detector" that is used to detect others' invisible mental states.

How these ideas might apply to animals awaits further study, but even if Gopnik's case is based entirely on imitation in human infants, there is ample evidence that animals engage in imitation (Byrne, 1995a; see also Galef, 1990/1996, 1998 for critical reviews of the literature). And, there seems to be little reason why, for example, in play, one dog might not be able to know that another dog wants to play by knowing what she feels like when she performs a play bow. Among the questions that need to be studied in detail is: "Does a dog need to have performed a bow (or other action) to know what a bow means and to be able to make attributions of mental states to other individuals—to know about others' beliefs, desires, expectations, feelings, thoughts, and plans? The following two hypotheses would have to be distinguished: (1) viewing a play bow induces a play mood in the recipient because of kinesthetic mapping; and, (2) viewing a play bow induces knowledge in the recipient of how the actor feels. (For discussion of possible neural bases for kinesthetic-visual matching, see Jeannerod, 1994 and accompanying commentaries. There is evidence that in monkeys, neurons respond to the performance of a specific action and to the same action when performed by another individual.) With respect to bows at least, there are data that suggest that there is a genetic component to them; the first bows that are observed to be performed by young canids are highly stereotyped and occur in the correct social context (Bekoff, 1977). Could these data support Gopnik's ideas about a primitive and foundational 'body scheme'? And, if so, how is learning incorporated into the development of social communication skills? Regardless of how nature and nurture mix, sparse evidence at hand supports the view that studies of animal cognition can inform the study of human cognition. Clearly, much more comparative research is needed.

There are other suggestions that Gopnik's ideas might enjoy some support from comparative research on animal cognition. For example, Savage-Rumbaugh (1990) noted: "Likewise, if Sherman screams when he is upset or hurt, Sherman may deduce that Austin is experiencing similar feelings when he hears Austin screams. This view is supported by the observation that Sherman, upon hearing Austin scream, does not just react, but searches for the cause of Austin's distress" (p. 59). This cause-effect relationship is generated after sufficient experience—if an animal screams when he is upset or hurt, he may deduce that another is experiencing similar feelings when he hears a scream. Tomasello, Gust, and Frost (1989) also note that some gestures in chimpanzees may be learned by "second-person imitation—an individual copying a behavior directed to it by another individual" (p. 35). They conclude that chimpanzees "rely on the sophisticated powers of social cognition they employ in determining what is perceived by a conspecific and how that conspecific is likely to react to various types of information" (p. 45).

In an interesting study of predator detection in mixed flocks of emberizid sparrows, Lima (1995) classified birds into different categories, based on whether or not an individual detects (detector) or does not detect (nondetector) an attack on the flock in which it is a member. According to Lima, nondetectors "infer the possibility of an approaching threat based on the occurrence of departures from the flock" (p. 1097). They seem to know that departures by others mean that a threat is impending. One wonders if the ability to make this inference is based on an individual's own knowledge of why it departs in certain contexts. Studies of naive birds, individuals who have no prior experience with threatening situations, might shed light on how this ability is acquired.

Others also have been interested in ways in which an individual might come to attribute states of mind to others. For example, in his discussion of research on the use of mirrors to study self-recognition, Byrne (1995a) asks: "How do mirror-self-recognizing organisms make the intuitive leap to treating self and other as equivalent in mind?" (p. 117). His discussion bears on some of what seems to be going on during play as well as Gopnik's ideas about how mental states may be shared between two individuals. Byrne (1995, 117) considers two possibilities: "A concept of self might be acquired by learning, first, that mental states are useful concepts in predicting the behaviour of others; then, by taking the others' point of view, the self, too, is viewed as having similar mental attributes." Learning that mental states are useful would seem to require having the concept of mental states already, and that might require more than we want to give at the beginning (Colin Allen, personal comm.). "Or, an intuitive understanding of self may come first, and later the individual finds it useful to attribute similar mental states to others—the better to understand their mind and behaviour" (Byrne 1995a, p. 117). Byrne notes that Humphrey (1983) defends this view, by holding that "we treat others as different versions of our own self, and therefore endow them with similar properties—knowledge, intentions and so on." The situation can become more complex when one engages in social referencing—"one person using another person's appraisal of a situation in order to form an understanding or interpretation of that situation" (Feinman, 1982, as cited by Itakura, 1995).

## Against Narrow Primatocentrism:
## Toward a Comparative Analysis of Mind

> After all, from an evolutionary point of view, there ought to be a high premium on the veridicality of cognitive processes. The perceiving, thinking organism ought, as far as possible, to get things right. Yet pretense flies in the face of this fundamental principle. In pretense we deliberately distort reality. How odd then that this ability is not the sober culmination of intellectual development but instead makes its appearance playfully and precociously at the very beginning of childhood. (Leslie, 1987, p. 412)

> [G]reat apes are certainly "special" in some way to do with mentally representing the minds of others. It *seems* that the great apes, especially the common chimpanzee can attribute mental states to other individuals; but no other group of animals can do so—apart from ourselves, and perhaps cetaceans. (Byrne, 1995a, p. 147; my emphases)

Attempts to place humans apart from and above nonhumans, have, in a sense, backfired. Comparative research in animal cognition has demonstrated evolutionary continuity in many cognitive abilities. It has also shown how connected humans are to other animals. Claims such as Byrne's in the above quotation simply are premature and may well prove wrong when necessary comparative research is completed. (It is important to note that Byrne actually equivocates in this and other statements in his otherwise excellent book. He also notes that little actually is known about the intellectual skills of, for example, carnivores.) It is a fact that very few nonprimate species have been studied to investigate the possibility that they have theories of mind. Species-fair tests need to be developed and applied widely before primatocentric claims that can be used to argue against evolutionary continuity can be assessed rigorously. It is unlikely that methods used to study theories of mind in nonhuman primates can be directly applied to nonprimates—dogs and wolves may have theories of mind, but it is highly unlikely that we will learn about them by using methods that are used on primates—and even among primates, it is clear that species-fair tests need to be developed to account for species differences in sensory and motor abilities, social organization, and habitat (Byrne, 1995a).

Suffice it to say, there already is ample evidence that comparative studies of animal cognition can be useful to learn about the evolution of cognition in humans and animals. As Watanabe, Lea, and Dittrich (1993) note in their research on pigeons: "The question is not whether pigeons have been proved beyond a reasonable doubt to possess and use concepts, but whether it has proved fruitful to ask whether they do" (p. 372). Surprises also might be forthcoming. Dharmaretnam and Andrew (1994), in their developmental study of vision in domestic chickens (Gallus gallus *domesticus*), recently discovered that one cerebral hemisphere seemed to be used by the other. Their important result shows how "phenomena which might have been considered as peculiarly human, and integral to the highest level of cognition, are in fact accessible to study in other vertebrates" (p. 1405).

There is little doubt that a broad comparative and evolutionary cognitive perspective will be very useful in future analyses of play (Bekoff, 1995b) and other behavioral phenotypes. Furthermore, these sorts of studies will be useful for those generally interested in the evolution of cognition. Evolutionary accounts of mental content (Allen, 1992a, 1992b) also are needed. There simply are no substitutes for careful observational and descriptive studies, as well as well-informed and well-executed experiments. They may be difficult to perform, but "difficult" should not be read to mean "impossible." Information about continuity of cognitive abilities will help to fill in the huge holes that exist in our current database. Individual variability also needs to be taken into account, for it would be misleading to conclude, on the basis of the behavior of a few members of a given species, that all members of that species are either unable to do something or do not perform specific behavior patterns that indicate well-developed cognitive abilities. To date, much research on animal cognition has been done on only a very limited number of species and on only a few members of those species in (often impoverished) laboratory environments (Kamil, 1987/1994). If research on animal cognition is to inform the study of human cognition, a broader database and broader evolutionary perspective is needed.

Broad comparative field studies are especially needed, for then we will have a good idea of what animals do in the wild. Byrne (1995b) stresses the importance of using naturally posed problems to learn about cognitive differences among species (see also Bekoff, 1995c, 1996). This knowledge will prevent some from making premature assumptions about what animals can and cannot do (for discussion, see Allen & Bekoff, 1997). Furthermore, while there certainly are good reasons to be concerned about the lack of control in field studies, there are also good reasons to worry about there being too much control in captive situations. Overcontrol, resulting in impoverished social environments and simplified stimulus situations might make it impossible to study the problems of interest in the social context in which individuals live (Bekoff, Townsend, & Jamieson, 1994). For example, controlling for possible interactions between visual and auditory stimuli might not allow individuals to have access to a more complex composite stimulus that is needed for eliciting certain types of behavior.

In this essay I have used social play as a candidate for further research in comparative animal cognition. I have asked: "What is it like to be a playing animal?" In some instances, animals seem to know what actions are likely to violate the terms of play, and they attempt to negotiate with their partner(s) so that play will continue—they seem to have the capacity to represent the mental states of others and make adjustments in their own behavior. This ability suggests an understanding of obligation or permission structures that may be crucial to understand human performance on tasks that require more abstract reasoning. When discussing behaviors such as play, it may be more economical or parsimonious to assume that an individual's situational needs need not be preprogrammed; cognitive explanations can be simpler than cumbersome stimulus-response explanations (de Waal, 1991; Bekoff & Allen, 1997). Indeed, it is the flexibility and versatility of play (and other behavior patterns, Bekoff, 1995c) that makes it a good candidate for comparative and evolutionary cognitive studies. While general rules of thumb may be laid down genetically during evolution, learned, specific rules of conduct that account for all possible contingencies may be too numerous to be hardwired. Furthermore, while behavioristic learning schemes appealing to notions such as conditioning, generalizing, and substituting can account (to a limited extent) for behavioral flexibility, behavioral integration, and the use of internal states and images of absent objects in some organisms (Holland, 1990), learning at high degrees of abstraction from sensory stimulation seems less amenable to behavioristic analysis (Bekoff & Allen, 1992; see also Kamil 1987/1994). Cognitive models of learning provide explanatory schemes for such cases. It might actually be more parsimonious to appeal to cognitive explanations in terms of accounting for complex patterns of behavior with fewer explanations. Moreover, this practice, motivated by research on cognition in animals, might find its way into studies of human cognition, many of which are unnecessarily embellished because of the lofty position in which researchers place humans.

Where to from here? Open-mindedness is the key. Single failures do not doom a field, nor do single successes warrant celebrations. Double standards that demand that cognitive ethology be more rigorous than other behavioral sciences are unlikely to be productive, especially when these sorts of biases lead to the demise of studies of nonhuman cognition. Double standards within the field of cognitive ethology also need to be dispensed with. Much of what we know about cognition in nonhuman primates is based on anecdotal reports and "scattered revelations" (Byrne, 1995a, p. 182); but for some, these sorts of stories carry more weight than they do for, say, domestic dogs or other companion animals. Brown (1996) has posed what he calls the "consistency axiom," in which evaluations of all explanations of behavior are subjected to the same degree of rigor. This seems to be a fair and obvious way to evaluate research. It is unlikely that all of humans' sophisticated cognitive abilities arose de novo. Only time will tell how useful different approaches are. Interaction among proponents of different views are essential if we are to make headway into learning more about animal cognition and how studies of animal cognition are able to inform and motivate the study of human cognition.

## Note

I thank Colin Allen, Denise Cummins, Gordon Burghardt, and Alison Gopnik for comments on an earlier draft of this paper. I also thank Dale Jamieson, Michael Pereira, Jack Hailman, Susan Townsend, Alex Rosenberg, and some students in my animal behavior classes for discussing some of the ideas contained herein. Others who have helped me along are mentioned in some of my other papers that deal with similar issues. Correspondence should be addressed to the author at the Department of Environmental, Population, and Organismic Biology, University of Colorado, Boulder, CO, 80309–0334 or bekoffm@spot.colorado.edu.

*References*

Allen, C. (1992a). Mental content. *British Journal of the Philosophy of Science, 43,* 537–553.

Allen, C. (1992b). Mental content and evolutionary explanation. *Biology and Philosophy, 7,* 1–12.

Allen, C. (1997). Animal cognition and animal minds. In P. Machamer & M. Carrier (Eds.), *Philosophy and the Sciences of the Mind: Pittsburgh-Konstanz Series in the Philosophy and History of Science,* vol. 4, pp. 227–243. Pittsburgh University Press and the Universitätsverlag Konstanz.

Allen, C., & Bekoff, M. (1994). Intentionality, social play, and definition. *Biology & Philosophy, 9,* 63–74.

Allen, C., & Bekoff, M. (1995a). Function, natural design, and animal behavior: philosophical and ethological considerations. *Perspectives in Ethology, 11,* 1–46.

Allen, C., & M. Bekoff. (1995b). Cognitive ethology and the intentionality of animal behaviour. *Mind and Language, 10,* 313–328.

Allen, C., & Bekoff, M. (1997). Species of mind: The philosophy and biology of cognitive ethnology. Cambridge, MA: MIT Press.

Altmann, S. A. (1962). Social behavior of anthropoid primates: Analysis of recent concepts. In E. L. Bliss (Ed.), *Roots of Behavior* (pp. 277–285). New York: Harper.

Atz, J. W. (1970). The application of the idea of homology to behavior. In L. R. Aronson, E. Tobach, D. S. Lehrman, & J. S. Rosenblatt (Eds.), *Development and evolution of behavior: Essays in honor of T. C. Schneirla* (pp. 53–74). San Francisco: W. H. Freeman.

Bekoff, M. (1974). Social play and play-soliciting by infant canids. *American Zoologist, 14,* 323–340.

Bekoff, M. (1975). The communication of play intention: Are play signals functional? *Semiotica, 15,* 231–239.

Bekoff, M. (1977). Social communication in canids: Evidence for the evolution of a stereotyped mammalian display. *Science, 197,* 1097–1099.

Bekoff, M. (1978). Social play: Structure, function, and the evolution of a cooperative social behavior. In G. Burghardt & M. Bekoff (Eds.), *The development of behavior: comparative and evolutionary aspects* (pp. 367–383). New York: Garland.

Bekoff, M. (1995a). Play signals as punctuation: The structure of social play in canids. *Behaviour, 132,* 419–429.

Bekoff, M. (1995b). Cognitive ethology and the explanation of nonhuman animal behavior. In J.-A. Meyer & H. Roitblat (Eds.), *Comparative approaches to cognitive science* (pp. 119–150). Cambridge, MA: MIT Press.

Bekoff, M. (1995c). Vigilance, flock size, and flock geometry: Information gathering by western evening grosbeaks (*Aves, fringillidae*). *Ethology, 99,* 150–161.

Bekoff, M. (1996). Cognitive ethology, vigilance, information gathering, and representation: Who might know what and why? *Behavioural Processes, 35,* 225–237.

Bekoff, M., & Allen, C. (1992). Intentional icons: Towards an evolutionary cognitive ethology. *Ethology, 91,* 1–16.

Bekoff, M., & Allen, C. (1997). Cognitive ethology: Slayers, skeptics, and proponents. In R. W. Mitchell, N. Thompson, & L. Miles (Eds), *Anthropomorphism, anecdote, and animals: The emperor's new clothes?* (pp. 313–334). Albany, NY: SUNY Press.

Bekoff, M., & Byers, J. A. (1981). A critical reanalysis of the ontogeny of mammalian social and locomotor play: An ethological hornet's nest. In K. Immelmann, G. W. Barlow, L. Petrinovich, & M. Main, (Eds.), *Behavioral development: The Bielefeld interdisciplinary project* (pp. 296–337). New York: Cambridge University Press.

Bekoff, M., & Jamieson, D. (Eds.). (1996). *Readings in animal cognition.* Cambridge, MA: MIT Press.

Bekoff, M., Townsend, S. E., & Jamieson, D. (1994). Beyond monkey minds: Towards a richer cognitive ethology. *Behavioral and Brain Sciences, 17,* 571–572.

Brown, A. (1996). *The minds of animals: Theoretical foundations of comparative psychology.* Ph.D. Dissertation, University of Colorado, Boulder.

Burghardt, G. M. (1988). Precocity, play, and the ectotherm-endotherm transition: profound reorganization or superficial adaptation. In E. M. Blass (Ed.), *Handbook of behavioral neurobiology,* vol. 9 (pp. 107–148). New York: Plenum.

Burghardt, G. M. (1991). Cognitive ethology and critical anthropomorphism: a snake with two heads and hognose snakes that play dead. In C. A. Ristau (Ed.), *Cognitive ethology: The minds of other animals. Essays in honor of Donald R. Griffin* (pp. 53–90).

Burghardt, G. M. (1998). Play. In G. Greenberg & M. Haraway (Eds.), *Encyclopedia of comparative psychology.* New York: Garland.

Burghardt, G. M. (1997). Amending Tinbergen: A fifth aim for ethology. In R. W. Mitchell, N. Thompson, & L. Miles, (Eds.), *Anthropomorphism, anecdote, and animals* (pp. 254–276). Albany, NY: SUNY Press.

Byrne, R. (1995a). *The thinking ape: Evolutionary origins of intelligence.* New York: Oxford University Press.

Byrne, R. (1995b). Primate cognition: Comparing problems and skills. *American Journal of Primatology, 37,* 127–141.

Caro, T. M. (1995). Short-term costs and correlates of play in cheetahs. *Animal Behaviour, 49,* 333–345.

Caudill, M. (1992). *In our own image: Building an artificial person.* New York: Oxford University Press.

Chalmers, N. R. (1980). The ontogeny of play in feral olive baboons. *Animal Behaviour, 28,* 570–585.

de Waal, F. B. (1991). Complementary methods and convergent evidence in the study of primate social cognition. *Behaviour, 118,* 297–320.

Darwin, C. (1871/1936). *The descent of man and selection in relation to sex.* Modern Library edition. New York: Random House.

Dennett, D. C. (1983). Intentional systems in cognitive ethology: The "Panglossian paradigm" defended. *Behavioral and Brain Sciences, 6,* 343–345.

Dharmaretnam, M., & Andrew, R. J. (1994). Age- and stimulus-specific use of right and left eyes by the domestic chick. *Animal Behaviour, 48,* 1395–1406.

Fagen, R. (1981). *Animal play behavior.* New York: Oxford University Press.

Fagen, R. (1993). Primate juveniles and primate play. In M. E. Pereira & L. A. Fairbanks (Eds.), *Juvenile primates: Life history, development, and behavior* (pp. 183–196). New York: Oxford University Press.

Feddersen-Petersen, D. (1991). The ontogeny of social play and agonistic behaviour in selected canid species. *Bonn Zoologische Beitrage, 42,* 97–114.

Flanagan, O. (1992). *Consciousness reconsidered.* Cambridge, MA: MIT Press.

Galef, B. G., Jr. (1990/1996). Tradition in animals: Field observations and laboratory analyses. In M. Bekoff & D. Jamieson (Ed.), *Readings in animal cognition* (pp. 91–105). Cambridge, MA: MIT Press.

Galef, B. G., Jr. (1998). Tradition and imitation in animals. In G. Greenberg & M. Haraway (Eds.), *Encyclopedia of comparative psychology*. New York: Garland.

Gopnik, A. (1993). Psychopsychology. *Consciousness and Cognition, 2,* 264–280.

Griffin, D. R. (1992). *Animal minds.* Chicago: University of Chicago Press.

Hailman, J. P. (1977). *Optical signals: animal communication and light.* Bloomington, IN: Indiana University Press.

Hill, H. L., & Bekoff, M. (1977). The variability of some motor components of social play and agonistic behaviour in infant eastern coyotes (*Canis latrans*). *Animal Behavior, 25,* 907–909.

Holland, P. C. (1990). Event representation in Pavlovian conditioning: Image and action. *Cognition, 37,* 105–131.

Humphrey, N. K. (1983). *Consciousness regained.* New York: Oxford University Press.

Ingold, T. (1988). The animal in the study of humanity. In T. Ingold (Ed.), *What is an animal?* (pp. 84–99). London: Unwin Hyman.

Itakura, S. (1995). An exploratory study of social referencing in chimpanzees. *Folia Primatologica, 64,* 44–48.

Jamieson, D., & Bekoff, M. (1993). On aims and methods of cognitive ethology. *Philosophy of Science Association, 2,* 110–124.

Jeannerod, M. (1994). The representing brain: neural correlates of motor intention and memory. *Behavioral and Brain Sciences, 17,* 187–245.

Jensvold, M. L. A., & Fouts, R. S. (1993). Imaginary play in chimpanzees (*Pan troglodyes*). *Human Evolution, 8,* 217–227.

Jerison, H. J. (1973). *Evolution of the brain and intelligence.* New York: Academic Press.

Kamil, A. C. (1987/1994). A synthetic approach to the study of animal intelligence. In L. Real (Ed.), *Behavioral mechanisms in evolutionary ecology* (pp. 11–45). Chicago: University of Chicago Press.

Leslie, A. M. (1987). Pretense and representation: The origins of "theory of mind." *Psychological Review, 94,* 412–426.

Lima, S. L. (1995). Collective detection of predatory attack by social foragers: Fraught with ambiguity. *Animal Behaviour, 50,* 1097–1108.

Lorenz, K. Z. (1996). *The natural science of the human species. An introduction to comparative behavioral research—The "Russian Manuscript"* (1944–1948). Cambridge, MA: MIT Press.

Martin, P. & Caro, T. M. (1985). On the functions of play and its role in behavioural development. *Advanced Study Behavior, 15,* pp. 59–103.

Meltzoff, A., & Gopnik, A. (1993). The role of imitation in understanding persons and developing a theory of mind. In S. Baron-Cohen, H. Tager-Flusberg, & D. Cohen (Eds.), *Understanding other minds* (pp. 335–366). New York: Oxford University Press.

Mitchell, R. W. (1990). A theory of play. In M. Bekoff & D. Jamieson (Eds.), *Interpretation and explanation in the study of animal behavior: Vol. I, interpretation, intentionality, and communication* (pp. 197–227). Boulder, CO: Westview Press.

Newberry, R. C., Wood-Gush, D. G. M., & Hall, J. W. (1988). Playful behaviour of piglets. *Behavioural Processes, 17,* 205–216.

Pearce, J. M. (1987). *Introduction to animal cognition.* Hillsdale, NJ: Erlbaum.

Pellegrini, A. D. (Ed.). (1995). *The future of play theory: A multidisciplinary inquiry into the contributions of Brian Sutton-Smith.* Albany, NY: SUNY Press.

Perner, M. (1993). *Understanding the representational mind.* Cambridge, MA: MIT Press.

Ristau, C. (Ed.). (1991a). *Cognitive ethology: The minds of other animals.* Hillsdale, NJ: Erlbaum.

Ristau, C. (1991b). Aspects of the cognitive ethology of an injury-feigning bird, the piping plover. In C. Ristau (Ed.), *Cognitive Ethology: The Minds of Other Animals* (pp. 91–126). Hillsdale, NJ: Erlbaum.

Rosenberg, A. (1990). Is there an evolutionary biology of play? In M. Bekoff & D. Jamieson (Eds.), *Interpretation and explanation in the study of animal behavior: vol. I, interpretation, intentionality, and communication* (pp. 180–196). Boulder, CO: Westview Press.

Savage-Rumbaugh, E. S. (1990). Language as a cause-effect communication system. *Philosophical Psychology, 3,* 55–76.

Steiner, A. L. (1971). Play activity of Columbian ground squirrels. *Zeitschrift für Tierpsychologie, 28,* 247–261.

Tanner, J., & R. Byrne. (1993). Concealing facial evidence of mood: Perspective-taking in a captive gorilla. *Primates, 3,* 451–457.

Thompson, K. V. (1996). Behavioral development and play. In D. G. Kleiman, M. E. Allen, K. V. Thompson, S. Lumpkin, & H. Harris (Eds.), *Wild mammals in captivity: Principles and techniques* (pp. 352–371). Chicago: University of Chicago Press.

Tinbergen, N. (1951/1989). *The study of instinct.* New York: Oxford University Press.

Tinbergen, N. (1963). On aims and methods of ethology. *Zeitschrift für Tierpsychologie, 20,* 410–433.

Tomasello, M., George, B. L., Kruger, A. C., Jeffry, M., & Evans, F. A. (1985). The development of gestural communication in young chimpanzees. *Journal of Human Evolution, 14,* 175–186.

Tomasello, M., Gust, D., & Frost, G. T. (1989). A longitudinal investigation of gestural communication in young chimpanzees. *Primates, 30,* 35–50.

Watanabe, S., Lea, S. E. G., & Dittrich, W. H. (1993). What can we learn from experiments on pigeon concept discrimination? In H. P. Zeigler and H.-J. Bischof (Eds.), *Vision, Brain, and Behavior in Birds* (pp. 351–376). Cambridge, MA: MIT Press.

Watson, D. M., & Croft, D. B. (1996). Age-related differences in playfighting strategies of captive male red-necked wallabie (*Macropus rufogriseus banksianus*). *Ethology, 102,* 33–346.

# 7

# The Evolution
of Reference

COLIN ALLEN & ERIC SAIDEL

The unrefined, untutored mind
Of *Homo javanensis*
Could only treat of things concrete
And present to the senses.

(WILLARD VAN ORMAN QUINE, 1953)

     Birds do it, bees do it, and specially educated chimpanzees do it. But how do nonhuman capacities for doing it compare to the seemingly infinite variety of human ways to do it? When the capacity in question is communication, there is little agreement on what we can learn about the human capacity for linguistic communication through studying animal communication. There is great skepticism among many linguists, psychologists, and philosophers about what the grunts, growls, whistles, and howls of our furry and feathered relatives can tell us about human language. There is even greater controversy about the significance of attempting to get members of other species to learn human languages.

    Some scientists contend that human language is the output of a special brain module whose evolutionary development lies buried with our hominid ancestors. This, they believe, makes human language so utterly unlike any other form of animal communication that there is no point trying to compare what we do with what other animals do. But not everyone agrees that the origins of language are as recent as the hominid line; and, there are many scientists who believe that much can be learned about human language by studying nonhuman communication, both in the laboratory and in the field.

    The authors of this chapter are philosophers interested in exploring the continuity between human minds and animal minds from a Darwinian perspective. The analysis of language is central to this project because it has often been claimed that the human capacity for language marks a difference in kind between human mentality and the mentality of nonhuman animals. Descartes, the founder of modern philosophy, thought that the human capacity for language was unexplainable in terms of the mechanical operations of a material body. He believed that this capacity could only be explained by the operations of an immaterial mind. The apparent inability of nonhuman animals to use language provided evidence for Descartes that they lacked minds (Descartes, 1637). Even contemporary philosophers who do not believe in Descartes's distinction between material bodies and immaterial minds assert that language is the basis of a unique mentality (Dennett, 1995).

To assess these claims of radical differences, it is important to know who is right: Is language a uniquely hominid innovation, or does it have a much older phylogenetic history? Our answer is neither a simple "yes" nor a simple "no." The human capacity for language is a complex mosaic of traits, each of which can be investigated independently. Such investigations provide insight into the ontogeny and phylogeny of language (Locke, 1995 makes a similar point). In this chapter, we will focus on one of those traits— the capacity for symbolic reference—to show what insights are available by taking a fully comparative, evolutionary approach.

## Three Views of Language

The "language-is-recent" perspective is recently exemplified by psycholinguist, Steven Pinker (1994), who has done a fine job to make the case that human language is an evolutionary adaptation. He repeatedly emphasizes the differences between human language and other forms of animal communication as part of his general argument that language is a recent, hominid adaptation. He lampoons attempts to teach human languages to members of other species with an analogy: Trying to teach languages to nonhumans is, he thinks, like trying to teach the nearest living relatives of elephants—the shrew-like hyraxes—to pick things up with their short, unremarkable snouts (pp. 332–333). This parody could easily be extended to naturalistic studies of animal communication. Ethologists who study animal communication in the field are like camouflaged researchers stalking wild hyraxes with field glasses and video recorders, hoping to catch them using their snouts in a prehensile way.

Many comparative psychologists disagree with the language-is-recent view that restricts its evolution to the hominid line. They see human language as built on top of more general cognitive and communicative abilities with a much longer evolutionary history. Their hunch is that much can be learned about the evolution of human language by studying both the natural communication capacities of nonhuman species and their ability to use artificial languages. This perspective is exemplified by Patricia Greenfield (1991). Greenfield argues that language and tool use share an underlying cognitive basis in the capacity to complete object manipulation tasks that are hierarchically structured, for instance tasks that involve the completion of subassemblies for combination into larger objects. Following Chomsky (1957), linguists agree that the syntax of human languages is best understood in terms of hierarchical relations between subassemblies (such as noun phrases and verb phrases) that can be combined into higher-level structures and a potentially infinite number of grammatical sentences. Greenfield suggests that the capacity for a hierarchically structured grammar has its origins in primate abilities to engage in structured manipulation of tools. She argues that the cognitive capacity for tasks with hierarchical structure has a neural basis that evolved well before the hominids and the pongids went their separate ways. Many of Greenfield's conclusions are based on laboratory studies that directly compare the cognitive skills and development of humans and other primates, particularly chimpanzees. These conclusions are controversial, but for our purposes it suffices that they represent a serious attempt to understand the phylogenetic origin of an important human linguistic capacity—the capacity to parse hierarchical syntactic structures—in terms of more general hierarchical capacities.

A third perspective is provided by biologists who are concerned with the evolution of behavior—the subdiscipline usually called "ethology." From an ethological perspective, human language is an adaptation to a specific regimen of natural selection, but it is nonetheless evolutionarily related to other forms of animal communication. Human language skills may share common origins with other forms of animal communication (human language and animal communication may be homologous), or there may been convergent evolution for similar functions (they may be examples of homoplasy or analogy). Although attempts to teach human languages to members of other species may provide interesting suggestions about the evolution of human language, ethologists prefer to compare the natural communication systems of different species. This perspective is exemplified by attempts to show that the communicative signals of the members of various species are what ethologists call "referential" signals. Cheney and Seyfarth (1990) use data collected from their field research on vervet monkeys to argue that some vervet vocalizations convey information about specific predators such as leopards, snakes, and eagles. Peter Marler and Christopher Evans have pressed a similar point about the alarm vocalizations of chickens that are different for aerial and terrestrial predators (Evans & Marler, 1995; Marler and Evans 1995). These and other ethologists are interested in the evolution of reference.

This third perspective is a response to an early but still common view of animal communication that takes signals to be involuntarily caused by immediate stimuli ("things concrete and present to the senses," to borrow the line from Quine). According to this view, a monkey's alarm call (or a chicken's) is simply an emotion-caused response to the appearance of a predator—a direct consequence, for example, of the fear that a predator causes in the monkey. Proponents of this "emotion" account of communication are not pressing any strong claims about the consciousness of the animal. Rather, they claim that it is not necessary to attribute complex information processing to explain nonhuman animal communication. They suppose that relatively simple mechanisms can explain the range of behaviors observed in instances of nonhuman animal communication, whereas, they argue that human communicative skills require much more complicated cognitive skills. Prominent in these arguments are claims about the amount of cortical involvement in processing signals and the degree of voluntary control that organisms have over their signalling behavior. Those who wish to emphasize the uniqueness and recency of human language evolution embrace the view that animal communication is involuntary, perhaps under the control of the limbic system (the subcortical parts of the brain that are also responsible for emotions) while human communication is highly voluntary and relatively detached from emotional responses (Pinker, 1994; see also Lieberman, 1995 for discussion).

Contemporary ethological research suggests, however, that animals have a much higher degree of voluntary control over their vocalizations than was originally supposed (Marler et al., 1991; Macedonia & Evans, 1993; Hauser & Marler, 1993a, 1993b; Marler & Evans, 1995). Additionally, neurological studies of nonhuman primates provide evidence that both comprehension and production of their vocalizations involve higher cortical parts of the brain, lending further credence to the view that there are closer parallels between human language and the vocalizations of other animals than the received view would suggest. For example, MacNeilage and colleagues (1991) present evidence that babbling in young human children is controlled by a part of the motor cortex that also controls the vocalizations of some primates. Hauser and Andersson (1994) established that adult rhesus macaques (but not infants) show left hemispheric dominance to process the vocalizations of their conspecifics, and Rauschecker and colleagues (1995) have shown that rhesus macaques possess cortical neurons that are selectively responsive to the vocalizations of conspecifics. These and other parallels can be used to identify general evolutionary principles that lead to the development of referential communication systems.

The relationships between human language and other forms of animal communication are undoubtedly complex. This suggests that it is appropriate to adopt an ethological perspective on language, exemplified by Evans and Marler (1995) when they write:

> Language is dependent upon such a complex package of cognitive and anatomical features that at first it seems to be the exception to the otherwise clear pattern of continuity apparent between humans and other vertebrates, particularly the higher primates. It is, however, possible to isolate the different functional attributes of language . . . and then to search for these traits in the cognitive and communicative abilities of other animals. This approach takes advantage of one of the most important legacies of the early ethologists, who demonstrated that comparative studies allow us to discriminate between attributes that are phylogenetically ancient and those that have evolved much more recently. (p. 341)

That our sympathies lie with this approach will be clear in the remainder of this chapter.

## What Is a Trait?

Any attempt to investigate relationships between the abilities of humans and those of other animals is faced with a challenging question: When are the traits of different species instances of the same (type) trait? In some cases, this question can be answered in a reasonably straightforward way on functional grounds. The upper appendages of birds, bats, and dragonflies are all considered wings because they play roughly the same role to enable these organisms to fly. In this case, a trait (the possession of wings) is identified on functional grounds, while questions of homoplasy versus homology are decided on grounds that indicate separate evolutionary development, such as the considerable anatomical differences between the wings of birds and the wings of insects.

When traits have easily recognized functions, their reidentification across species is a relatively straightforward matter. Questions of homoplasy versus homology can also be settled in a relatively straightforward manner if there are obvious anatomical structures associated with the functions. But language provides a special difficulty for the comparative method because the capacity for language has very many functions whose dependencies on each other are not clear. Naively, one might ask: Is the capacity of humans to communicate via language the same (type) trait as that of vervets to communicate via alarm calls? But this question is not as straightforward as it seems; before answering it, one must determine which of the multiple functions of human and animal communication systems fix the identity of the trait. The determination of functions can perhaps be placed on an objective footing (see Allen & Bekoff, 1995), but the choice of functions used to determine the trait identity seems to be a largely pragmatic decision—it is interest-relative. Comparisons between human language and vervet communication are further clouded by the fact that while there is much overlap in function, there is also divergence at many points. To be sure, humans can do things with their languages that other animals cannot do with their communication systems. But so too can hummingbirds do things with their wings that eagles cannot do with theirs, and they share a common trait despite these differences.

Those concerned with defending the uniqueness of human language often deny the equivalency of the traits studied in other animals. With respect to ape language research, this has led to lengthy battles over the definition of "language." But it is our view that such disputes are off the point. It's not so much a matter of what language is, but what language *does* that is important for its evolutionary analysis. And because there are many things that language does, and many features of language that support these functions, it is a mistake to dismiss the relevance of animal studies wholesale. Different features and functions of language can be investigated from an evolutionary perspective, and there may be different answers about the usefulness of comparing each feature to the capacities of nonhuman animals. Some features of human language may turn out to be homologous with animal communication; others may turn out to be homoplasies; and, still other features may turn out to be entirely unique to human language. But this latter category does not entail that there is no sense in comparing them; if the wings of hummingbirds have unique features, it does not follow that it is fruitless to compare hummingbird wings to the wings of other birds or to the wings of insects.

Participants on both sides of this discussion recognize that disputes about the definition of language are usually pointless. Pinker, for example, declares that the debate "over what qualifies as True Language" is "fruitless and boring" (p. 347). It is worth noting, however, that this follows an earlier statement that "[g]enuine language ... is seated in the cerebral cortex, primarily the left perisylvian region," and is thus distinguished from primate vocalizations that are (he alleges) involuntarily controlled by subcortical structures (p. 334). If the debate about "True Language" really is fruitless and boring, then it's really just as pointless to hold up control by the cerebral cortex as a criterion of "genuine" language. These facts are, of course, relevant to questions about homoplasy versus homology. But the more interesting topic is the extent to which various functions of language can be teased apart and then shown to exist in different phylogenetic groups, not whether humans are categorically different from other animals (see also Hauser, 1996).

Those who take a hard line about the relationship between human language and nonhuman animal communication also suggest that the study of animal communication is of no interest to understand the evolution of human language unless the traits are homologous; mere homoplasy—parallel or convergent evolution—is deemed irrelevant. But this is too hasty. It is true that homologies provide more direct evidence about the actual historical trajectory along which current traits developed, but it is false that homoplasies provide no relevant information. Ethologists are interested in general principles of evolution and selection. Homoplasy between the traits of different organisms results from similar selective pressures. Thus the study of homoplasies can reveal general principles about the effects of selection on organisms. A better understanding of those general principles can be used to inform the construction of hypotheses about specific historical trajectories. Comparative studies of vocal development in birds and humans provide a wealth of examples of how fruitful this approach can be (Hauser, 1996).

## Reference and Language

In trying to defend the view that reference is a basic functional property of language, we note that many words in human language refer to actions or objects that are external to the speaker. The twentieth-century philosopher,

Ludwig Wittgenstein, famously argued that philosophers (including his own younger self) mistakenly tend to think of reference as the sole function of words in a language, a view of language that he associates at the beginning of his *Philosophical Investigations* (1953) with St. Augustine's theory of language acquisition. While we agree that it is a mistake to forget that words do help to fulfill other functions, we want to suggest that the ability to refer is basic, and that in a very interesting sense, all the more sophisticated functions of language are dependent on this ability. Because of the basic role of reference, one might also suspect that the capacity to refer to external objects or events is phylogenetically older than other features of language, and that it might therefore be a property of other forms of animal communication. This, in turn, suggests that it may be fruitful to study the role of reference in other forms of animal communication in order to understand the evolution of human language.

Pinker grants that the apparently referential vervet alarm calls are as good a place as any to begin thinking about the evolution of human language. He writes: "Perhaps a set of quasi-referential calls such as these came under the voluntary control of the cerebral cortex, and came to be produced in combination for complicated events; the ability to analyze combinations of calls was then applied to the parts of each call" (p. 352). Underlying Pinker's description of the vervet calls as "quasi-referential" seems to be the now familiar concern with the alleged lack of voluntary control, coupled with the fact that vervet communication lacks a structured, combinatorial syntax. Although the combination of voluntary control and complex syntactic abilities plausibly allows organisms to exploit a wider range of communicative abilities for various biological functions, the issues of signal reference, volitional control of signal production, and combinatorial syntax can be treated independently. Lumping different features together and considering them all essential to language reinforces the view that human language is unique. After all, nothing else has *precisely* this combination of features. In a similar vein, absolutely any trait could be deemed unique to a particular species. But appeals to such a weak standard of uniqueness may obscure evolutionary continuity for the various features considered independently.

The hardliner may continue to deny that the communication systems of other species share interesting features with human language. But if features exemplified by the vervets are conceded to be (at least) homoplasies for similar features of human languages, then this weakens the case for the uniqueness of human language. To move toward treating those features as homologies would be to deny the independent evolution of human language. Using Pinker's analogy of the elephant's trunk, the corresponding issue here is whether the common ancestor of elephant and hyrax passed on any traits that predisposed its descendants towards the evolutionary development of a trunk, given selective pressures favoring a prehensile snout. If not, then the trunk can be viewed as a trait that evolved independently in the elephant branch of the evolutionary tree. Similarly at issue for language is whether the prehominid ancestors of humans possessed and transmitted traits that predisposed their descendants towards the evolution of human language, given selective pressures favoring such a development (either directly or indirectly). To settle this question it is necessary to do comparative work involving humans, apes, monkeys, and nonprimates.

Hardliners who claim that language is a uniquely human trait may seek to bolster their case by pointing out that the apparent reference of animal signals is assessed by criteria that do not apply to the referential uses of words in human languages. In particular, biologists seeking to establish that the signals of nonhuman animals are referential often apply a criterion that Quine's fictional *Homo javanensis* would satisfy but that modern human languages do not satisfy. For example, Macedonia and Evans write (1993): "The 'production' criterion is that referential signals should exhibit a degree of stimulus specificity. This requires that all eliciting stimuli must belong to a common category. . . . One clear correlate of the 'production specificity criterion' is that referential signals should not occur at appreciable rates in inappropriate contexts. We would not expect them to be produced in the absence of the putative referent" (179). But as a matter of fact, in cases of modern human language, one might very well expect that signals are used more often in the absence of their referents than in their presence. One of the advanced functions of a language is to allow us to talk about people and things in their absence. Without this capacity, gossip would be next to impossible! So, are biologists wrong to place such a restriction on reference? Or, are they talking about a different phenomenon entirely? We think that the answers to these questions are both negative. It is the same phenomenon, but the cases of reference that satisfy the *javanensian* "production specificity criterion" are (as Quine versified) more primitive in evolutionary development, and it is perfectly acceptable for biologists to seek evidence for these more primitive capacities.

That signals are often present in the absence of their putative referents is evidence either that those signals do not refer to the putative referent, or that the organism using those signals has advanced beyond *javanensian* reference. It would be a mistake to conclude that because the signal, "airplane," is most commonly used in the absence of direct stimulation by airplanes (and therefore fails the *javanensian* production specificity criterion) it does not refer to airplanes. It is important when applying this criterion to recognize the fact that the absence of *javanensian* reference alone does not indicate that there is no reference. One must consider the evidence for both of these rival hypotheses—that reference has advanced beyond the here and now, or that reference is absent. One place to look for evidence of the former is in the development of reference in the young of the species. A suggestion that might (if treated with caution) guide this research is that ontogeny recapitulates phylogeny.

This old saw, that ontogeny recapitulates phylogeny, is at best a rough heuristic and at worst thoroughly misleading (Deacon, 1991). Nonetheless, in this case there are some interesting comparisons to be drawn between human language acquisition, and the role of *javanensian* reference in the evolution of reference. A standard philosophical view of language acquisition is traced in the very first paragraphs of Wittgenstein's *Philosophical Investigations*. The "Augustinian" picture is suggested by St. Augustine's claim that he learned his language from adults who pointed to things and named them. The process of ostensive definition is caricatured by Wittgenstein in his example of "the block world." In this world, a teacher points to stones cut into different shapes and utters a word, allowing a pupil to learn the correlation between the words and the stones. The blockworld language has three key features: (1) it contains referring terms (loosely called "names"); (2) it has no syntax; (3) it is acquired by a process of ostensive definition. Wittgenstein complains that the Augustinian picture of language stresses the importance of naming and plays down other aspects of language. He points out that even in such a restricted language there is much more to language than naming; there are also, for example, complex relationships between linguistic expression and action, such as fetching or carving a particular shaped stone. Different "language games" may even involve varying responses to the same expressions. By stressing naming, the Augustinian picture gives an incomplete and therefore misleading view of language.

Wittgenstein's premise—that there is more to language than just the names of objects—is correct. However, his ensuing de-emphasis of language's naming function may be as misleading as the view it is intended to replace. While Augustinian ostensive definition may not apply to all of language, it may still provide the best account of a foundational stage of language acquisition. So, while there may be more to learning a language than learning the names for various referents, learning those names may be a necessary stage in the process of learning a language.

Learning to associate names and referents is necessary for organisms who are not born with complete knowledge of their vocabulary and its use. Such organisms must learn to correlate the referring terms with those events or objects beyond the speaker to which they refer. Without knowing that "dog" refers to dogs, the speaker of English is at a loss to understand sentences and utterances which use the word "dog." But how central is ostensive definition for the process by which a competent language user comes to learn the relationship between terms and referents? What role in language learning does ostensive definition play? Is the naming of objects a necessary ontogenetic precursor to other language functions? And, if it is, we're led to wonder if ontogeny does recapitulate phylogeny. Is what we find in many nonhuman species a primitive blockworld language? If so, was something like this blockworld language a step in the evolution of human language? Did language evolve by first being something akin to a primitive blockworld language that we might find in nonhuman species?

Does the previously mentioned communication system of vervet monkeys lend credence to the suggestion that animals might use something resembling a blockworld language? Cheney and Seyfarth (1986) report that infant vervets learn to refine the application of their calls to correspond to the call use of adults in the group. Initially, an infant will make the bird of prey alarm whenever something is moving in the sky. However, adults in the group ignore the call in most cases in which the object in the sky is not a predator. If it is a predator, the call is typically repeated by an adult. It seems likely that nothing like explicit pedagogy is occuring between adults and infants, and Cheney and Seyfarth do not claim, on the basis of their data, that there is a connection between adults' repetitions of calls and infants' learning when to use them. Caro and Hauser (1992) do, however, present evidence that adult repetition is necessary for the infants to acquire the same patterns of use as the adults. Despite the lack of explicit instruction, we believe that there are some important similarities to the blockworld language game. The reinforcement provided (perhaps unintentionally) by adult vervets depends on infants and adults sharing attention to the same environmental features. The limited vocabulary of the vervets is similar to the limited vocabulary of the block world. And although the extent to which the vervets could be said to have a language is clearly very limited, nonetheless the referential function of the vervets' communicative utterances appears to be shaped by an ostensive process, albeit one that does not involve any overt pointing. But how is this fact about the acquisition of the vervet communication system related to the acquisition of human language? Is their apparently Augustinian acquisition process merely vaguely similar to human language acquisition? Is it a homologous process? Or, is it homoplastic? How might advocates of the three views discussed above answer these questions? The questions assume, of course, that there is a shared function of vervet "language" and human language. The evidence supports this assumption: both have the function to refer to objects and events external to the "speaker."

Those who propose the hardline view that human language is a unique and recent adaptation are likely to argue that there are still considerable differences between the (possible) conditioning of young vervets by adult reinforcement and the kind of ostensive definition that Augustine described, involving active pointing and naming of objects. But pointing is a gesture that is highly species-specific to humans. Its function is to draw attention to some feature of the environment. In the case of the vervets, there is no need for adults to draw the attention of an infant to the cause of the infant's vocalization because they already share attention to the relevant environmental condition. We return to the issue of shared attention below. But for now our point is that the absence of pointing does not preclude other mechanisms to establish shared attention. Once there is shared attention, then adult vocalizations bear the same relationship to the attentional object or event in both humans and vervets.

Comparative psychologists and cognitive ethologists are likely to be more comfortable with the idea of drawing inferences about phylogeny from ontogeny. Such inferences must be treated with extreme caution, but if the language learning of humans passes through an Augustinian phase, and a similar mode of learning is found in animal communication systems, then the idea that this mode of learning is phylogenetically quite old demands further investigation. Comparable to Greenfield's view that language development is evolutionarily related to the development of the ability to reason hierarchically about objects, one might also view both *javanensian* reference and learning from ostension as necessary precursors to more sophisticated linguistic abilities. The cognitive ethologist may also argue that the development of these abilities in other species provides important evidence about the possible precursors of the more varied language abilities found in hominids. Not only is there reason to think that the vervets (and other organisms) possess a communication system that shares features with the primitive blockworld language—a language that contains referring terms and is learned ostensively, but lacks syntactic structure—but there is also reason to think that these capacities are advantageous. For example, all other things being equal, the organism who can warn her offspring of an approaching predator stands a much better chance of passing her genes on to future generations than does the organism who lacks even the capacity for *javanensian* reference to predators.

## Three Kinds of Reference

The questions we have asked thus far have had to do with the relation between the referential properties of animal communicative systems and reference by human language. But we could approach this issue from another direction. We might ask about the attitude reflected in the ditty which begins this paper: Can organisms whose communication skills match those of the speaker of a blockworld language (vervets, for example, or perhaps, very young humans) manage to refer to objects that are not present? Or, is the user of a blockworld language doomed to refer only to objects that are present to the senses? Under what conditions can reference extend to objects that are absent? To investigate these questions we consider three varieties of reference.

The first kind of reference to consider we shall call "mimetic reference;" this occurs when a signal closely resembles the referent so that it is capable of directly causing the same kind of response. As Dawkins and Krebs (1978) point out, a substantial part of signalling in nonhuman animals is the evolutionarily designed attempt by one animal to use another animal's muscle power to achieve the ends of the first. So, an angler fish that attracts prey by means of a lure has certain behavior patterns and looks a certain way so that it may conserve its own energy while using the muscles of its prey to do work for the angler fish. This is an example of mimetic reference. And, in a nontrivial sense, the angler fish's lure makes reference to something (food for the prey) that is not present. Likewise, the broken-wing distraction display of plovers described by Carolyn Ristau (1991) constitutes a reference to an injured animal, and in doing so it provides an attractive alternative prey for predators near the plover's nest. Both the broken-wing display and the angler fish lure work by providing a stimulus that is not discriminated by the intended audience from a stimulus that would accompany the presence of a suitable prey item. This signalling strategy works because there is a nonarbitrary relationship between signal and referent. There may, however, be a considerable difference in the degree of sophistication with respect to voluntary control. Ristau's results suggest that the plover's deployment of its broken-wing strategy depends on a complex assessment of intruder intention that is partly based on previous experience with individual predators. The point that interests us here, however, is that mimetic reference is possible in the absence of complex intentionality and in the absence of a blockworld language; it may, in some species, lack the sophistication of even involuntary, emotional communication systems. Although this kind of reference is, of course, available to possessors of a blockworld language, it seems appropriate to treat it as an independent trait.

The second kind of reference we shall call "proxy reference;" this occurs when signals function as proxies for their referents, in the sense that signals elicit the same kind of response that the referents would but do so by a different cognitive mechanism. This is in contrast to mimetic reference, which works by stimulating the same sensory/cognitive pathways as the referent would. Proxy reference represents a step toward the more arbitrary relationship between words and their referents that is common to all human languages. Many species of birds and mammals have such signals, but much more work is necessary to find out the extent to which the arbitrary relationships between signal and referent are innate or learned. Proxy reference may also be exploited to refer to absent or nonexistent referents to provide a benefit for the signaller. For example, in mixed-flock species of birds, Munn (1986) observed that members of a sentinel species would sometimes emit an alarm call when in direct competition with birds of other species for a particular prey item. In many cases there was no predator present, and when the other birds took anti-predatory action, the individuals who gave the spurious alarm calls were able to catch the insects for which they were competing. (This behavior seems to persist because the costs of ignoring a threat far outweigh the benefits of eating a bug.) There is also anecdotal evidence of similar behavior by monkeys during intergroup conflicts (Dennett, 1983). All that is necessary for successful proxy reference is the ability to make the link between a signal and the object or behavior to which the signal refers. Proxy reference is thus within the capability of organisms limited to a blockworld language.

The third sort of reference is what we call "conceptual reference;" this occurs when signals may refer to external conditions without it being normal for such uses to elicit the responses that the referents themselves would elicit if they were present. This kind of reference is the norm for everyday human conversation. When someone says the word "tiger," the listener is not expected to get scared, begin evasive maneuvers, or to look for cat food. Because of the independence of conceptual reference from behavioral response, conceptual reference enables a whole new range of references to things that are not physically present. Bob is able to tell Jane about the spectacular sunset he saw last week, thereby making her think that he is a romantic. Whereas, if his description simply evoked her typical responses to sunsets, the point about his character might be lost (although bonding could still occur). Is conceptual reference possible for an organism that is limited to a blockworld language? There seems to be no principled reason the Augustinian organism would be unable to exploit conceptual reference. Indeed, one can imagine a Wittgenstinian language game where the utterance of "slab" would invoke different responses according to whether or not it is uttered in the presence of a slab. In this case, the word is not simply a proxy for the object. Whether actual Augustinian organisms do show evidence of conceptual reference is another question—one that we believe could be investigated profitably by ethologists and comparative psychologists. The demonstration of conceptual reference would not amount to a demonstration of more than a blockworld language, and the absence of conceptual reference would raise interesting questions and suggest interesting research into why that capacity is absent.

Because both proxy and conceptual reference require the organism to make an arbitrary connection between signal and referent, and because it is often ecologically inadvisable to hardwire such connections, both these kinds of reference are likely to involve the kind of learning from ostension that concerned Wittgenstein. In order to learn the name of something ostensively, the referent of the name must be clear to the student. This ostensive definition requires, at minimum, some shared attention—both participants must be attending to the same condition in the environment. If the infant vervet and the adult are attending to different conditions when the adult repeats the infant's warning cry, the infant will fail to learn what are the correct referents of the warning cry. Indeed Caro and Hauser (1992) observed a case in which an infant vervet saw a herd of stampeding elephants, gave a leopard alarm call, and then immediately after, the alpha male vervet saw a leopard and gave a leopard alarm call. The infant persisted giving leopard alarm calls to approaching elephants for several months.

One interesting issue for future study is the evolution and development of shared attention. How much does the infant know innately about what to pay attention to, and how much is learned? And how is the ontogeny of shared attention related to the ontogeny of language? We turn to these questions below. Before doing so, however, we want to ask what the shared attention is attention to.

*Attention and Reference*

Our tendency, as language-using adults, is to think of reference stereotypically as reference to objects; but we shall argue that both phylogenetically and ontogenetically, reference to behaviors may be more basic than reference to objects. Consider, first, human infants. Studies of the attention of human infants show that they are more likely to attend to lights moving in an animated pattern (as if they are positioned at the joints of a moving animal, human, or nonhuman) than they are to attend to lights that are either static or moving linearly (Johannson, 1973). This suggests that the attention of human infants is drawn naturally to objects engaged in certain kinds of behavior rather than to objects themselves. Furthermore, this suggests that the motion that human infants find most captivating is animate motion—motion, that is, that might be of something animate in the infant's environment rather than the motion of something inanimate (such as a tree branch blowing in the wind). A natural predisposition to attend to animate motion more readily than inanimate motion or to static objects would provide evolutionary advantages under certain ecological conditions. Some of those things that are moving are predators. The organism that is naturally predisposed to attend to animate motion is the organism that is going to monitor a predator more closely. Does this predisposition extend to nonhuman primates? Do vervet infants prefer to attend to lights moving in an animate pattern over lights that are static or lights that are moving in a linear pattern? We don't know of any research specific to vervets, but Johansson's methods applied to cats showed that they can discriminate animate motion from nonanimate motion (Blake, 1993). Hauser and Carey (this volume) discuss their own experiments with monkeys (tamarins) that seem to differentiate between animate motion and other forms of motion.

There is some evidence from field studies that nonhuman primates are similarly concerned with motion. Part of the vocal behavioral repertoire of the vervet is the "moving-into-the-open" (MIO) grunt. This is used by a vervet to indicate that it is about to move into an open area, or that it is following another into an open area. The grunts do not indicate the open areas themselves. They're not performed in most contexts when the vervets are simply near or in an open area, but are reserved for contexts that involve motion into the open areas. The referential properties of the grunts would be a mystery if the vervets were limited to referring to objects. There is no one object (or type of object) that is the referent of an MIO grunt, instead there is a change in the spatial relationship between the open area and various vervets. What moves into the open might be the animal producing the grunt, or it might be another vervet. The MIO grunt captures the changing relationship between the two. Because this is one signal that refers to different objects in different situations in which the common element is not just how the objects are related, but also how that relationship is changing, the vervet could not successfully make an MIO grunt with a blockworld language that refers only to objects, and not behaviors. If we hypothesize instead that their language takes behaviors or movements as its primitives, then we could have an atmosphere that facilitates understanding the MIO grunt, and one that doesn't demand any language of greater complexity than blockworld language. (While this result may please those hardliners who prefer to distance human linguistic abilities from those of nonhuman animals, we suggest below that the support this provides for the hardliner about human uniqueness is less than may seem at first blush;

remember, evidence also suggests that human infants attend to events rather than objects).

Other ethological evidence supports the conclusion that the vervet communication system takes events rather than objects as a primitive. Careful analysis of the ontogeny of vervet alarm calling shows that the infants don't make mistakes about everything in the sky (when making bird of prey alarm calls) or everything in the trees (when making beast of prey alarm calls); instead, analysis of the ontogeny of eagle alarm calls shows that vervet infants' "mistakes" (when making bird of prey alarm calls) are most common for nonpredatory species diving rapidly from the sky or closely approaching the vervets, and that such errors are not associated merely with morphological similarity (Seyfarth, Cheney, & Marler, 1980; Seyfarth & Cheney, 1986; Cheney & Seyfarth, 1986; Hauser, 1989). Because these are behaviors that may reasonably be associated with predation, and because moving objects are more easily discriminated from background than static objects, it makes sense that vervets would be innately disposed to react to such events. Again, it is the nature of the events that is noteworthy from the point of view of the vervet, not the nature of the object performing the behavior. In order that the infant vervet learn which objects are the correct referents of the alarm calls, it is apparently predisposed to pay attention to objects behaving in a certain manner. This would also explain how it could happen that an infant vervet would learn to make the leopard alarm call to approaching elephants (as observed by Caro & Hauser, 1992): what it was predisposed to notice was a kind of behavior, not a kind of morphology. This is also consistent with discovery by Evans and Marler (1995) that a chicken shown a moving image of a raccoon on a video monitor mounted overhead will make aerial predator calls at a higher rate than terrestrial predator calls. This is not to say that morphology is irrelevant: alarm calls were more reliably elicited by video footage of a raptor on the overhead monitor than by footage of the raccoon. Similarly, realistic, artificially-generated, raptor-shaped images were significantly more effective to elicit alarm calls than disk-like images with the same surface area moving at the same velocity. (Evans & Marler don't tell us, but it would also be interesting to know how the animals would respond to video of raptors in the eye-level monitor).

The evidence from chickens indicates that event type of the stimulus is a more important determinant of call type than is object type. (Remember that the raccoon and the disk moving overhead both produce aerial predator alarms, albeit at a lower rate than hawks or artificial hawk shapes). The evolution of reference to events of these categories as distinct may have been driven by the different anti-predatory strategies that are appropriate for chickens faced by these different predators (Macedonia & Evans, 1993). Similarly, infant vervets seem to begin with an action-oriented classification scheme. In vervets, reinforcement of infant vocalizations may lead to a classification scheme that is based more on perceptual characteristics abstracted away from behavior. The ability to categorize and refer to objects independently of behavior would be an adaptive trait when the costs of responding to false positives (such as nonpredators behaving in a predatory fashion) or of failing to respond to false negatives (such as predators behaving in nontypical ways) are relatively high.

If both human infants and nonhuman primate infants naturally (perhaps even innately) attend to behaviors rather than to objects, this may be a result of a common cognitive attentional ability. We see two possibilities here. Either this trait (the trait of attending to behaviors) is found in both human and nonhuman primate infants because it is a homoplastic development, or because it is a homologous development. The first is certainly possible: as suggested above, there is clear advantage to attending to behaviors rather than to objects. But the second is equally possible: this development may well have first come about in some ancestor common to both human and nonhuman primates. What is needed to answer this question is some comparative study of these cognitive abilities in both humans and other primates. Such a study would attempt to map the co-occurrence and dissociations between the different types of referential abilities described above. This makes possible inferences about the phylogenetic relationships between these traits.

To see how this applies to the particular case of human language, consider the importance of infant attention for the development of language. Without shared attention between infant and adult, learning from ostension is impossible (in fact, this was Wittgenstein's point when he objected to a blockworld language). In order to learn some basic vocabulary, both parties to the interaction must each be attending to the same thing. Because attention to motion is a very basic necessity for a wide range of organisms (but not all), it is not surprising to find that mechanisms that depend on *shared* attention should be built on top of the capacity to attend to motion. If the infant's attention is naturally drawn to behaviors, an adult will be able to draw upon that in her ostensive definition. It seems likely, then, that studying the cognitive mechanisms of attention is an important task to understand the development of language. Supposing that language depends on shared attention, and that mechanisms for establishing shared attention are found in many nonhuman organisms, if it is further found that these mechanisms are especially well developed in primates, then language can be seen as built on top of an ability that we share with other primates. Even if the shared attention mechanisms of primates are merely homoplastic and not homologous to the human trait, the comparative studies may nonetheless establish that the capacity for shared attention is a necessary precursor to learn relationships between signals and referents. Thus, it is too hasty for hardliners about human language uniqueness to dismiss the relevance of animal studies on the grounds that the communicative capacities of animals are mere homoplasies of human language. And while it is possible that human attentional mechanisms are only analogous to those found in other primates, this conclusion should be supported by comparative studies of humans and other primates, not by an a priori conviction about the nature and origins of human language.

## Concluding Remarks

We've been pursuing two apparently distinct lines of inquiry in our discussion of the evolution of reference, one about reference to absent objects, and another about the primitive objects of reference. Now it is time to draw these lines together. When an adult vervet makes an alarm call, the other vervets respond to that call as if they were responding directly to the predator (their behavior differs, of course, with the kind of alarm call). This is what we have called "proxy reference." Some vervets have apparently learned to exploit proxy reference to their advantage, relying on alarm calls to cause the same reaction in other vervets that a predator would cause. The same is true for members of sentinel species of birds: they have learned to use their alarm calls to their advantage when there is no predator. This kind of behavior can only be advantageous if the recipient of the alarm call treats it as a sign caused by the presence of the predator, not as a false signal of some absent object. Compare this use of an alarm call to shouting "Fire!" in a theater in order to get a seat. The false "Fire!" cry only works if the recipients of this cry treat it as a reference to something present, rather than as a reference to something absent. The successful use of false alarms depends on the audience treating them as signals of a present, not absent object. The sentinel bird and the (anecdotal) monkey are able to rely on their audience responding in that way.

What we learn from the discussion of the primitive objects of reference is that these alarm calls, at least when they are being learned, refer not to the predators per se, but to predator-like behavior. This realization helps us complete an ontogenetic picture. For vervets, at least, reference starts with reference to certain behavioral patterns. Through a process that involves ostensive definition, this gets modified so that it applies to either specific behavioral patterns or to a combination of behavior and morphology (we think the latter is more likely, but this is an open question and one that should be easily testable). It seems likely that only after the ability to refer correctly has been learned is the vervet able to refer to absent objects in the false signalling sense discussed above. And only after the vervet can refer to absent objects in false signals, could it engage in the kind of reference that we have labelled as "conceptual." Notice that even if the vervet could engage in conceptual reference, the signals it produced would evoke behavior as if the referent were actually present. Its audience, in other words, is unable to comprehend reference as anything beyond proxy reference. There are two lessons here: (1) successful reference is a product of an interaction between the producer of the reference and the producer's audience; (2) there are developmental stages in the ontogenesis of reference. Does ontogeny recapitulate phylogeny? Are the ontogenetic stages reflections of the phylogenetic development of reference? If so, we might expect to find organisms that have developed referential abilities of the first stage, but not the second, the way vervets have apparently developed abilities at the second stage and not the third. This also raises questions about human development. We have pointed out that there are these stages in the ontogeny of reference for vervets; are there the same stages in the ontogeny of human reference? Finally, this raises questions for the evolution of language: if we find that these stages do occur in humans as well as in other species, this would suggest that the development of language is neither highly unique nor highly modular. We think comparative psychology and ethology are on the right track here; these are interesting questions, and the comparative evidence is well worth looking at.

Further support for the idea that reference to behaviors is more basic in the early stages of the evolution of language comes from the work of Tanner and Byrne (1996), who have studied the spontaneous gestures of lowland gorillas. Their analysis reveals that these gestures typically refer to desired behaviors such as play or copulation. They remark that: "It is likely that the earliest iconic depiction by human ancestors was of actions rather than objects, since it is representation of action that we find in the gestures of extant apes" (p. 163). Tanner and Byrne are engaging in exactly the kind of study that would shed light on the questions we're raising here: a comparative study that looks at the development of reference. We find it encouraging that their results confirm the hypotheses we draw from other research into the development of reference.

Thus far we have raised more questions than we have answered. This suits our purposes well, for we are more interested in presenting interesting directions for future research than in defending specific theories. In this vein, it is also worth pointing out some implications of these ideas about the evolution of reference for a puzzle about ostensive definition that exercised Wittgenstein and Quine, and that continues to exercise those who are interested in the acquisition of language by children. Human children show a remarkable ability to identify the correct reference of learned count nouns such as "dog" or "bird" (Hall, 1994). To explain this ability, it is common to appeal to the concept of a "medium-sized" or "basic-level" category, specified in terms of perceived similarity to a morphologically identified prototype (Rosch, 1978). But the designations "medium-sized" and "basic level" can seem suspiciously ad hoc. In some cases, the category is at the taxonomic level of species or family (e.g., "dog") and sometimes at the level of a class (e.g., "bird"), and the only reason for picking these levels as basic is that these are what the language learners in fact latch onto. The degree of abstraction in these categories does, however, correspond closely to those categories identified by Cheney and Seyfarth as the referents of vervet monkey alarm calls (e.g., "leopard," "snake," or "eagle") which also correspond to different taxonomic levels, and they are considerably less abstract than the categories identified by Marler and Evans as referents of the alarm calls of chickens (e.g., "avian predator" and "terrestrial predator"). It is possible that these translational differences reflect nothing more than a lack of knowledge about the vocalizations of chickens and vervets. But if the differences are real, then data about the ontogeny of vervet alarm calls suggest an interesting hypothesis about the evolution of communication systems and the ability to conceptualize objects independently of their typical behaviors.

The hypothesis is that if the ontogeny of sophisticated referential skills recapitulates the phylogeny in a transition from action-based categories to feature-based categories, then it may not be necessary to postulate morphologically specified, innate "middle-sized" or "basic-level" categories to explain how children settle on a reasonable level of interpretation for count nouns. The behavioral differences between dogs and cows (although belonging to the same taxonomic order) may have been evolutionarily salient to humans in ways that differences between behavior in different species of birds was not. Thus humans might innately be disposed to categorize initially according to such behaviorally specified categories. An evolutionary and comparative approach to the notion of reference, and similarities to various nonhuman communication systems, may thus help provide a specification of the basic categories that facilitate the earliest stages of language acquisition. Furthermore, worries about just how it is that language learners manage to latch onto the correct referents may be mitigated by appeal to behaviors. Because motion against a background is more easily discriminated than the boundaries of a static object, it may be possible for language learners and language teachers to rely on the innate tendency to attend to behaviors in order to bootstrap reference to its first stage. The next stage, reference to objects, may then be learned as a consequence of exposure to uses of a word or other signal in cases in which the object is not behaving in its typical fashion.

In the end we've told a partial story about the complex mosaic of traits that make up human language. We've tried to pick on one of these traits, reference, to describe the variety of forms that it might take in organisms belonging to various species. Our understanding of these forms has been helped immensely by empirical research that was conducted with an explicitly comparative agenda and that would have been unavailable from a purely hardline approach. Finally, we have a second verse that we wrote for Quine's ditty that summarizes our findings, and although we're still a bit embarrassed about revealing it, here it is:

> The well refined and tutored mind
> Of *homo sapiens* is
> Evolved to treat things inconcrete
> From moving references.

## Note

We thank Marc Bekoff, Denise Cummins, Heather Gert, Patricia Greenfield, and Marc Hauser for comments.

## References

Allen, C., & Bekoff, M. (1995). Function, natural design, and animal behavior: Philosophical and ethological considerations. *Perspectives in Etholology*, *11*, 1–46.

Blake, R. (1993). Cats perceive biological motion. *Psychological Science*, *4*, 54–57.

Caro, T. M., & Hauser, M. D. (1992). Is there teaching in nonhuman animals? *Quarterly Review of Biology*, *67*, 151–174.

Cheney, D. L., & Seyfarth, R. M. (1986). Vocal development in vervet monkeys. *Animal Behavior*, *34*, 1640–1658.

Cheney, D. L., & Seyfarth, R. M. (1990). *How monkeys see the world: Inside the mind of another species*. Chicago: University of Chicago Press.

Chomsky, N. (1957). *Syntactic Structures*. The Hague: Mouton.

Dawkins, R., & Krebs, J. (1978). Animal Signals: Information or manipulation? In J. R. Krebs and N. B. Davies (Eds.), *Behavioural Ecology: An evolutionary approach* (1st ed.). Sunderland, MA: Sinauer Associates.

Deacon, T. W. (1991). Anatomy of hierarchical information processing. *Behavioral and Brain Sciences*, *14*, 555–557.

Dennett, D. C. (1983). Intentional systems in cognitive ethology: The "Panglossian paradigm" defended. *Behavioral and Brain Sciences*, *6*, 343–390.

Dennett, D. C. (1995). *Darwin's dangerous idea: Evolution and the meanings of life*. New York: Simon & Schuster.

Descartes, R. (1637/1985). *Discourse and Essays*, published in *The Philosophical Writings of Descartes*, vol 1., J. Cottingham, R. Stoothoff, & D. Murdoch (Trans.). Cambridge: Cambridge University Press.

Evans, C., & Marler, P. (1995). Language and animal communication: Parallels and contrasts. In J.-A. Meyer & H. L. Roitblat (Eds.), *Comparative Approaches to Cognitive Science* (pp. 341–383). Cambridge, MA: MIT Press.

Greenfield, P. (1991). Language, tools and brain: The ontogeny and phylogeny of hierarchically organized sequential behavior. *Behavioral and Brain Sciences*, *14*, 531–595.

Hall, D. G. (1994). How children learn common nouns and proper names: a review of the experimental evidence. In J. Macnamara & G. E. Reyes (Eds.), *The Logical Foundations of Cognition* (pp. 212–240). New York: Oxford University Press,

Hauser, M. D. (1989). Ontogenetic changes in the comprehension and production of vervet monkey (*Cercopithecus aethiops*) vocalizations. *Journal of Comparative Psychology*, *103*, 149–158.

Hauser, M. D. (1996). *The Evolution of Communication*. Cambridge, MA: MIT Press.

Hauser, M. D., & Andersson, K. (1994). Left hemisphere dominance for processing vocalizations in adult, but not infant, rhesus monkeys: Field experiments. *Proceedings of the National Academy of Sciences*, *91*, 3946–3948.

Hauser, M. D., & Marler, P. (1993a). Food associated calls in rhesus macaques (*Macaca mulatta*). I. Socioecological factors. *Behavioral Ecology*, *4*, 194–205.

Hauser, M. D., & Marler, P. (1993b). Food associated calls in rhesus macaques (*Macaca mulatta*). II. Costs and benefits of call production and suppression. *Behavioral Ecology*, *4*, 206–212.

Johansson, G. (1973). Visual perception of biological motion and a model for its analysis. *Perception and Psychophysics*, *14*, 201–211.

Lieberman, P. (1995). What primate calls can tell us about human evolution. In E. Zimmerman, J. D. Newman, & U. Jurgens (Eds.), *Current topics in primate vocal communication* (pp. 273–282). New York: Plenum Press.

Locke, J. (1995). Linguistic capacity: An ontogenetic theory with evolutionary implications. In E. Zimmerman, J. D. Newman, & U. Jurgens (Eds.), *Current topics in primate vocal communication* (pp. 253–272). New York: Plenum Press.

MacNeilage, P. F., Studdert-Kennedy, M., & Lindblom, B. (1991). Primate handedness reconsidered. *Behavioral and Brain Sciences, 10,* 247–263.

Marler, C., & Evans, P. (1995). Bird calls: just emotional displays or something more? *Ibis, 138,* 26–33.

Marler, P., Karakashian, S., & Gyger, M. (1991). Do animals have the option of withholding signals when communication is inappropriate? The audience effect. In C. A. Ristau (Ed.), *Cognitive ethology: The minds of other animals. Essays in honor of Donald R. Griffin* (pp. 187–208). Hillsdale, NJ: Erlbaum.

Munn, C. A. (1986). The Deceptive Use of Alarm Calls by Sentinel Species in Mixed-species Flocks of Neotropical Birds. In R. W. Mitchell & N. S. Thompson (Eds.), *Deception* (pp. 169–175). New York: SUNY Press.

Pinker, S. (1994). *The language instinct.* New York: Morrow.

Quine, W. V. O. (1953). Identity, ostension and hypostasis. In *From a logical point of view.* Cambridge, MA: Harvard University Press.

Rauschecker, J. P., Tian, B., & Hauser, M. (1995). Processing of complex sounds in the macaque nonprimary auditory cortex. *Science, 268,* 111–114.

Ristau, C. (1991). Aspects of the cognitive ethology of an injury-feigning bird, the piping plovers. In C. A. Ristau (Ed.), *Cognitive ethology: The minds of other animals. Essays in honor of Donald R. Griffin* (pp. 91–126). Hillsdale, NJ: Erlbaum.

Rosch, E. (1978). Principles of categorization. In E. Rosch & B. B. Lloyd (Eds.), *Cognition and categorization* (pp. 27–48). Hillsdale, NJ: Erlbaum.

Seyfarth, R. M., Cheney, D. L., & Marler, P. (1980). Vervet monkey alarm calls: Semantic communication in a free-ranging primate. *Animal Behaviour, 28,* 1070–1094.

Seyfarth, R. M., & Cheney, D. L. (1986). Vocal development in vervet monkeys. *Animal Behavior, 34,* 1640–1658.

Tanner, J. E., & Byrne, R. W. (1996). Representation of action through iconic gesture in a captive lowland gorilla. *Current Anthropology, 37,* 162–173.

Wittgenstein, L. (1953). *Philosophical investigations.* New York: Macmillan.

# 8

# Some Issues in the Evolution of Language and Thought

PAUL BLOOM

Language and thought are intimately related. Without language, much of what we think about (such as science and politics) would not exist. And without thoughts to convey, language would be worthless. What use are words without concepts or sentences without propositions? It is likely that language and other aspects of the human mind entered into a competitive feedback loop over the course of human evolution. As our ancestors' abilities to communicate increased, this may have led to selective pressure for increased social and conceptual capacities—which in turn created more pressure for greater communicative abilities, and so on. Many of the design features of language itself, such as the inventory of syntactic categories that all languages possess, exist in part through mappings with aspects of nonlinguistic thought, and children's language learning relies on their appreciation of such mappings (Bloom, 1994a; Jackendoff, 1990).

There is no doubt, then, that language and thought are related. This chapter is about how they are independent. I will suggest here that, despite their obvious connections, language and nonlinguistic aspects of human mental life have distinct evolutionary histories. This chapter naturally divides into two parts—one concerning language, and the other concerning certain other cognitive capacities.

## Language

There are several theories of how humans evolved the ability to learn and use language. The dominant theory in the social sciences is that language is a human invention. It is a good idea that was invented one or more times, spreading across the world, like agriculture and beer brewing. An alternative theory is that language is a by-product of a more general property of humans, such as our accelerated general intelligence or our big brains. A third theory is that language emerged through some freak biological event— a macromutation, perhaps. A fourth theory is that language has evolved primarily as a system of reasoning and representation, as an enhanced mode of thought. A fifth theory, which I will argue is the correct one, is that language evolved through natural selection for the function of communication. Though language is plainly related to culture, social cognition, and all manners of abstract thought, it is nevertheless a distinct adaptation.

Many scholars are skeptical that such an account can be defended. Some have said that we are not in a position to know how any aspect of the mind has evolved and most likely never will be (Lewontin, 1990). Others have speculated that explaining the emergence of language and other aspects of the mind poses a special mystery for evolutionary theory, requiring perhaps advances in molecular biology (Chomsky, 1988) or quantum physics (Penrose, 1989). And still other scholars believe that the very notion of adaptation is out-dated and irrelevant. Doesn't the theory of complex systems show that natural selection plays no interesting role in evolution? Aren't all selectionist proposals nothing more than just-so stories? Aren't we post-Darwinian by now? (e.g., Piattelli-Palmarini, 1989).

It is an interesting sociological question why this skepticism about natural selection is so much more prevalent within linguistics and psycholinguistics than it is within biology itself, but this issue will not be addressed here (see Dennett, 1995). Instead, I will try to defuse these skeptical concerns by showing that the evolution of language can be studied in much the same way we would study the evolution of any other biological trait, such as the wings of insects (e.g., Kingsolver & Koehl, 1985) or the peacock's tail (e.g., Cronin, 1991). It turns out that there are data from linguistics, psychology, and neuroscience that bear directly on the question of how language evolved. These data allow us to evaluate critically the theories described above.

## Language as an Invention

One idea is that language is an invention—a cultural innovation. This view has led to many proposals about the moment when language was first used. In a recent New Yorker cartoon, a cavewoman and a caveman are sitting together, the cavewoman saying sternly: "We have to talk." The cartoon is titled, "The Origin of Language." The more traditional theories of first utterances, such as the proposals made in the nineteenth century that language somehow originated out of grunts of exertion or imitations of animal sounds, are not much more compelling.

In the following section, I will argue that language is a distinct capacity of the human brain, sometimes called a mental organ, or module. If this is right, then it is plainly not an invention. But the mental organ proposal is admittedly controversial, and we can reject the invention account on simpler grounds.

No society lacks language. The languages of technologically advanced societies are no more complex than those of hunter-gatherer societies, and there is no sense in which Modern English is an improvement over Old English. Although languages differ in certain regards, these differences cannot be explained in terms of diffusion from an original source. Instead, "there appears to be a fairly poor correlation between language typology and historical relatedness of languages, except over very short time spans . . . languages change according to a random walk within a circumscribed set of possibilities; they do not systematically and cumulatively diverge according to their family tree" (Pinker, in press). For instance, languages cycle back and forth between having relatively fixed word order (like Modern English) and relatively free word order with case-marking (like Warlpiri and English hundreds of years ago). This is all quite different from what one finds with cultural innovations, such as writing and agriculture, which are typically not universal, vary in complexity across societies, and show progress and diffusion over the course of history.

In fact, the capacity to create language exists in every neurologically normal human. Even young children appreciate highly abstract universals of grammar, suggesting that they start off with certain expectations about the nature of language (e.g., Chomsky, 1988; Crain, 1991; Pinker, 1994). And they can use these expectations to create a language even in cases in which they are not exposed to one in the course of development. Some children are only exposed to a "pidgin," an ad hoc system created for the purpose of communication by adult speakers of different languages. This was typically the case when plantation owners deliberately mixed slaves from diverse backgrounds (Bickerton, 1981). There are also deaf children whose sole linguistic input consists of a distorted and rudimentary sign system, which often occurs when hearing parents give birth to a deaf child and must quickly (and inadequately) learn some sign language to attempt to communicate with their child (Singleton & Newport, 1993). What one finds in such cases is that children develop a full-blown language with abstract structural properties not present in the sentences they are exposed to—a process called "creolization." Once again, this does not happen with cultural innovations, which are learned as the result of careful tutelage, not invented anew each generation.

The final problem with the invention theory is that it begs the question. Suppose language were an invention. We are still faced with the fact that humans are able to make use of this invention, while chimpanzees, cats, and goldfish are not. Attempts to teach language to members of our most related species, chimpanzees, have led to unimpressive results. Even the most enthusiastic claims about these animals put them at the linguistic level of slow three-year-olds, and such claims are most likely overstatements (Pinker, 1994; Seidenberg & Petitto, 1979). So the question remains: What happened in the evolutionary history of our species that gave rise to the unique ability to learn and use language?

## Language as a By-product

The fact that humans possess language does not entail that this ability has been selected for, and it certainly does not entail that there is some special part of human psychology devoted to language learning. Evolutionary theorists have long understood that an indefinite number of biological traits exist that have not been specifically selected for. For instance, an organ can evolve for one purpose and then be co-opted for another. This is what Darwin (1859) called "preadaptation" and Gould and Vrba (1982) termed "exaptation." In the most extreme case, this occurs without natural selection playing any further role. Humans are unique in that we can learn to play chess, for instance, but it would be madness to say that we have evolved a specific capacity to do so; our chess ability is, instead, an accidental by-product of other cognitive capacities that *have* evolved as adaptations. Much of the debate within contemporary psychology is about which aspects of the mind are specific adaptations and which are by-products of mental systems that have evolved for other, perhaps more general, purposes.

It is sometimes suggested that language is an exaptation, either of some more general intellectual capacity that humans possess or of our large brains. But there are reasons to reject this view.

Consider first the claim that language is a by-product of our general intelligence (e.g., Gould, 1979). We know immediately that this cannot be entirely correct, because aspects of language can be linked to distinct regions of human anatomy. Darwin himself pointed out that the human vocal tract is tailored to the demands of speech. This is at the expense of swallowing, which is why humans are the only primate who frequently die by choking on meat. In his "Natural Theology" (1802, p. 81), William Paley rhapsodized about the extent to which our anatomy seems crafted for speech: "we have a passage opened . . . for the admission of air, exclusively of every other substance; we have muscles, some in the larynx, and without number in the tongue, for the purpose of modulating that air in its passage, with a variety, a compass and precision, of which no other musical instrument is capable" (see also Lieberman, 1984).

The evidence that language is special is not restricted to speech, however. The ability to acquire grammar emerges at about the age of one and a half, but starts to diminish at about the age of seven. Studies from first- and second-language learning suggest that this critical period is the result of neural maturation, not cultural or environmental factors, and it exists for both spoken and signed languages (Newport, 1990). Also, as discussed above, there is evidence from studies of normal language development that children quickly acquire highly abstract properties of grammar even when these properties are absent in the input. These considerations suggest that the human capacity for language learning is distinct from other, more general, systems of knowledge acquisition.

Studies of language pathologies motivate a similar conclusion. There are disorders caused by stroke or trauma in which people suffer severe language deficits but are of otherwise normal intelligence (Caplan, 1995). Other disorders are genetically transmitted. Many members of one family studied by Gopnik (1990) show a severe deficit in their understanding of certain core aspects of language, but have normal nonverbal intelligence. The fact that language can be selectively impaired (as well as selectively spared; see Smith & Tsimpli, 1995) is further evidence that it is not the result of more general intellectual abilities.

If not intelligence, what about brain size? A different suggestion is that language might be an emergent property of the human brain's large size or the way in which the neurons are crammed together (e.g., Chomsky, 1988). But there are good reasons to dismiss this proposal (Bickerton, 1990; Pinker & Bloom, 1990). A large brain is neither necessary nor sufficient for language. Some nanencephalic dwarfs, people with brain-sizes in the range of chimpanzees, have little language impairment (Lenneberg, 1967), and, as mentioned above, there are people with brains of perfectly normal size who have severe impairments of language.

More generally, the whole idea that a big brain makes you smart is dubious. There is obviously some minimum number of neurons that the brain needs in order to solve certain problems, but once one gets past this minimum, there is no reason to expect more neurons to be of further benefit. In fact, neural network modeling suggests the opposite—for many computational problems, smaller systems do better than larger ones, since they are better at making generalizations (Elman, 1993). Large brains are bad for other reasons, since they consume an inordinate amount of oxygen, blood, and metabolic energy. Most likely, as Pinker (1994) argues, the "big brain" theory of language is exactly backwards. It is not that the brain got big and language mysteriously emerged as a by-product. Instead, language has evolved through standard Darwinian processes. The human brain is big because it has to contain language and other specialized mental organs. It is brain size that is the by-product, not language.

### Language and Natural Selection

The conclusion up to now is that language is a distinct capacity. The standard explanation of the origin of distinct capacities is natural selection—descent with modification. But there are alternatives. For instance, Bickerton (1995) has argued that full-fledged human language emerged from a more rudimentary protolanguage in a single step, as a "catastrophic event." He notes that his view has received a lot of criticism, but goes on to defend it as follows: "I became aware that the theory of punctuated equilibrium (Eldridge & Gould, 1972) was a respectable alternative to neo-Darwinian gradualist orthodoxy. Although many evolutionary developments come about very gradually, through a slow-building mosaic of cumulative adaptations, not all of them do. . . . In many evolutionary lines, what we see is countless millennia of stagnation, followed by quite sudden shifts to new plateaus of stability" (p. 69).

Can language emerge in a single step? Actually, Bickerton's idea that punctuated equilibrium is an alternative to natural selection is a common misinterpretation of this theory, prompted in part by over-enthusiastic statements by its supporters (see Dennett, 1995 for discussion). More recently, however, Gould (1982) has stated that "punctuated equilibrium is not a theory of macromutation," it is "a theory about ordinary speciation (taking tens of thousands of years) and its abrupt appearance at low scales of geological resolution, not about ecological catastrophe and sudden genetic changes" (1987a). Even if the theory of punctuated equilibrium is right, then, it provides no support for Bickerton's proposal, which is a macromutation theory and has nothing to do with speciation.

There is a more general problem with Bickerton's theory, as well as with any theory that posits a non-selectionist process, like macromutation or genetic drift to explain the evolution of human language. The argument, outlined by Pinker and Bloom (1990), goes as follows:

- Natural selection is the only explanation for the origin of adaptive complexity.
- Human language shows complex design for the adaptive goal of communication.
- Hence, language has evolved through natural selection.

There are two premises that need to be defended here—one about evolution, and one about language. Evolution first. One of the fundamental problems in the study of the natural world has been to explain the existence of intricate structures that have the appearance of design (see Dawkins, 1986). The classic solution has been to posit a divine intentional designer, God. As Paley (1802) suggested, if someone came across a watch, precisely fashioned to fit on the wrist and tell time, the person would not be satisfied with the claim that it had emerged by accident. Its intricacy of design would lead to the belief that it had a designer. Paley noted further that organs such as the eye, the hand, and the heart are far more complicated than a watch, and hence it is reasonable to posit an intentional explanation for their existence. Saying that the eye is the result of a random process would be like saying that a watch came into being when a bolt of lighting hit a pile of scrap metal; it would be appealing to a miracle.

Darwin was familiar with Paley's writings, and he responded by explaining how "organs of extreme perfection and complication" could arise from the purely physical process of natural selection. Although the materials that natural selection draws upon are random mutations, natural selection is not itself a random process. Natural selection works through the retention of variations that give rise to minute changes in reproductive success. This allows an organism to move gradually through the landscape of possible forms toward the possession of biological traits of ever-increasing functional utility. In fact, natural selection is the only nonintentional process we know of that is capable of producing such traits (Cronin, 1991; Dawkins, 1983, 1986; Dennett, 1995). Historically, all alternatives to natural selection—saltationism, directed mutation, and the inheritance of acquired character-istics—have either ignored the question of design altogether or "solved" it by sneaking in some unexplained principle that miraculously guides organ-isms to more perfect states (Cronin, 1991).

None of this is to deny that biological and physical factors serve to constrain evolutionary processes, as argued by Goodwin (1994) and Kaufmann (1993), among others. But such constraints cannot, in them-selves, explain how adaptations arise because they are inherently insensi-tive to functional demands at the level of the whole organism. From the standpoint of principles acting at the level of molecular interactions, for instance, there would be no reason at all to expect that we would possess biological structures that enable us to see and talk and walk, as opposed to any of the extraordinarily vast number of possible structures that do noth-ing at all.

The notion that natural selection is the explanation for complex de-sign is not controversial among practicing evolutionary theorists. Even Gould and Lewontin (1979), in their classic attack on adaptationism, are explicit that they agree with Darwin that natural selection is the most im-portant of evolutionary mechanisms, presumably because it is the only ex-planation for adaptively complex organs such as the eye (see also Gould, 1977). The real debate over the role of natural selection in the evolution of language is not a debate about evolution, then; it is a debate about *lan-guage*. The reason why Gould (1987b), Lewontin (1990), and others are so skeptical about language being an adaptation is that they do not see lan-guage as exhibiting special design in the way that organs like the eye do.

This brings us to the second premise—the adaptive complexity of lan-guage. Chomsky (1975) once described the language organ as "marvelous and intricate." I will not try to convince the reader here that language is "marvelous," but I will try to give a flavor of its intricacy, in the sense that it is composed of many distinct parts arranged together to fulfill the func-tion of communication (see Jackendoff, 1993; Pinker, 1994 for more com-prehensive reviews).

Language breaks down into three distinct components. *Phonology* re-fers to the principles that govern the physical expression of language—typi-cally sound, although in sign languages the identical principles apply over basic physical movements. Some principles dictate the sorts of sequences that are possible, both universally and in specific languages. This is how we know that "gorp" is a possible English word, but "vlorf" is not. Other prin-ciples concern prosody—the patterns of intonation, stress, and timing that apply within and across words. Prosody has many communicative purposes: it allows us to disambiguate sentences that have more than one meaning;

to distinguish between old information and new information through emphasis; and to convey distinctions such as asking, "He's got a gun?", versus stating, "He's got a gun!"

*Morphology* deals with words and parts of words. Inflectional morphology is the capacity to modify the meaning of an existing word, as in the change from "dog" to "dogs," while derivational morphology is the capacity to create new words from pre-existing forms, as with "pro-democracy." English has a relatively impoverished morphological system when compared to languages such as Navajo, Turkish, and American Sign Language. These languages have richer systems that can generate complex words by combining several morphemes, just as English typically conveys complex notions through combining words into sentences.

*Syntax* governs the combination of words and phrases. Principles of phrase structure dictate properties of order and hierarchical structure. For instance, in the sentence, "John hit the duck," there is a verb phrase ("hit the duck") that includes as a subpart the noun phrase ("the duck"), and the noun phrase itself includes as a subpart the noun, "duck." The recursive power of syntax allows us to describe objects to a potentially infinite level of precision, to attribute mental states at a potentially infinite degree of embedding ("he thinks that she knows that he persuaded . . .", and so on). Other aspects of syntax determine how thematic roles—who is the agent of an action, what is the goal, and so on—are expressed in sentences. Thus we distinguish between "John hit Bill" and "Bill hit John." Finally, dependencies show up in a range of contexts, including the interpretation of questions. For instance, in "Who did John hit?", we know there is a semantic relationship between the question word "who" and the object of the verb "hit." There are universal syntactic constraints as to which dependencies are and are not possible; and in many linguistic theories, they are computed via derivations or transformations that establish mappings between different levels of syntactic representation.

In addition to phonology, morphology, and syntax, there are interface mechanisms. These allow for the transduction of sensory input into linguistic code in the course of comprehension, the transduction of linguistic code into motoric sequences in the course of production, and the interaction between language and nonlinguistic conceptual structures.

Within contemporary linguistic theory, the motivation to distinguish between these aspects of language is computational—they appear to use distinct representations and principles, and they are most elegantly characterized independent from one another. But there are other motivations as well. There are cases in which some aspects of language are selectively impaired, while others are fully functional. Some children, for example, have severe problems with morphology, particularly inflectional morphology, while their syntax is intact (Gopnik, 1990). Adults learning a second language find phonology extremely difficult to acquire, but not phrase structure. Some types of aphasia lead to impairments of syntax with no corresponding deficit in other aspects of language, such as phonology (Caplan, 1995). In the course of normal child development, these modules come online at different times, starting with phonology, next morphology, and then different aspects of syntax (Bloom, 1994a). These findings support the linguist's conclusion that human language is composed of several interdependent submodules or mechanisms—it is not an undifferentiated entity.

In sum, the position that language is intricate is not an after-the-fact claim, motivated by an adaptationist bias. It is instead based on data from linguistic theory, and supported by studies of development, processing, and pathology. The complexity of language is unsurprising when you look at human language from an engineering standpoint. Mapping complex propositional structures onto a serial channel is an extraordinarily complicated task. We have only a limited grasp of how the human system solves this problem, and attempts by philosophers and scientists to create a usable alternative to human language have been abysmal failures (Eco, 1995). All artificial languages, to the extent that they are useful for communication, are highly parasitic on natural language.

Language meets the criterion of adaptive complexity, then, suggesting that it evolved through natural selection. This does not, of course, lead us to the absurd position that every aspect of language is an adaptation, any more than visual psychologists believe that every aspect of the visual system is an adaptation. What the adaptive complexity of language does motivate is a serious examination of its different structures from a functional point of view, so that we can parcel out which features of language have been specifically selected for, which are by-products, and which exist due to properties of growth and development.

## Language as Thought

It is often assumed that language is an adaptation for the purpose of communication. This is a claim about language's evolutionary history, not its current use. The fact that we can use language in other ways, such as talking to ourselves, is not a problem for this view. (After all, we can use our eyes for purposes other than seeing, such as intimidating people by staring at them, and this does not refute the claim that eyes evolved for seeing). To say that language is an adaptation for communication does entail that its existence and design are best explained as having evolved to fulfill that function.

One alternative, proposed by Bickerton (1990, 1995), is that language evolved as an internal system of mental representation, what psychologists often call a "language of thought" or "mentalese" (Fodor, 1975). It is a lucky accident that we can give voice to this internal medium and use it to communicate, but communication is not why language evolved in the first place.

In support of this alternative, there is an important distinction between the content of a language (the notions it can express) and its form (how it expresses them). It is likely that much of the content of language—in particular, the concepts that words express and the propositions that sentences express—did not evolve for communicative purposes, but instead is part of human thought itself. Similarly, the generative nature of language, often cited as resulting from language evolution, may be better explained as a *conceptual* accomplishment; we can produce a potentially infinite number of sentences just because we can entertain a potentially infinite number of propositions (Bloom, 1994b). Finally, certain notions that principles of syntax and morphology draw upon, such as the thematic roles, "agent" and "goal," and the semantic categories, "individual" and "event," most likely are also not specific to language.

Nevertheless, there are reasons to reject the more radical proposal that languages like English and ASL are simply the physical expressions of mentalese. This leaves too much of the form of language unexplained (Jackendoff, in press; Pinker, 1992). What about phonology and phonetics? These principles are for sound and sign, not thought, and an internal medium of computation has no need for them. What about principles of word order? Different languages use different word orders to express the same meaning, showing that word order cannot be a property of thought. What about subject-verb agreement, case-marking, principles of pronoun interpretation? It would make no sense for a system of computation, something akin to the assembler language of a computer, to have these properties. Instead, they most likely exist to ease the time and memory demands posed by transmitting thoughts along a serial channel. The "s" in "John eats" is computationally irrelevant, but it adds a touch of redundancy that can aid a listener in sentence comprehension; pronouns like "it" and "he" introduce an ambiguity that would be fatal for a system of thought, but which saves time and effort in sentence production.

Consider also universal syntactic constraints that only permit certain ways of expressing our thoughts (e.g., Chomsky, 1988). Some of these may be accidents, computational spandrels that result from the conflicting purposes that syntax has to fulfill. But others might exist to serve communicative goals, since they often exclude sentences that are difficult to parse. In fact, Newmeyer (1991) convincingly argues that syntax itself has evolved as an intermediate level of representation that facilitates the mapping from structures of phonology to conceptual representations—something akin to the intermediate levels of representation that exist in the visual cortex to facilitate mapping from the retinal image to systems of object recognition. In contrast, one cannot make sense of syntax and syntactic principles (and phonology, phonetics, morphology, and the like) as properties of a language of thought.

*Abstract Thought*

Humans are unique in domains other than language. Most obviously, we possess what can be called—for lack of a more precise expression—a rich mental life. This is manifested in many ways. Consider the sorts of entities we think about, the notions that play a role in our beliefs and desires. Like other animals, we think about perceptible material entities, like objects and substances, but we are not limited to these. We can also think about more abstract entities, such as arguments, alimony, jokes, stories, conferences, and evolution. We also differ from other animals in the extent of our ability to consciously reflect on the past, to plan and imagine the future, and to create and appreciate fictional and fantasy worlds. Finally, we possess what Corballis (1991) calls generative systems, systems composed of primitive elements and rules for recursively combining them, such as music, number, some forms of visual art, and formal logic.

Above, I addressed the view that language is a by-product of other aspects of human mental life. But consider now the opposite view—could it be that some of the human intellectual capacities described above are the by-product of human language? Bickerton (1990) notes that this view was proposed by Darwin (1871): "Nevertheless, the difference in mind between man and the higher animals, great as it is, is certainly one of degree and not of kind. . . . If it be maintained that certain powers, such as self-consciousness, abstraction, etc . . . are particular to man, it may well be that these are the incidental results of other highly-advanced intellectual faculties; and these again are mainly the result of the continued use of a highly developed language."

If Darwin were right, it would have profound implications. One implication would be that we would not need multiple evolutionary accounts—one for self-consciousness, one for abstraction, one for language, and so on. We would need only to explain how language evolved, and all else would follow from this. Darwin's view also suggests that the sole important difference between humans and other primates is linguistic. If one could somehow give chimpanzees the ability to talk, soon they would be playing chess, planning bank robberies, debating evolutionary theory, and doing everything else that people can do.

There are different versions of Darwin's proposal. One version is Bickerton's, which is that language is just the externalization of abstract thought. This was discussed above. Another version is that the generative properties that have evolved as part of human language have somehow moved to domains such as music and number, giving them their generative nature (for discussion, see Bloom, 1994b; Chomsky, 1988; Corballis, 1991, 1992). Below, I will focus on three further variants of Darwin's view, all of which concern the origin of human conceptual capacities. I will argue that only the weaker versions of Darwin's claim are correct.

### How Language Might Affect Thought

Language is a superb mechanism for the transmission and accumulation of information; thus it has had a profound influence on human life. As Tomasello and colleagues (1993) put it: "The very large difference in product between animal and human societies may be most directly explained by a small but very important difference in process. . . . Human beings 'transmit' ontogenetically acquired behavior and information, both within and across generations, with a much higher degree of fidelity than other animal species" (p. 495). The point raised here is both correct and important. Without language, most of human culture—everything from scientific inquiry to professional football—would not exist. For an adult human to lose language is a tragedy, because this person is isolated from the social world.

Nevertheless, there is an important distinction between saying that language is an excellent tool for information transfer and the much stronger claim that language explains people's ability to understand or generate this information in the first place. There is a useful analogy with vision, also an excellent tool for the transfer and storage of information. Blind people find it harder to pick up certain aspects of human culture than people who can see, because they lack the same access to books, diagrams, maps, and so on. But it does not follow from this that blind people have diminished cognitive capacities. Nor does anybody believe that explaining how vision has evolved is tantamount to explaining how abstract thought has evolved. Language may be useful in the same sense that vision is useful, and similar to how technological mechanisms of information transfer, such as e-mail and cable television, are useful. Language is a tool for the expression and storage of ideas, but not a mechanism that could give rise to the capacity to generate and appreciate these ideas.

A stronger hypothesis about the relationship between language and thought is that there is an important sense in which we think in the language we speak (e.g., Dennett, 1991; Vygotsky, 1962; Whorf, 1956). This is intuitively plausible. Perhaps everyone has the subjective impression of thinking in a natural language or at least some of the time; of planning, drawing inferences, and so on, as in the thought-bubbles of cartoon characters.

Nevertheless, there is almost no psychological evidence to support the thinking-in-natural-language claim. If it were true, one would expect that lexical and grammatical differences across languages would lead to corresponding differences in the thought processes of native speakers of these languages. But studies in domains as disparate as color memory and counterfactual reasoning have either failed to find that speakers of different languages differ in nonlinguistic capacities (e.g., Au, 1983; Brown, 1958), or found differences only in tasks that are themselves language-dependent, such as explicit recall memory (e.g., Kay & Kempton, 1984). There is but one good case of cross linguistic differences leading to interesting cognitive differences, in the domain of spatial cognition. Levinson (1996) reports a series of studies comparing the spatial cognition of speakers of Dutch with speakers of Tzeltal, a Mayan language spoken in Chiapas, Mexico. In Dutch, as in English, objects in close proximity are typically described with relative frames of reference, as in: "The boy is in front of me." Tzeltal works differently. In this language, an absolute system, roughly akin to "North," "South," "East/West," is the typical way to describe objects in close proximity; so, one would say the equivalent of: "The boy is to the north of me."

Levinson finds that Dutch speakers differ substantially from Tzeltal speakers in nonlinguistic tasks requiring spatial inference, as well as in their visual recall and gesture. He argues convincingly that such tasks are not mediated by verbal memory, concluding that Dutch speakers tend to encode their world, using a relative spatial system, while Tzeltal speakers use an absolute spatial system.

This is an impressive finding, though in order for it to be a conclusive demonstration of an effect of language on spatial cognition, one would have to rule out the possibility that some third nonlinguistic factor—such as differences in early spatial experience—could account for both the linguistic and the cognitive differences between members of the two cultures. But assume for the moment that Levinson's analysis of these differences is right. Still, it would be a mistake to take this to show that language *creates* systems of spatial thought. After all, both relative and absolute systems are encoded in brain mechanisms that underlie the navigation of species other than humans; and hence, both are independent of language (O'Keefe & Nadel, 1978; Peterson et al., 1996). Furthermore, Dutch speakers can think in absolute terms and Tzeltal speakers can think in relative terms—it is just that they tend not to. Perhaps the best way to make sense of the Levinson finding is that it suggests that language can *exercise* certain preexisting ways of thinking about the world, affecting what Whorf (1956) called "habitual thought and behavior."

Whorf himself made strong claims about the effect of language on thought such as: "We dissect nature along lines laid down by our native languages. . . . The world is presented as a kaleidoscopic flux of impressions which has to be organized by our minds—and this means largely by the linguistic systems in our minds" (p. 214).

Not many scholars would endorse this claim in such extreme terms; there is now abundant evidence that prelinguistic infants and nonhuman primates are capable of imposing structure in our world without the aid of language (e.g., Premack, 1983; Spelke, 1994). But there are weaker versions of this hypothesis that many do defend. Some developmental psychologists, such as Gentner & Boroditsky (in press), would argue that this is true of abstract concepts. So, while our notions of physical objects are given prior to language, most abstract concepts only arise as the result of learning language. Other scholars might defend this view for just those concepts that are *consciously* apprehended, those concepts that are the objects of our experience, as opposed to those involved in unconscious mental processes.

Again, this is a tempting view, in part because there is some truth to it—language *is* sometimes sufficient to motivate the origin of a new concept. Words are excellent signals about the existence and boundaries of a category. Markman and Hutchinson (1984), for instance, have found that if a two-year-old is shown a novel object and told, "See this one; find another one," she will typically reach for something that has a spatial or thematic relationship with that object (such as finding a bone to go with a dog). But if a new word is used, as with, "See this fendle; find another fendle," she typically seeks something from the same category (such as finding another dog to go with the first dog). In this sense, the presence of a word can motivate categorization.

A different domain is that of perceptual learning (see Bedford, 1993). In wine tasting, for instance, linguistic labeling can give rise to both conceptual and phenomenological distinctions. If you are a wine novice, all wines might taste the same. But because of the linguistic cues repeatedly provided in the context of a wine tasting class—this is a Merlot; this is a Beaujolais; this is dry; this is sweet—you can come both to organize the "flux of impressions" that you experience into discrete categories and to appreciate the ways in which wines differ. As a result of this, you can both acquire the functional ability to distinguish the wines and come to have a different, richer, phenomenal experience of the taste of these wines. This is a further demonstration of how words can have a profound effect of thought.

Words thus serve as a useful and effective means of signaling the boundaries of categories. But this is not because of any special powers that language possesses; any signaling device would do just as well. One can induce categorization in the situation developed by Markman and Hutchinson (1984) without novel words, saying merely, "Find something of the same kind" (Bloom, in press). And one can also conduct a wine tasting class without words, by using colored lights or different sounds to mark the relevant distinctions. Words are just much easier to use, as well as being highly familiar even to very young children.

The moral here is that language (qua signaling device) can sometimes lead to the origin of some concepts. But is language necessary, as suggested by Whorf, Quine (1960), and others, in order for humans to possess certain sorts of concepts? To put the question differently, what sorts of concepts exist independently of language?

### Abstract Thought without Language

One source of evidence comes from linguistic isolates—typically, congenitally deaf adults who have grown up having never been exposed to sign language. As Sacks (1988) reviews, the cognitive abilities of these isolates was a central topic of debate in the nineteenth century. One classic case study was that of Theophilus d'Estrella, who did not acquire a formal sign language until the age of nine. After he had acquired language, he wrote an autobiographical account of his early experience, describing elaborate ruminations that he had about religion and other matters. This profoundly impressed William James, who wrote (1893): "His narrative tends to discountenance the notion that no abstract thought is possible without words. Abstract thought of a decidedly subtle kind, both scientific and moral, went on here in advance of the means of expressing it to others."

This account is hardly decisive, as one should always be skeptical about autobiographical reports (and many of James's contemporaries rejected his conclusion for this reason). But there is more recent support for James's conclusion. Schaller (1991), who studied contemporary deaf isolates living in California, on the border between the United States and Mexico, observes that they show all signs of possessing a rich mental life. They have elaborate spatial knowledge and skills, including the ability to repair complicated machinery, and they can handle money. In fact, many of them can do well enough to live on their own. Furthermore, they can actively describe events from the past, using pantomimed narratives (see also Pinker, 1994 for discussion).

Schaller also found that when one of these adults without language was taught new words for the first time, he learned them quickly, acquiring an adult vocabulary in the space of just a few years. This suggests that he was mapping words onto pre-existing concepts. Such rapid acquisition is similar to what happens in the course of normal language learning by young children. Preschoolers are extremely good at learning the meanings of words through only limited and sporadic experience, a phenomenon described as fast mapping (Carey, 1978). From about 18 months to 6 years of age, children learn an average of five new words a day. With the onset of schooling, this rate of word learning increases radically, to about 20 new words a day (Anglin, 1993; Carey, 1978).

The vocabularies of young children include many names for middle-sized objects—words such as "dog" and "truck." But they also include words that refer to events, times, spatial relations, mental states, and all sorts of abstract entities. In fact, by the time a child is about two years of age, roughly half of her words refer to these more abstract kinds of entities (Bloom, in press). There is also experimental evidence that such words are acquired rapidly. After being given only a few exposures, children can learn new action words (Bloom, 1994a), new collective nouns (Bloom & Kelemen, 1995), and new words for social institutions (Soja, 1994). These findings support the notion that much of word learning involves mapping words onto concepts that exist prior to language, and do not support to the alternative that such concepts must be created through the shaping powers of words.

Finally, prior to any grasp of language, infants have a surprisingly rich mental life. They expect objects to continue to exist once they go out of sight (Baillargeon, 1987), and they can predict the trajectories of moving objects (Spelke, 1994). They can determine the numerosities of small arrays of objects (Starkey et al., 1990), and they can even compute the results of simple additions and subtractions performed over these arrays (Wynn, 1992). But their conceptual abilities are not limited to objects. For instance, they can determine the numerosities of sequences of distinct sounds (Starkey et al., 1990), and they can also individuate and enumerate distinct actions, such as the jumps of a continuously moving puppet (Wynn, 1996). Infants also show some ability to recall spatial location (Wilcox et al., 1994), can make simple causal inferences (Leslie, 1982), and can even predict the actions of an agent, based on its previous intentional behavior (Premack, 1990).

Of course, infants have a lot to learn. Their mental life is limited in many ways, and there are many concepts that emerge only as the result of conceptual development; in many cases, this is facilitated by language (see Bloom, 1996). Nevertheless, the infant research provides dramatic evidence against the Whorfian theory, demonstrating that abstract conceptualization exists prior to the acquisition of language.

## Conclusion

In the discussion of the evolution of language, I argued that language is a distinct adaptation, not a by-product of some other aspect of human mental life. The conclusion here is similar. Although I have not presented a theory of how the human capacity to entertain abstract concepts has evolved, I have summarized evidence from different sources that Darwin's speculation was mistaken. At least some of the unique aspects of human mental life cannot be explained as by-products of the evolution of language.

It is common for scholars interested in the origin of the human mind to look for a single factor—high intelligence, big brains, language—from which everything else special to humans follows. The evidence presented above supports a quite different picture. Language is not a by-product of intelligence or brain size; certain conceptual capacities of humans are not by-products of language. This hints that the correct account of human cognitive evolution is going to be more complicated than many scholars would expect. My hunch is that, just as with different bodily organs, each of these different aspects of the human mind (language, different types of abstract concepts, self-consciousness, social cognition, number) will have its own history, leaving many problems in the evolution of cognition, not just one.

## Note

I am grateful to Colin Allen, Denise Cummins, Lori Markson, Mary Peterson, and especially Karen Wynn for comments on an earlier draft. Preparation of this manuscript was supported by a grant from the Spencer Foundation. Address correspondence to: Paul Bloom, Department of Psychology, University of Arizona, Tucson AZ 85721, or "bloom@u.arizona.edu."

## References

Anglin, J. (1993). Vocabulary development: A morphological analysis. *Monographs of the Society for Research in Child Development, 238,* 1–166.

Au, T. K-F. (1983). Chinese and English counterfactuals: The Sapir-Whorf hypothesis revisited. *Cognition, 15,* 155–187.

Baillargeon, R. (1987). Object permanence in 3.5 and 4.5 month old infants. *Child Development, 23,* 655–664.

Bedford, F. (1993). Perceptual learning. In D. Medin (Ed.), *The Psychology of Learning and Motivation, 30,* 1–60. San Diego, CA: Academic Press.

Bickerton, D. (1981). *Roots of language*. Ann Arbor, MI: Karoma.

Bickerton, D. (1990). *Language and species*. Chicago: University of Chicago Press.

Bickerton, D. (1995). *Language and human behavior*. Seattle: University of Washington Press.

Bloom, P. (1994a). Recent controversies in the study of language acquisition. In M. A. Gernsbacher (Ed.), *Handbook of Psycholinguistics*. San Diego, CA: Academic Press.

Bloom, P. (1994b). Generativity within language and other cognitive domains. *Cognition, 51,* 177–189.

Bloom, P. (1996). Possible individuals in language and cognition. *Current Directions in Psychological Science, 5,* 90–94.

Bloom, P. (in press). Roots of word learning. In M. Bowerman & S. Levinson (Eds.), *Conceptual development and language acquisition*. Cambridge: Cambridge University Press.

Bloom, P., & Kelemen, D. (1995). Syntactic cues in the acquisition of collective nouns. *Cognition, 56,* 1–30.

Brown, R. (1958). *Words and things*. New York: Free Press.

Caplan, D. (1995). The cognitive neuroscience of syntactic process. In M. Gazzaniga (Ed.), *The Cognitive Neurosciences* (pp. 871–879). Cambridge, MA: MIT Press.

Carey, S. (1978). The child as word-learner. In M. Halle, J. Bresnan, & G. A. Miller (Eds.), *Linguistic theory and psychological reality*. Cambridge, MA: MIT Press.

Chomsky, N. (1975). *Reflections on language*. New York: Pantheon.

Chomsky, N. (1988). *Language and problems of knowledge: The Managua lectures*. Cambridge, MA: MIT Press.

Corballis, M. (1991). *The lopsided ape: Evolution of the generative mind*. New York: Oxford University Press.

Corballis, M. (1992). On the evolution of language and generativity. *Cognition, 44,* 197–226.

Crain, S. (1991). Language acquisition in the absence of experience. *Behavioral and Brain Sciences, 14,* 597–650.

Cronin, H. (1991). *The ant and the peacock: Altruism and sexual selection from Darwin to today*. Cambridge: Cambridge University Press.

Darwin, C. R. (1859/1964). *On the origin of species*. Cambridge, MA: Harvard University Press.

Darwin, C. R. (1871). *The descent of man and selection in relation in sex*. New York: Hurst and Co.

Dawkins, R. (1983). Universal Darwinism. In D. S. Bendall (Ed.), *Evolution from molecules to men*. New York: Cambridge University Press.

Dawkins, R. (1986). *The blind watchmaker*. New York: W. W. Norton.

Dennett, D. C. (1991). *Consciousness explained*. Boston: Little, Brown & Co.

Dennett, D. C. (1995). *Darwin's dangerous idea*. New York: Simon & Schuster.

Eco, U. (1995). *The search for the perfect language*. Oxford: Blackwell.

Eldredge, N., & Gould, S. J. (1972). Punctuated equilibrium: An alternative to phylectic gradualism. In T. J. M. Schopf (Ed.), *Models in paleobiology*. San Francisco: Freeman.

Elman, J. L. (1993). Learning and development in neural networks: The importance of starting small. *Cognition, 48,* 71–99.

Fodor, J. A. (1975). *The language of thought*. New York: Crowell.

Gentner, D., & Boroditsky, L. (in press). Individuation, relativity, and early word learning. In M. Bowerman & S. Levinson (Eds.), *Conceptual development and language acquisition.* Cambridge: Cambridge University Press.

Goodwin, B. C. (1994). *How the leopard changed its spots: The evolution of complexity.* New York: Charles Scribner's Sons.

Gopnik, M. (1990). Feature blindness: A case study. *Language acquisition, 1,* 139–164.

Gould, S. J. (1977). Darwin's untimely burial. In S. J. Gould (Ed.), *Ever since Darwin: Reflections on natural history.* New York: W. W. Norton.

Gould, S. J. (1979). Panselectionist pitfalls in Parker and Gibson's model of the evolution of intelligence. *Behavioral and Brain Sciences, 2,* 385–386.

Gould, S. J. (1982). The meaning of punctuated equilibrium and its role in validating a hierarchical approach to macroevolution. In R. Milkman (Ed.), *Perspectives on evolution* (pp. 83–104). Sunderland, MA: Sinauer.

Gould, S. J. (1987a). Integrity and Mr. Rifkin. In S. J. Gould (Ed.), *An urchin in the storm: Essays about books and ideas.* New York: W. W. Norton.

Gould, S. J. (1987b). *The limits of adaptationism: Is language a spandrel of the human brain?* Paper presented to the Cognitive Science seminar, Center for Cognitive Science, Massachusetts Institute of Technology, October.

Gould, S. J., & Lewontin, R. (1979). The spandrels of San Marco and the Panglossian Paradigm: A critique of the Adaptationist Programme. *Proceedings of the Royal Society, 205,* 581–598.

Gould, S. J., & Vrba, E. (1982). Exaptation: A missing term in the science of form. *Paleobiology, 8,* 4–15.

Jackendoff, R. (1990). *Semantic Structures.* Cambridge, MA: MIT Press.

Jackendoff, R. (1993). *Patterns in the mind: Language and human nature.* New York: Harvester-Wheatsheaf.

Jackendoff, R. (in press). How language helps us think. *Pragmatics and Cognition.*

James, W. (1893). Thought before language: A deaf-mute's recollections. *American Annals of the Deaf, 38,* 135–145.

Kay, P., & Kempton, W. (1984). What is the Sapir-Whorf hypothesis? *American Anthropologist, 86,* 65–79.

Kaufmann, S. (1993). *The origins of order: Self-organization and selection in evolution.* New York: Oxford University Press.

Kingsolver, J. G., & Koehl, M. A. R. (1985). Aerodynamics, thermoregulation, and the evolution of insect wings: Differential scaling and evolutionary change. *Evolution, 39,* 488–504.

Lenneberg, E. H. (1967). *Biological foundations of language.* New York: Wiley.

Leslie, A. M. (1982). The perception of causality in infants. *Perception, 11,* 173–186.

Levinson, S. C. (1996). Frames of reference and Molyneux's question: Cross-linguistic evidence. In P. Bloom, M. Peterson, L. Nadel, & M. Garrett (Eds.), *Language and space* (pp. 109–169). Cambridge, MA: MIT Press.

Lewontin, R. C. (1990). Evolution of cognition. In D. Osherson & E. E. Smith (Eds.), *Thinking: An invitation to cognitive science,* vol. 3. Cambridge, MA: MIT Press.

Lieberman, P. (1984). *The biology and evolution of language.* Cambridge, MA: Harvard University Press.

Markman, E. M., & Hutchinson, J. E. (1984). Children's sensitivity to constraints in word meaning: Taxonomic versus thematic relations. *Cognitive Psychology, 16,* 1–27.

Newmeyer, F. J. (1991). Functional explanations in linguistics and the origin of language. *Language and Communication, 11*, 1–28.

Newport, E. (1990). Maturational constraints on language learning. *Cognitive Science, 14*, 11–28.

O'Keefe, J., & Nadel, L. (1978). *The hippocampus as a cognitive map.* Oxford: Clarendon Press.

Paley, W. (1802/1851). *Natural theology: Evidence of the existences and attributes of the deity, collected from the appearances of nature.* Boston: Gould & Lincoln.

Penrose, R. (1989). *The emperor's new mind.* Oxford: Oxford University Press.

Peterson, M., Nadel, L., Bloom, P., & Garrett, M. (1996). Space and language. In P. Bloom, M. Peterson, L. Nadel, & M. Garrett (Eds.), *Language and space* (pp. 553–577). Cambridge, MA: MIT Press.

Piattelli-Palmarini, M. (1989). Evolution, selection, and cognition: From "learning" to parameter-setting in biology and the study of language. *Cognition, 31*, 1–44.

Pinker, S. (1989). *Learnability and cognition: The acquisition of argument structure.* Cambridge, MA: MIT Press.

Pinker, S. (1992). Review of Language and Species. *Language, 68*, 375–382.

Pinker, S. (1994). *The language instinct.* New York: Morrow.

Pinker, S. (in press). Facts about human language relevant to its evolution. In J.-P Changeux (Ed.), *Origins of the human brain.* New York: Oxford University Press.

Pinker, S., & Bloom, P. (1990). Natural language and natural selection. *Behavioral and Brain Sciences, 13*, 585–642.

Premack, D. (1983). The codes of man and beasts. *Behavioral & Brain Sciences, 6*, 125–167.

Premack, D. (1990). The infant's theory of self-propelled objects. *Cognition, 36*, 1–16.

Quine, W. V. O. (1960). *Word and object.* Cambridge, MA: MIT Press.

Sacks, O. (1988). *Seeing voices: A journey into the world of the deaf.* Berkeley: University of California Press.

Schaller, S. (1991). *A man without words.* New York: Summit Press.

Seidenberg, M. S., & Petitto, L. A. (1979). Singing behavior in apes: A critical review. *Cognition, 7*, 177–215.

Singleton, J., & Newport, E. (1993). When learners surpass their models: The acquisition of sign language from impoverished output. Unpublished manuscript, Department of Psychology, University of Rochester.

Smith, N., & Tsimpli, I.-M. (1995). *The mind of a savant.* Oxford: Blackwell.

Soja, N. N. (1994). Evidence for a distinct kind of noun. *Cognition, 51*, 267–284.

Soja, N. N., Carey, S., & Spelke, E. S. (1991). Ontological categories guide young children's inductions of word meaning: Object terms and substance terms. *Cognition, 38*, 179–211.

Spelke, E. S. (1994). Initial knowledge: Six suggestions. *Cognition, 50*, 431–445.

Starkey, P., Spelke, E. S., & Gelman, R. (1990). Numerical abstraction by human infants. *Cognition, 36*, 97–127.

Tomasello, M., Kruger, A. C., & Ratner, H. H. (1993). Cultural learning. *Behavioral & Brain Sciences, 16*, 495–552.

Vygotsky, L. (1962). *Thought and language.* Cambridge, MA: MIT Press.

Whorf, B. L. (1956). *Language, thought, and reality.* Cambridge, MA: MIT Press.

Wilcox, T., Rosser, R., & Nadel, L. (1994). Representation of object location in 6.5-month-old infants. *Cognitive Development, 9,* 193–209.

Wynn, K. (1992). Addition and subtraction by human infants. *Nature, 358,* 749–750.

Wynn, K. (1996). Infants' individuation and enumeration of actions. *Psychological Science, 7,* 164–169.

# 9

# Morgan's Canon

ELLIOTT SOBER

When an ant in the species *Solenopsis saevissima* dies, its fellow workers carry the body out of the nest to discard it. Why do they do so? One possibility is that the workers believe that the immobile organism is dead, and they have the desire to rid the nest of dead individuals. A better explanation is provided by the fact that the dead ant exudes oleic acid. Workers are disposed to pick up and discard anything that smells of this compound, even living ants that perverse biologists have daubed with the tell-tale substance (Wilson, 1971, p. 279).

When a piping plover (*Charadrius melodus*) sees a predator approach its nest, it will produce a broken wing display, dragging its intact wing along the sand as if the wing were injured (Ristau, 1991). Why does the bird do this? One possibility is that the plover wants to protect its young and believes that the display will induce a false belief in the predator. A better explanation is that the plover wants to protect her young, and believes that the broken wing display will have that effect.

In the first of these examples, a nonmentalistic explanation is preferable to a mentalistic explanation; the hypothesis that the ants are engaging in a fixed action pattern, triggered by a chemical trace, seems more plausible than the hypothesis that they are acting on the basis of beliefs and desires. In the second example, we prefer to explain the plover's behavior by attributing to it a belief about its own action, rather than by attributing to it a belief about the mind of the predator it confronts. Both these inferences obey a principle that C. Lloyd Morgan espoused in his *Introduction to Comparative Psychology*: "In no case may we interpret an action as the outcome of the exercise of a higher psychical faculty, if it can be interpreted as the outcome of the exercise of one which stands lower in the psychological scale" (Morgan, 1894, p. 53).[1] Morgan called this his canon, and the name has stuck. In this paper, I want to explore what the canon says and whether it is justified.

The two examples I have sketched (both drawn from Dennett, 1987) may make Morgan's principle seem self-evident. However, there are two considerations, each of them biological in character, that suggest that the canon is less than transparently obvious.

First, there is Morgan's use of the terms "higher" and "lower." Morgan thought of himself as developing an evolutionary perspective on the explanation of behavior. Indeed, he believed that his canon depends on specifically Darwinian ideas, not on a general maxim that bids us prefer simpler theories (Morgan, 1894, p. 54). Yet, when we consult the words of the master, we find Darwin writing himself a memo to never say "higher" and "lower" (Ghiselin, 1969, p. 70). This was no mere passing scribble, but characterized a deep and enduring implication of the hypotheses that Darwin developed. The theory of evolution by natural selection undermines the idea of a linear scale of nature in which each stage is either higher or lower than every other. Darwin replaced the ladder with the tree; lineages diverge from each other and develop adaptations that suit them to their peculiar conditions of life. In this framework, it makes no sense to ask whether the ant's use of pheromones is higher or lower than the plover's use of deception.[2] Both have their place in life's diversity.

These worries about the concepts of *higher* and *lower* are not assuaged by what Morgan says. Although Morgan was less than totally explicit about what these concepts mean, it is clear that he was very much in the grip of the Spencerian doctrine that evolution always marches from simple to complex (Gottlieb, 1979, p. 150; Boakes, 1984, p. 40). To the degree that Morgan's canon depends on this claim of directionality, the canon is in trouble. Although life started simple, and thus had to show a net increase in complexity (it had nowhere to go but up), the history of life is peppered with cases of evolutionary simplification. For example, the evolution of parasites typically involves a transition from complex to simple, as the parasite loses features of its free-living ancestor. So the first reason to pause over Morgan's canon is his use of the concepts of higher and lower. How should they be understood; and, once they are clarified, how justified does the canon turn out to be?

A second reason for wondering about the correctness of Morgan's canon is provided by patterns of reasoning frequently used in comparative biology. Comparative biologists attempt to infer the phylogenetic relationships that different species bear to each other from data concerning their similarities and differences. They also use hypotheses about phylogenetic relationship to help infer the characteristics of extinct species that cannot be ascertained by direct observation. These biologists usually do not think about psychological characteristics; more commonly, they focus on morphological, physiological, genetic, and molecular traits. Nonetheless, their modes of reasoning can be applied perfectly well to psychological features. I suggest that if Morgan's canon makes sense, it should make sense for any trait, whether the trait is psychological or not. For example, if an organism is able to digest a particular protein, we may ask what internal mechanism enables it to do so. Morgan tells us to prefer a hypothesis that attributes a lower digestive mechanism over a hypothesis that attributes a higher mechanism. Comparative psychology is a branch of comparative biology.

With this point in mind, let's consider the inference problem depicted in Figure 9.1. We know by observation that the eggs of modern turtles, birds, and mammals have amniotic sacs, whereas the eggs of modern amphibians and fish do not. Now let's consider the protorothyrids, a group of small fossil reptiles thought to be closely related to the group that includes turtles, birds, and mammals (Carroll, 1988, pp. 192–198). Since fossils preserve hard parts and nothing else, we cannot tell by observation whether protorothyrids possessed an amnion. Should we attribute an amniotic sac to them, or not? Morgan's canon apparently says that we should decline to do so. If having an amniotic sac is "higher" and lacking a sac is "lower," and if our observations do not decide between these two hypotheses, then the canon evidently recommends the conclusion that the fossil resembled fish and amphibia in this regard.

Many comparative biologists would find this preference for the lower hypothesis less than compelling. Systematists who call themselves "cladists" would evaluate the hypotheses by applying considerations of parsimony, which

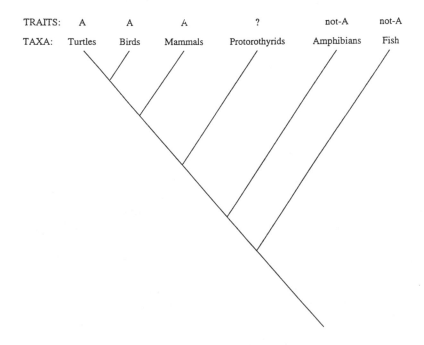

Figure 9.1   *The protorothyrids are closely related to turtles, birds, and mammals. Do protorothyrids have amnions, or not?*

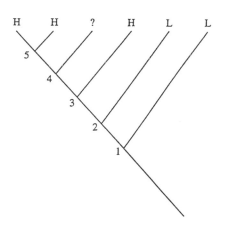

Figure 9.2 *The question-mark taxon falls within a genealogical group whose other members are known to have trait H. What character state should this taxon be assigned?*

they measure by counting the number of independent originations of traits that a hypothesis demands.[3] Notice that the tree depicted in Figure 9.1 requires only a single origination in the trait in question, regardless of whether protorothyrids are assigned an amnion or not. In this example, cladistic parsimony is quite indifferent to the distinction between higher and lower.

Many systematists would not wish to let the question about whether protorothyrids have amnions go at that. Even though cladistic parsimony is an important inferential tool, it is not the only game in town. Here is a fairly conventional piece of reasoning that biologists use to solve this problem: the amnion is thought to have evolved because it helps prevent eggs from drying out. The sac allows organisms to lay eggs on land, thus avoiding an aquatic larval stage. The fossils of protorothyrids suggest that they were land-dwelling and so they probably laid their eggs on land. So, in all likelihood, protorothyrid eggs had amnions. The point of this example is that biologists assign a character state to protorothyrids by considering specific biological details; they do not invoke a general preference for "lower" over "higher."

Figure 9.2 depicts a different problem. Once again, we are asked to assign a character state to a taxon whose phylogenetic relationship to other taxa is known. However, in this instance, the question mark taxon falls within a group that is otherwise characterized by the "higher" character state *H*.[4] The most parsimonious assignment of character states to the ancestors represented as interior nodes in this phylogenetic tree is $1=L$, $2=L$, $3=H$, $4=H$, and $5=H$. This set of assignments requires that the *H* character state evolved only once. Parsimony favors assigning *H* to the question mark taxon as well. In this problem, the principle of cladistic parsimony leads us to prefer "higher" over "lower" because the target taxon belongs to a phylogenetic group whose other members exhibit the higher character state.

The two inferences just discussed differ in structure and in the types of biological information that are relevant. Nonetheless, they have something in common. With biological information of the requisite type, a character state can be assigned to the target taxon. This assignment is made in accordance with principles that embody no particular preference for "lower" over "higher." But suppose that such biological details were not available in the inference problems just described. It is here that Morgan's principle might be expected to play the role of a tie-breaker—of discriminating between hypotheses that fit the available evidence equally well. However, when no biological evidence is available, I would expect many biologists to remain agnostic about the character state of the question mark taxon. Morgan's canon reaches the wrong conclusion in the two problems I just sketched when biological details are available; in similar problems in which biological details are *not* available, the canon seems to license inferences in which the proper conclusion is that no inference can be drawn.

These critical remarks are not meant to show that Morgan's canon is mistaken. Rather, the point so far is that the canon presents a puzzle. The problem is to understand what "higher" and "lower" mean, and to see why it makes sense to favor lower over higher. At the end of this paper, I'll try to construct a justification of Morgan's idea. But before I get to that, I want to describe the role that the canon played in Morgan's own thought and also examine in detail the justifying argument that Morgan himself constructed. Morgan's canon has had a long and influential history in psychology. As the examples at the beginning of this paper suggest, the canon was a weapon that behaviorists used against hypotheses that postulate inner mental states; it currently plays a role in cognitive ethology, guiding inference towards hypotheses that are "conservative" in the psychological mechanisms they assign. It is worth trying to understand the canon in its historical context. It also is worth seeing whether the canon can be defended in ways that its originator never imagined.

To understand Morgan's canon historically, we must understand what Morgan was reacting *against*. Darwin had argued for the mental continuity of human and nonhuman organisms. His chosen successor, Romanes, continued to emphasize this idea. Darwin's objective was to show that evolutionary ideas apply to mental characteristics no less than they apply to morphology and physiology. If all living things are related genealogically, we can locate the emergence of novelties in the interior branches of phylogenetic trees like the one depicted in Figure 9.1. According to this evolutionary conception, new traits emerge from old ones; we should be able to find the vestiges of ancient forms in more modern adaptations.

Darwin and Romanes defended this point about psychological evolution by relating anecdotes about animal behavior that were saturated with anthropomorphism (Richards, 1987). For example, in Chapter Two of *The Descent of Man*, Darwin tells stories about animal behavior to support the claim that language, self-consciousness, an aesthetic sense, and belief in God are qualitatively similar (though not identical) to mental faculties found in nonhuman organisms. Morgan also wished to defend the evolutionary hypothesis that all life is genealogically related, but he saw that the case for evolution does not require one to gloss over the differences that separate human beings from the rest of nature. One branch of a phylogenetic tree can develop novelties that do not emerge on others; a shared genealogy does not require that there be no qualitative differences among the traits exhibited by related species (Gottlieb, 1979, p. 150).

Although Morgan's insight accords well with a modern evolutionary point of view, there is something decidedly unmodern about Morgan's ideas on the foundations of psychology. Like many psychologists writing at the time, Morgan maintained that attribution of mental states to others depends on an introspective examination of one's self. When I raise a cup to my lips, this is because I believe that the cup contains a palatable liquid that I desire to drink. When I see another human being perform the same action, I infer a similar mental cause. Morgan saw that this pattern of inference extends across species boundaries. What Morgan termed the *double inductive method* leads one to interpret the behavior of organisms in other species as stem-ming from the same causes that move human beings to action. The net result is that my interpretation of nonhuman organisms is prey to a bias—the bias of *anthropomorphism*.[5]

This bias requires a counterbalance, and that was the role that the canon played in Morgan's thought (Burghardt, 1985, p. 912). Morgan believed that the *simplest* hypothesis would be that other organisms are just like us. If I drink water because I believe that water is thirst quenching and I want to stop being thirsty, then the simplest inference is that other organisms drink water for the very same reason. It is Morgan's canon that leads one to ask whether drinking behavior in other species can be explained by a psy-chological mechanism that is less elevated than the beliefs and desires that animate human beings. If the behavior *can* be so explained, then it *should* be so explained. We should conclude that other organisms are *not* like us psychologically. The proximate mechanism that drives drinking behavior in human beings differs from the mechanisms at work in other creatures.

Seen in this historical context, it is evident that Morgan's canon served a useful function; it provided a needed corrective to the anthropomorphism that introspective methods and uncritical anecdote-mongering tended to engender. However, this point is not enough to justify the canon. Although the canon helps one avoid the bias of anthropomorphism, the question needs to be asked whether it introduces an opposite bias of its own. If other crea-tures really are like us in certain respects, perhaps the canon will lead one to miss this fact about nature. The canon would not make sense if it merely avoided one bias by embracing another.

At this point, it is worth considering the idea that Morgan's canon is a version of Occam's razor—the principle of parsimony. As I've mentioned, Morgan claimed that the canon leads one to reject a simple theory, not accept it. Nonetheless, many commentators have thought that the canon is justified because of its connection to the principle of parsimony. For example, Skinner (1938) says: "Darwin, insisting upon the continuity of mind, attributed mental faculties to subhuman species. Lloyd Morgan, with his law of parsimony, dispensed with them in a reasonably successful attempt to account for characteristic animal behavior without them" (4).[6] Boring (1950) also thinks that the canon is a version of the razor, but denies that the principle of parsimony is legitimate when the problem is to infer the mental capacities of nonhuman organisms. Boring says that "nature is notoriously prodigal; why should we interpret it only parsimoniously?" (p. 474). Boring's criticism, I suggest, involves a misunderstanding of what the principle of parsimony asserts. Roughly speaking, Occam's razor tells one to accept the simplest theory that fits the evidence; it places no upper bound on how complex that theory will have to be. Even if nature is prodigal, Occam's razor tells us to find the simplest theory that is consistent with its observed prodigality (Sober, 1988).

Boring is not the only psychologist to have thought that Morgan's canon is defective because it is a version of Occam's razor. Walker (1983) provides an interesting elaboration of this line of argument:

> Clearly, because sticklebacks and chimpanzees both build nests, we should not be obliged to believe that the psychological processes available to the chimpanzee are the same as those utilized by the stickleback. . . . There is a very general, and a very difficult problem behind all this, which infects the roots of behaviourist systems of explanation of animal activities. It may be described as the "same behavior—same mechanism" fallacy. (p. 57)

It might be replied that the similarity in behavior here described between sticklebacks and chimpanzees is superficial; a fuller profile of their respective behaviors would show that the similarities are slight. So, postulating the same psychological processes is in fact *not* demanded by Morgan's canon. In contrast, when two organisms exhibit a detailed set of behavioral similarities, there seems to be a presumption in favor of postulating similar underlying processes. This apparently is why we explain behavioral similarities among conspecifics by saying that they have similar psychological mechanisms. What is true for conspecifics also is true for different species in the same genus, and so on, up the taxonomic hierarchy.[7]

The conclusion I draw is that Walker's point about chimp and stickleback nest building does not undermine the idea that common cause explanations are often preferable to explanations that postulate separate causal mechanisms (Sober, 1994b). Still, the question remains of what this has to do with "higher" and "lower." In this regard, it is worth asking whether Morgan's canon really is an instance of Occam's razor at all. Newbury (1954), for example, suggests that the razor "is applied when we adhere to a *paucity* of assumptions, whereas Morgan's Canon refers to *lower* processes of development" (p. 72). Newbury's point is an excellent one. If parsimony is assessed by counting mechanisms, then attributing a single lower mechanism and attributing a single higher mechanism are equally parsimonious. And how should we compare a hypothesis that explains a set of behaviors by postulating a single higher mechanism and a hypothesis that explains those behaviors by postulating twelve separate, lower, mechanisms? The hypothesis that involves a single higher mechanism seems to be simpler than the hypothesis of a dozen lower mechanisms. Pending clarification of what "higher" and "lower" mean, it is quite unclear how Morgan's canon is related to Occam's razor.

As I have already mentioned, Morgan argues that his canon rests on a specifically evolutionary foundation. He formulates the problem of justification by asking the reader to consider three "divergently ascending grades of organisms." Species *a*, man, has ascended to a higher level than *b*, and *b* has risen higher than *c*. Each of these organisms may exhibit, to some degree, each of three "ascending faculties or stadia in mental development," numbered 1, 2, and 3. How might these three faculties be represented in the three taxa? Morgan describes three possible patterns by which psychological faculties might be distributed across species; Morgan calls each distribution pattern a "method." I've reproduced his graphical representation of the problem (Morgan 1894, p. 56) as my Figure 9.3.[8]

Morgan calls the first possibility the *Method of Levels*. Here, "the faculties or stadia are of constant value. In the diagram, *b* has not quite reached the level of the beginning of the third or highest faculty, while *c* has only just entered upon the second stadium" (p. 57). The Method of Levels apparently says that an organism must attain a certain level of development of a lower faculty before it can have any trace whatever of a higher faculty.

The second alternative Morgan dubs the *Method of Uniform Reduction*. In this arrangement "in both *b* and *c* we have all three faculties represented in the same ratio as in a, but all uniformly reduced" (p. 57). The idea here is that a lower organism has all the faculties that a higher organism possesses, but it has them developed to a lesser extent.

The third alternative is the *Method of Variation*, "according to which any one of the faculties 1, 2, or 3, may in *b* and *c* be either increased or reduced relative to its development in a" (p. 57). This pattern seems to be the least constraining of the three; evidently, the method of variation is the method of *anything goes*.

Morgan summarizes how the above methods differ by asking us to suppose that:

> *b* represents the psychic stature of a dog. Then, according to the interpretation on the method of levels, he possesses the lowest faculty (1) in the same degree as man; in the faculty (2) he somewhat falls short of man; while in the highest faculty (3) he is altogether wanting. According to the interpretation on the method of uniform reduction he possesses all the faculties of man but in reduced degree. And according to the interpretation on the method of variation he excels man in the lowest faculty, while the other two faculties are both reduced but in different degrees. (p. 57)

Morgan then asserts that the process of evolution by natural selection entails that "it is the third method . . . which we should expect *a priori* to accord most nearly with observed facts." He notes that "in the diagram by

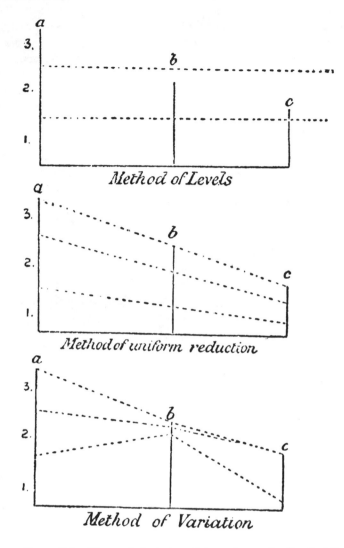

*Figure 9.3   Morgan's depiction of three alternative "methods" that describe how psychological faculties 1, 2, and 3 might be distributed among three species a, b, and c.*

which the Method of Variation is illustrated, the highest faculty 3 is in *c* reduced to zero;" the total absence of higher faculties in lower organisms is entirely possible.

Morgan now is able to bring his argument for the canon to its conclusion. If the Method of Variation is correct, then "it is clear that any animal may be at a stage where certain higher faculties have not yet been evolved from their lower precursors; and hence we are logically bound not to assume the existence of these higher faculties until good reasons shall have been shown for such existence" (p. 59).

It is here that we can see the slippage in Morgan's logic. The Method of Variation does say that it is possible for an organism to have lower but not higher faculties. However, the Method also seems to allow for the possibility that an organism will have a higher faculty but not a lower one. This alternative happens not to be represented in Morgan's diagram; it is depicted in Figure 9.4. If "any . . . of the faculties . . . may in *b* and *c* be either increased or reduced relative to its development in *a*," then *a* may have none of a lower faculty that is found in *b*.

Although Morgan's Method of Variation is too permissive to justify the canon, it is possible to construe the concepts of higher and lower so that this objection to Morgan's argument can be finessed. In the problems depicted in Figures 9.1 and 9.2, "lower" and "higher" were mutually exclusive characteristics. Let us now stipulate new meanings for those terms:

Trait *X* is higher than trait *Y* if and only if *X* entails *Y*, but not conversely.

Lower traits can be present without higher traits, but higher traits cannot be present without lower ones. For example, if (as Morgan thought) "abstract reasoning" is higher than "sense perception," then a creature that reasons must be capable of sense perception, but it is possible for an organism to have sense perception without being able to reason abstractly. If we define "higher" and "lower" in this way, there is no Spencerian implication that evolution always moves in the direction of adding higher traits to lower ones. A parasite may lose some of the "higher" characteristics of its free-living ancestors. What an organism cannot do is lose lower traits while retaining higher ones.

This definition seems to accord fairly well with at least some of what Morgan says, and it entails that it is more probable that an organism has a

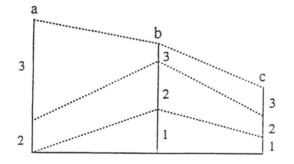

*Figure 9.4   A pattern of distribution that is not depicted in Morgan's figure. Here a higher species (a) lacks a lower faculty (1) that is present in lower species (b and c).*

lower faculty than that it has a higher faculty, relative to any evidence one might have available:

> If Higher entails Lower, but not conversely, then
> Pr(Higher|Evidence) < Pr(Lower|Evidence).

Ironically, there is no need to appeal to evolutionary processes if this is what "higher" and "lower" mean. The proposed definition entails that Lower is more probable than Higher, even if organisms are separately created by God.

It is no objection to Morgan's canon that its justification does not depend on the evolutionary matters that Morgan thought germane. However, the justification we are considering is limited in an important respect. Even when Higher entails Lower, but not conversely, it is still an open question how probable it is that a species should have both Higher *and* Lower, rather than Lower only. Figure 9.5 depicts a group of species in which every organism with the Higher trait also possesses the Lower trait, but not conversely. If we sample a species at random from the tips of the tree, it is more probable that the species will have Lower than that it will have Higher. However, the same sampling procedure entails that Pr(Higher & Lower) > Pr(-Higher & Lower). In a phylogenetic group of this sort, Morgan's canon would be misleading, if the canon is taken to require one to *assert* the presence of Lower and *deny* the presence of Higher. If Lower and Higher are internal mechanisms that might produce a behavior, and at least one of them is needed to produce the behavior one observes, then the most probable inference is that the organism possesses *both* of them.

In spite of the point illustrated by Figure 9.5, there is a special circumstance in which it is possible to explain why (Higher & Lower) is a less probable hypothesis than (-Higher & Lower). This is the case in which Higher entails Lower *and* the two internal mechanisms are behaviorally equivalent—not only are both able to explain the behaviors one presently observes, but they have the same implications about all possible behaviors.[9] As noted earlier, it is not an implication of probability theory that having exactly one mechanism is more probable than having exactly two. However, there is an evolutionary reason to expect an organism to deploy one mechanism rather than two if their behavioral consequences are exactly the same. The reason is *energetic efficiency*. It costs energy to build and maintain a machine. This is as true for organisms as it is for automobiles. If one machine produces precisely the same range of behaviors as would occur if that machine were supplemented by a second machine, then there is no adaptive reason why that supplement should evolve. In fact, the *internal costs* (Sober, 1994a) involved suggest that the supplement should *not* evolve. Here, it is a specifically evolutionary consideration that justifies a preference for monism over pluralism with respect to internal mechanisms. Maybe Morgan would have been pleased.

The argument just presented applies to the problem of discriminating between behaviorally equivalent hypotheses. I want to emphasize, however, that this is rarely a situation that ethologists know themselves to confront.

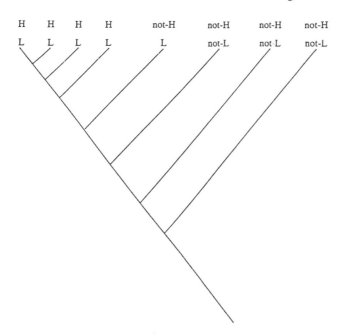

*Figure 9.5  Since the presence of H entails the presence of L, but not conversely, Pr(H) < Pr(L). However, in this example, it is nonetheless true that Pr(H&L) > Pr(-H&L).*

Biologists construct alternative hypotheses that may be able to explain the data at hand; that these hypotheses do equally well with respect to all possible data, however, is not at all obvious. One should be circumspect about endorsing the claim that two alternative mechanisms are in fact behaviorally equivalent; it is difficult to survey in an instant all the environmental circumstances that may arise. Mechanisms that seem to perform similarly in one range of environments may turn out to perform differently in others.

When two devices influence the same behaviors, causing the organism to perform a given behavior in a given environmental circumstance, it is often true that two control devices do a better job than one. When internal mechanisms are subject to error, redundancy can increase precision (Sober & Wilson, 1997). I suspect that it is virtually never the case that a pair of mechanisms is behaviorally equivalent with one of them acting alone. Even if two mechanisms are more energetically costly than just one, there still may be a fitness advantage in having the two rather than the one. No general principle can be stated about this tradeoff; whether one is better than two will depend on details that may vary from trait to trait and from species to species.

For this reason, I want to consider a different approach to the problem of explicating and justifying Morgan's canon. Figure 9.6 reproduces a cartoon by S. Gross that appeared in *The New Yorker* (September 4, 1995,

42). Some penguins stand in a group, watching one of their number flying overhead. The airborne bird is saying, "We just haven't been flapping them hard enough." Gross's cartoon suggests that he may have read Chomsky's *Rules and Representations*, in which Chomsky (1980, p. 239) asks whether nonhuman organisms possess something like the human capacity for language. Here is his answer:

> It is conceivable, but not very likely. This would constitute a kind of biological miracle, rather similar to the discovery on some unexplored island of a species of bird that had never thought to fly until instructed to do so through human intervention. . . . It is difficult to imagine that some other species, say the chimpanzee, has the capacity for language but has never thought to put it to use.

Gross' joke is based on Chomsky's principle—a useful ability does not go unused.

To bring this idea into contact with Morgan's canon, let's consider a new definition of the concepts of *higher* and *lower*:

> One internal mechanism is higher than another if and only if
> the behavioral capacities entailed by the former properly
> include the behavioral capacities entailed by the latter.

*"We just haven't been flapping them hard enough."*

*Figure 9.6   An illustration of the principle that useful capacities get used. Drawing by S. Gross; © 1995. The New Yorker Magazine, Inc.*

According to this construal, "higher" faculties allow an organism to do more. The present proposal does not assume that "higher" faculties always evolve after "lower" ones. Nor does it assume that an organism with a "higher" mechanism also must possess a "lower" mechanism; even though the behaviors provided by the higher mechanism properly contain the behaviors provided by the lower mechanism, there is no implication relation between the mechanisms themselves.

Let us suppose that the internal mechanisms, $H$ and $L$, have the following behavioral consequences. $H$ allows an organism to perform the behaviors in set $B_1$ and those in set $B_2$. In contrast, if an organism has $L$ but lacks $H$, then its behavioral repertoire shrinks to $B_1$. Let us assume, with Gross and Chomsky, that what an organism *can* do, it *will* do, given the right circumstances.

What can we infer about the presence of $H$ and $L$, if we see an organism perform the behaviors in $B_1$? I suggest that no conclusion can be drawn as to whether the organism has $H$ alone, or $L$ alone, or both together. However, suppose we observe the organism for a long time under varied circumstances, never seeing it perform the behaviors in $B_2$. I take it that we now are entitled to an additional inference: since we have not observed the organism perform these behaviors, we have observed it not performing them. We have observed a nonevent. This involves something more than merely not observing an event. Someone who has never looked at the organism has failed to observe it perform $B_2$. However, only those who have observed the organism are entitled to say that they have seen the organism not perform $B_2$. If we now have the premiss $-B_2$—that these behaviors are outside the organism's repertoire—then we can deduce $L \& -H$ (assuming that $H$ and $L \& -H$ are the only two alternatives). There is no need for a special principle of nondeductive inference to derive this consequence. Deductive logic suffices.[10]

It is important to bear in mind that this line of reasoning requires that one has observed the organism in "appropriate circumstances." As far as we know, the human beings who lived 100,000 years ago were anatomically modern. Their fossil traces are indistinguishable in shape from the bones that modern human beings possess. Let us suppose, then, that their brains were just as big as ours, and that they had all the same cognitive capacities. In spite of this similarity, an observer of these organisms would notice that they fail to do a number of things that modern people do. Apparently, these human beings had no decorative arts; the oldest examples arose some 60,000 years later, with most examples (e.g., cave paintings) appearing a mere 10,000 to 17,000 years ago (Bahn, 1992). Agriculture and written language are even more recent developments. However, it does not follow from these behavioral facts that the human beings of 100,000 years ago lacked the capacities we have. It is perfectly possible that the circumstances in which they lived explain why some of their capacities never surfaced in behavior.

So, on second thought, the idea underlying Gross's cartoon and Chomsky's claim is not entirely unproblematic. Capacities are manifested in behavior only when the circumstances are right. And a pervasive theme in the history of life is the existence of evolutionary spin-off. Perhaps our big brain evolved in ancestral human beings for one set of reasons, but then, in novel circumstances, this big brain has allowed us to do other things. We now use our brains to do science, philosophy, and the arts, but this is not why the big brain evolved. Our ancestors had the same big brains we have, but their behavior was quite different. This point must always temper the inference that an organism's failure to exhibit a behavior shows that the organism is incapable of performing the behavior.

The argument I have given uses a definition of "higher" and "lower" according to which the behavioral capacities of a higher internal mechanism properly include those associated with a lower mechanism. Although this definition fits some examples in which we may be disposed to talk of higher and lower, it fails to fit others. Perhaps the ability to fly is "higher" than the ability to glide, but even so, there may be things that gliders can do that flyers cannot. Fortunately, there is no need to insist on the definition of higher and lower that I have used, since the epistemological point remains the same even for internal mechanisms whose associated behavioral capacities overlap only partially. If one observes a behavior that is part of the repertoires associated with both $L$ and $H$, then no conclusion can be drawn. However, if the organism fails to perform a behavior that should have occurred if it had $H$, but could not have occurred if it had $L$ alone, this is evidence that favors $L$ and goes against $H$. We may leave behind the question of how "higher" and "lower" should be defined and recognize that this simple point is fundamental.[11]

Let me bring this analysis of Morgan's canon down to earth by applying it to the piping plovers that I discussed at the beginning of the chapter.

When a predator approaches their nest, piping plovers move away from the nest and peep loudly. They engage in "false nesting"; that is, they make it look as if they are sitting on their eggs when, in fact, they are just sitting on sand. And they produce the broken-wing display (Ristau, 1991). Consider two possible explanations of these behaviors. The first hypothesis ($H_1$) says that the birds want to protect their young, and believe that these actions will have that effect. The second hypothesis ($H_2$) is that the plovers want to protect their young and believe that deceiving the predator is the best way to accomplish this; they perform the actions listed because they think that these actions will deceive the predator and thereby protect their young. This second hypothesis attributes second-order intentionality (Dennett, 1987) to the birds—the hypothesis says that they form representations about the mental states of other organisms. The first hypothesis limits itself to a claim of first-order intentionality; it says only that the birds have beliefs about nonmental subjects.

Most philosophers believe that second-order intentionality entails first-order intentionality, but not conversely. For example, if a plover is able to form beliefs about what predators *think* about whether its wing is broken, then the bird is also able to form beliefs about whether its wing is in fact broken. However, the converse does not hold; it is possible to form beliefs about wings without also forming beliefs about beliefs about wings.

Morgan's canon, applied to this problem, suggests that we should endorse the first hypothesis, and reject the second. Since $H_2$ entails $H_1$, but not conversely, it is a theorem of probability theory that $\Pr(H_1) > \Pr(H_2)$. However, nothing follows, so far, as to whether $\Pr(H_1 \& \text{-} H_2) > \Pr(H_1 \& H_2)$. Nor is it at all obvious that the conjunction $H_1 \& \text{-} H_2$ is behaviorally equivalent with the conjunction $H_1 \& H_2$. So, energetic efficiency cannot be used to argue that the hypothesis of second-order intentionality is false. Presumably, the second-order ability underwrites behavioral capacities not provided by first-order intentionality alone.

It is tempting to think that some nondeductive principle of inference needs to be imported here; since the plover's behavior can be explained by both hypotheses, some such principle may seem to be needed to underwrite the conclusion that plovers have first-order intentionality and lack the second-order ability. I agree that the more "conservative" hypothesis is the one that is more plausible; however, I suggest that no special principle of inference is needed.

It isn't the plover's broken-wing behavior that is doing the work here, but the fact that the plover is *not* producing the sorts of behavior that only second-order intentionality would be able to generate. It is this *non*event that ethologists implicitly take into account when they favor the hypothesis that only first-order intentionality is present. Let me try to persuade the reader of this diagnosis with a thought experiment. Suppose I told you, "I am thinking of an organism that is able to protect its young by performing actions that have the effect of misleading predators." I then ask: "Am I thinking of an organism that has first-order intentionality only, or am I thinking of one that has first- and second-order intentionality both?" My opinion is that you should decline to answer my question. For all you know, I am thinking of a human being; alternatively, I may be thinking of a plover. When the problem is stripped of background information in this way, there is little inclination to think that a behavior that could occur with only first-order intentionality is in fact produced in that way.

It may be replied that there are many organisms that have first-order intentionality, but only a few that have second-order intentionality. I agree that this consideration would be relevant, if you thought I had chosen my example by drawing an organism at random. However, you have no reason to think this. Furthermore, Morgan's canon cannot rely on the assumption that it is more common for organisms to have lower abilities alone than for them to have lower and higher abilities together. This may be true for the example of first- and second-order intentionality, but there is no reason why the claim should be true in general. In any event, I take it that the canon is intended to guide our inferences about internal mechanisms when we don't have this type of prior knowledge.

If this reconstruction of the meaning and justification of Morgan's canon is correct, then the canon has been widely misunderstood. Morgan thought that the canon rests on a specifically evolutionary rationale; however, we have seen that his evolutionary justification does not work, and the justification I am suggesting does not depend on any evolutionary assumption. Many others have seen the canon as an instance of Occam's razor, the principle of parsimony. But there is no *need* to understand the canon in this way. If we take Morgan's terms "lower" and "higher" to mark a difference in the behavioral capacities that a psychological mechanism provides, and if we are entitled to expect an organism to exhibit its behavioral capacities in suitable circumstances, then observed behavior will sometimes tell us to attribute a lower rather than a higher psychological mechanism. It isn't that observing $B_1$ tips the scale in favor of $L$ and against $H$, with the principle of parsimony underwriting the inference. Rather, it is the observation of the nonoccurrence of $B_2$ that points to $L$ and away from $H$, with the inference proceeding deductively. Construed in this way, Morgan's canon makes sense, but neither evolution nor parsimony is the reason why.

## Notes

I am grateful to Colin Allen, Robin Andreasen, Andre Ariew, Marc Bekoff, Len Berkowitz, Ned Block, Paul Bloom, Denise Cummins, Berent Ençn, Ted Everett, David Papineau, Larry Shapiro, Peter Godfrey-Smith, Chris Stephens, and Denis Walsh for useful discussion, and to Denis Walsh, in addition, for the example of the protorothyrids.

   1. In the book's second edition, Morgan (1903) rephrases the canon and then adds an important clarification: "To this, however, it should be added, lest the range of the principle be misunderstood, that the canon by no means excludes the interpretation of a particular activity in terms of the higher processes, if we already have independent evidence of the occurrence of these higher processes in the animal under observation" (p. 59). If methodological behaviorism is the view that human behavior should be explained without appealing to inner mental states, even though we know that human beings in fact occupy such states, then the rider that Morgan appended entails that the canon cannot be used to justify methodological behaviorism. Similar remarks apply to the use of Morgan's canon in spurious justifications of psychological egoism. See Chapter 10 of Sober and Wilson (1998) for discussion.

   2. This is not to say that Darwin disavowed the idea of evolutionary progress; see Ospovat (1981, chapter 9). Sober (1994e) discusses modern evolutionary theory's attitude to this concept; see also the essays in Nitecki (1988).

   3. For an explanation of the conceptual framework of cladistic parsimony, see Sober (1988).

   4. The group comprised of the question mark taxon and the taxa that have the character state $H$ are said to be *monophyletic*; a monophyletic group is composed of an ancestor and all its descendants. The members of the monophyletic group just described are more closely related genealogically to each other than any of them is to the taxa in the figure that lie outside.

   5. Morgan's brief for the indispensability of introspection (which rehearses a traditional solution to the philosopher's problem of other minds) arguably pertains to the *context of discovery*, not the *context of justification*. If so, the eviden-

tial warrant of third person attributions of mental states may depend not at all on introspection. In Sober (1995), I argue that the analogy argument for the existence of other minds is better construed as an *abductive* argument than as an argument based on *inductive sampling*. Introspection plays no essential role in the former; moreover, the standard objection to the argument—that the sample size is too small (i.e., $n=1$)—has no bite when the argument is understood in this way.

6. See note 1.

7. There is no precise degree of similarity that is necessary or sufficient to postulate a common underlying mechanism. Some similarities that unite chimps and sticklebacks *are* homologies, though building a nest is not one of them. See Sober (1988) for further discussion.

8. It is an unfortunate feature of Morgan's graphical representation that the overall "highness" of a species is a sum of the degree to which it has developed different mental faculties. This implies a type of commensurability that is quite unjustifiable—namely, that a "unit" of change in one faculty has the same effect on "highness" as a "unit" of change in any other.

9. In saying that the mechanisms are *behaviorally* equivalent, I am not saying that the two hypotheses are *observationally* equivalent. After all, there is more to observation than observing an organism's behavior; one can open the black box and observe the organism's physical make-up. I would be loathe to endorse a principle for discriminating between observationally equivalent theories, but I have no problem with the idea that there may be reasons for saying that two behaviorally equivalent theories differ in plausibility; see Sober (1994c) for details.

10. The argument here resembles the one developed in Sober (1994d), in which two influential arguments in evolutionary biology that appeal to the principle of parsimony are reformulated so that no such appeal is required.

11. It is worth noticing that this construal of Morgan's Canon does not license a wholesale preference for purely physiological explanations over explanations that attribute representational content. Suppose that $H$ and $L$ are psychological mechanisms, each involving the formation of representations. Suppose further that the organism under study implements $H$ if it has physiological structure $P_1$ and implements L if it has physiological structure $P_2$. Morgan's canon concerns the choice between $H$ and $L$ and the choice between $P_1$ and $P_2$; physiological hypotheses entail behavioral capacities just as much as representational hypotheses in psychology do. However, the canon does *not* entail a preference for $P_1$ over $H$; these are equally "high" in any reasonable sense of the term.

## References

Bahn, P. (1992). Ancient Art. In S. Jones, R. Martin, & D. Pilbeam (Eds.), *Human evolution* (pp. 361–364). Cambridge: Cambridge University Press.

Boakes, (1984). *From Darwin to Behaviorism*. Cambridge: Cambridge University Press.

Boring, E. G. (1950). *A history of experimental psychology* (2nd ed.). New York: Appleton Century Crofts.

Burghardt, G. (1985). Animal Awareness—Current Perceptions and Historical Perspective. *American Psychologist*, *40*, 905–919.

Carroll, R. (1988). *Vertebrate paleontology and evolution*. New York: W. H. Freeman.

Cheney, D., & Seyfarth, R. (1990). *How monkeys see the world*. Chicago: University of Chicago Press.

Chomsky, N. (1980). *Rules and representations.* New York: Columbia University Press.

Darwin, C. (1871/1981). *The descent of man and selection in relation to sex.* Princeton: Princeton University Press.

Dennett, D. (1987). *The intentional stance.* Cambridge, MA: MIT Press.

Ghiselin, M. (1969). *The triumph of the Darwinian method.* Berkeley: University of California Press.

Gottlieb, G. (1979). Comparative Psychology and Ethology. In E. Hearst (Ed.), *The first century of experimental psychology* (pp. 147–174). Hillsdale, NJ: Erlbaum.

Heyes, C. (1994). Social Cognition in Primates. In N. J. Mackintosh (Ed.), *The handbook of perception and cognition, vol. 9, Animal learning and cognition* (pp. 281–304). New York: Academic Press.

Morgan, C. Lloyd (1894). *An introduction to comparative psychology.* London: Walter Scott.

Morgan, C. Lloyd (1903). *An introduction to comparative psychology* (2nd ed.). London: Walter Scott.

Newbury, E. (1954). Current Interpretation and Significance of Morgan's Canon. *Psychological Bulletin, 51,* 70–74.

Nitecki, M. (Ed.) (1988). *Evolutionary progress.* Chicago: University of Chicago Press.

Ospovat, D. (1981). *The development of Darwin's theory.* Cambridge: Cambridge University Press.

Richards. R. (1987). *Darwin and the emergence of evolutionary theories of mind and behavior.* Chicago: University of Chicago Press.

Ristau, C. (1991). Aspects of the Cognitive Ethology of an Injury-Feigning Bird, the Piping Plover. In C. Ristau (Ed.), *Cognitive ethology—the minds of other animals* (pp. 91–126). Hillsdale, NJ: Erlbaum.

Skinner, B. (1938). *The behavior of organisms.* New York: Appleton Crofts.

Sober, E. (1988). *Reconstructing the past—parsimony, evolution, and inference.* Cambridge, MA: MIT Press.

Sober, E. (1994a). The Adaptive Advantage of Learning and A Priori Prejudice. In *From a biological point of view* (pp. 50–70). Cambridge: Cambridge University Press.

Sober, E. (1994b). The Principle of the Common Cause. In *From a biological point of view* (pp. 158–174). Cambridge: Cambridge University Press.

Sober, E. (1994c). Contrastive Empiricism. In *From a biological point of view* (pp. 114–135). Cambridge: Cambridge University Press.

Sober, E. (1994d). Let's Razor Ockham's Razor. In *From a biological point of view* (pp. 136–157). Cambridge: Cambridge University Press.

Sober, E. (1994e). Progress and Direction in Evolution. In J. Campbell (Ed.), *Progressive evolution?* Boston: Jones & Bartlett.

Sober, E. (1995). *Core questions in philosophy* (2nd ed.). Englewood Cliffs, NJ: Prentice-Hall.

Sober, E., & Wilson, D. (1998). *Unto others—The evolution and psychology of unselfish behavior.* Cambridge, MA: Harvard University Press.

Walker, S. (1983). *Animal thought.* London: Routledge.

Williams, G. (1966). *Adaptation and natural selection.* Princeton: Princeton University Press.

Wilson, E. (1971). *The insect societies.* Cambridge: Harvard University Press.

# 10

# Do's and Don'ts for Darwinizing Psychology

LAWRENCE A. SHAPIRO

Darwin's claims about the evolution of *homo sapiens* by natural selection apply as much to human minds as they do to human morphology. Many of our morphological similarities to members of other species owe to our shared ancestry. Likewise, although we have no direct acquaintance with the minds of nonhuman animals, our common ancestry should lead us to expect remarkable mental similarities. This continuity in human and nonhuman minds, repellent as it may have appeared to an unsuspecting nineteenth-century audience, is a reason for celebration in our life sciences today. Ethology, which once limited itself to cumbersome, mechanistic explanations of animal behavior, now avails itself of cognitive psychology's mentalistic vocabulary to study topics such as memory and imagery in animals (Yoerg & Kamil, 1991). Cognitive psychology, correlatively, gains from the stepping stones that investigations of nonhuman minds afford (e.g., Parker & Gibson, 1979). In short, Darwin's discovery that human and nonhuman minds differ in degree rather than kind (provided they are phylogenetically related) allows the possibility that the study of any mind will inform the study of any other mind, regardless of species. For this latter point alone, Darwin's importance in the history of psychology is most widely, and easily, recognized.[1]

This said, I wish now to suggest that the theory of natural selection makes another significant contribution to psychology that only few have appreciated despite the fact (maybe because of the fact?) that it is even more obvious than the connection between human and nonhuman minds. What Darwin did for psychology is to license and ground the ascription of teleological functions to mental processes. Mental processes, Darwin allows us to say, are purposeful. Accordingly, thanks to Darwin, one of psychology's main jobs is to tell us what these purposes are and how they are achieved.

I foresee a likely reaction to this claim. One might dismiss it as anachronistic. After all, long before Darwin, people had known about mental processes—perception, attention, memory, and so on—and had conceived of them in functional terms. A good deal of the history of philosophy, for instance, can be read as a history of debate about the *function* of the senses. Clearly, then, it was not *Darwin's* insight that mental processes like perception have functions. Yet, this is not my claim. I claim that prior to Darwin people did not know how to analyze the purposiveness of these functions in a way that coheres with our current scientific understanding of the world. Imagine a psychology that attributed the purposes of mental processes to God's design. The extent to which such a psychology could be scientific is limited by its invocation of a supernatural artificer. Insofar as God exists outside of nature, this psychology could not, I claim, be a natural science. In contrast, as we shall see, Darwin's theory of evolution by natural selection underwrites a naturalistically respectable explication of functions. Consequently, while Darwin was not the first to realize that mental processes have functions, he, more than anyone, deserves credit for making their investigation a subject for a natural science.

In this chapter, I will make explicit (1) why teleological thinking is important for psychology, (2) how Darwin's theory of natural selection makes talk of teleology naturalistically respectable, and (3) how an examination of human evolutionary history can contribute to psychological investigations. I will close with a discussion of two precautions psychologists should take when availing themselves of an explanatory framework that incorporates a teleological view of mind.

## Teleology in Psychology

Some sciences aim to describe how things are. Astronomy tells us about the initial conditions of the universe, about the development of stars, and about the trajectories of planets. Physics tells us about the forces that hold atoms together, about the shape of space-time, and about the kinds and characteristics of fundamental particles. Other sciences describe how things are, doing so against a background assumption, however, that there is a way things should be. Physiology tells us not only that hearts pump blood, but that they should pump blood (i.e., hearts have been designed for the sake of pumping blood). Likewise, ethology tells us that certain behavioral patterns serve particular purposes. For instance, Bekoff (1995) argues that play bows among canids communicate the message that subsequent bites are to be interpreted as play rather than aggression. It is because play bows are supposed to convey this message that dogs engaged in social play will bow. So, while some sciences simply describe how things behave, other sciences tell us how things are supposed to behave.

This difference between solely descriptive sciences and sciences that assume the presence of functions, designs, and purposes is grounded in more than just a way of speaking.[2] One might object to the distinction I am drawing by claiming that talk of design and purpose is just metaphorical and thus can be eliminated in favor of a purely descriptive account (Hempel, 1965; Nagel, 1979). Surely, the objection goes, we can *say* that hearts are supposed to pump blood and play bows are supposed to send certain messages. But we can also *say* both that bodies in free fall (on Earth) are supposed to fall at $9.80\text{m}/\text{sec}^2$ and that light is supposed to travel at 483,600km/sec. Ascriptions of purposes are on a par in all sciences, and since no harm comes from their elimination in some sciences, we should be able to dispense with them in all sciences.

While I do not intend here to launch a full-scale defense of the need for teleological reasoning in some sciences, it is useful when considering this objection to reflect upon the distinct attitudes we have toward various kinds of recalcitrant observations. In particular, there is an asymmetry in the way that we account for a particular heart that does not pump and a particular object that does not fall at $9.80\text{m}/\text{sec}^2$. We say of the heart that it is malfunctioning—that it is not behaving as things of its kind ought to behave. On the other hand, the object that falls at a rate other than $9.80\text{m}/\text{sec}^2$ is not misbehaving. Rather, we assume that other forces are acting upon the object to cause its rate of fall to diverge from its expected rate. Indeed, in the incredible event that many or most hearts no longer pump, we may continue to assert that the function of the heart is to pump blood and, accordingly, we may still describe these hearts as malfunctioning. In contrast, if we find that many or most objects do not, *ceteris paribus*, fall at $9.80\text{m}/\text{sec}^2$, we should decide that our initial description of free fall was wrong. It is not that these objects are malfunctioning; rather, our original calculations of how objects fall are inaccurate.

This contrast between things that misbehave and things that do not behave as our prior descriptions would lead us to expect them to marks a real difference—a difference, as we shall see in the next section, that is a consequence of the unique kinds of history certain things have. Because some things develop as a result of a certain kind of process it is appropriate to assign to them functions and purposes. Teleological talk is not just metaphorical. Its application is possible because functions, designs, and purposes really do exist in the world.

Moreover, psychology must avail itself of teleological reasoning because psychological phenomena are the result of the same sort of process that has produced hearts, play bows, and other traits that carry the obvious stamp of design. Of course, it is possible to learn something about psychological phenomena without presupposing that psychological capacities have purposes, just as it is possible to say something about the heart without knowing what hearts are supposed to do. But, by the same token, descriptions of our psychology that ignore functions are as incomplete and uninformative as descriptions of the heart that fail to make salient the importance of its pumping.

The rest of this chapter is devoted to consider the extent to which evolutionary theory can inform psychological theorizing. However, before turning to this discussion, it is necessary to show the connection between teleological thinking (by which I mean the sort of thinking that is guided by questions about purposes, functions, etc.), and evolutionary theory.

### Teleology and Evolution

As I noted in the introduction, one can believe that organisms have been designed even though one has no view (or even a negative view) of the theory of evolution by natural selection. When William Harvey discovered the function of the heart in 1628, he did so without any knowledge of the theory of evolution by natural selection. Likewise, in 1800 William Paley drew the public's attention to the intricacies of organismic design. However, for Paley, this intricacy of design implied not evolution by natural selection but the existence of an omnipotent being: "There cannot be design without a designer; contrivance without a contriver; order without choice" (as quoted in Feinberg, 1996, 43).

Yet despite the independence of teleology and evolution, it is both desirable and possible to understand the former in terms of the latter. The desirability of analyzing teleology in terms of evolution has already been noted. Insofar as psychology is to be a natural science, it is imperative that it not make reference to *super*natural beings. A psychology that attributes the design of psychological systems to an omnipotent being is not a naturalistic psychology.[3] The complaint is not trivial. In the first place, we have no empirical means by which to study things outside of nature. Hence, a psychology that incorporated a supernatural element would, from the perspective of empirical science, suffer a cavernous and mysterious lacuna. Not only would it be a science without completion in principle, but one we wouldn't even know how to start. Second, it is important that psychology cohere with our other natural sciences. Sciences draw from each other and tend to blend together at their boundaries. A science based on the supernatural could not fully engage in the give-and-take that facilitates growth in the other natural sciences.

Fortunately, the theory of evolution by natural selection paves the way to understand teleology in completely natural terms. Evolution by natural selection, as the name implies, does not require any divine intervention. It is a process that occurs in any population with members that (1) exhibit variation in those traits that affect the number of offspring they can produce, and, (2) have offspring that resemble themselves more than others (Lewontin, 1978). But, it is appropriate to wonder, what does this process have to do with functions? Why is it legitimate to attribute design to the products of such a process?

Larry Wright (1973) offers an analysis of function that goes hand-in-hand with the theory of evolution by natural selection; and, although Wright's analysis has undergone revisions (Matthen, 1988; Godfrey-Smith,

1994; Allen & Bekoff 1995a, 1995b), and similar analyses have been derived independently (Millikan, 1984), his original proposal suffices for
present purposes. According to Wright, to say that something either has a
function or has been designed is to offer an explanation of why that thing
is present or continues to be present. This is true regardless of whether we
are talking about man-made artifacts or the parts of naturally occurring
organisms. So, for instance, the statements, "a stapler has the function of
joining pieces of paper" and "the heart has the function of pumping blood,"
both make claims about why something exists. Staplers and hearts both
exist because of what they do. This observation constitutes the first part
of Wright's analysis of functions:

> The function of X is Z means
> (1) X is there because it does Z.

Wright claims that the "because" in (1) is to be understood etiologically.
That is, the "because" is intended to answer questions about how X came
to be. For this reason, Wright's account of function and the others similar
to it are called etiological accounts of function.

Wright's analysis includes a second clause necessary to resolve the following sort of ambiguity. Suppose one were to ask why there are staplers.
Surely the function of staplers is to join pieces of paper. However, there is
another reason staplers are present: there are manufacturers who produce
them. Likewise, though the function of hearts is to pump blood, hearts are
present also because of the genes that code for their construction. In order
to specify the right sort of answer to the question, "why is something here?"
(i.e., an answer that illuminates something's function), Wright adds to his
analysis of function:

> (2) Z is a consequence (or result) of X's being there.

With the addition of (2), Wright insures that the etiology introduced by
the word "because" in statement (1) is of the proper sort to define functions. To say that staplers have the function of joining pieces of paper is to
say that staplers are present because they join papers, and joined papers are
a consequence of their presence. Likewise, hearts have the function of pumping blood, meaning that hearts are present because they pump blood, and
blood pumping is a consequence of the presence of hearts.

As we should expect, Wright's analysis of function seems to do a good
job both to distinguish things with functions from things without and to
distinguish those effects of a thing that are functional from those that are
not. For instance, consider the fact that light travels at 483,600km/sec. Is
traveling at this rate a function of light? We should think not; and, happily,
Wright's analysis precludes such a possibility, for traveling at 483,600km/
sec. is not a reason light is present. Similarly, it is true of hearts not only
that they pump blood, but also that they make throbbing noises. However,
it is not because they make such noises that they are in the chests of mam-

mals. Accordingly, Wright's analysis tells us that throbbing is not a function of hearts, despite the fact it is something hearts do.

Although Wright was not explicitly concerned with developing an analysis of function that defines the concept as it appears in biology and psychology, his analysis does capture admirably a sense of function that is prominent in these sciences.[4] Significantly, Wright's analysis is suitable for biology and psychology *because* our bodies and minds have evolved by natural selection. Consider again how evolution by natural selection proceeds. There is a population in which certain traits vary along dimensions that make a difference in individual fitness (i.e., in an organism's propensity to reproduce). If the organism's offspring resemble it more than they resemble others in the population, then some traits will increase in frequency in the population while others will decrease. At any moment in the duration of this population, there will be some trait type present because of what it has contributed to fitness. Moreover, what it has contributed to fitness will be a consequence of its presence. These traits (i.e., those that evolutionary biologists call *adaptations*), will, on Wright's analysis, have functions.

In sum, combining Wright's analysis of function with the theory of natural selection provides an account of teleology suitable for a natural science. Functions, as I mentioned in the previous section, emerge as the result of a kind of process—a process in which types of traits persist in a population because of what they do. When this process is itself natural, when it is not, for example, God who determines which traits persist, the resulting functions of these traits will also be natural.

## Putting Evolutionary Theory to Work in Psychology

The previous two sections have laid the groundwork to understand why evolutionary theory might be expected to contribute something to psychology. In the first place, some things in the world have functions. Scientific talk of design is more than mere metaphor, it is essential in a world in which design is present. In the second place, a naturalistic psychology can and should avail itself of teleological reasoning. It can do so because the theory of evolution by natural selection affords a naturalistic analysis of teleology. It should do so because, according to this analysis, traits that are the product of natural selection will have functions, and many psychological traits *are* the product of natural selection.[5] In short, psychology can benefit from evolutionary theory because psychological systems owe their design to their evolution. The more we understand their evolution, the more we'll understand their design.

Yet while it is one thing to agree in the abstract that psychology can benefit from evolutionary theory, it is another to say how evolutionary theory can be applied to psychology in practice. In this section, I will argue that evolutionary theory offers an important methodological heuristic for psychological theorizing on the one hand, and makes possible more complete psychological explanations on the other hand. (For further discussion of these points, see Shapiro & Epstein, forthcoming.)

Let's first consider the methodological importance of evolutionary theory for psychology. I shall assume that psychology is in the business of discovering how the mind works. In particular, psychologists study processes like perception, memory, attention, language acquisition, categorization, and reasoning. Among contemporary psychologists, the vision scientist David Marr (1982) has been especially clear about the first step one must take to study a mental capacity. Before doing anything else, the psychologist must have in hand a clear statement of the purpose or function of the capacity under investigation. This point is obvious upon reflection. No matter how brilliant the investigator, she would likely be unable to explain how a simple thermostat works unless she knew what thermostats are for. To be sure, digging around inside a thermostat will reveal something about what thermostats *can* do, but an account of how a thermostat works will be an account of how a thermostat does what it is designed to do. Accordingly, one cannot hope to offer such an account without first knowing what a thermostat is designed to do. It's also worth mentioning that one might think one has correctly described how something works, when, in fact, one has only described how some nonfunctional capacity of the thing is produced. If one thought the thermostat were designed to hold a hat, one's explanation of how the thermostat serves this function might be correct, though one would still be wrong about how thermostats (*qua* temperature regulators) work.

The lesson for psychology is equally clear. For example, until one can say what perception is for, one cannot hope to explain how perception is achieved. Moreover, one's theory of perception might correctly describe how perception accomplishes some tasks, but, as with the description of how a thermostat can serve as a hat hook, the theory might still fail to be the *right* theory of perception—the theory that explains how perception does what it is truly supposed to do.

We now come to the significance of evolutionary theory as a methodological heuristic. It is one thing to agree with Marr that we can't say how something works unless we know what it is supposed to do. It is another to develop hypotheses about what something is supposed to do. We can't know the function of something simply by looking at it, so how might we discern something's function? A promising strategy to specify functions is to ask what good a given trait might have done for a type of organism in its evolutionary history. Certainly this strategy is easy to apply in the case of things like wings and thumbs so we should expect it to apply as readily to psychological traits. An example will make clear the methodological value of evolutionary theory in the study of psychological traits.

Hatfield (1992) discusses two distinct approaches to the study of color vision in vertebrates. While both approaches investigate color vision from a teleological perspective (i.e., a perspective that assigns to color vision some purpose), only one approach looks to evolutionary theory for direction in its function assignments. Just as an explanation of how a thermostat regulates temperature differs considerably from an explanation of how it holds hats, so will accounts of color vision differ, depending upon what one thinks color vision is for. Furthermore, though there is a sense in which the explanation of how a thermostat holds hats may be correct, it is not an explanation a scientist concerned with design would seek, because it is not an explanation of how the thermostat does what it was designed to do. Analogously, we shall see that though some explanations of color vision might succeed to tell us how color vision does accomplish some tasks, it is the account of color vision that is grounded in evolutionary theory that the psychologist should prefer, for it is this account that strives to tell us how color vision does what it was in fact designed to do.

The two approaches to color vision that Hatfield contrasts are those of Barlow and those more in line with Marr's work in early vision. The contrast comes into clear relief when considering the phenomenon of metameric matching. Metamers are color samples that reflect distinct combinations of wavelengths under the same illumination, but are nevertheless indiscriminable to the vertebrate eye. So, for instance, two surfaces that appear to the human eye as identical shades of green might, in fact, be reflecting very different distributions of wavelengths. For Barlow, metameric matches are something of an embarrassment for color vision. Metamers mark a deficiency in our ability to distinguish between spectral energy distributions (combinations of wavelengths and intensities). Notably, this view of metamers assumes something about the function of color vision. If metameric matches are "mistakes" the color system makes, the function of the color system must be something like the discrimination of spectral energy distributions. Indeed, as Hatfield observes, Barlow seems to endorse just such a view: "For colour vision, the task of the eye is to discriminate different distributions of energy over the spectrum" (1982, p. 635).

The alternative view to color vision that Hatfield discusses begins with a speculation about the adaptive function of color vision. What good might color vision have served our evolutionary ancestors? Hatfield suggests that we "assume that one function of color vision is to enhance the discriminability of objects and surface features, and that a particular color system serves to promote the discrimination of healthy green plants from soil and rocks" (1992, p. 497). He also notes the common view that color vision helped our ancestors to distinguish ripened fruit from their green surround. From this evolutionary perspective, metamerism is not a malfunction of the color system because it is not a function of the color system to discriminate any and all distinct spectral energy distributions: "it would be of no consequence if various types of soil and rocks possessed metameric surface reflectances. Indeed, it might well be an advantage if classes of surfaces that were biologically equivalent in relation to a given organism appeared to be of the same color to that organism, despite spectrophotometric variations in surface-reflective properties . . . Under this analysis, an adaptively better color system would be one that allowed the organism to do a better job of discriminating environmentally-significant objects or surface characteristics than could a conspecific with less sensitive or no color vision" [1992, pp. 497–498]. Apparently, depending upon the function one takes color vision to have, metamerism is either a breakdown or a boon.

As one might imagine, Barlow's account of how the color system works is likely to vary considerably from the evolutionarily inspired approach to color vision. An explanation of color vision, for Barlow, will emphasize the discriminative capacities of color vision: "It treats the problem of color encoding much as a video engineer might treat the problem of building a good television camera: as the problem of accurately encoding the physical characteristics of a signal within given dimensions of variation" (1992, p. 496). In contrast, the evolutionary perspective on color vision will high-light the aspects of color vision that make it well suited to discriminate those ecologically salient features of an organism's environment. While Barlow's approach encourages us to examine the raw discriminatory power of cones, the evolutionary approach requires that we examine why cones have the range of sensitivities that they do. Of course, even though guided by an evolutionarily implausible view, it must be conceded that Barlow has con-tributed much to our understanding of color vision. However, assuming that he is incorrect about the function of color vision, the information he has collected about color vision must be picked through in order to secure those bits that prove relevant to understand how color vision does what it has in fact been designed to do.

I believe the example of color vision has general applicability in psychol-ogy and, indeed, in any science that studies functional capacities. Before we can explain how something works, we must know what it was designed to do, but to say what something was designed to do it helps to acquaint our-selves with the forces that have done the designing. When investigating psy-chological systems, the designing force has been natural selection. Accord-ingly, psychologists do well to learn something about our evolutionary history.

Before turning to the importance of evolutionary theory for purposes of explanatory completeness, I should justify characterizing the method-ological role of evolutionary theory as *heuristic* only. In my view, evolu-tionary theory helps the scientist to discover the functions of evolved ca-pacities, but it is not essential for this purpose. We have already observed that Harvey was able to state correctly the function of the heart despite not knowing anything about evolution by natural selection. Indeed, despite Marr's emphasis upon the need to articulate clearly the function of vision, evolutionary theory seems to play no explicit role in the development of his theory of vision. In the section of his book in which he discusses the purpose of vision (1982, pp. 32–36), Marr credits his formulation of the function of early vision to Warrington's work on aphasics. Like Harvey, Marr's conjectures about function rest on evidence uninformed by evolu-tionary theory. Had Marr perhaps thought more deeply about the evolu-tionary history of the visual system, he would have arrived at a statement of the purpose of vision earlier. Yet whatever the case *might* have been, the fact remains that it is possible to characterize correctly the function of a system without knowing anything about its evolution.

In contrast to the merely heuristic role of evolutionary theory in the methodology of function determination, its role is essential when demanding a complete explanation of a psychological capacity. The reason for this becomes clear when we recall Wright's motivation for the second clause in his analysis of function. We saw that the need for this second clause is to insure that the cause cited for something's presence is something that members of the thing's kind can themselves effect. Staplers are present because they can join pieces of paper. True, staplers are also present because someone has constructed them, but this second explanation of their presence is not one that is relevant in an analysis of a stapler's function.

Evolutionary biologists mark the distinction between these two sorts of explanation by distinguishing between ultimate and proximate factors (Mayr, 1961; Tinbergen, 1963). Ultimate factors are those that influence the survival value of a trait. The theory of natural selection answers questions about the ultimate factors that have shaped the characteristics of a trait. On the other hand, the proximate factors that determine the characteristics of a trait are developmental—they are the genes and other complex molecules that direct the ontogeny of an organism. The ultimate factors that are responsible for the characteristics of hearts today are the selective forces that made the heart an efficient pump. The proximate factors are the genes and proteins that create individual hearts.

A more complete explanation of a psychological capacity will include an explanation of not just the proximate factors that are responsible for the presence of the capacity, but an explanation of the ultimate factors as well. We have already seen how evolutionary theory contributes to an explanation of the ultimate factors that may have shaped the properties of vertebrate color vision. Why do vertebrate eyes have the sensitivities that they do? A discussion of the proximate factors producing these sensitivities will not provide a complete answer to this question. In addition, we should like to know what ultimate factors have also had a hand in making the color system sensitive to one class of spectral energy distributions rather than another.

Cosmides's work (1989) on the Wason selection task provides another example of the completeness evolutionary theory adds to an explanation of a psychological ability. The Wason selection task reveals curious facts about human subjects' abilities to evaluate conditional rules (i.e., rules of the form *if p then q*). Wason & Johnson-Laird (1972), as well as many others using the Wason selection task, had discovered that subjects are quite good at applying this rule in some contexts but are remarkably bad in other contexts. However, Wason and Johnson-Laird had no explanation for these discrepancies. As Cosmides and Tooby observe: "the literature on the Wason selection task was full of reports of a wide variety of content effects, and there was no satisfying theory or empirical generalization that could account for these content effects" (1992, p. 183).

Consequently, Cosmides turned to the theory of natural selection in an effort to unify the disparate results psychologists working with the selection task had accumulated. Cosmides considered subjects' performance in an evolutionary framework. That is, she asked what value correct application of conditional rules might have had in our evolutionary past. Examination of subjects' performance suggested to Cosmides that their evaluation of conditional rules was best when these rules expressed a social contract. More specifically, when the rule is of the form "If you take the benefit, then you pay the cost," subjects are quite good at detecting violations of the rule. In general, Cosmides and Tooby conclude: "human reasoning is well designed for detecting violations of conditional rules when these can be interpreted as cheating on a social contract" (1992, p. 205).

In the present context, Cosmides' work on the Wason selection task provides a nice example of the kind of explanatory contribution the theory of evolution can offer psychology. Cosmides's hypothesis that our competence with conditional rules that evolved as an adaptation to detect cheaters unifies previous work that had revealed content-sensitive performance on the Wason selection task. Prior to bringing evolutionary theory to bear on the results from the Wason selection task, work in this area was undirected. Subsequently, we have testable answers to questions about why subjects perform well with some contents and poorly with others.[6]

In sum, not only does evolutionary theory help the psychologist to figure out what the functions of psychological traits are, but it also is essential for a complete understanding of why our psychological traits have the characteristics that they do. It's one thing to understand how the vertebrate eye sees color; another to understand why it sees the colors it does. Similarly, it's one thing to know how subjects perform on various reasoning tasks, but it's another to know why performance is constrained in the ways that it is. The lesson is general. Understanding linguistic ability involves more than understanding how we acquire language and how we make judgments of grammatical correctness. We need also to ask why we have language. What is it for? Why does it have the syntactic structure that it does? Why do human beings rely on mental imagery to perform some tasks but not others? Why are some things easier to recognize than others? What makes some concepts easy to learn while others are difficult or impossible to learn? Answers to questions like these—questions that a mature psychology should pursue—demand that we attend to human evolutionary history.

*Precautions to Take When Applying Evolutionary Theory*

Despite all that psychology has to gain from appreciation of human evolutionary history, it is nevertheless possible to be overly zealous when applying evolutionary theory to psychological questions. In this final section I will consider two dangers one must take care to avoid when looking to evolutionary theory for a deeper understanding of our psychology.

The first danger is that of assuming design when no design is in fact present. Adaptationism in biology is the thesis that natural selection has been the only important force in the evolution of most biological traits

(Sober, 1993). Construed in this way, adaptationism is an empirical thesis, and, while many biologists have taken sides in the debate over adaptationism, it is safe to say that enough data are not yet available to determine whether adaptationism is true. One thing we can say, however, is that there are certain to be *some* biological traits for which there has not been selection. So, for instance, the biologists Gould and Lewontin (1979) claim that the human chin, which is clearly a biological trait, has nevertheless not been selected for. Rather, the chin is an artifact of a functional organization for which there has been selection. As Sober observes: "One salient fact about biological function is this: where there is functional organization, there also will be artifacts of functional organization—items that have no function at all. . . . Since biology studies not just the fact of functional organization, but also the consequences of functional organization, biology will study artifacts" (1985, p. 104 in Lycan).

Sober conjectures that this point is as likely to hold for psychology. It is only a premature belief in the truth of adaptationism that could lead a psychologist to assume that most psychological traits are principally the products of design. Wherever there is psychological organization there are likely to be accompanying psychological artifacts.[7] This means that psychologists must be ready to accept the presence of psychological *junk*: psychological phenomena that do not contribute to the function of the capacity under investigation. When analyzing a psychological system, one must not feel the need to give a role to all observed psychological phenomena.

For instance, in 1956, George Miller published the ground-breaking paper, "The Magical Number Seven, Plus or Minus Two: Some Limits on Our Capacity for Processing Information." In this paper, Miller drew together research from a number of different sources that, together, suggested that short term memory has a capacity of about seven items. Hence, whether one is trying to remember numbers, letters, words, tones, or names, one can remember approximately only seven such items at a time. Miller summarizes this fascinating discovery as follows: "There seems to be some limitation built into us either by learning or by the design of our nervous systems, a limit that keeps our channel capacities in this general range" (1956, p. 86). Given the generality of this limit, it seems reasonable to ask *why* our nervous systems have been designed to store no more than about seven items at a time. What function does the storage of seven items, plus or minus two, serve? While this appears to be a good question, it may in fact have no evolutionarily significant answer. Perhaps the storage limitation of short term memory is an artifact of its design, in the same way that chins are artifacts of the design of our jaw.

Of course, simply because there may be no purpose to the "heptic" limit of short term memory, this does not preclude the need to learn more about the origins of this limit. The capacity of short term memory is a psychological trait of great interest, suggesting as it does something about how short term memory works, why there is a need for other kinds of memory, and so on. The point to draw from the example is that there will almost certainly be some facts about our psychology that a selectionist perspective will not illuminate. Hence, assumptions of design, while perhaps a reasonable default, should not go unchallenged.

The second danger one confronts when applying evolutionary theory to psychology concerns the inference from the nature of the task an organism performs to the structure the solution to the task must take. Care must be taken not to be unduly profligate in descriptions of the components an organism's psychology must possess, or the stages a psychological process must pass through, in order to produce adaptive behavior. Simply because an organism succeeds in some task, we should not jump to the conclusion that the organism is equipped with a special psychological mechanism designed for the sole purpose of performing that task; nor should we jump to conclusions about how this mechanism, if it does exist, performs its job.

Consider, for instance, Cosmides and Tooby's description of the psychology involved in kin selection behavior. Members of many species confer benefits upon their kin, and Cosmides and Tooby are interested in characterizing the psychological system that produces such behavior:

> To confer benefits on kin in accordance with the evolvability constraints of kin selection theory, the organism must have cognitive programs that allow it to extract certain specific information from its environment: Who are its relatives? Which kin are close and which distant? What are the costs and benefits of an action to itself? To its kin? The organism's behavior will be random with respect to the constraints of kin selection theory unless (1) it has some means of extracting information relevant to these questions from its environment, and (2) it has well-defined decision rules that use this information in ways that instantiate the theory's constraints. We are one of the species that has evolved the ability to help kin. Consequently, we can be expected to have evolved mechanisms that are dedicated to solving such problems. (1994, pp. 97–98)

In this passage, Cosmides and Tooby seem to reason in the following way.

1. Kin-helping behavior is evident in many species.
2. To help kin successfully, an organism must be able to perform a variety of tasks that provide information about (a) who its relatives are; (b) how closely related it is to individual kin; (c) what the costs and benefits of its actions to itself are; (d) what the costs and benefits of its actions to its kin are.
3. Because information about points (a) through (d) is necessary for successful kin-helping behavior, there must be mechanisms dedicated to gathering information about these points. Moreover, there must exist special rules for processing the information these mechanisms gather.

While I would not dispute that many species display kin-helping behavior, this ability does not require the truth of either (2) or (3). It is quite possible that members of a species confer benefits upon their kin without having at their disposal any information about (a) through (d). Moreover, even if kin selection behavior did occur as a result of mechanisms designed for collecting such information, these mechanisms need not provide information in the sense that Cosmides and Tooby assume (i.e., information that is processed by decision rules).

As an example of a species in which kin-helping behavior occurs, but not as a product of psychological mechanisms designed specifically for this purpose, consider the wasp, *Nasonia vitripennis*. According to the biologist Steven Orzack (personal comm.), females of this species lay eggs in the pupa of a fly. When the eggs hatch, the wasp larvae consume the contents of the host pupa. Orzack conjectures that it is likely that all the larvae are related to each other because of the ecology of the situation: it is unlikely that more than one female will lay eggs in the same pupa. Furthermore, kin help each other by eating their share of the pupal contents. If individual larvae did not each consume a sufficient amount of the pupa, then the leftover contents would literally get in the way when the wasps were finally ready to exit the pupa: they would die in the same goop that once nourished them. Here, then, is a case of kin helping kin in which none of the kin requires information about (a)–(d). Kin help kin simply by eating their fill. They do not need to calculate relatedness. They do not need to calculate costs and benefits of their actions.

Some may object that the above example does not illustrate a case in which an organism distinguishes kin from nonkin. I have two responses. First, despite having no need to distinguish cognitively between kin and nonkin, there is no denying that *Nasonia's* behavior is directed preferentially towards kin. The point is important, for it argues against Cosmides and Tooby's unfortunate tendency to characterize many adaptive behaviors as necessarily quite complex. To be sure, portraying behaviors in this light makes more persuasive their inference to the existence of complex and cognitive behavior-producing mechanisms. Yet, insofar as many of the adaptive behaviors Cosmides and Tooby describe might be far less involved than first appearances suggest, the inference to complex mechanisms is dubious.

Second, even if Cosmides and Tooby are right that kin-helping behavior does require the existence of dedicated mechanisms, these mechanisms need not, as suggested in the third step of the reasoning above, be part of a sophisticated information-processing system. Many insects, for instance, have evolved mechanisms that allow them to distinguish kin from nonkin. These mechanisms, however, are simply odor detectors. Wasps that smell "good" are kin, and those that smell "bad" are not. Presumably, good smells cause one series of reflexive behaviors, and bad smells cause another. There is simply no need to adopt a level of explanation that drags in information-processing apparatuses to explain kin selection of this sort.

In sum, when offering an analysis of a given capacity, it is essential that the adaptive utility of the capacity not bewitch one into crediting its source with more complexity than it in fact has. Many capacities with obvious adaptive value may occur as a result of no special psychological equipment at all. Other capacities that are the product of dedicated equipment may, nevertheless, not be appropriate targets for psychological analyses. Exactly when a psychological rather than a more basic biological account is necessary for understanding a given behavior is itself a matter for empirical inquiry.

## Conclusion

There is no doubt that minds have evolved as a result of the same kinds of processes that have shaped our bodies. In this chapter I have tried to draw some consequences of this fact for psychology. Evolutionary theory, I have argued, provides psychology with both an important methodological heuristic as well as an essential explanatory tool. However, proper application of evolutionary theory to psychological questions requires first, that we avoid unreflective adaptationist impulses, and second, that we do not immediately infer from the complexity of adaptive behavior the need for correspondingly complex psychological systems.

## Notes

For helpful comments on drafts of this chapter, I wish to thank William Epstein, Elliott Sober, and the editors of this volume.

1. See Riley, Brown, and Yoerg (1986) for a nice discussion of the value of comparative psychology.

2. Allen and Bekoff (1995a, 1995b) distinguish function from design. While I believe their distinction is a sound one, it is one I shall overlook in the following discussion.

3. In the philosophical psychology literature, "naturalizing" psychology often is equated with analyzing intentional language in nonintentional terms. However, this goal seems to me quite distinct from the goal of showing psychology to be a natural science (see Shapiro (1996) and Shapiro (1997)).

4. Walsh (1996) and Walsh and Ariew (1996) argue convincingly that biology, at least, contains senses of function for which Wright's analysis is not appropriate.

5. I think it is likely that not all psychological traits are the product of natural selection. I will return to this point in the next section.

6. Note that the point I am making in this paragraph does not commit me to the truth of Cosmides's hypothesis. Cummins (1996) has recently challenged Cosmides's evolutionary hypotheses, suggesting that we must look even further into our evolutionary past than the Pleistocene to account for current human performance with conditional rules.

7. See Shapiro (1997) for a discussion of junk representations: representations that are spin offs of a system designed to produce representations but that themselves never contribute to the function of the system.

## References

Allen, C., & Bekoff, M. (1995a). Function, natural design, and animal behavior: philosophical and ethological considerations. In N. Thompson (Ed.), *Perspectives in Ethology*, *11* (pp. 1–46). New York: Plenum Press.

Allen, C., & Bekoff, M. (1995b). Biological function, adaptation, and natural design. *Philosophy of Science*, 62, 609–622.

Barlow, H. (1982). What Causes Trichromacy? A theoretical analysis using comb-filtered spectra. *Vision Research*, 22, 635–644.

Bekoff, M. (1995). Play signals as punctuation: The structure of social play in canids. *Behaviour*, 132, 419–429.

Cosmides, L. (1989). The logic of social exchange: Has natural selection shaped how humans reason? Studies with the Wason selection task. *Cognition*, 31, 187–276.

Cosmides, L., & Tooby, J. (1992). Cognitive adaptations for social exchange. In J. Barkow, L. Cosmides, & J. Tooby (Eds.), *The adapted mind* (pp. 163–228). New York: Oxford University Press.

Cosmides, L., & Tooby, J. (1994). Origins of domain specificity: The evolution of functional organization. In L. Hirschfeld & S. Gelman (Eds.), *Mapping the mind* (pp. 85–116). New York: Cambridge University Press.

Cummins, D. (1996). Evidence for the innateness of deontic reasoning. *Mind and Language*, 11, 160–190.

Godfrey-Smith, P. (1994). A modern history theory of functions. *Noûs*, 28, 344–362.

Gould, S. J., & Lewontin, R. (1979). The spandrels of San Marco and the panglossian paradigm: A critique of the adaptationist programme. *Proceedings of the Royal Society*, 205, 581–598.

Hatfield, G. (1992). Color perception and neural encoding: Does metameric matching entail a loss of information? *Philosophy of Science Association, vol. 1*, 492–504.

Hempel, C. (1965). *Aspects of scientific explanation*. New York: Free Press.

Lewontin, R. (1978). Adaptation. *Scientific American*, 293, 213–230.

Marr, D. (1982). *Vision*. San Francisco: W. H. Freeman & Co.

Matthen, M. (1988). Biological functions and perceptual content. *The Journal of Philosophy*, 85, 5–27.

Mayr, E. (1961). Cause and effect in biology. *Science*, 134, 1501–1506.

Miller, G. (1956). The magical number seven, plus or minus two: Some limits on our capacity for processing information. *Psychological Review*, 63, 81–97.

Millikan, R. (1984). *Language, thought, and other biological categories*. Cambridge, MA: MIT Press.

Nagel, E. (1979). *The structure of science*. Indianapolis: Hackett.

Paley, W. (1800/1996). Natural theology. As reprinted in J. Feinberg (Ed.), *Reason and responsibility* (9th ed., pp. 40–45). Belmont: Wadsworth.

Parker, S., & Gibson, K. (1979). A developmental model for the evolution of language and intelligence in early hominids. *The Behavioral and Brain Sciences*, 2, 367–408.

Riley, D., Brown, M., & Yoerg, S. (1986). Understanding animal cognition. In T. Knapp & L. Robertson (Eds.), *Approaches to cognition: Controversies and contrasts* (pp. 111–136). Hillsdale, NJ: Erlbaum.

Shapiro, L. (1996). Representation from bottom to top. *Canadian Journal of Philosophy*, 26, 523–542.

Shapiro, L. (1997). The nature of nature: Rethinking naturalistic theories of intentionality. *Philosophical Psychology*, 10, 365–378.

Shapiro, L. (1997). Junk representations. *The British Journal for the Philosophy of Science*, 48, 345–361.

Shapiro, L., & Epstein, W. (forthcoming). Evolutionary theory meets cognitive psychology: A more selective perspective. *Mind and language.*

Sober, E. (1985). Putting the function back into functionalism. In W. Lycan (Ed.), *Mind and cognition* (pp. 97–106). Cambridge: Basil Blackwell.

Sober, E. (1993). *Philosophy of biology.* Boulder, CO: Westview Press.

Tinbergen, N. (1963). On aims and methods of ethology. *Zeitschrift für Tierpsychologie, 20,* 410–429.

Walsh, D. (1996). Fitness and function. *The British Journal for the Philosophy of Science, 47,* 553–574.

Walsh, D., & Ariew, A. (1996). A taxonomy of functions. *Canadian Journal of Philosophy, 26,* 493–514.

Wason, P., & Johnson-Laird, P. (1972). *Psychology of reasoning: Structure and content.* Cambridge, MA: Harvard University Press.

Wright, L. (1973). Functions. *Philosophical Review, 82,* 139–168.

Yoerg, S., & Kamil, A. (1991). Integrating cognitive ethology with cognitive psychology. In C. Ristau (Ed.), *Cognitive ethology: The minds of other animals* (pp. 273–289). Hillsdale, NJ: Erlbaum.

# Index

Adaptationism, 253–254
Animal communication. *See* Communication
Anthropomorphism, 84, 166, 229
Attention
  joint, 6, 156, 198
  and referential signaling, 195
  selective, 132
Autism, 32, 44

Bayes theorem
  frequency format, 12
  probability format, 10

Causal reasoning. *See* Reasoning, causal
Cheater detection
  in deontic reasoning, 40
  and memory for cheaters, 41
  and social status or rank, 41–42
Cognition
  and behavioral flexibility, 168
  cognitive vs. noncognitive explanation of behavior, 177–178, 224, 255–256
  field study of, 153
  "higher" and "lower", 224–240

human compared to nonhuman, 4, 51–101, 127–156, 162–177
looking time methodology, 54–101, 154
play and, 164
psychological vs. biological approaches, 3
relation to brain function, 3
species-fair tests for, 176
Cognitive bias, 130
Color vision, 155, 249–251
  adaptive function of, 250
  adaptive vs. engineering approach to, 251
  color constancy, 9
Communication
  animal, compared to human language, 183–201
  emotional theory of animal communication, 185
  evolution of, 183–201
  gestural, 200
  of intention, 169
  meaning of signals, 140
  play signals and, 163–177
  voluntary control of, 186

Concepts
  of agency, 54, 83–98
  of alive, 137
  of animacy, 85, 97, 128, 137,
      196
  cross-linguistic differences in,
      214–217
  fast-mapping of, 218
  innate, 218–219
  and language, 217–219
  of medium-sized objects,
      200–201
  nonlinguistic concepts, 54, 56,
      63–68, 72–77, 89–93,
      94–98
  of number, 54–83
  of object, 54–83
Cooperation
  and cheater detection, 36
  in forming alliances, 33–34
  in play, 165, 170–172
  and reciprocity, 35–36

Deaf isolates, 218
Deception
  and levels of intentionality, 37–38
  in nonhuman animals, 38–39
  and relation to belief, 38
  in thwarting dominance hierarchies,
      36–37
  types of, 38
Deontic effect
  in children, 40
  definition, 39–40
  example of, 40
Dominance hierarchies
  in children, 42
  correlation with size, 34, 39
  deception in, 36–39
  definition, 33
  as dynamic structures, 34
  as implicit social norms, 34–35
  and "Machiavellian" intelligence,
      36
  and "male authority", 45
  monarchies as example of, 45
  and play, 164
  as priority of access, 33
  relation to evolution of
      intelligence, 34–39

relation to permissions,
      prohibitions, and obligations,
      35
  relation to reproductive success,
      33–34
  role of reciprocal obligations in
      formation and maintenance of,
      35
  and sexism, 45
  street gangs as examples of, 45
  as transitive structures, 33
Dominance rank. *See* Dominance
      hierarchies; Social status

Emotion
  bonding, 149
  and communication, 185
  and empathy in chimpanzees, 174–
      175
  mood contagion, 148
Environment of Evolutionary
      Adaptiveness (EEA)
  effect on cognitive function, 9, 52
  effect on human morphology, 9

False belief task, 43, 99–100, 151–
      152
  nonverbal version of task, 99
Frequencies
  effect on reasoning performance,
      10–12, 17–25
  monitoring as an automatic process,
      14
Function
  analyses of, 244–248
  functional approach to cognition,
      154, 242–256
  of reference, 187–201

Garcia effect, 129
Gaze direction. *See* Visual orientation

Homologies
  compared to homoplasies, 4, 53, 187

Imitation, 150, 174
Individual variation, 177
Intelligence
  Machiavellian, 32
  and neocortex ratio, 32

Intentionality
  attribution to others, 84–101, 139,
    151, 166, 173, 175
  and goal-direction, 85
  levels of, 37–38, 238
  relation to deception, 37–39
  in theory of mind reasoning,
    42–45
  and visual orientation, 141

Kin helping, 255
Kinesthetic-visual matching. *See*
    Imitation

Language
  acquisition of, 52–54, 216–217,
    218
  as  biological adaptation, 7, 204–
    219
  and brain size, 7, 208
  as by-product of higher cognition,
    184–185, 212–214
  and chimpanzee use of lexigrams,
    132
  complexity of, 210–212
  and concepts, 216–219
  and counting, 82
  creolization, 206
  as a cultural invention, 204–207
  effect of neurological impairment
    on, 208, 211
  evolution of, 52–53, 183–201
  as exaptation, 207–208
  generative nature of, 213–214
  hierarchical structure of, 185
  as instance of punctuated
    equilibrium, 208–209
  and intelligence, 208
  morphology, 7, 211, 213
  naming function of, 190–192
  and natural selection, 208–210
  phonology, 7, 210–211
  pidgins, 206
  prosody, 210–211
  and representation of number, 74–
    77
  syntax, 7, 211, 213
  theories of, 204–205, 213, 215
  and thought, 7, 204, 212–219
  uniqueness of, 187, 192

  universal syntactic constraints, 213
  vocal tract tailored to demands of,
    207

Limbic system, 31

Mental algorithms. *See* Reasoning,
    statistical
Mind reading, 149
Modularity of mind, 3,
  caution in inferring, 7
Morgan's Canon, 224–240
  and Occam's Razor, 229
  relation to parsimony, 7, 226–230
  role of deductive reasoning in, 237
Motion detection, 128, 136, 155
  and agency, 86–98
  and animacy, 86–98, 196
  and object permanence, 136

Natural Selection
  in making functional attributions,
    7
  *See also* Function
Negotiation
  of agreements to play, 168
Neocortex, 31
Neocortex ratio, 32
Numerical competence
  accumulator model of, 68–74,
    116–119
  adaptive benefits of, 119–120
  addition and subtraction, 64–68
  and counting system, 82, 121–124
  evolutionary building blocks for,
    81–83
  of infants, 6, 55–61, 66–72, 107–
    113
  of nonhuman animals, 6, 55–61,
    63–68, 72–75, 114–116
  numeron list model of, 68–77
  object file model of, 69–74
  relation to duration estimates, 118,
    120
  symbolic vs. nonsymbolic, 118–119
  *See also* Concepts, of number

Object classification schemes, 6, 77–
    81
  *See also* Concepts, of object

Object permanence, 56–65, 132–137
  and attention to motion, 136
  biologically relevant tests for, 134
  vs. delayed match to sample test, 136
  social factors in, 135
Obligations, 35–36
  in deontic reasoning, 39–42
  in dominance hierarchies, 36
  reciprocal, 36, 41–42
Occam's Razor, 229
  absence of evolutionary rationale for, 240
Ontogeny
  relation to phylogeny, 190, 192

Perception/action cycle, 31
Permission, 35–36
  in deontic reasoning, 39
  in dominance hierarchies, 36
  in play, 178
Prefrontal lobe syndrome
  in humans, 31
  in nonhuman primates, 31–32
Play, 162–177
  cooperation during, 170–172
  definition of social play, 166–167
  and dominance, 164
  and intentionality, 166
  pretend play, 165
  self-handicapping, 165
  solicitation signals, 163–177
Predator detection, 175
Prisoner's Dilemma
  in rational choice theory, 40–41
  and violations of reciprocity, 40–41
Probabilities and percentages, as cultural inventions, 11–12
Prohibitions, 35–36
  in deontic reasoning, 39
  in dominance hierarchies, 36

Reasoning, causal, 86–101
  in human infants, 88–89
  in nonhuman primates, 89–93
Reasoning, logical, 5, 30–50
  and cheater detection, 40
  and confirmation bias, 40
  deontic vs. indicative, 39–40

and hypothesis-testing, 40
  *See also* Deontic effect
Reasoning, statistical, 5, 9–29
  base rates, 11, 13
  Bayes theorem
    frequency format, 12
    probability format, 10
  and "cognitive illusions", 11, 24–25
  examples:
    AIDS counseling, 20–22
    breast cancer, 10, 15
    colon cancer, 17–18
    expert witnesses, 22–24
    "Linda" problem, 24–25
    O. J. Simpson and wife-battering, 18–20
  and mental algorithms, 11
  natural sampling, 12–13
  physician performance, 10–11, 15, 17–18
  probabilities and percentages, as cultural inventions, 11–12
  probability vs. frequency format, effect on, 10–12, 17–25
  standard menu vs. short menu, 13
  teaching of, 25–26
Reasoning, theory of mind, 5, 42–45
  autistic impairment, 44
  development of, 42–43
  effect of birth order, 44
  false belief task, 43, 99–100, 151–152
  in nonhuman primates, 94–101
  relation to deception, 36–39, 43–44
  relation to evolution of intelligence, 36–39
  relation to sabotage, 43–44
Reasoning, transitive
  in children, 42
Referential signals, 183–201
  and attention, 195
  conceptual reference, 194, 199
  false signals, 199
  reference to events vs. objects, 197

Social environment
  effect on object permanence tests, 135
  and evolution of brain, 31–32
  *See also* Dominance hierarchies

Social status
    and effect of retaliation on
        frustration level, 41
    and memory for cheaters, 41
    and reasoning performance, 41–42
Sociality
    advantages and costs, 33
    definition, 33
    and dominance hierarchies, 33–34
    impact on evolution of brain
        structure, 31–33
    impact on evolution of cognitive
        function, 31
Spatial cognition, 130–131, 153, 215

Teleology
    dangers of teleological approach to
        psychology, 253–256
    design of psychological traits, 248
    naturalistic theories of, 245–248
    in psychology, 244–252
    relation to proximate vs. ultimate
        explanations, 252

Theory of body mechanism. *See*
    Reasoning, causal
Theory of mind. *See* Intentionality,
    attribution to others;
    Reasoning, theory of mind
Thought
    cross-cultural studies, 214–216
    in deaf isolates, 217–218
    independent of language,
        217–219
    "language of thought",
        212–213
Trait
    definition of, 187

Validity, 5, 39–40
Visual orientation
    and attribution of intentional
        states, 141
    human and animal monitoring of,
        142

Wason selection task, 252–253